Lecture Notes in Computer Science 6673

Commenced Publication in 1973
Founding and Former Series Editors:
Gerhard Goos, Juris Hartmanis, and Jan van Leeuwen

Serge Fehr (Ed.)

Information Theoretic Security

5th International Conference, ICITS 2011
Amsterdam, The Netherlands, May 21-24, 2011
Proceedings

 Springer

Volume Editor

Serge Fehr
Centrum Wiskunde & Informatica (CWI)
Science Park 123, 1098 XG Amsterdam, The Netherlands
E-mail: serge.fehr@cwi.nl

ISSN 0302-9743   e-ISSN 1611-3349
ISBN 978-3-642-20727-3   ISBN 978-3-642-20728-0 (eBook)
DOI 10.1007/978-3-642-20728-0
Springer Heidelberg Dordrecht London New York

Library of Congress Control Number: 2011926693

CR Subject Classification (1998): E.3, D.4.6, F.2.1, C.2, K.4.4, K.6.5

LNCS Sublibrary: SL 4 – Security and Cryptology

Typesetting: Camera-ready by author, data conversion by Scientific Publishing Services, Chennai, India

Printed on acid-free paper

Springer is part of Springer Science+Business Media (www.springer.com)

Preface

ICITS 2011, the 5th International Conference on Information Theoretic Security, was held in the city of Amsterdam, The Netherlands, during May 21–24, 2011. The conference took place at CWI, the Dutch Center for Mathematics and Computer Science, and at the Trippenhuis, the headquarters of the Royal Dutch Academy of Arts and Sciences.

The goal of this conference series is to bring together the leading researchers in the field of information-theoretic cryptography. This area of cryptography aims at understanding the possibility and impossibility of cryptographic schemes that offer information-theoretic security. Such a strong level of security, sometimes also referred to as unconditional security, is very attractive as it does not rely on unproven computational hardness assumptions, and in particular also withstands attacks by quantum computers. The price for this level of security often comes in the form of less efficiency and/or some physical assumption. Understanding the minimal requirements for information-theoretic security is a central part of this line of research. Personally, what I find very attractive is the mathematical neatness of the field, and its rich connections to other areas of mathematics, such as probability and information theory, algebra, combinatorics, coding theory, and quantum information processing, just to mention the most prominent ones.

There were 27 submitted papers of which 10 were selected. Each contributed paper was reviewed by at least three members of the Program Committee. Submissions co-authored by Program Committee members were reviewed by at least five members. The Program Committee worked hard to review and discuss the submissions, and to finally select the best papers among them. It was a pleasure to work together with such a motivated and professional Program Committee. I would like to thank each member for his/her contribution. I also thank the external reviewers who assisted the Program Committee members during the reviewing process.

In addition to the accepted papers, the conference also featured nine invited speakers. Each invited speaker provided a summary of his presentation as a contribution to these proceedings. The invited speakers were: Benny Applebaum, Alexander Barg, Imre Csiszár, Ivan Damgård, Yuval Ishai, Renato Renner, Leonid Reyzin, Amin Shokrollahi, and Ronald de Wolf.

As a new component, ICITS 2011 featured a Rump Session: an informal afternoon program that gave all the attendees the possibility for a short presentation on a topic of their choosing. I hope that this turns into a tradition for future ICITS conferences.

I would like to thank the two General Chairs, Ronald Cramer and Krzysztof Pietrzak, for organizing the conference and for ensuring a smooth running of the event. I would also like to thank Niek Bouman for chairing the Rump Session, and Joachim Schipper for his work behind the scenes. Furthermore, my thanks go to the local support staff at CWI, in particular to Susanne van Dam for her unwavering organizational assistances, and to Maarten Dijkema and Chris Wesseling for setting-up and maintaining the submission system. I used Shai Halevi's Web Submission And Review Software; this is a very handy system which was of great help to me to perform my work as Program Chair, and Shai was always very prompt in answering questions.

Last but not least, I would like to thank all the authors who submitted papers to the conference and all the attendees of the conference; you are the ones that make ICITS possible.

May 2011   Serge Fehr

ICITS 2011

The 5th International Conference on Information Theoretic Security
CWI Amsterdam, The Netherlands
May 21–24, 2011.

Supported by an NWO[1] VICI grant

General Chairs

Ronald Cramer	CWI Amsterdam, and Mathematical Institute Leiden University, The Netherlands
Krzysztof Pietrzak	CWI Amsterdam, The Netherlands

Program Chair

Serge Fehr	CWI Amsterdam, The Netherlands

Program Committee

Amos Beimel	Ben-Gurion University, Israel
Nishanth Chandran	UCLA, USA
Hao Chen	East China Normal University, China
Paolo D'Arco	University of Salerno, Italy
Stefan Dziembowski	La Sapienza, Italy
Serge Fehr, Chair	CWI, The Netherlands
Juan Garay	AT&T Labs – Research, USA
Vipul Goyal	Microsoft Research, India
Maria Isabel González Vasco	University Rey Juan Carlos, Spain
Kaoru Kurosava	Ibaraki University, Japan
Eyal Kushilevitz	Technion, Israel
Keith Martin	Royal Holloway, UK
Jesper Buus Nielsen	Aarhus University, Denmark
Carles Padró	Nanyang Technological University, Singapore
Reihaneh Safavi-Naini	University of Calgary, Canada
Louis Salvail	University of Montreal, Canada
Christian Schaffner	CWI, The Netherlands
Berry Schoenmakers	TU Eindhoven, The Netherlands
Adam Smith	Pennsylvania State University, USA
Tamir Tassa	The Open University, Israel
Dominique Unruh	Saarland University, Germany
Daniel Wichs	New York University, USA
Jürg Wullschleger	Université de Montréal and McGill, Canada

---

[1] Netherlands Organisation for Scientific Research.

Steering Committee

Carlo Blundo	University of Salerno, Italy
Gilles Brassard	University of Montreal, Canada
Ronald Cramer	CWI and Leiden University, The Netherlands
Yvo Desmedt, Chair	University College London, UK
Hideki Imai	AIST and Chuo University, Japan
Kaoru Kurosawa	Ibaraki University, Japan
Ueli Maurer	ETH, Switzerland
C. Pandu Rangan	IIT, Madras and IIT, Hyderabad, India
Reihaneh Safavi-Naini	University of Calgary, Canada
Doug Stinson	University of Waterloo, Canada
Moti Yung	Google and Columbia University, USA
Yuliang Zheng	University of North Carolina at Charlotte, USA

External Referees

Hadi Ahmadi	Matthias Fitzi	Gil Segev
Mohsen Alimomeni	Goichiro Hanaoka	Ashraful Tuhin
Gilad Asharov	Michael Langberg	Severin Winkler
Seung Geol Choi	Steve Lu	He Xiang
Ashish Choudhury	Hemanta Maji	Vassilis Zikas
Stelvio Cimato	Ilan Orlov	
Frédéric Dupuis	Anat Paskin	
Sebastian Faust	Angel L. Perez del Pozo	

Table of Contents

Correlation Extractors and Their Applications*
(Invited Talk)

Yuval Ishai**

Technion
yuvali@cs.technion.il

Abstract. Randomness extractors convert dirty sources of randomness
into clean sources of randomness. Motivated by the usefulness of correlated randomness in cryptography, we introduce an extension of randomness extraction and the related notion of privacy amplification to the
case of correlated sources. Our main result is an efficient interactive two-
party protocol which extracts m clean independent instances of a given
joint distribution (X, Y) from $n = O(m)$ dirty (or "leaky") instances of
the same distribution. The classical case corresponds to X and Y being identical random bits. We present several applications of correlation
extractors to cryptography.

1 Background

The problem we consider is best explained as an extension of *privacy amplification* [2,1], the first application of randomness extractors [19] in cryptography.
Suppose that Alice and Bob initially share an n-bit secret random key k. This
key is partially compromised by an adversary Eve, who applies some leakage
function $L : \{0,1\}^n \to \{0,1\}^t$ to k and learns the output $z = L(k)$. Now Alice
and Bob would like to engage in a public discussion which results in agreement
on a shorter m-bit key k' on which Eve has essentially no information. (Ideally,
$m \approx n - t$.) This problem can be solved by having Alice communicate a short
random seed r for a (strong) randomness extractor Ext, and defining the new
key as $k' = \text{Ext}(k, r)$. The extractor Ext should guarantee that for every admis-
sible leakage function L, the final key k' is almost uniformly distributed when
conditioned on Eve's view (z, r).

2 How to Clean Noise

Standard privacy amplification can be thought of as the question of building
a clean secure communication channel from a leaky secure channel. The question we ask is whether this can be generalized to other types of channels. This

---

* Based on a joint work with Eyal Kushilevitz, Rafail Ostrovsky, and Amit Sahai [16].
** Supported by ERC Starting Grant 259426, ISF grant 1361/10, and BSF grant
2008411.

question is motivated by the usefulness of noisy channels and correlated randomness in cryptography [20,7]. Similarly to the use of a common source of secret randomness as a resource for secure *communication*, correlated randomness is useful as a resource for secure *computation* [22,12,17]. To illustrate the question of cleaning channels, consider the simple case of a binary symmetric channel (BSC). Here Alice sends a random n-bit string a and Bob receives an n-bit string b obtained from a by flipping each bit (independently) with some fixed probability $0 < p < 1/2$. Can we build a clean BSC from a leaky BSC which may reveal arbitrary t bits of information about (a, b)?

A natural solution that comes to mind is to have Alice and Bob first use their leaky BSC to agree on a common random string k on which Eve has essentially no information, and then use k to generate a pair of local outputs (a', b') whose joint distribution is statistically close to that of an m-bit BSC, for some $m < n$. This solution is acceptable if we are only concerned about protecting Alice and Bob against an *external* Eve. In the classical privacy amplification scenario, this is indeed the only relevant concern. The current case of a BSC is qualitatively different in that an ideal BSC keeps secrets from both parties. Since the above solution allows each of Alice and Bob to fully learn (a', b'), it falls short of faithfully emulating an ideal BSC. Instead, we would like the outputs to be distributed correctly not only from the point of view of an external Eve, but also from the point of view of Alice or Bob.

3   Extracting Correlations

The above example leads us to the notion of *correlation extractors*. Given a joint distribution (X, Y) which specifies an atomic correlation, or a "channel," the goal is to realize m clean independent instances of (X, Y) given n leaky instances of (X, Y). More precisely, suppose that Alice holds a and Bob holds b, where (a, b) are obtained by taking n independent samples from (X, Y) and letting a include all X instances and b include all Y instances. An adversary Eve gets partial information on Alice and Bob's inputs by applying a global leakage function L with output length t to (a, b) and learning its output $z = L(a, b)$.[1] The goal is to design an interactive protocol between Alice and Bob which uses a public communication channel and a small amount of fresh randomness, such that for every L as above the following holds. In the end of the protocol, Alice outputs a' and Bob outputs b' such that (a', b') are statistically indistinguishable from m independent instances of (X, Y) even when conditioned on Eve's view, and *even when conditioned on the joint view of Eve together with either Alice or Bob*. We refer to such a protocol as a correlation extractor for (X, Y). The notion

---

[1] Our results apply (with the same asymptotic parameters) also to a stronger notion of correlation extractors, allowing (a, b) to be taken from any joint distribution (A, B) such that $\Pr[(A, B) = (a, b)] \leq 2^t \cdot \Pr[(X, Y)^n = (a, b)]$ for all (a, b). The latter notion of an imperfect (X, Y)-source generalizes the standard notion of a weak n-bit source with min-entropy $n - t$ [19].

of correlation extractors can also be captured using the standard simulation-based paradigm for defining secure computation [12,11,4]. In the terminology of secure computation, an (n, m, t, ϵ) correlation extractor for (X, Y) is a two-party protocol which ϵ-securely realizes $(X, Y)^m$ given a single call to a "t-leaky oracle" for $(X, Y)^n$. Here we assume that the adversary is *semi-honest*: it can observe all information available to corrupted parties but cannot modify the messages they send to each other.

4   OT Extractors

An *OT extractor* is a correlation extractor for the correlation defined by a random instance of oblivious transfer [20,8]. That is, $X = (X_0, X_1)$ is uniformly random over $\{0, 1\}^2$ and $Y = (b, X_b)$ for a random bit b. It is instructive to compare OT extractors with previous related notions from the literature. When the leakage function L can only contain *physical bits* of its input, extracting OTs coincides with the previously studied goal of *combining* OTs [14], namely generating secure instances of OT from multiple candidates of which a bounded number may be faulty and leak information. Thus, OT extractors can be viewed as a common generalization of OT combiners and standard randomness extractors, which in turn both generalize the notion of extractors for bit-fixing sources [6].

5   Main Result

Our main result is a construction of a "constant-rate" correlation extractor for any distribution (X, Y) with constant-size support and rational probabilities. More precisely, for any such (X, Y) there exist constants $c_1, c_2, c_3 > 0$ and $c > 1$ for which there is an explicit constant-round (n, m, t, ϵ) correlation extractor with $m(n) = c_1 n$, $t(n) = c_2 n$, $\epsilon(n) = 2^{-c_3 n}$ and cn bits of communication. The construction modifies a previous OT combiner from [13] by providing the additional guarantee that the inputs fed into the OT candidates are taken from a small-bias space [18]. Constant rate is achieved by employing "MPC-friendly" algebraic-geometric codes over constant-size fields [9,5].

6   Applications

As discussed above, correlation extractors can be applied for purifying imperfect correlated random sources that can be useful for cryptographic applications. For instance, when basing unconditionally secure cryptographic protocols on a physical BSC, correlation extractors can be used to accommodate an imperfect or leaky implementation of the BSC. As another example, one can think of using an expensive process of generating many precomputed random OTs for the purpose of a very fast "non-cryptographic" secure computation which should be done in the future. To eliminate the effect of leakage which may have occurred during the generation and storage of the precomputed OTs, an OT extractor can be applied shortly before the OTs are consumed. Similarly to the case of privacy amplification, it is crucial that correlation extraction be done *strictly after* leakage occurs, so that the fresh randomness used by the extractor is independent of the leakage.

We also show a somewhat surprising application to eliminating leakage caused by a computationally secure two-party protocol. Under a variant of the Φ-Hiding Assumption [3,10], we apply our constant-rate OT extractor to realize n instances of OT with only $O(n)$ bits of communication. Such a protocol was previously known only under the (nonstandard) assumption that there exists a pseudorandom generator with polynomial stretch in NC^0 [15].

Finally, our main result implies constant-rate leakage-resilient secure reductions (in the semi-honest model) between any pair of nontrivial finite correlations, or "channels".

References

1. Bennett, C.H., Brassard, G., Crépeau, C., Maurer, U.: Generalized privacy amplification. IEEE Transactions on Information Theory 41, 1915–1923 (1995)
2. Bennett, C.H., Brassard, G., Robert, J.-M.: Privacy Amplification by Public Discussion. SIAM J. Comput. 17(2), 210–229 (1988)
3. Cachin, C., Micali, S., Stadler, M.A.: Computationally private information retrieval with polylogarithmic communication. In: Stern, J. (ed.) EUROCRYPT 1999. LNCS, vol. 1592, pp. 402–414. Springer, Heidelberg (1999)
4. Canetti, R.: Universally Composable Security: A New Paradigm for Cryptographic Protocols. In: FOCS 2001, pp. 136–145 (2001)
5. Chen, H., Cramer, R.: Algebraic geometric secret sharing schemes and secure multiparty computations over small fields. In: Dwork, C. (ed.) CRYPTO 2006. LNCS, vol. 4117, pp. 521–536. Springer, Heidelberg (2006)
6. Chor, B., Goldreich, O., Hastad, J., Friedman, J., Rudich, S., Smolensky, R.: The Bit Extraction Problem of t-Resilient Functions. In: FOCS 1985, pp. 396–407 (1985)
7. Crépeau, C., Kilian, J.: Achieving oblivious transfer using weakened security assumptions. In: FOCS 1988, pp. 42–52 (1988)
8. Even, S., Goldreich, O., Lempel, A.: A randomized protocol for signing contracts. Communications of the ACM 28(6), 637–647 (1985)
9. Garcia, A., Stichtenoth, H.: On the asymptotic behavior of some towers of function fields over finite fields. Journal of Number Theory 61(2), 248–273 (1996)
10. Gentry, C., Ramzan, Z.: Single-database private information retrieval with constant communication rate. In: Caires, L., Italiano, G.F., Monteiro, L., Palamidessi, C., Yung, M. (eds.) ICALP 2005. LNCS, vol. 3580, pp. 803–815. Springer, Heidelberg (2005)
11. Goldreich, O.: Foundations of Cryptography - Volume 2. Cambridge University Press, Cambridge (2004)
12. Goldreich, O., Micali, S., Wigderson, A.: How to play any mental game. In: STOC 1987, pp. 218–229 (1987)
13. Harnik, D., Ishai, Y., Kushilevitz, E., Nielsen, J.B.: OT-combiners via secure computation. In: Canetti, R. (ed.) TCC 2008. LNCS, vol. 4948, pp. 393–411. Springer, Heidelberg (2008)

14. Harnik, D., Kilian, J., Naor, M., Reingold, O., Rosen, A.: On tolerant combiners for oblivious transfer and other primitives. In: Cramer, R. (ed.) EUROCRYPT 2005. LNCS, vol. 3494, pp. 96–113. Springer, Heidelberg (2005)
15. Ishai, Y., Kushilevitz, E., Ostrovsky, R., Sahai, A.: Cryptography with constant computational overhead. In: STOC 2008, pp. 433–442 (2008)
16. Ishai, Y., Kushilevitz, E., Ostrovsky, R., Sahai, A.: Extracting Correlations. In: FOCS 2009, pp. 261–270 (2009)
17. Kilian, J.: Founding cryptography on oblivious transfer. In: STOC 1988, pp. 20–31 (1988)
18. Naor, J., Naor, M.: Small-bias probability spaces: Efficient constructions and applications. SIAM J. Comput. 22(4), 838–856 (1993)
19. Nisan, N., Zuckerman, D.: Randomness is linear in space. J. Computer and System Sciences 52(1), 43–52 (1996)
20. Rabin, M.O.: How to exchange secrets by oblivious transfer. TR-81, Harvard (1981)
21. Wyner, A.D.: The wire-tap channel. Bell Cyst. Tech. J. 54, 1355–1387 (1975)
22. Yao, A.C.: How to generate and exchange secrets. In: FOCS 1986, pp. 162–167 (1986)

Characterization of the Relations between Information-Theoretic Non-malleability, Secrecy, and Authenticity

Akinori Kawachi, Christopher Portmann, and Keisuke Tanaka

Department of Mathematical and Computing Sciences, Tokyo Institute of
Technology, 2-12-1 Ookayama, Meguro-ku, Tokyo 152-8552, Japan
{kawachi,christo5,keisuke}@is.titech.ac.jp

Abstract. Roughly speaking, an encryption scheme is said to be non-malleable, if no adversary can modify a ciphertext so that the resulting message is meaningfully related to the original message. We compare this notion of security to secrecy and authenticity, and provide a complete characterization of their relative strengths. In particular, we show that information-theoretic perfect non-malleability is equivalent to perfect secrecy of two different messages. This implies that for n-bit messages a shared secret key of length roughly $2n$ is necessary to achieve non-malleability, which meets the previously known upper bound. We define approximate non-malleability by relaxing the security conditions and only requiring non-malleability to hold with high probability (over the choice of secret key), and show that any authentication scheme implies approximate non-malleability. Since authentication is possible with a shared secret key of length roughly $\log n$, the same applies to approximate non-malleability.

1 Introduction

There exist many different cryptographic goals to protect information. The most basic is *secrecy*, namely, that the desired information remain unknown to an adversary. Information-theoretic perfect secrecy was already fully characterized by Shannon in the 40's [14]. *Authentication* is another important task, which consists in guaranteeing that the information was not tampered with, that it really comes from who it claims. Wegman and Carter's seminal work [18] is considered the corner stone in information-theoretic authentication, since it is the first paper to show that the secret key needed can be much shorter than the message. *Non-malleability* is yet another goal. This notion of security was introduced by Dolev, Dwork and Naor [4] for computational security, and has received quite a lot of attention since.

Roughly speaking, non-malleability is the requirement that an adversary cannot perform a "controlled modification" of a message when given the corresponding ciphertext. Or, in other words, the adversary should not be able to produce a new ciphertext such that the two underlying messages are "meaningfully related." For example, if a document such as a contract is encrypted, a dishonest

S. Fehr (Ed.): ICITS 2011, LNCS 6673, pp. 6–24, 2011.

party might try to modify the ciphertext in such a way that he only modifies the amount of money due in the contract. With encryption schemes such as the one-time pad this is perfectly possible, because flipping a bit of the ciphertext flips a bit of the underlying message, even though perfect secrecy is guaranteed.

Shared secret keys are considered a very expensive resource, and thus bounding the length of the key needed and finding schemes which meet this bound are amongst the most important tasks when studying information-theoretic security. In his much celebrated work, Shannon [14] showed that to provide (perfect) secrecy for one message, an encryption scheme requires a shared key at least as long as that message.

Perfect security can be an expensive or sometimes even an impossible goal to achieve. Relaxing the security conditions and only requiring the security criteria to be met with high probability over the choice of keys often results in great improvements. For example, perfect authentication is impossible: there is always a small chance that a forged message and authentication code (MAC) match.[1] Therefore we can at best guarantee with probability $1 - 1/|\mathcal{Z}|$ that a correctly authenticated message has not been tampered with, where $\mathcal{Z}$ is the alphabet of the MAC appended to the message. To achieve an error of exactly $1/|\mathcal{Z}|$, a shared secret key of length at least n bits is needed [15], where $n = \log |\mathcal{X}|$ is the length of the message. By simply increasing the error from $1/|\mathcal{Z}|$ to $2/|\mathcal{Z}|$, Wegman and Carter [18] showed that the shared secret key needed can be reduced from n to roughly $\log n$ bits.

Previous Work on Non-malleability. In the case of computational security, several non-malleable schemes have been proposed with semantical "simulation based" security definitions [4] and indistinguishability or "comparison based" security definitions [1,11]. Many papers focus on comparing and classifying the relative strengths of these different notions of security, both in the public-key setting [2,12] and computational private-key setting [8].

In the case of information-theoretic security, Hanaoka, Shikata, Hanaoka, and Imai [7,5] were the first to formalize non-malleable security.[2] McAven, Safavi-Naini, and Yung [10] generalized their definition to the case of ciphertexts longer than the message and approximate security. Schemes exist which are known to provide non-malleability and secrecy [7,5] or non-malleability and authenticity [6]. However, prior to this work, there existed no security reduction between these different notions. These previous works on information-theoretic non-malleability [7,5,10] did not consider the optimality of the secret key length, and no lower bound on this key length was known.

---

[1] To authenticate a message m, a pair $(m, h_k(m))$ is generated and sent, where k corresponds to the shared secret key, and $h_k(m)$ is the message authentication code (MAC). An adversary wishing to modify the message also has to guess the correct $h_k(m')$ corresponding to the new message m' for it to be accepted.

[2] The standard information-theoretic definition of non-malleability (Definition 4) is not an immediate adaption of one of the computational definitions, but differs somewhat in the details. We refer to Sect. 6 for further comments on this.

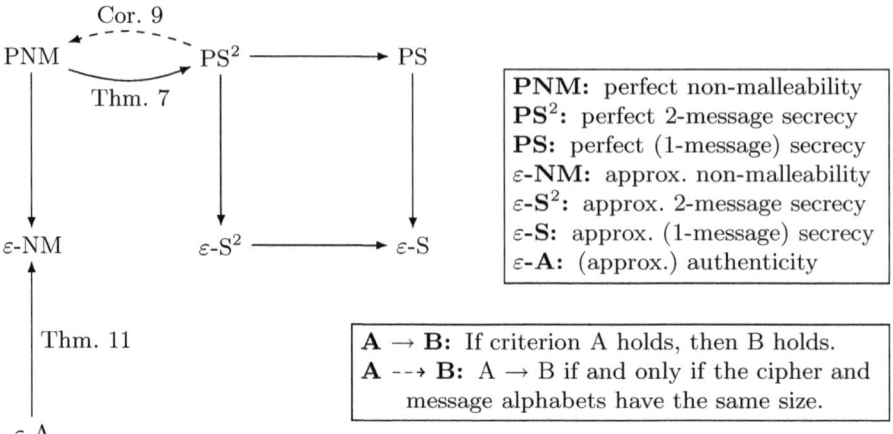

Fig. 1. *Complete characterization of the relations between different notions of information-theoretic non-malleability, secrecy, and authenticity.* A directed path between two notions of security means that any scheme providing the first also provides the second. If there is no directed path from one security criterion to another, then there is an example of a scheme that satisfies the first security definition, but not the second. The dashed arrow means that this relation only holds if the message and ciphertext alphabets have the same cardinality.

New Results. In this work we provide a complete characterization of the relations between perfect and approximate information-theoretic non-malleability, secrecy, and authenticity, which we illustrate in Fig. 1. Only the trivial relations (depicted in Fig. 1 by arrows without any reference to a theorem) were previously known.

We first study perfect non-malleability and show that it is equivalent to requiring that the encryption function uniformly maps any two different messages to all possible pairs of two different ciphertexts. This is equivalent to perfect secrecy of two different messages (PS^2 in Fig. 1) when the message and ciphertext alphabets have the same size, and strictly stronger if the size of the ciphertext alphabet is larger than that of the message.

An immediate consequence of this is a lower bound on the key needed for perfect non-malleability, namely $\log\left[|\mathcal{X}|(|\mathcal{X}| - 1)\right]$ bits, where $\mathcal{X}$ is the message alphabet, since this is the key length needed for perfect secrecy of two different messages. This also proves that a scheme by Hanaoka et al. [7,5] is optimal in the key size.

The converse yields a very easy way to design perfect non-malleable schemes, since we do not need to consider adversary strategies or invalid ciphertexts.

We then relax the security definition of non-malleability to only hold with high probability over the choice of secret key, and define approximate non-malleability

(ε-NM in Fig. 1).[3] We prove that any authentication scheme with error ε (ε-A in Fig. 1) is a non-malleable scheme with error $\varepsilon' \le 2\sqrt{\varepsilon}$, even though the formal definition of non-malleability does not consider the adversary to have failed if his choice of forged ciphertext is invalid. This answers an open question by Hanaoka [5].

This also means that authentication techniques such as almost strong 2-universal hashing provide approximate non-malleability with a shared secret key of length roughly $2 \log \log |\mathcal{X}| + 3 \log \frac{1}{\varepsilon}$ [3], where $\mathcal{X}$ is the message alphabet and ε the error probability.[4]

We show in the full version of this work [9, Section 6] that Fig. 1 is indeed complete: if there is no directed path from one security criterion to another, then there is an example of a scheme that satisfies the first security definition, but not the second.

Structure of this Paper. We start in Sect. 2 by introducing the notation and defining the symmetric-key encryption model used for information-theoretic security. In Sect. 3 we then define the different notions of perfect and approximate security needed in this work, namely secrecy, non-malleability, and authenticity. In Sect. 4 we prove the first main result about the relation between perfect non-malleability and perfect secrecy of two messages. In Sect. 5 we consider approximate security, and prove the second main result, that approximate non-malleability can be achieved by any authentication scheme. And finally in Sect. 6 we conclude with several remarks on the consequences of these results and a discussion of alternative information-theoretic non-malleable security definitions.

2   Preliminaries

2.1   Notation

In this paper we use calligraphic letters for alphabets (e.g., $\mathcal{X}$), lowercase letters for elements of these sets (e.g., $x \in \mathcal{X}$) and uppercase letters for random variables (e.g., X). We write $P_X(x)$ for the probability that X takes the value x. For two random variables X and Y with joint probability distribution $P_{XY}(\cdot, \cdot)$, we write $X|_{Y=y}$ to denote the random variable X given $Y = y$, and $P_{X|Y}(\cdot|y) := \frac{P_{XY}(\cdot, y)}{P_Y(y)}$ for the corresponding distribution. We also denote by $X \cdot Y$ the random variable with distribution $P_{X \cdot Y}(x, y) := P_X(x)P_Y(y)$. Note that unless X and Y are independent, $X \cdot Y \ne XY$.

To measure the distance between two random variables over a common alphabet we use the variational distance (sometimes also called statistical distance)

---

[3] We note that McAven et al.'s definition of approximate non-malleability [10] does not capture the notion of "security with high probability." We therefore redefine approximate non-malleability to reflect this concept.

[4] Since authentication does not imply secrecy, approximate non-malleability does not imply secrecy either. We refer to Sect. 5 for more details on this.

and write

$$d(X,Y) = \frac{1}{2} \sum_{x \in \mathcal{X}} |P_X(x) - P_Y(x)| \ .$$

We denote the expected variational distance between X and Y over a third random variable Z by

$$d(X,Y|Z) := \frac{1}{2} \sum_{x,z} P_Z(z) \left| P_{X|Z}(x|z) - P_{Y|Z}(x|z) \right| \ .$$

This will be used in particular to measure how close two random variables (over possibly different alphabets) are to being independent from each other, i.e., we are interested in $d(XY, X \cdot Y)$. In this case, conditioning on a third random variable Z results in

$$d(XY, X \cdot Y|Z) = \frac{1}{2} \sum_{x,y,z} P_Z(z) \left| P_{XY|Z}(x,y|z) - P_{X|Z}(x|z)P_{Y|Z}(y|z) \right| \ .$$

For an alphabet $\mathcal{X}$ and a random variable X distributed over $\mathcal{X}$, we call *domain of X* and write $\mathscr{D}(X)$ the subset of $\mathcal{X}$ with non-zero probability, that is $\mathscr{D}(X) = \{x \in \mathcal{X} : P_X(x) > 0\}$. We will often be interested in several random variables (usually two) $X_1 \cdots X_\ell$, each one defined over the same alphabet $\mathcal{X}$, but such that $\mathscr{D}(X_1 \cdots X_\ell)$ consists only of tuples of all different elements, i.e., for any $i,j \in [\ell]$, $i \neq j$, $\Pr[X_i = X_j] = 0$. So we will introduce the notation

$$\mathcal{X}_{\text{diff}}^{\times \ell} := \{(x_1, \ldots, x_\ell) \in \mathcal{X}^{\times \ell} : \forall i,j \in [\ell], i \neq j \Rightarrow x_i \neq x_j\}$$

for the subset over which these random variables are defined, and say that they are *different*.

We write $H(X)$ for the (Shannon) entropy of X and $I(X;Y) := H(X) + H(Y) - H(XY)$ for the mutual information between X and Y. This notation extends in the usual way for conditional entropies, e.g., $H(X|Y)$, $I(X;Y|Z)$.

2.2 Symmetric-Key Model

To achieve information-theoretic security, we consider the symmetric-key model, in which the two honest parties wishing to communicate share a secret key $k \in \mathcal{K}$. No matter what notion of security is desired – whether it be secrecy, non-malleability, or authenticity – the protocol follows the same steps. To transmit a message m, the sender applies a function f_k to the message, obtaining $c = f_k(m)$, which we will refer to as the ciphertext. This is transmitted on an insecure channel to the receiver, who applies the inverse function, $m = f_k^{-1}(c)$. Since decryption must always be possible (if the ciphertext was not tampered with during transmission), the functions $\{f_k\}_{k \in \mathcal{K}}$ must be injective. If c has been modified, then there might not be any corresponding message m, in which case the decryption results in $\perp$.

In the following we will loosely refer to any such scheme as an encryption scheme, and to the corresponding operations as encryption and decryption, even when secrecy is not required.

Definition 1. *A symmetric-key encryption scheme is defined by a set of keys* $k \in \mathcal{K}$, *a probability distributions* $P_K(\cdot)$ *over these keys and injective encryption functions* $f_k : \mathcal{X} \to \mathcal{Y}$ *associated with each key. The decryption functions are defined as*

$$g_k : \mathcal{Y} \to \mathcal{X} \cup \{\bot\}$$
$$c \mapsto \begin{cases} f_k^{-1}(c) & \text{if this is well defined.} \\ \bot & \text{otherwise.} \end{cases}$$

The two legitimate players wishing to securely communicate a message m must share the key $k \in \mathcal{K}$ *with probability* $P_K(k)$ *at the beginning of the protocol. The sender creates the ciphertext* $c = f_k(m)$ *and transmits it on an insecure channel to the receiver, who applies the decryption function* $\tilde{m} = g_k(\tilde{c})$ *to whatever (possibly modified) ciphertext* $\tilde{c}$ *he receives.*

In the following we will usually describe the messages, ciphertexts and keys by random variables M, C and K respectively, with $C = f_K(M)$.

3 Information-Theoretic Security Notions

In this section we define the three notions of security, secrecy, non-malleability, and authenticity, in Sects. 3.1, 3.2, and 3.3 respectively. All these definitions already appear in the literature, except the definition of approximate non-malleability (Definition 5), which is slightly different from previous ones [10]. Definition 5 is however a straightforward generalization of perfect non-malleability (Definition 4, [7,5]).

3.1 Secrecy

Since in the symmetric-key model described in Sect. 2.2 the ciphertext is sent on an insecure channel, an adversary can intercept it, and try to gain information about the message from it. So for a given message random variable M, an encryption scheme is considered to provide perfect secrecy if the adversary cannot learn anything about the message given the ciphertext, no matter how much time and computation power he has, that is, if

$$H(M|C) = H(M) \text{ or } I(M;C) = 0 \ , \tag{1}$$

as already defined by Shannon [14] in the 40's.

When we design an encryption scheme, we do not want it to be secure for some random variable M_1 with distribution $P_{M_1}(\cdot)$, but insecure for some other random variable M_2 with distribution $P_{M_2}(\cdot)$. Ideally, the scheme should still be secure, no matter how the messages are distributed over the message space, as long as they are independent from the key. We will therefore require that (1) be fulfilled for all distributions $P_M(\cdot)$ on $\mathcal{X}$ independent from the key, i.e., for all M such that $I(M;K) = 0$.

Equation (1) is called *perfect* secrecy, since the adversary's information is zero. However, in most practical situation, it is sufficient to have *approximate* secrecy, in which the adversary's probability (over the choice of keys) of noticing a difference between the real situation and the ideal one in which the ciphertext is independent from the message, is bounded by some very small ε. We therefore do not require any more that the message and ciphertext be perfectly independent, but that they be ε-close to independent according to the variational distance.[5]

Definition 2. *An encryption scheme is said to provide ε-secrecy (ε-S) if for all message random variables M on $\mathcal{X}$ independent from the key – i.e., $I(M; K) = 0$ – we have*

$$d(MC, M \cdot C) \leq \varepsilon \ , \tag{2}$$

where C is the resulting ciphertext random variable.

If $\varepsilon = 0$, (2) is equivalent to (1), and we say that the scheme provides perfect secrecy *(PS).*

This secrecy criterion is defined for encrypting one message. If the key is much larger than the message, the same encryption function and key could be used several times to encrypt different messages and still preserve secrecy. Since we only need a security definition for the secrecy of two messages in this work, we restrict the following definition to two messages. Generalizing it to any number of messages is however straightforward.

Definition 3. *An encryption scheme is said to provide* 2-message ε-secrecy *(ε-S^2) if for all pairs of* different *message random variables $M_1 M_2$ on $\mathcal{X}_{\text{diff}}^{\times 2}$ independent from the key – i.e., $I(M_1 M_2; K) = 0$ and $\Pr[M_1 = M_2] = 0$ – we have*

$$d(M_1 M_2 C_1 C_2, M_1 M_2 \cdot C_1 C_2) \leq \varepsilon \ , \tag{3}$$

where C_1 and C_2 are the resulting ciphertext random variables, i.e., $C_i = f_K(M_i)$ for $i = 1, 2$.

If $\varepsilon = 0$, (3) is equivalent to

$$I(M_1 M_2; C_1 C_2) = 0 \ ,$$

and we say that the encryption scheme provides 2-message perfect secrecy *(PS²).*

When the same key is used to encrypt two messages, and these messages are identical (respectively different), their ciphertexts will necessarily be identical (respectively different) too, since the encryption scheme is deterministic and uses the same key each time. It is therefore impossible for $I(M_1 M_2; C_1 C_2) = 0$ for all random variables $M_1 M_2$ defined over $\mathcal{X}^{\times 2}$, since the adversary can always learn which messages are identical or different, hence the restriction to *different* messages defined on $\mathcal{X}_{\text{diff}}^{\times 2}$.

---

[5] There exist several alternative ways to formulate approximate secrecy. We give a brief overview of these in the full version of this work [9, Appendix A.1], and show that they are equivalent.

3.2   Non-malleability

As briefly explained in Sect. 1, an encryption scheme is said to be malleable if an adversary can perform a controlled modification of an encrypted message, that is, modify a ciphertext in such a way that the new message resulting from decrypting the modified ciphertext is meaningfully related to the original message. An encryption scheme is then non-malleable, if the adversary cannot perform such a controlled modification of the message.

Let the original message be given by a random variable M, and let C be the corresponding ciphertext when encrypted with the key K. An adversary trying to perform a controlled modification of the message will replace the ciphertext with another ciphertext $\tilde{C}$, which, after decryption, becomes the message $\tilde{M}$. For simplicity we will assume for the moment that the message and ciphertext alphabets have the same size, since otherwise the ciphertext $\tilde{C}$ generated by the adversary might be invalid.

If the encryption scheme is malleable, the adversary can thus create an $\tilde{M}$ which is meaningfully related to M, that is, which satisfies some specific relation $\mathcal{R}(M, \tilde{M})$ with high probability. Thus, if we give M to this adversary (who already holds C and $\tilde{C}$) he will have some information about $\tilde{M}$ – he knows that it satisfies this relation $\mathcal{R}$ – more information than if he had not created $\tilde{C}$ to satisfy $\mathcal{R}$ and only held M and C. If on the other hand the scheme is non-malleable, then he cannot create an $\tilde{M}$ to satisfy any relation $\mathcal{R}$. So given M, C and $\tilde{C}$, he does not know any more about $\tilde{M}$ than if he only has M and C.

Let us illustrate this with the one-time pad. The one-time pad is a malleable encryption scheme, because if an adversary flips some bits of the ciphertext, he also flips the same bits of the message, and can thus decide how to modify the message even without knowing what this message is. So if after flipping some bits of the ciphertext C to create $\tilde{C}$, the adversary is then given the message M, he can reconstruct $\tilde{M}$ by flipping the same bits of M. An observer who does not know how the adversary created $\tilde{C}$ would only learn from M that $\tilde{M}$ is different, but no more. So an adversary who holds $MC\tilde{C}$ would know more about $\tilde{M}$ than an observer who only holds MC, but does not know how $\tilde{C}$ was created, i.e.,

$$H(\tilde{M}|MC\tilde{C}) < H(\tilde{M}|MC) \ .$$

On the other hand, if the encryption scheme is non-malleable, then as described above, the adversary does not know more about $\tilde{M}$ than had he not created $\tilde{C}$, so

$$H(\tilde{M}|MC\tilde{C}) = H(\tilde{M}|MC) \ . \tag{4}$$

Note that this is equivalent to $I(\tilde{M};\tilde{C}|MC) = 0$. Criterion (4) was first proposed by Hanaoka et al. [7] (see also [5]) to define information-theoretic non-malleability. Following [10], we generalize their definition to the case where the ciphertext alphabet can be larger than the message alphabet, by extending the message alphabet to $\bar{\mathcal{X}} := \mathcal{X} \cup \{\perp\}$, as described in Sect. 2.2.

Definition 4. *An encryption scheme is said to provide* perfect non-malleability *(PNM), if for all message random variables M on $\mathcal{X}$ independent from the* *key – i.e., $I(M;K) = 0$ – and all ciphertexts $\tilde{C}$ on $\mathcal{Y}$ different from C and independent from the key given MC – i.e., $\Pr[C = \tilde{C}] = 0$ and $I(\tilde{C};K|MC) = 0$ – we have*

$$I(\tilde{M};\tilde{C}|MC) = 0 \ ,$$

where $\tilde{M}$ is defined on $\mathcal{X} \cup \{\perp\}$ and takes the value $\tilde{M} = \perp$ whenever $\tilde{C}$ is invalid.

There are several important remarks to make about this definition. The first concerns the domains of M and $\tilde{C}$. M is chosen by the legitimate players, so we can require that they choose it independently from the key. $\tilde{C}$ is however chosen by the adversary, who might make it depend on whatever information he holds about the secret key, i.e., in general we have $H(K|\tilde{C}) < H(K)$, or equivalently $I(\tilde{C};K) > 0$. Information about the key is leaked to him from the ciphertext C. We can however not exclude that the legitimate players decide to make (part of) the message public, or that the adversary knows it by some other means. The pair MC leaks (much) more information about the key, and hence we need to allow the adversary to make his choice of $\tilde{C}$ depend on this. But the adversary should not get any information about K from any other source than MC, i.e., $\tilde{C}$ should not depend on any other part of K than that leaked by MC. Expressed with entropies, this means that we must have $H(K|MC\tilde{C}) = H(K|MC)$, or equivalently $I(\tilde{C};K|MC) = H(K|MC) - H(K|MC\tilde{C}) = 0$, which is one of the conditions of Definition 4.

The second remark concerns the condition $\Pr[C = \tilde{C}] = 0$. The adversary can always choose whether to modify the ciphertext or not, and hence can always decide whether $\tilde{M}$ is equal to or different from M. Criterion (4) can thus never be satisfied for a general ciphertext $\tilde{C}$, since learning $\tilde{C}$ (given C) will always tell us whether $M = \tilde{M}$ or $M \neq \tilde{M}$. But since this cannot be avoided, it is of no concern either. As the informal definition of non-malleability states, we are only interested in modifications of the original message, and hence restrict our attention to this case.

Thirdly, we consider it important to extend the message alphabet to include "$\perp$" and not simply declare the adversary to be unsuccessful if he produces an invalid ciphertext. This is because we do not want the adversary to have the ability to generate an invalid ciphertext given that the message has certain properties, but not for other messages. We refer to Sect. 6 for a more detailed discussion of this.

As in Sect. 3.1, we are interested in generalizing the security notion to hold only with high probability over the choice of keys. Instead of requiring $\tilde{M}$ and $\tilde{C}$ to be perfectly independent given M and C, we require them to be ε-close to independent.

Definition 5. *An encryption scheme is said to provide ε-non-malleability (ε-NM), if for all message random variables M on $\mathcal{X}$ independent from the key – i.e., $I(M;K) = 0$ – and all ciphertexts $\tilde{C}$ on $\mathcal{Y}$ different from C and independent from the key given MC – i.e., $\Pr[C = \tilde{C}] = 0$ and $I(\tilde{C};K|MC) = 0$ – we have*

$$d\left(\tilde{M}\tilde{C}, \tilde{M}\cdot\tilde{C}\big|MC\right) \leq \varepsilon \ ,$$

where $\tilde{M}$ is defined on $\mathcal{X}\cup\{\bot\}$ and takes the value $\tilde{m} = \bot$ whenever $\tilde{C}$ is invalid.

It is immediate from this definition that 0-NM is equivalent to PNM. We refer to the full version of this work [9, Appendix A.2] for a discussion of alternative approximate non-malleability definitions.

3.3   Authentication

In an authentication protocol, the goal is not to provide any form of secrecy, but to be sure that the message has not been tampered with, i.e., that it really comes from the legitimate party. Since no secrecy is needed, authentication schemes usually append some MAC to the message, which is sent in clear, i.e., $f_k(m) = (m, h_k(m))$, where h_k is some hash function. Upon reception of $\tilde{c} = (\tilde{m}, \tilde{s})$, the party sharing the secret key k and wishing to authenticate the message will simply check if $\tilde{s} = h_k(\tilde{m})$, thus

$$g_k(\tilde{c}) = \begin{cases} \tilde{m} & \text{if } \tilde{s} = h_k(\tilde{m}) \\ \bot & \text{otherwise.} \end{cases}$$

In terms of random variables, the adversary who intercepts the ciphertext to replace it with his own obtains C. But even if C does not contain a clear copy of M, just like for non-malleability we have to assume that (part of) the message might be public, or that the adversary knows it by some other means. Hence when he creates the ciphertext $\tilde{C}$ he can make it depend on the part of the key leaked by MC, but not on any other part of K, i.e., $H(K|MC\tilde{C}) = H(K|MC)$, or equivalently $I(\tilde{C}; K|MC) = H(K|MC) - H(K|MC\tilde{C}) = 0$. The authentication scheme is successful if $\tilde{M} = \bot$ whenever the adversary modifies C.

Definition 6. *An encryption scheme is said to provide ε-authenticity (ε-A), if for all message random variables M on $\mathcal{X}$ independent from the key – i.e., $I(M; K) = 0$ – and all ciphertexts $\tilde{C}$ on $\mathcal{Y}$ different from C and independent from the key given MC – i.e., $\Pr[C = \tilde{C}] = 0$ and $I(\tilde{C}; K|MC) = 0$ – we have*

$$P_{\tilde{M}}(\bot) \geq 1 - \varepsilon \ .$$

Unlike secrecy, authenticity can only be defined with high probability over the choice of keys, since it is always possible that an adversary might be lucky and choose a valid ciphertext. Definition 6 can however still be strengthened a little, since it corresponds to average case security over C. We discuss this further in the full version of this work [9, Appendix A.3].

We note that this definition could equivalently have been written with the variational distance notation. Abusing slightly notation, we write $\bot$ for the random variable on $\mathcal{X} \cup \{\bot\}$ which takes value $\bot$ with probability 1. Then Definition 6 is equivalent to $d(\tilde{M}, \bot) \leq \varepsilon$.

The notation used in this definition – in particular the use of random variables – is not quite standard. We use it for compatibility with the definitions of non-malleability. This definition and the alternative from [9, Appendix A.3] are however identical to what is found in textbooks, e.g., [17]. We additionally give a proof in [9, Appendix B.2] that ε-almost 2-strong universal hashing forms an ε-authentication scheme according to both these definitions.

4   Non-Malleability and 2-Message Secrecy

The main result of this section, stated here under as Theorem 7 is that information-theoretic perfect non-malleability (PNM) is equivalent to uniformly mapping any pair of different messages to all possible pairs of different ciphertexts. As noted in Corollary 9, this means PNM is equivalent to 2-message perfect secrecy (PS^2) if the message and ciphertext alphabets have the same size, and strictly stronger than PS^2 if the ciphertext alphabet is larger. This immediately gives a lower bound on the necessary key size for PNM, and an easy way to design and prove the secrecy of these schemes.

Theorem 7. *Let* $\{f_k : \mathcal{X} \to \mathcal{Y}\}_{k \in \mathcal{K}}$ *be a set of encryption functions with key given by K and $|\mathcal{Y}| > 2$. The corresponding encryption scheme provides perfect non-malleability (PNM) if and only if for any two different random variables M_1 and M_2 with domain $\mathscr{D}(M_1 M_2) \subseteq \mathcal{X}_{\mathrm{diff}}^{\times 2}$ and independent from the key – i.e., $\Pr[M_1 = M_2] = 0$ and $I(M_1 M_2; K) = 0$ – and any values $(m_1, m_2) \in \mathscr{D}(M_1 M_2)$ and $(c_1, c_2) \in \mathcal{Y}_{\mathrm{diff}}^{\times 2}$,*

$$P_{C_1 C_2 | M_1 M_2}(c_1, c_2 | m_1, m_2) = \frac{1}{\left|\mathcal{Y}_{\mathrm{diff}}^{\times 2}\right|} \; . \tag{5}$$

Note that this theorem immediately implies the equivalence between PNM and PS^2 if $|\mathcal{X}| = |\mathcal{Y}|$.

Equation (5) makes a statement about the distribution of two ciphertext random variables $C_1 C_2$, given that the messages $M_1 M_2$ are independent from the key. PNM on the other hand, makes a statement about the distribution of some message $\tilde{M}$, given that the corresponding ciphertext $\tilde{C}$ is somewhat independent from the key. In both cases the random variables $M_1 M_2 C_1 C_2 K$ and $M \tilde{M} C \tilde{C} K$ are defined over different domains, e.g., M_2 is independent from the key but $\tilde{M}$ can be correlated. So to simplify the proof of Theorem 7, we will use a proposition which will allows us to convert more easily between the two domains, namely Lemma 8 here below.

Lemma 8. *Let* $\{f_k : \mathcal{X} \to \mathcal{Y}\}_{k \in \mathcal{K}}$ *be the encryption functions from a symmetric-key encryption scheme. For any random variable M on $\mathcal{X}$ independent from the key – i.e., $I(M; K) = 0$ – and any $m \in \mathcal{X}$ and $c \in \mathcal{Y}$, we have*

$$P_{C|M}(c|m) = \frac{1}{|\mathcal{Y}|} \tag{6}$$

if and only if for any random variable $\tilde{C}$ on the ciphertext alphabet $\mathcal{Y}$ independent from the key – i.e., $I(\tilde{C}; K) = 0$ – we have

$$I(\tilde{M}; \tilde{C}) = 0 \; , \tag{7}$$

where $\tilde{M} = g_K(\tilde{C})$ and g_k is the decryption function corresponding to f_k with range $\mathcal{X} \cup \{\bot\}$.

We provide a proof of Lemma 8 in Appendix A as Lemma 12.

Imagine that the random variables M_1 and C_1 in (5) are fixed and fall out of the equation. The result would be (6). In the definition of PNM, namely in $I(\tilde{M}; \tilde{C}|MC) = 0$, imagine that M and C are fixed and also fall out of the equation. The result would be (7). This proposition basically shows that Theorem 7 holds for fixed values of MC and M_1C_1. To finish the proof, we still need to show that it holds for arbitrary MC and M_1C_1 on the given domains.

Proof (Proof of Theorem 7). We start with the "if direction" ((5) $\implies$ PNM). Note that for any random variables X, Y and Z, $I(X;Y|Z) = 0$ if and only if for all $z \in \mathscr{D}(Z)$, $I(X;Y|Z = z) = 0$. So to prove PNM, it is sufficient to fix m_1 and c_1 arbitrarily, and show that $I(\tilde{M}; \tilde{C}|MC = m_1c_1) = 0$.

We define new random variables M', C' and K' on alphabets $\mathcal{X}' := \mathcal{X} \setminus \{m_1\}$, $\mathcal{Y}' := \mathcal{Y} \setminus \{c_1\}$ and $\mathcal{K}' := \{k \in \mathcal{K} : f_k(m_1) = c_1\}$ with joint distribution

$$P_{M'C'K'}(m, c, k) := P_{M_2 C_2 K|M_1 C_1}(m, c, k|m_1, c_1) . \tag{8}$$

It follows from (5) that $P_{C_2|M_1 M_2 C_1}(c_2|m_1, m_2, c_1) = \frac{1}{|\mathcal{Y}|-1}$. Hence from (8),

$$P_{C'|M'}(c|m) = \frac{P_{M_2 C_2|M_1 C_1}(m, c|m_1, c_1)}{P_{M_2|M_1 C_1}(m|m_1, c_1)} = P_{C_2|M_1 M_2 C_1}(c|m_1, m, c_1) = \frac{1}{|\mathcal{Y}'|} .$$

All the conditions are gathered to apply Lemma 8, which tells us that for any $\tilde{C}'$ defined on $\mathcal{Y}'$ with $I(\tilde{C}'; K') = 0$, $I(\tilde{M}'; \tilde{C}') = 0$. By repeating this for different values of M_1 and C_1, we can extend $\tilde{C}'$ to any random variable $\tilde{C}$ such that $I(\tilde{C}; K|M_1 C_1) = 0$, but otherwise arbitrarily correlated to M_1 and C_1, and with $I(\tilde{M}; \tilde{C}|M_1 C_1) = 0$.

Now for the "only if direction" (PNM $\implies$ (5)). Let M_1 be any random variable with $\mathscr{D}(M_1) = \mathcal{X}$ and pick any values $(m_1, m_2) \in \mathcal{X}_{\text{diff}}^{\times 2}$ and $(c_1, c_2) \in \mathcal{Y}_{\text{diff}}^{\times 2}$. Since the scheme provides PNM we have $I(\tilde{M}; \tilde{C}|M_1 C_1)$ for any $\tilde{C}$ with $I(\tilde{C}; K|M_1 C_1) = 0$ and $\Pr[\tilde{C} = C_1] = 0$. Similar to what we did above, we define random variables $\tilde{M}', \tilde{C}', K'$ and $\tilde{M}'', \tilde{C}'', K''$ as

$$P_{\tilde{M}'\tilde{C}'K'}(m, c, k) := P_{\tilde{M}\tilde{C}K|M_1 C_1}(m, c, k|m_1, c_1) ,$$

$$P_{\tilde{M}''\tilde{C}''K''}(m, c, k) := P_{\tilde{M}\tilde{C}K|M_1 C_1}(m, c, k|m_2, c_2) .$$

So $I(\tilde{M}'; \tilde{C}') = I(\tilde{M}''; \tilde{C}'') = 0$. We can now apply Lemma 8 to the encryption functions of K' and K'' respectively, and get that for any M' and M'' on $\mathcal{X} \setminus \{m_1\}$ and $\mathcal{X} \setminus \{m_2\}$ and independent from K' and K'' respectively,

$$P_{C'|M'}(c'|m') = \frac{1}{|\mathcal{Y}| - 1} ,$$

$$P_{C''|M''}(c''|m'') = \frac{1}{|\mathcal{Y}| - 1} . \tag{9}$$

Let M_2 be any random variable such that $\mathscr{D}(M_1M_2) \subseteq \mathcal{X}_{\text{diff}}^{\times 2}$, $m_1, m_2 \in \mathscr{D}(M_2)$ and $I(M_1M_2; K) = 0$, and choose the M' and M'' from (9) such that

$$P_{M'C'}(m,c) = P_{M_2C_2|M_1C_1}(m,c|m_1,c_1)$$
$$\text{and } P_{M''C''}(m,c) = P_{M_2C_2|M_1C_1}(m,c|m_2,c_2) \ .$$

We then have

$$P_{C_1C_2|M_1M_2}(c_1,c_2|m_1,m_2) = P_{C_1|M_1M_2}(c_1|m_1,m_2)P_{C_2|M_1M_2C_1}(c_2|m_1,m_2,c_1)$$

$$= P_{C_1|M_1}(c_1|m_1)\frac{1}{|\mathcal{Y}|-1} \ , \tag{10}$$

$$P_{C_1C_2|M_1M_2}(c_2,c_1|m_2,m_1) = P_{C_1|M_1}(c_2|m_2)\frac{1}{|\mathcal{Y}|-1} \ .$$

Since the same encryption function with the same key is applied to m_1 and m_2, we must have $P_{C_1C_2|M_1M_2}(c_1,c_2|m_1,m_2) = P_{C_1C_2|M_1M_2}(c_2,c_1|m_2,m_1)$, and hence for all $(m_1,m_2) \in \mathcal{X}_{\text{diff}}^{\times 2}$ and $(c_1,c_2) \in \mathcal{Y}_{\text{diff}}^{\times 2}$,

$$P_{C_1|M_1}(c_1|m_1) = P_{C_1|M_1}(c_2|m_2) \ .$$

Since $|\mathcal{Y}| > 2$, this implies that for any $(m_1,m_2) \in \mathcal{X}_{\text{diff}}^{\times 2}$ and $(c_1,c_2,c_3) \in \mathcal{Y}_{\text{diff}}^{\times 3}$,

$$P_{C_1|M_1}(c_1|m_1) = P_{C_1|M_1}(c_3|m_2) = P_{C_1|M_1}(c_2|m_1) \ .$$

Since $\sum_c P_{C_1|M_1}(c|m) = 1$, we get $P_{C_1|M_1}(c|m) = \frac{1}{|\mathcal{Y}|}$. Putting this in (10) proves the theorem. □

Theorem 7 equates PNM with a uniform mapping from pairs of different messages to different ciphertexts ((5)). This latter condition is slightly different from PS^2. Corollary 9 makes the correspondence between PNM and PS^2 explicit.

Corollary 9. *For any symmetric-key encryption scheme with ciphertext alphabet size $|\mathcal{Y}| > 2$,*[6]

$$PNM_{|\mathcal{X}|=|\mathcal{Y}|} \Leftrightarrow PS^2_{|\mathcal{X}|=|\mathcal{Y}|} \ ,$$
$$PNM_{|\mathcal{X}|<|\mathcal{Y}|} \Rightarrow PS^2_{|\mathcal{X}|<|\mathcal{Y}|} \ ,$$
$$PNM_{|\mathcal{X}|<|\mathcal{Y}|} \nLeftarrow PS^2_{|\mathcal{X}|<|\mathcal{Y}|} \ .$$

Proof. Equation (5) is clearly a sufficient condition to imply PS^2, no matter what the ciphertext length is. So from Theorem 7 we immediately have

$$\text{PNM}_{|\mathcal{X}|=|\mathcal{Y}|} \Rightarrow \text{PS}^2_{|\mathcal{X}|=|\mathcal{Y}|} \ ,$$
$$\text{PNM}_{|\mathcal{X}|<|\mathcal{Y}|} \Rightarrow \text{PS}^2_{|\mathcal{X}|<|\mathcal{Y}|} \ .$$

---

[6] By $\text{PNM}_{|\mathcal{X}|=|\mathcal{Y}|}$, $\text{PNM}_{|\mathcal{X}|<|\mathcal{Y}|}$, etc., we simply mean encryption functions with message and ciphertext alphabet sizes corresponding to the subscript and meeting the corresponding security definitions. We did not formally introduce this notation, because it is quite intuitive and is not used anywhere else. All other results about PNM, PS^2, etc., apply to all message and ciphertext alphabet sizes if not clearly stated otherwise.

If $|\mathcal{X}| = |\mathcal{Y}|$, then for any scheme providing PS^2, and random variables $M_1 M_2$ uniformly distributed on $\mathcal{X}_{\text{diff}}^{\times 2}$,

$$H(C_1 C_2 | M_1 M_2) = H(C_1 C_2) \geq \log |\mathcal{X}_{\text{diff}}^{\times 2}| = \log |\mathcal{Y}_{\text{diff}}^{\times 2}| .$$

The inequality above holds because the entropy of the ciphertexts must be at least as large as the entropy of the messages. Thus (5) holds as well, which means that

$$\text{PNM}_{|\mathcal{X}|=|\mathcal{Y}|} \Leftarrow \text{PS}^2_{|\mathcal{X}|=|\mathcal{Y}|} .$$

Finally, to show that

$$\text{PNM}_{|\mathcal{X}|<|\mathcal{Y}|} \nLeftarrow \text{PS}^2_{|\mathcal{X}|<|\mathcal{Y}|} ,$$

we give an example in the full version of this work [9, Lemma 6.1] of an encryption scheme with $|\mathcal{X}| < |\mathcal{Y}|$ and providing PS^2, but not satisfying (5).   □

We note that the requirement that $|\mathcal{Y}| > 2$ is essential, since otherwise PNM does not even imply PS. This can easily be seen by considering the following example. Let $\mathcal{X} = \mathcal{Y} = \{0, 1\}$ and the encryption function be the identity function. For such a small alphabet $H(\tilde{M}|MC) = H(\tilde{M}|MC\tilde{C}) = 0$, because as $\Pr[\tilde{M} = M] = 0$, once $M = m$ is fixed, $\tilde{M}$ can only take the other value, and hence has zero entropy. This scheme thus provides PNM, because the ciphertext $\tilde{C}$ chosen by the adversary provides no information about $\tilde{M}$.

An important consequence of Theorem 7 is that we get an immediate lower bound on the size of the secret key needed for PNM for any ciphertext size.

Corollary 10. *If an encryption scheme with key K provides PNM, then*

$$H(K) \geq \log |\mathcal{Y}_{\text{diff}}^{\times 2}| = \log |\mathcal{Y}| (|\mathcal{Y}| - 1) .$$

This immediately implies that the perfect non-malleable scheme proposed by Hanaoka et al. [7,5] is optimal in the key size.[7] We describe this scheme in the full version of this work [9, Appendix B.1] for completeness.

5   Non-Malleability and Authentication

We show in this section that any authentication scheme provides approximate non-malleability. In the full version of this work [9, Appendix A.3] we provide a proof that the same holds when we replace the notions of authenticity and non-malleability with strong authenticity and strong approximate non-malleability.

Theorem 11. *Any scheme which provides ε-authenticity also provides $(\sqrt{\varepsilon}+\varepsilon)$-non-malleability.*

---

[7] This scheme is also optimal in the ciphertext size, since $|\mathcal{X}| = |\mathcal{Y}|$.

Proof. For all $(m,c) \in \mathscr{D}(MC)$, let $\varepsilon_{m,c} := 1 - P_{\tilde{M}|MC}(\bot|m,c)$. So we have $\sum_{m,c} P_{MC}(m,c)\varepsilon_{m,c} \le \varepsilon$. Note that

$$P_{\tilde{M}|MC}(\bot|m,c) = \frac{\sum_{\tilde{c}} P_{\tilde{M}\tilde{C}MC}(\bot,\tilde{c},m,c)}{P_{MC}(m,c)}$$

$$= \sum_{\tilde{c}} P_{\tilde{C}|MC}(\tilde{c}|m,c) P_{\tilde{M}|MC\tilde{C}}(\bot|m,c,\tilde{c}) \ .$$

From Lemma 13 in Appendix A we then have that

$$\frac{1}{2} \sum_{\tilde{c}} P_{\tilde{C}|MC}(\tilde{c}|m,c) \left| P_{\tilde{M}|MC\tilde{C}}(\bot|m,c,\tilde{c}) - P_{\tilde{M}|MC}(\bot|m,c) \right| \le \sqrt{\varepsilon_{m,c}}.$$

Using Jensen's inequality we get

$$\frac{1}{2} \sum_{m,c,\tilde{c}} P_{MC\tilde{C}}(m,c,\tilde{c}) \left| P_{\tilde{M}|MC\tilde{C}}(\bot|m,c,\tilde{c}) - P_{\tilde{M}|MC}(\bot|m,c) \right| \le \sqrt{\varepsilon} \ .$$

Putting this in the definition of non-malleability we finally obtain

$$\frac{1}{2} \sum_{m,c,\tilde{m},\tilde{c}} P_{MC\tilde{C}}(m,c,\tilde{c}) \left| P_{\tilde{M}|MC\tilde{C}}(\tilde{m}|m,c,\tilde{c}) - P_{\tilde{M}|MC}(\tilde{m}|m,c) \right|$$

$$\le \frac{1}{2} \sum_{m,c,\tilde{c}} P_{MC\tilde{C}}(m,c,\tilde{c}) \left| P_{\tilde{M}|MC\tilde{C}}(\bot|m,c,\tilde{c}) - P_{\tilde{M}|MC}(\bot|m,c) \right|$$

$$+ \sum_{\tilde{m}\in\mathcal{X}} P_{\tilde{M}}(\tilde{m})$$

$$\le \sqrt{\varepsilon} + \varepsilon \ .$$

$\square$

ε-authentication can be achieved with a shared key of length

$$\log|\mathcal{K}| \le 2\log\log|\mathcal{X}| + 3\log\frac{1}{\varepsilon} \tag{11}$$

by using almost strong 2-universal hashing. For completeness we show this in the full version of this work [9, Appendix B.2]. The parameters of (11) are from a specific family of almost strong 2-universal hash functions by Bierbrauer et al. [3]. We refer to an expository paper on 2-universal hashing by Stinson [16] for an overview of constructions.

We note that since (approximate) secrecy is only possible if the key is as long as the message, this means that ε-NM does not imply secrecy. This might seem surprising at first, because in the public-key setting non-malleability does imply secrecy [2]. This difference between non-malleability and secrecy in the private-key setting has however already been noted by Katz and Yung [8].[8]

---

[8] In [8], the adversary is declared unsuccessful if the message produced is invalid, in which case it is trivial that authenticity is sufficient to achieve approximate non-malleability. We refer to Sect. 6 for a further discussion of how to handle invalid messages.

6   Concluding Remarks

In this work we studied information-theoretic non-malleability, extending a line of research initiated by Hanaoka et al. [7]. The formal definitions used to capture the intuitive notion of non-malleability follow these previous works [7,5,10]. There exist however alternative ways to characterize the same notion. We discuss them briefly in this section.

Unifying the Definitions. Although the works on computational and information-theoretic non-malleability in the private-key setting use the same informal definition, the tools used to formalize this definition are different: the former computes the probability that the falsified message is related to the original message in the real and ideal case [8], the latter measures the indistinguishability of message and ciphertext distributions between the real and ideal case. It remains open to prove formally that these definitions are indeed equivalent when the distinguisher in the computational security definition is unlimited, and does not access oracles.

Invalid Ciphertexts. In the formal definition of non-malleability, we chose that the adversary is allowed to pick invalid ciphertexts and still be successful. We could have considered an alternative weaker definition, in which the adversary automatically fails when this happens. In the public-key setting, both ways of treating invalid ciphertexts can be found, and there is no clear consensus as to how to deal with this case. Pass et al. [12] investigate the differences between the two notions in detail. They point out how the stronger notion in which the adversary can produce an invalid ciphertext makes a critical difference in certain situations, in particular for composability.

In the case of information-theoretic security, if we had defined the adversary to be unsuccessful when he picks an invalid ciphertext, then perfect non-malleability would have been exactly equivalent to 2-message perfect secrecy, and not strictly strong for a ciphertext longer than the message. And authenticity would trivially imply approximate non-malleability, instead of requiring some work.

Accessing Oracles. When considering computational security, the adversary usually has access at various stages to a decryption oracle.[9] In information-theoretic security, when the adversary is computationally unbounded, unlimited access to an oracle is not possible. McAven et al. [10] and Portmann and Tanaka [13] propose security definitions in which the adversary can make ℓ queries to an oracle. The definitions of non-malleability used in this work can be seen as allowing the adversary 1 query to an encryption oracle, after which he has to choose his forged ciphertext $\tilde{C}$. By generalizing this to ℓ-queries to either encryption or decryption oracles, we can define various notions of ℓ-non-malleability.

---

[9] In the case of computational private-key cryptography, he may also access an encryption oracle.

We conjecture that the results from this work on the relations between 1-non-malleability, 2-message security, and the 2-universal hashing used for authentication, directly generalize to ℓ-non-malleability, $(\ell + 1)$-message security and $(\ell + 1)$-universal hashing.

Acknowledgments. AK was partially supported by the Ministry of Education, Science, Sports and Culture, Grant-in-Aid for Scientific Research (B), 18300002. KT was supported in part by I-System Co. Ltd.

References

1. Bellare, M., Desai, A., Pointcheval, D., Rogaway, P.: Relations among notions of security for public-key encryption schemes. In: Krawczyk, H. (ed.) CRYPTO 1998. LNCS, vol. 1462, pp. 26–45. Springer, Heidelberg (1998)
2. Bellare, M., Sahai, A.: Non-malleable encryption: Equivalence between two notions, and an indistinguishability-based characterization. In: Wiener, M. (ed.) CRYPTO 1999. LNCS, vol. 1666, pp. 519–536. Springer, Heidelberg (1999), full version available at http://eprint.iacr.org/2006/228
3. Bierbrauer, J., Johansson, T., Kabatianskii, G.A., Smeets, B.J.M.: On families of hash functions via geometric codes and concatenation. In: Stinson, D.R. (ed.) CRYPTO 1993. LNCS, vol. 773, pp. 331–342. Springer, Heidelberg (1994)
4. Dolev, D., Dwork, C., Naor, M.: Non-malleable cryptography. SIAM Journal on Computing 30(2), 391–437 (2000); a preliminary version appeared at STOC 1991
5. Hanaoka, G.: Some information theoretic arguments for encryption: Non-malleability and chosen-ciphertext security (invited talk). In: Safavi-Naini, R. (ed.) ICITS 2008. LNCS, vol. 5155, pp. 223–231. Springer, Heidelberg (2008)
6. Hanaoka, G., Hanaoka, Y., Hagiwara, M., Watanabe, H., Imai, H.: Unconditionally secure chaffing-and-winnowing: A relationship between encryption and authentication. In: Fossorier, M.P.C., Imai, H., Lin, S., Poli, A. (eds.) AAECC 2006. LNCS, vol. 3857, pp. 154–162. Springer, Heidelberg (2006)
7. Hanaoka, G., Shikata, J., Hanaoka, Y., Imai, H.: Unconditionally secure anonymous encryption and group authentication. The Computer Journal 49(3), 310–321 (2006); a preliminary version appeared at Asiacrypt 2002
8. Katz, J., Yung, M.: Characterization of security notions for probabilistic private-key encryption. Journal of Cryptology 19(1), 67–95 (2006)
9. Kawachi, A., Portmann, C., Tanaka, K.: Characterization of the relations between information-theoretic non-malleability, secrecy, and authenticity. Cryptology ePrint Archive, Report 2011/092 (2011); full version of the current paper, http://eprint.iacr.org/2011/092
10. McAven, L., Safavi-Naini, R., Yung, M.: Unconditionally secure encryption under strong attacks. In: Wang, H., Pieprzyk, J., Varadharajan, V. (eds.) ACISP 2004. LNCS, vol. 3108, pp. 427–439. Springer, Heidelberg (2004)
11. Pass, R., Shelat, A., Vaikuntanathan, V.: Construction of a non-malleable encryption scheme from any semantically secure one. In: Dwork, C. (ed.) CRYPTO 2006. LNCS, vol. 4117, pp. 271–289. Springer, Heidelberg (2006)
12. Pass, R., Shelat, A., Vaikuntanathan, V.: Relations among notions of non-malleability for encryption. In: Kurosawa, K. (ed.) ASIACRYPT 2007. LNCS, vol. 4833, pp. 519–535. Springer, Heidelberg (2007)

13. Portmann, C., Tanaka, K.: Information-theoretic secrecy with access to decryption oracles. To appear in IEICE Transactions A, Fundamentals of Electronics, Communications and Computer Sciences (2011)
14. Shannon, C.: Communication theory of secrecy systems. Bell System Technical Journal 28(4), 656–715 (1949)
15. Stinson, D.R.: Universal hashing and authentication codes. Designs, Codes and Cryptography 4(3), 369–380 (1994); a preliminary version appeared at CRYPTO 1991
16. Stinson, D.R.: On the connections between universal hashing, combinatorial designs and error-correcting codes. Proceedings of Congressus Numerantium 114, 7–27 (1996)
17. Stinson, D.R.: Cryptography: Theory and Practice, 2 edn. Chapman & Hall/CRC (2002)
18. Wegman, M.N., Carter, L.: New hash functions and their use in authentication and set equality. Journal of Computer and System Sciences 22(3), 265–279 (1981)

A   Technical Lemmas

In this section we provide a few technical lemmas needed in the main body of this work. The following lemma shows that a ciphertext chosen by an adversary is independent from the corresponding message after decryption if and only if the encryption scheme maps every message to all ciphertext with equal probability.

Lemma 12. *Let $\{f_k : \mathcal{X} \to \mathcal{Y}\}_{k \in \mathcal{K}}$ be the encryption functions from a symmetric-key encryption scheme. For any random variable M on $\mathcal{X}$ independent from the key – i.e., $I(M; K) = 0$ – and any $m \in \mathcal{X}$ and $c \in \mathcal{Y}$, we have*

$$P_{C|M}(c|m) = \frac{1}{|\mathcal{Y}|}$$

if and only if for any random variable $\tilde{C}$ on the ciphertext alphabet $\mathcal{Y}$ independent from the key – i.e., $I(\tilde{C}; K) = 0$ – we have

$$I(\tilde{M}; \tilde{C}) = 0 \ ,$$

where $\tilde{M} = g_K(\tilde{C})$ and g_k is the decryption function corresponding to f_k with range $\mathcal{X} \cup \{\perp\}$.

Proof. We start with the "if direction" ($I(\tilde{M}; \tilde{C}) = 0 \implies P_{C|M}(c|m) = \frac{1}{|\mathcal{Y}|}$). If $I(\tilde{M}; \tilde{C}) = 0$ then for any $m \in \bar{\mathcal{X}}$ and $c \in \mathcal{Y}$, $P_{\tilde{M}|\tilde{C}}(m|c) = P_{\tilde{M}}(m)$ and hence for any two $c, c' \in \mathcal{Y}$ and any $m \in \bar{\mathcal{X}}$,

$$P_{\tilde{M}|\tilde{C}}(m|c) = P_{\tilde{M}|\tilde{C}}(m|c') \ . \tag{12}$$

Since $I(\tilde{C}; K) = 0$, for any $m \in \mathcal{X}$ and $c \in \mathcal{Y}$ we have

$$P_{\tilde{M}|\tilde{C}}(m|c) = \sum_{\substack{k \in \mathcal{K} \\ f_k^{-1}(c) = m}} P_K(k) = \sum_{\substack{k \in \mathcal{K} \\ f_k(m) = c}} P_K(k) = P_{C|M}(c|m) \tag{13}$$

for any M with $I(M; K) = 0$. Since the distribution $P_{C|M}$ is well defined, we have for any $m \in \mathcal{X}$ that

$$\sum_{c \in \mathcal{Y}} P_{C|M}(c|m) = 1 \ . \tag{14}$$

Combining (12), (13) and (14) we get that for any $m \in \mathcal{X}$ and any $c \in \mathcal{Y}$, $P_{C|M}(c|m) = \frac{1}{|\mathcal{Y}|}$.

The "only if direction" ($P_{C|M}(c|m) = \frac{1}{|\mathcal{Y}|} \implies I(\tilde{M}; \tilde{C}) = 0$) works similarly. We have for any $m \in \mathcal{X}$ and $c \in \mathcal{Y}$ that

$$\frac{1}{|\mathcal{Y}|} = P_{C|M}(c|m) = \sum_{\substack{k \in \mathcal{K} \\ f_k(m)=c}} P_K(k) = \sum_{\substack{k \in \mathcal{K} \\ f_k^{-1}(c)=m}} P_K(k) = P_{\tilde{M}|\tilde{C}}(m|c)$$

for any $\tilde{C}$ independent from the key. Furthermore

$$P_{\tilde{M}|\tilde{C}}(\perp|c) = 1 - \sum_{m \in \mathcal{X}} P_{\tilde{M}|\tilde{C}}(m|c) = 1 - \frac{|\mathcal{X}|}{|\mathcal{Y}|}$$

for every $c \in \mathcal{Y}$. Hence $I(\tilde{M}; \tilde{C}) = 0$. ☐

This last lemma is needed in the proof of Theorem 11.

Lemma 13. *For $i \in [n]$, let $0 \le a_i \le 1$ and have weighted average $\sum_i w_i a_i = a$, where $0 \le w_i \le 1$ and $\sum_i w_i = 1$. Then*

$$\sum_{i=1}^n w_i |a_i - a| \le 2 \min\{\sqrt{a}, \sqrt{1-a}\} \ .$$

Proof. Without loss of generality, let $a \le \frac{1}{2}$. If $a > \frac{1}{2}$, set $a_i^{\text{new}} := 1 - a_i^{\text{old}}$ for all i, which leaves $|a_i - a|$ unchanged.

Define $\mathcal{I} := \{i \in [n] : a_i \ge \sqrt{a}\}$. Then

$$\sum_{i=1}^n w_i a_i \ge \sum_{i \in \mathcal{I}} w_i \sqrt{a} \ ,$$

hence $\sum_{i \in \mathcal{I}} w_i \le \sqrt{a}$. We then have

$$\sum_{i=1}^n w_i |a_i - a| = \sum_{i \in \mathcal{I}} w_i |a_i - a| + \sum_{i \in [n] \backslash \mathcal{I}} w_i |a_i - a|$$

$$\le \sum_{i \in \mathcal{I}} w_i (1 - a) + \sum_{i \in [n] \backslash \mathcal{I}} w_i \max\{\sqrt{a} - a, a\}$$

$$\le \sqrt{a}(1 - a) + (1 - \sqrt{a}) \max\{\sqrt{a} - a, a\}$$

$$= 2\sqrt{a} \ .$$

☐

Randomly Encoding Functions:
A New Cryptographic Paradigm⋆
(Invited Talk)

Benny Applebaum

School of Electrical Engineering, Tel-Aviv University
benny.applebaum@gmail.com

Abstract. The notion of *randomized encoding* allows to represent a "complex" function $f(x)$ by a "simpler" randomized mapping $\hat{f}(x; r)$ whose output distribution on an input x encodes the value of $f(x)$. We survey several cryptographic applications of this paradigm.

1 Introduction

To what extent can one simplify the task of computing a function f by settling for computing some (possibly randomized) *encoding* of its output? This question can be formalized as follows: We say that a function $\hat{f}(x; r)$ is a *randomized encoding* (RE) of a function $f(x)$, if its output distribution depends only on the output of f. More precisely, we require the existence of an efficient recovery algorithm Rec and an efficient randomized simulator Sim that satisfy the following conditions:

- (**Correctness**) For every (x, r), given $\hat{f}(x; r)$ the algorithm Rec recovers $f(x)$;
- (**Privacy**) For every x, given $f(x)$ the simulator Sim samples from the distribution of $\hat{f}(x; r)$ induced by a uniform choice of r.

This notion of randomized encoding was introduced by Ishai and Kushilevitz [21] (under the algebraic framework of *randomizing polynomials*) and was implicitly used, in weaker forms, in the context of secure multiparty computation (e.g., [23,19]). Observe that each of the above requirements alone can be satisfied by a trivial function $\hat{f}$ (e.g., $\hat{f}(x; r) = x$ and $\hat{f}(x; r) = 0$, respectively). However, the combination of the two requirements can be viewed as a non-trivial natural relaxation of the usual notion of computing. This gives rise to the following question: Can we encode "complex" functions f by "simple" functions $\hat{f}$?

It is not hard to show that if one is restricted to *deterministic* encoding the answer is in general negative. For example, let us call a function "simple" if each of its output bits depends on a small constant number of input bits, e.g., 4. In this case, if a boolean function $f : \{0, 1\}^n \to \{0, 1\}$ can be deterministically encoded by some (possibly non-boolean) simple function $\hat{f}$, then f itself is simple. Indeed

---

⋆ Supported by Alon Fellowship.

S. Fehr (Ed.): ICITS 2011, LNCS 6673, pp. 25–31, 2011.

if the encoding is deterministic then, by privacy, there is a pair of strings z_0 and z_1 such that for every x we have $\hat{f}(x) = z_{f(x)}$. By correctness, z_0 and z_1 should differ in at least a single location i (assuming that f is non-degenerate). Hence, $f(x)$ can be computed by the 4-local function which projects the i-th bit of $\hat{f}(x)$ and, possibly, flips the result. A similar argument holds for any notion of simplicity that is closed under bit-projection and negation.

On the other hand, the use of randomness allows us to encode non-simple functions by simple ones. For example, the sum-function

$$f(x) = x_1 + \ldots + x_n,$$

where x_i is the i-th bit of x and addition is over $\mathbb{F}_2$, can be encoded by the 3-local function

$$\hat{f}(x; (r_1, \ldots, r_{n-1})) = (x_1 - r_1, r_1 + x_2 - r_2, \ldots, r_{n-1} + x_n),$$

which uses $n - 1$ random inputs $r = (r_1, \ldots, r_{n-1})$ and outputs n bits. To prove correctness, note that the sum of the output bits of $\hat{f}(x; r)$ equals to $\sum x_i$ as the r_i's cancel out. On the other hand, when r is random, the vector $\hat{f}(x; r)$ is uniformly distributed over all n-bit vectors whose components add to $f(x)$, and so privacy follows.

Perhaps surprisingly, it turns out that REs are powerful enough to encode rich classes of functions. In [21,22,4,3] it is shown that 4-local functions can encode log-space computations, and even poly-time computations if one settles for computational privacy, i.e., the simulator's output is only required to be computationally indistinguishable from $\hat{f}(x; r)$.[1] Similar results hold for other notions of simplicity that will be mentioned later.

The ability to encode complex functions by simple ones is extremely useful. In this short survey we will focus on the applications of REs (and ignore the way REs are constructed). In the next sections we will demonstrate several interesting ways in which this tool can be employed. We consider the archetypal cryptographic setting where Alice and Bob wish to accomplish some computational goal (e.g., a functionality f) at the presence of an adversary. We will see that REs can be beneficial when they are applied to each component of this system: to the functionality, to the honest parties, and even to the adversary.

2   Encoding the Functionality

Delegating computations. Suppose that Bob is a computationally weak device (client) who wishes to compute a complex function f on an input x. Bob is too weak to compute f on his own and so he delegates the computation to a computationally strong server Alice. Since Bob does not trust Alice, he wishes to

---

[1] The latter requires to assume the existence of log-space computable one-way function, an assumption which is implied by most standard intractability assumptions used in cryptography.

guarantee the following: (1) Secrecy: Alice should learn nothing on the input x; and (2) Verifiability: Bob should be able to verify the correctness of the output (i.e., a cheating Alice should be caught whp). Similar problems were extensively studied in various settings, originating from the early works on interactive proofs, program checking and instance-hiding schemes (see references in [6]).

Let us start with secrecy and consider a variant where both parties should learn the output $f(x)$ but x should remain private. In this case, a randomized encoding $\hat{f}$ immediately solves the problem via the following single-round protocol: Bob selects private randomness r, computes $\hat{f}(x; r)$ and sends the result to Alice who applies the recovery algorithm and outputs the result. The privacy of the RE guarantees that Alice learns nothing beyond $f(x)$. We refer to this protocol as the *basic RE protocol*. Jumping ahead, we note that the protocol has a non-trivial correctness guarantee: even if the server Alice deviates from the protocol and violates correctness she cannot force an erroneous output which violates privacy; that is, it is possible to simulate erroneous outputs solely based on the correct outputs.

It is not hard to modify the basic protocol and obtain full secrecy: instead of encoding f, encode an encrypted version of f. Namely, define a function $g(x, s) = f(x) \oplus s$, where s plays the role of a one-time pad (OTP), and apply the previous protocol as follows: Bob uniformly chooses the pad s and the randomness r, and sends the encoding $\hat{g}(x, s; r)$ of g to Alice, who recovers the result $y = g(x, s) = f(x) \oplus s$, and sends it back to Bob. Finally, Bob removes the pad s and terminates with $f(x)$. (See [3] for more details.)

Achieving verifiability is slightly more tricky. The idea, due to [6], is to combine an RE with a private-key signature scheme (also known as message authentication code or MAC) and ask the server to sign the output of the computation under the client's private key. Here the privacy property of the RE will be used to hide the secret key. Specifically, given an input x, Bob asks Alice to compute $y = f(x)$ (via the previous protocol) and, in addition, to generate a signature on $f(x)$ under a private key k which is chosen randomly by the client. The latter request is computed via the basic RE protocol that hides the private key from Alice. More precisely, Bob, who holds both x and k, invokes an RE protocol in which both parties learn the function $g(x, k) = \mathtt{MAC}_k(f(x))$. Bob then accepts the answer y if and only if the result of the protocol is a valid signature on y under the key k. (The latter computation is typically cheap). The soundness of the protocol follows by showing that a cheating Alice, which fools Bob to accept an erroneous $y^* \neq f(x)$, can be used to either break the privacy of the RE or to forge a valid signature on a new message. For this argument to hold, we crucially relies on the ability to simulate erroneous outputs based on the correct outputs.

The main advantage of this approach over alternative solutions is the ability to achieve good soundness with low computational overhead. For example, $2^{-\tau}$ soundness error introduce an additive overhead of τ in the communication whereas the overhead in competing approaches is multiplicative in τ. (See [6] a more detailed comparison.) Instantiating these approaches with known constructions of REs lead to protocols with an $\mathbf{NC^0}$ client[2] for either log-space functions or poly-time functions depending on the level of security needed (information-theoretic or computational). In fact, in the computational setting we can even reduce the *sequential*-complexity of the client Bob, assuming that he is allowed to invest a lot of computational resources in a preprocessing phase before seeing the actual input x. We also mention that REs can achieve other related properties such as *correctability* [6]: i.e., Bob is able to *correct* Alice's errors as long as Alice is somewhat correct with respect to a predefined distribution over the inputs. In the latter case REs yield $\mathbf{NC^0}$ correctors for log-space computations strengthening the results of [20].

Secure computation [21]. Let us move to a more general setting where the roles of Alice and Bob are symmetric and none of them is computationally weak. The main observation is that instead of securely computing f it suffices to securely compute the randomized encoding $\hat{f}(x;r)$. Indeed, if Alice and Bob learn a sample from $\hat{f}(x;r)$ then they can locally recover the value of $f(x)$ and nothing else. In other words, the task of securely computing f *reduces* to the task of securely computing a simpler randomized functionality $\hat{f}(x;r)$. As protocol designers, we get a powerful tool which allows us to construct a complex interactive object (protocol) by arguing about a simpler *non-interactive* object (RE).

This paradigm, which was introduced in [21] (and motivated the original definition of REs), yields several new results in the domain of secure computation. As an example, if the algebraic degree of $\hat{f}$ is constant then it can be computed in constant number of rounds [9,15]. By instantiating this approach with known RE constructions [22,16], we derive constant-round protocols for boolean or arithmetic log-space functions with information-theoretic security. In the computational setting, this yields a new constant round protocol for poly-time functions [3] providing an alternative construction to the classical protocol of [8].[3] The RE based approach also simplifies the proofs of classical results such as Yao's garbled-circuit protocol [24] and Kilian's completeness theorem [23].

3   Encoding the Primitive: Parallel Cryptography

Suppose now that we already have an implementation of some cryptographic protocol. A key observation made in [4] is that we can "simplify" some of the computations in the protocol by replacing them with their encodings. Consider, for example, the case of public-key encryption: Alice publishes a public/private key pair (pk, sk); Bob uses the public-key pk and a sequence of random coins s to "garble" a message m into a ciphertext $c = \mathsf{E}(\mathsf{pk}, m, s)$; Finally, Alice recovers m by applying the decryption algorithm to the ciphertext $\mathsf{D}(\mathsf{sk}, c)$. Suppose

---

[2] Functions in $\mathbf{NC^0}$ are computable by constant-depth circuits of bounded fan-in, and so they capture a strong notion of constant parallel-time computation.

[3] The RE based solution requires slightly stronger assumption – one-way function computable in log-space rather in poly-time – but can also lead to efficiency improvements as shown in [17].

that Bob sends an encoding of his ciphertext $\widehat{\mathsf{E}}(\mathsf{pk}, m, s; r)$ instead of sending c. This does not violate semantic-security as all the information available to an adversary in the modified protocol can be emulated by an adversary who attacks the original protocol (thanks to the simulator of the RE). On the other hand, Alice can still decrypt the message: first she recovers the original ciphertext (via the recovery algorithm) and then she applies the original decryption algorithm. As a result, we "pushed" the complexity of the sender (encryption algorithm) to the receiver (decryption algorithm).

By employing REs with some additional properties, it is possible to prove similar results for many other cryptographic protocols (e.g., one-way functions, pseudorandom generators, collision-resistance hash functions, signatures, commitments, zero-knowledge proofs) and even information-theoretic primitives (e.g., ε-biased generators and randomness extractors). In the case of stand-alone primitives (e.g., one-way functions and pseudorandom generators) there is no receiver and so the gain in efficiency comes for "free".

Being security preserving, REs give rise to the following paradigm. In order to construct some cryptographic primitive $\mathcal{P}$ in some low complexity class $\mathcal{WEAK}$, first encode functions from a higher complexity class $\mathcal{STRONG}$ by functions from $\mathcal{WEAK}$; then, show that $\mathcal{P}$ has an implementation f in $\mathcal{STRONG}$, and finally replace f by its encoding $\hat{f} \in \mathcal{WEAK}$ and obtain a low-complexity implementation of $\mathcal{P}$. This approach was used in [4,3,5] to obtain cryptographic primitives in $\mathbf{NC^0}$ and even in weaker complexity classes. The fact that REs preserve cryptographic hardness was also used to reduce the complexity of cryptographic *reductions* [4,3] and to reduce the complexity of complete problems for sub-classes of statistical zero-knowledge [18].

4   Encoding the Adversary: Key-Dependent Security

Key-dependent message (KDM) secure encryption schemes [14,10] provide secrecy even when the attacker sees encryptions of messages related to the secret-key sk. Namely, we say that an encryption is KDM secure with respect to a function class $\mathcal{F}$ if semantic security holds even when the adversary can ask for an encryption of the message $f(\mathsf{sk})$ where f is an arbitrary function in $\mathcal{F}$. Until recently, it was only known how to achieve KDM security for simple linear (or affine) function families [11,2,12]. To improve this situation, we would like to have an *amplification* procedure which starts with $\hat{\mathcal{F}}$-KDM secure encryption scheme and boost it into an $\mathcal{F}$-KDM secure scheme, where the function class $\mathcal{F}$ should be richer than $\hat{\mathcal{F}}$. It was recently shown [13,7] that a strong form of amplification is possible, provided that the underlying encryption scheme satisfies some special *additional* properties. We show [1] how to use REs in order to achieve a *generic* KDM amplification theorem.

Let $f(x)$ be a function and let us view the encoding $\hat{f}(x; r)$ as a *collection* of functions $\hat{\mathcal{F}} = \left\{ \hat{f}_r(x) \right\}_r$, where each member of the collection corresponds to some possible fixing of the randomness r, i.e., $\hat{f}_r(x) = \hat{f}(x; r)$. Now suppose that our scheme is KDM secure with respect to the family $\hat{\mathcal{F}}$, and we would like to immunize it against the (more complicated) function f. This can be easily achieved by modifying the encryption scheme as follows: to encrypt a message m we first translate it into the $\hat{f}$-encoding by applying the RE simulator $\mathsf{Sim}(m)$, and then encrypt the result under the original encryption scheme. Decryption is done by applying the original decryption algorithm, and then applying the recovery algorithm Rec to translate the result back to its original form. Observe that an encryption of $f(\mathsf{sk})$ in the new scheme is the same as an encryption of $S(f(\mathsf{sk})) = \hat{f}(\mathsf{sk}; r)$ under the original scheme. Hence, a KDM query for f in the new scheme is emulated by an old KDM query for a *randomly chosen* function $\hat{f}_r$. It follows that the KDM security of the new scheme with respect to f reduces to the KDM security of the original scheme with respect to $\hat{\mathcal{F}}$.

This idea easily generalizes to the case where instead of a single function f we have a class of functions $\mathcal{F}$ which are all encoded by functions in $\hat{\mathcal{F}}$. Moreover, the simple structure of the reduction (i.e., a single KDM query of the new scheme translates to a single KDM query of the original scheme) allows to obtain a strong amplification theorem which is insensitive to the exact setting of KDM security, including the symmetric-key/public-key setting, the CPA/CCA cases and the case of multiple-keys. Using known constructions of REs, we can amplify KDM security with respect to linear functions (or even bit-projections) into functions computable by circuits of arbitrary fixed polynomial-size (e.g., n^2).

Acknowledgements. I thank to the conference organizers for inviting this survey, and to Yuval Ishai and Eyal Kushilevitz for introducing me to the notion of randomized encoding and for fruitful and enjoyable collaborations.

References

1. Applebaum, B.: Key-dependent message security: Generic amplification and completeness. In: Paterson, K.G. (ed.) EUROCRYPT 2011. LNCS, vol. 6632, pp. 527–546. Springer, Heidelberg (2011)
2. Applebaum, B., Cash, D., Peikert, C., Sahai, A.: Fast cryptographic primitives and circular-secure encryption based on hard learning problems. In: Halevi, S. (ed.) CRYPTO 2009. LNCS, vol. 5677, pp. 595–618. Springer, Heidelberg (2009)
3. Applebaum, B., Ishai, Y., Kushilevitz, E.: Computationally private randomizing polynomials and their applications. Journal of Computional Complexity 15(2), 115–162 (2006)
4. Applebaum, B., Ishai, Y., Kushilevitz, E.: Cryptography in NC^0. SIAM Journal on Computing 36(4), 845–888 (2006)
5. Applebaum, B., Ishai, Y., Kushilevitz, E.: Cryptography by cellular automata or how fast can complexity emerge in nature? In: ICS 2010 (2010)
6. Applebaum, B., Ishai, Y., Kushilevitz, E.: From secrecy to soundness: Efficient verification via secure computation. In: Abramsky, S., Gavoille, C., Kirchner, C., Meyer auf der Heide, F., Spirakis, P.G. (eds.) ICALP 2010. LNCS, vol. 6198, pp. 152–163. Springer, Heidelberg (2010); draft of full version available at the authors home page
7. Barak, B., Haitner, I., Hofheinz, D., Ishai, Y.: Bounded key-dependent message security. In: Gilbert, H. (ed.) EUROCRYPT 2010. LNCS, vol. 6110, pp. 423–444. Springer, Heidelberg (2010)

8. Beaver, D., Micali, S., Rogaway, P.: The round complexity of secure protocols (extended abstract). In: STOC 1990 (1990)
9. Ben-Or, M., Goldwasser, S., Wigderson, A.: Completeness theorems for non-cryptographic fault-tolerant distributed computation. In: STOC 1988 (1988)
10. Black, J., Rogaway, P., Shrimpton, T.: Encryption-scheme security in the presence of key-dependent messages. In: Nyberg, K., Heys, H.M. (eds.) SAC 2002. LNCS, vol. 2595, pp. 62–75. Springer, Heidelberg (2003)
11. Boneh, D., Halevi, S., Hamburg, M., Ostrovsky, R.: Circular-secure encryption from decision diffie-hellman. In: Wagner, D. (ed.) CRYPTO 2008. LNCS, vol. 5157, pp. 108–125. Springer, Heidelberg (2008)
12. Brakerski, Z., Goldwasser, S.: Circular and leakage resilient public-key encryption under subgroup indistinguishability (or: Quadratic residuosity strikes back). In: Rabin, T. (ed.) CRYPTO 2010. LNCS, vol. 6223, pp. 1–20. Springer, Heidelberg (2010)
13. Brakerski, Z., Goldwasser, S., Kalai, Y.: Black-Box Circular-secure encryption beyond affine functions. In: Ishai, Y. (ed.) TCC 2011. LNCS, vol. 6597, pp. 201–218. Springer, Heidelberg (2011)
14. Camenisch, J.L., Lysyanskaya, A.: An efficient system for non-transferable anonymous credentials with optional anonymity revocation. In: Pfitzmann, B. (ed.) EUROCRYPT 2001. LNCS, vol. 2045, p. 93. Springer, Heidelberg (2001)
15. Chaum, D., Crépeau, C., Damgård, I.: Multiparty unconditionally secure protocols (extended abstract). In: STOC 1988 (1988)
16. Cramer, R., Fehr, S., Ishai, Y., Kushilevitz, E.: Efficient multi-party computation over rings. In: Biham, E. (ed.) EUROCRYPT 2003. LNCS, vol. 2656, pp. 596–613. Springer, Heidelberg (2003)
17. Damgård, I.B., Ishai, Y.: Scalable secure multiparty computation. In: Dwork, C. (ed.) CRYPTO 2006. LNCS, vol. 4117, pp. 501–520. Springer, Heidelberg (2006)
18. Dvir, Z., Gutfreund, D., Rothblum, G., Vadhan, S.: On Approximating the Entropy of Polynomial Mappings. In: ICS 2011 (2011)
19. Feige, U., Killian, J., Naor, M.: A minimal model for secure computation (extended abstract). In: STOC 1994 (1994)
20. Goldwasser, S., Gutfreund, D., Healy, A., Kaufman, T., Rothblum, G.N.: A (de)constructive approach to program checking. In: STOC 2008 (2008)
21. Ishai, Y., Kushilevitz, E.: Randomizing polynomials: A new representation with applications to round-efficient secure computation. In: FOCS 2000 (2000)
22. Ishai, Y., Kushilevitz, E.: Perfect constant-round secure computation via perfect randomizing polynomials. In: Widmayer, P., Triguero, F., Morales, R., Hennessy, M., Eidenbenz, S., Conejo, R. (eds.) ICALP 2002. LNCS, vol. 2380, p. 244. Springer, Heidelberg (2002)
23. Kilian, J.: Founding cryptography on oblivious transfer. In: STOC 1988 (1988)
24. Yao, A.C.C.: Theory and application of trapdoor functions. In: FOCS 1982 (1982)

Minimal Connectivity for Unconditionally Secure Message Transmission in Synchronous Directed Networks

Manan Nayak, Shashank Agrawal, and Kannan Srinathan

Center for Security, Theory and Algorithmic Research (C-STAR),
International Institute of Information Technology, Hyderabad, 500032, India
{manan.nayak@research.,shashank.agrawal@research.,srinathan@}iiit.ac.in

Abstract. In this paper we give the minimal connectivity required in a synchronous directed network, which is under the influence of a computationally unbounded *Byzantine* adversary that can corrupt a subset of nodes, so that Secure Message Transmission is possible between sender S and receiver R. We also show that secure communication between a pair of nodes in a given synchronous directed network is possible in both directions if and only if reliable communication is possible between them. We assume that in a network, every node is capable of computation and we model the network along the lines of [14].

Keywords: Directed networks, Connectivity, Information-theoretic security.

1 Introduction

Achieving reliable and private communication is one of the fundamental problems in distributed computing. Most solutions to the problem of Secure Multi-Party Computation assume that nodes are connected by secure channels ([1],[2], [5],[10]). However, in practice, such a channel may not be present between every pair of nodes. In such a case we need to simulate the channel using a protocol. The problem of point-to-point Secure Message Transmission (SMT) studies the possibility, optimality and feasibility of protocols in which – given a distributed network where a subset of nodes may be faulty, and given a sender node S and a receiver node R – S should be able to send any message m to R such that even if all the faulty players collude with each other, R receives m reliably and the faulty players get no information about m (privacy or secrecy). The general form of this problem is usually denoted by (ϵ, δ)-SMT where ϵ denotes the error in secrecy and δ the error in reliability [4].

The problem of Secure Message Transmission has been studied under various network and corruption models. The case of synchronous directed (unicast) networks under the influence of a computationally unbounded *Byzantine* adversary has been studied in depth by the research community, beginning with the work of Desmedt and Wang [3]. In [3], the authors abstract a directed network as a

S. Fehr (Ed.): ICITS 2011, LNCS 6673, pp. 32–51, 2011.

collection of directed channels between S and R, and find the minimum number of forward and backward channels required in a network, affected by a threshold adversary, for $(0,0)$-SMT and for $(0,\delta)$-SMT. They also give protocols over networks which satisfy the minimum connectivity requirements. Subsequently, Patra et al. [9] and Yang and Desmedt [15] generalize these results to the case of non-threshold adversary.

While the abstraction of a directed network as a collection of directed channels between S and R is suitable for networks where intermediate nodes are routers, who can only forward messages and do not have any computing power of their own, a more general way of modelling the network as digraphs with computationally capable intermediate nodes is proposed in [14]. The main result of [14] is a characterization of directed networks, under the control of a non-threshold *mixed* adversary, over which reliable message transmission (or $(1,\delta)$-SMT using the standard notation) is possible. Subsequently, in [13], the minimal connectivity requirement in a network for $(0,\delta)$-SMT is studied.

Our work is mainly inspired by the following analogous existing result: the minimum connectivity requirement for $(1,\delta)$-SMT in digraphs (characterized in [14]) is strictly *weaker* than that required for $(1,0)$-SMT in digraphs. Similarly, we ask if the minimum connectivity requirement for (ϵ,δ)-SMT in digraphs is strictly *weaker* than that required for $(0,\delta)$-SMT. The existing results appear to hint at a negative answer to the above question. Specifically, it is known that "$(0,\delta)$-SMT if and only if (ϵ,δ)-SMT" if (a) the network is abstracted as a collection of disjoint directed paths between sender and receiver [15] or if (b) the network is modelled as an undirected graph [4].

Notwithstanding, we present a characterization of the possibility of (ϵ,δ)-SMT and find that in the case of digraphs influenced by a non-threshold Byzantine adversary, there exist graphs in which (ϵ,δ)-SMT is possible while no $(0,\delta)$-SMT protocol is known. For instance, consider the network $\mathcal{G}$ given in Figure 1 with adversary structure $\mathbb{A} = \{\{b_1\},\{b_2\}\}$. We show that this digraph satisfies the necessary and sufficient condition for the existence of a (ϵ,δ)-SMT protocol as given in Theorem 5. On the other hand, no $(0,\delta)$-SMT protocol is known over $\mathcal{G}$ ([13]).

Further, to see why if intermediate nodes can compute, the results of [15] are not applicable, again consider the network $\mathcal{G}$ with the same adversary structure

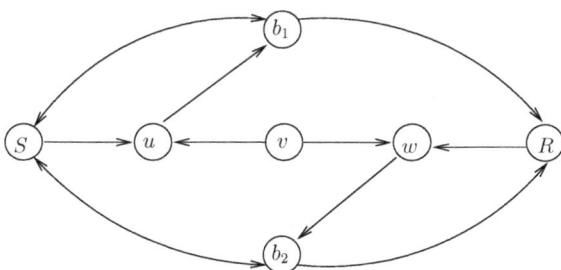

Fig. 1. Network $\mathcal{G}$

A. According to Theorem 6 and Corollary 1 in [15], (ϵ, δ)-SMT from S to R tolerating $\mathbb{A}$ is possible if and only if there exists a path from S to R, or from R to S, avoiding both the nodes b_1 and b_2. Since no such path is present in the network, no protocol exists for (ϵ, δ)-SMT in $\mathcal{G}$ according to [15]. However, if we assume that every node in the network can compute, there does exist an (ϵ, δ)-SMT protocol in $\mathcal{G}$ as shown in Section 4.1.

We would like to emphasize that the main focus of this work is on the (im)possibility and not the feasibility of SMT protocols. The protocols that we give to prove the possibility of SMT are inefficient in both message and round complexity. Previous results on SMT shed some light on the anomalous behaviour of protocols when "randomness meets directedness" [14, 12], which makes it extremely hard to design worst case efficient protocols.

2   Model and Definitions

Network: The network is modelled as a directed graph $\mathcal{N} = (\mathbb{V}, \mathcal{E})$, where the set of vertices $\mathbb{V}$ represents the set of players and the set of edges $\mathcal{E}$ represents the perfectly secure, point-to-point, directed channels in the network. The network is assumed to be synchronous and any protocol is executed in a sequence of rounds. In each round a player can send messages to its out-neighbours, receive messages sent to it by its in-neighbours in that round and perform computations, in that order. It is assumed that the network topology is known to every player. Throughout the paper we represent the sender node by S and the receiver node by R.

Adversary: Fault in the network is modelled via a computationally unbounded *centralized* adversary that can corrupt a subset of nodes, excluding S and R, in *Byzantine* fashion [8]. This means that the corrupted nodes are in complete control of the adversary and the adversary can make them behave in any arbitrary manner. The adversary is *non-threshold* [6, 7] and is represented by an adversary structure which is the collection of all possible subsets of nodes that can be corrupted by the adversary. More formally, an adversary structure $\mathbb{A}$ is defined as: $\mathbb{A} = \{B_1, B_2, ..., B_n\}$ where $\forall i$, $B_i \subseteq \mathbb{V} \setminus \{S, R\}$. The adversary can choose to corrupt any *one* subset of players from $\mathbb{A}$ and can control their behaviour throughout the execution of the protocol. Note that the adversary is not allowed to change the subset in the middle of an execution. These subsets are also known as *failure patterns* in distributed computing. The adversary structure is monotone which means that if $B_1 \in \mathbb{A}$ then $\forall B_2$ such that $B_2 \subseteq B_1$, $B_2 \in \mathbb{A}$. The players are assumed to have no information about the corrupt subset before the beginning of the protocol. It is assumed that the adversary knows the complete protocol specification and the network topology.

We note that an adversary structure can be uniquely and concisely represented by its maximal basis.

Definition 1 (Maximal basis of $\mathbb{A}$). *The maximal basis $\overline{\mathbb{A}}$ for an adversary structure $\mathbb{A}$ is defined as:* $\overline{\mathbb{A}} = \{B \mid B \in \mathbb{A} \text{ and } \nexists X \in \mathbb{A} \text{ s.t. } B \subsetneq X\}$

Throughout this paper we use $\mathbb{A}$ to denote the adversary structure and $\overline{\mathbb{A}}$ to denote its maximal basis. Following [4], the **adversary's view** consists of the messages sent and received and the coin tosses made by the corrupt nodes in each round of the protocol. Random variable $adv(m, r)$ denotes the view of the adversary when S chooses to send m and the coin tosses made by the adversary is r.

Message Space: Let $\mathbb{F}$ be the message space where $< \mathbb{F}, +, * >$ is a large finite field. All the computations are done in this field. The sender S can select any element from $\mathbb{F}$ to send to R. In any message transmission protocol we assume that S starts with a message m_S and R outputs m_R at the end. Throughout the paper we write $|H|$ to denote the cardinality of the set H and $h \in_R H$ denotes that h is uniformly chosen from H.

Definition 2 (Reliability). *A message transmission protocol is said to be δ-reliable if the probability that $m_R = m_S$ is at least $(1-\delta)$, where the probability is taken over the random coin tosses of all the players and the random coin tosses of the adversary.*

Definition 3 (Privacy). *Again following [4], a message transmission protocol is said to be ϵ-private if, for every two messages m and $m' \in \mathbb{F}$ and every r, $\sum_c |Pr[adv(m, r) = c] - Pr[adv(m', r) = c]| \leq 2\epsilon$. The probabilities are over the coin tosses of the honest players and the sum is over all possible views of the adversary.*

Definition 4 $((\epsilon, \delta)$-SMT). *A message transmission protocol is said to be (ϵ, δ)-SMT if it is ϵ-private and δ-reliable, where ϵ and δ are negligibly small.*

Definition 5 (δ-URMT). *A message transmission protocol is said to be δ-URMT (Unconditionally Reliable Message Transmission) if it is δ-reliable.*

Definition 6 (δ-URMT$_{FK}$). *We say that a message transmission protocol tolerating adversary structure $\mathbb{A}$ is δ-URMT$_{FK}$ if for all valid Byzantine corruptions of any $B \in \mathbb{A}$, the probability that R outputs $m_R = m_S$ or knows that the set B is faulty is at least $(1 - \delta)$.*[1]

Throughout this paper we use the following terms interchangeably: (a) δ-URMT and URMT (b) δ-URMT$_{FK}$ and URMT$_{FK}$.

It should be noted that protocols with error probabilities greater than $\frac{1}{2}$ or negligibly close to $\frac{1}{2}$ in reliability or secrecy are not interesting. Instead, we would like to have protocols with these error probabilities negligibly small.

Authentication Scheme: Our protocols use the following information theoretically secure authentication code to circumvent the low connectivity in the graph. Suppose two random keys k_1 and k_2 are privately shared between two

---

[1] FK stands for Fault Knowledge.

parties S and R.[2] Let S send $(m, m*k_1+k_2)$ to R and let R receive (x, y). Then, R can easily check if adversary has tampered with the authenticated message by verifying if $y \overset{?}{=} x * k_1 + k_2$. If adversary has altered the messages en-route then with probability at least $1 - \frac{1}{|\mathbb{F}|}$, verification will fail and R will find out (see [11] for proof). In addition to this if one more key k_3 is privately shared and S sends $(m + k_3, (m + k_3) * k_1 + k_2)$ to R, then the message m remains perfectly secret, since $m + k_3$ is independent of m. We use the following notations in the paper: (i) $\chi(m, k_1, k_2) = (m, m * k_1 + k_2)$; (ii) $\zeta(m, k_1, k_2, k_3) = \chi(m+k_3, k_1, k_2) = (m+k_3, (m+k_3)*k_1+k_2)$; where $m, k_1, k_2, k_3 \in \mathbb{F}$. For brevity, we sometimes abuse the notation and write $\zeta(m, K)$ to denote $\zeta(m, k_1, k_2, k_3)$ where $K = (k_1, k_2, k_3)$.

3 URMT

In [14], Srinathan and Pandu Rangan gave the characterization of directed graphs for URMT tolerating mixed adversary (*Byzantine* and *Fail-stop*). In that paper, they prove the following theorem that reduces the problem of URMT tolerating adversary structures of arbitrary size to URMT tolerating two-sized adversary structures.

Theorem 1. *In a digraph $\mathcal{N} = (\mathbb{V}, \mathcal{E})$, a δ-URMT protocol from S to R tolerating an arbitrary adversary structure $\mathbb{A}$ ($|\mathbb{A}| \geq 2$) exists iff δ-URMT protocols tolerating every $\mathcal{A}$ s.t. $\mathcal{A} \subseteq \overline{\mathbb{A}}$ and $|\mathcal{A}| = 2$ exist, where $\delta < \frac{1}{2}$.*

Once the problem is reduced to tolerating two-sized adversary structures only, they give three constructions using which we can add virtual nodes and edges in the graph. Finally a very simple condition remains to be checked in the augmented graph which shows whether or not URMT is possible in the graph.

Since in this paper we are dealing with *Byzantine* adversary only, the three constructions in [14] collapse to a single construction. We now give that construction which shall be used extensively in the characterization for (ϵ, δ)-SMT in Section 4.

Construction of Y: For a given adversary structure $\mathcal{A} = \{B_1, B_2\}$ and a given node $u \in \mathbb{V} \setminus (B_1 \cup B_2)$ we construct the set $Y(u)$ as follows: $Y(u)$ is initialized to $\{u\}$; a node $v \in \mathbb{V} \setminus (B_1 \cup B_2)$ is added to $Y(u)$ if one of the following holds:

1. $\exists a \in Y(u)$ s.t. $(v, a) \in \mathcal{E}$
2. $\exists b \in Y(u)$ s.t. $(b, v) \in \mathcal{E}$ and $\exists a \in Y(u), \exists \alpha \in \{1, 2\}$ s.t. v has a path to a avoiding the set $B_{\overline{\alpha}}$ where $\overline{\alpha} = 3 - \alpha$. This path may contain nodes from B_α (see Figure 2).

The above steps are executed iteratively until no more nodes can be added. Note that nodes in $B_1 \cup B_2$ are never considered.

---

[2] We take no such assumption in our protocols. The protocols establish keys between parties on their own before using them.

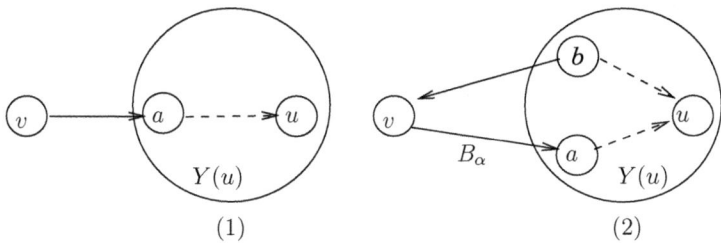

Fig. 2. Constructions for $Y(u)$

Remark: Unlike [14], where virtual paths with certain properties are added in the graph for the above construction, we used the set notation, Y. Nevertheless, the set notation is equivalent to what is done in [14], i.e. a node v added to $Y(u)$ is equivalent to adding a virtual path from v to u in the graph.

The following two Lemmas act as the basic blocks for the (ϵ, δ)-SMT characterization.

Lemma 1. *If a node $v \in Y(u)$, then v can do δ-$URMT_{FK}$ to u, for any $\delta \geq \frac{1}{|\mathbb{F}|}$, with the additional property that the message sent will remain perfectly secret from the adversary.*

The proof of this lemma appears in [14]. They give a protocol, with the above mentioned properties, that simulates the virtual path added in the graph. Although the message remains perfectly secret throughout the protocol, it is not mentioned explicitly in the proof. Nevertheless, for the sake of completeness, we give the proof of this lemma in Appendix A.1.

Lemma 2. *If a node $v \notin Y(u)$ then there does not exist any δ-$URMT$ protocol with $\delta < \frac{1}{2}$.*

Proof appears in [14]. It assumes that the adversary knows the message that is being transmitted. We can do away with that assumption and show that any URMT protocol with $\delta < \frac{1}{2}(1 - \frac{1}{|\mathbb{F}|})$ does not exist (a similar proof is given in [4]).

The key idea used in the proof is that if $v \notin Y(u)$, then for any message transmission protocol from v to u, the adversary can simulate a copy of the node v (which we call $\bar{v}$) on a message of its own choice in such a way that u can't distinguish between the "actual" v and the "simulated" $\bar{v}$. In this way if v intends to send message m and adversary simulates the node $\bar{v}$ on some message m' such that $m \neq m'$ [3], then u cannot do better than guessing between m and m'.

Finally, using the construction of $Y(R)$ we can restate the main theorem of [14] as follows:

Theorem 2. *In a digraph $\mathcal{N} = (\mathbb{V}, \mathcal{E})$, for $\delta < \frac{1}{2}(1 - \frac{1}{|\mathbb{F}|})$, δ-$URMT$ from S to R tolerating two-sized adversary structure $\mathcal{A} = \{B_1, B_2\}$ is possible if and only if $S \in Y(R)$ and there exist two paths p_1 and p_2 from S to R with path p_α avoiding B_α for $\alpha \in \{1, 2\}$.*

---

[3] Adversary can do that with probability $1 - \frac{1}{|\mathbb{F}|}$ by choosing $m' \in_R \mathbb{F}$.

4 (ϵ, δ)-SMT

We now characterize the family of graphs in which (ϵ, δ)-SMT from S to R tolerating an adversary structure $\mathbb{A}$ is possible. As done in Section 3, we again start with the theorem that reduces the adversary structures of arbitrary size to two-sized adversary structures. Similar theorem has been proved in [13] for $(0, \delta)$-SMT.

Theorem 3. *In digraph $\mathcal{N} = (\mathbb{V}, \mathcal{E})$, (ϵ, δ)-SMT tolerating an arbitrary adversary structure $\mathbb{A}$ ($|\mathbb{A}| \geq 2$) is possible if and only if (ϵ, δ)-SMT tolerating $\mathcal{A}$ for all $\mathcal{A} \subseteq \overline{\mathbb{A}}$, such that $|\mathcal{A}| = 2$, is possible, where $\epsilon \leq \frac{1}{648}$ and $\delta \leq \frac{1}{864}$.*

Proof. The *only-if* part is obvious. We prove the *if* part here. Suppose that (ϵ, δ)-SMT protocols tolerating all two-sized subsets of $\overline{\mathbb{A}}$ exist. Let $\overline{\mathbb{A}} = \{B_1, B_2, ..., B_n\}$ and let $\Pi_{i,j}$ be the (ϵ, δ)-SMT protocol tolerating $\{B_i, B_j\}$ where $1 \leq i, j \leq n$. Using these as the subprotocols we construct a (ϵ, δ)-SMT protocol Π tolerating $\overline{\mathbb{A}}$ (which is also the protocol tolerating $\mathbb{A}$).

We show how to construct a (ϵ, δ)-SMT protocol $\Pi'_{i,j,k}$ tolerating $\{B_i, B_j, B_k\}$ using $\Pi_{i,j}, \Pi_{j,k}$ and $\Pi_{k,i}$. The protocol $\Pi'_{i,j,k}$ is a $(6\epsilon, 12\delta)$-SMT protocol as will be shown in Lemmas 3 and 4. Further, in Lemma 5, we will show how this protocol can be used to construct an (ϵ, δ)-SMT protocol $\Pi_{i,j,k}$ (the upper bounds on ϵ and δ become critical here). The key idea used in the construction of $\Pi'_{i,j,k}$ is that each of the subsets B_i, B_j and B_k are tolerated in two of the three protocols which means that no matter which set is corrupt, two of them will be successful. Similar process can be used to construct a protocol $\Pi_{i,j,k,l}$ using protocols $\Pi_{i,j,k}, \Pi_{i,j,l}$ and $\Pi_{j,k,l}$. In general for any $\mu > 2$, a μ-sized set H can be divided into three $\lceil \frac{2\mu}{3} \rceil$-sized subsets H_1, H_2 and H_3 such that every element $h \in H$ occurs in at least two of H_1, H_2 and H_3. In this way, ultimately the grand protocol Π that tolerates all the n subsets simultaneously is constructed. It can be easily shown that $poly(n)$ sub-protocols are used to construct the protocol Π.

The protocol $\Pi'_{i,j,k}$ consists of 3 phases where in each phase, protocols $\Pi_{i,j}$, $\Pi_{j,k}$ and $\Pi_{k,i}$ are run in parallel. Phase 2 begins only after the completion of Phase 1 and similarly Phase 3 begins only after the completion of Phase 2.[4] The protocol proceeds in the following steps:

- S chooses 3 set of keys K_1, K_2 and K_3 randomly from $\mathbb{F}^3$ where $K_i = (k_{i1}, k_{i2}, k_{i3})$, $i \in \{1, 2, 3\}$.
- S sends $\zeta(m_S, K_1)$, $\zeta(m_S, K_2)$ and K_3 through the protocol $\Pi_{i,j}$ in phases 1, 2 and 3 respectively. Similarly S sends $\zeta(m_S, K_2)$, $\zeta(m_S, K_3)$ and K_1 through the protocol $\Pi_{j,k}$ and sends $\zeta(m_S, K_3)$, $\zeta(m_S, K_1)$ and K_2 through the protocol $\Pi_{k,i}$ in phases 1, 2 and 3 respectively.
- Let R receive $(x_1^{i,j}, y_1^{i,j}), (x_2^{i,j}, y_2^{i,j})$ and K_3' from $\Pi_{i,j}$ in phases 1, 2 and 3 respectively. Similarly R receives $(x_2^{j,k}, y_2^{j,k}), (x_3^{j,k}, y_3^{j,k})$ and K_1' from $\Pi_{j,k}$, and $(x_3^{k,i}, y_3^{k,i}), (x_1^{k,i}, y_1^{k,i})$ and K_2' from $\Pi_{k,i}$ in phases 1, 2 and 3 respectively (see Figure 3) where $K_i' = (k_{i1}', k_{i2}', k_{i3}')$.

---

[4] Although Phase 1 and 2 are separated just for better understanding, it is crucial that Phase 3 begins only after Phases 1 and 2 have ended.

- R tries to find an $\alpha \in \{i, j, k\}$ such that the messages received through the two protocols tolerating B_α are *consistent* with each other. For instance, the messages received through two protocols tolerating B_i ($\Pi_{i,j}$ and $\Pi_{k,i}$) are *consistent* with each other when $(x_2^{i,j}, y_2^{i,j}) = \chi(x_2^{i,j}, k'_{21}, k'_{22})$ and $(x_3^{k,i}, y_3^{k,i}) = \chi(x_3^{k,i}, k'_{31}, k'_{32})$ and $x_2^{i,j} - k'_{23} = x_3^{k,i} - k'_{33}$.
  - If more than one such α exists, proceed with any one of them. If no such α exists then choose $\alpha \in_R \{i, j, k\}$ and proceed.
  - If α is i then output $x_2^{i,j} - k'_{23}$. Similarly if α is j then output $x_3^{j,k} - k'_{33}$ and if α is k then output $x_1^{k,i} - k'_{13}$.   □

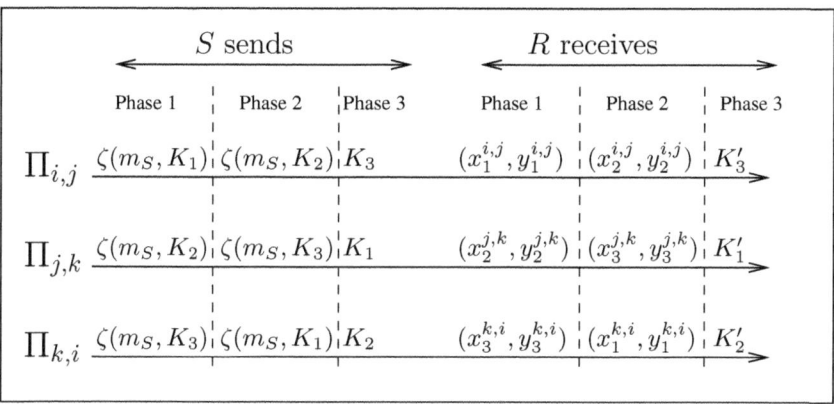

Fig. 3. Protocol $\Pi'_{i,j,k}$

We give proof ideas for the following three lemmas here. Formal proofs of Lemma 3 and Lemma 4 appear in Appendix A.2 and A.3 respectively. Proof of Lemma 5 appears in the full version of this paper.

Lemma 3. *Protocol $\Pi'_{i,j,k}$ is (12δ)-reliable.*

Proof idea: With probability at least $(1 - \delta)^{12}$, R will be able to find a pair of protocols such that the messages received through them are *consistent* and the message that R finally outputs is m_S.

Lemma 4. *Protocol $\Pi'_{i,j,k}$ is (6ϵ)-secure.*

Proof idea: The messages sent through the protocol, that is not tolerating the corrupt set, can be completely revealed to the adversary. In that case there are six messages that are sent along the other two ϵ-secret protocols that are such that m_S remains secret iff these 6 messages remain secret. This in turn shows that $\Pi'_{i,j,k}$ is (6ϵ)-secure.

Lemma 5. *An (ϵ, δ)-SMT protocol $\Pi_{i,j,k}$ can be constructed using a $(6\epsilon, 12\delta)$-SMT protocol $\Pi'_{i,j,k}$.*

Proof idea: To enhance reliability we can repeat the protocol thrice and let R output the majority element. This brings the error in reliability down to $432\delta^2$ but increases the error in secrecy to 18ϵ. Next, to enhance security, any message m is sent by sending f and $m + f$ in separate executions, where $f \in_R \mathbb{F}$. This reduces the error in secrecy to $648\epsilon^2$ but increases the error in reliability to $864\delta^2$. For the given upper bounds on ϵ and δ, the protocol becomes (ϵ, δ)-SMT.

4.1 (ϵ, δ)-SMT Characterization

Following Theorem 3, it is now sufficient to give only a characterization for (ϵ, δ)-SMT tolerating two-sized adversary structures of the form $\mathcal{A} = \{B_1, B_2\}$.

We make use of the set Y defined in Section 3. In addition, we define two more sets Z_1 and Z_2.

Construction of Z_1: For a given adversary structure $\mathcal{A} = \{B_1, B_2\}$ and a given node $u \in \mathbb{V} \setminus (B_1 \cup B_2)$ we construct $Z_1(u)$ as follows: $Z_1(u)$ is initialized to $\{u\}$; a node $v \in \mathbb{V} \setminus (B_1 \cup B_2)$ is added to $Z_1(u)$ if one of the following hold:

1. $\exists\, a \in Z_1(u)$ s.t. $(v, a) \in \mathcal{E}$, or,
2. $\exists\, b \in Z_1(u)$ s.t. b can do $URMT_{FK}$ to v (in other words, $b \in Y(v)$) and v has a path to u avoiding the set B_2. This path may contain nodes from B_1.

The above steps are executed iteratively until no new node can be added. Nodes in $(B_1 \cup B_2)$ are never considered. This completes the construction of $Z_1(u)$. The set $Z_2(u)$ is constructed along similar lines (replacing B_2 with B_1 and vice-versa in step (2) of the iteration).

Figure 4 describes the situations in which S can be added to $Z_1(R)$.

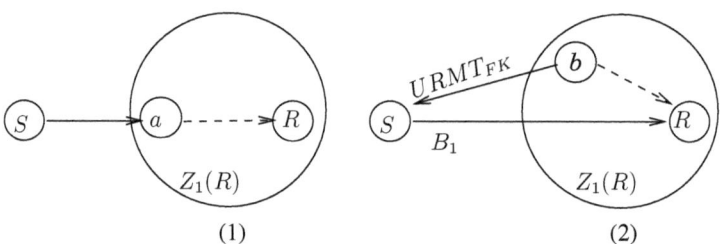

(1)   (2)

Fig. 4. Constructions for $Z_1(R)$

Theorem 4. *In a directed network $\mathcal{N} = (\mathbb{V}, \mathcal{E})$, (ϵ, δ)-SMT from S to R tolerating $\mathcal{A} = \{B_1, B_2\}$ is possible if and only if $S \in Y(R) \cap Z_1(R) \cap Z_2(R)$.*

The proof is divided into two parts - Sufficiency (*if* part) and Necessity (*only if* part).

Sufficiency. To prove the sufficiency of the theorem we give a protocol for (ϵ, δ)-SMT from S to R, with $\epsilon \le \frac{1}{648}$ and $\delta \le \frac{1}{864}$. The upper bounds on the error probabilities ensure that these protocols, tolerating two-sized adversary structures, can then be used to build the final protocol tolerating the complete adversary structure. The protocol makes use of the 3 properties of S viz. $S \in Y(R)$, $S \in Z_1(R)$ and $S \in Z_2(R)$ in 3 distinct subprotocols and at the end, R, from its view of the entire protocol, outputs m_R such that $m_R = m_S$ with a very high probability and m_S remains secret.

The 3 subprotocols (corresponding to $S \in Y(R)$, $S \in Z_1(R)$ and $S \in Z_2(R)$) are as follows:

1. Subprotocol P_F: S sends m_S to R through the $URMT_{FK}$ protocol.
2. Subprotocol P_1: If S was added to $Z_1(R)$ by:
   - Construction (1), then it simply sends the message m_S to the node a through the honest edge (see Figure 4). The node a then starts another instance of the protocol P_1 to send m_S to R.
   - Construction (2), then b first chooses a random set of keys $K = (k_1, k_2, k_3)$ and sends it to S through $URMT_{FK}$ (see Figure 4). Let S receive K'. Since $S \in Z_1(R)$, S has a path to R that avoids B_2. Let that path be p_2.
     • If S successfully verifies K', it sends $\zeta(m_S, K')$ to R along the path p_2. In addition to this it also sends $m' \in_R \mathbb{F}$ to R along p_2.
     • If the verification fails then S knows the identity of the corrupt set with very high probability. Let $\mathcal{I}_S$ denote the identity knowledge of S. First S chooses $(f_1, f_2) \in_R \mathbb{F}^2$ on its own and sends (f_1, f_2) to R through p_2 (thus, tries to inform R that it didn't receive the keys from b). Next, if $\mathcal{I}_S = B_1$ then S sends $m' \in_R \mathbb{F}$ to R through p_2. But if $\mathcal{I}_S = B_2$ then S sends m_S to R through that path.
   Let R receive (x, y) and m_p. Now b starts new instances of protocol P_1 to send the elements of key K to R.
3. Subprotocol P_2: P_2 is exactly same as P_1 with B_1 replaced with B_2 and vice-versa.

COMPUTATION BY R: At the end of the subprotocol P_F, R either receives m_S or knows the identity of the corrupt set with probability at least $1 - \frac{1}{|\mathbb{F}|}$. Let $\mathcal{I}_R$ be its identity knowledge. If R receives m' which it is able to verify then it outputs $m_R = m'$ and stops. Otherwise, if $\mathcal{I}_R = B_2$ it ignores all the messages it received from P_2 and does the following computation on the messages received through P_1 (analogous behaviour when $\mathcal{I}_R = B_1$). If S was added to $Z_1(R)$ by Construction (1), then R simply receives m_S (recursively) from node a. In case of Construction (2), it receives a set of keys $K^R = (k_1^R, k_2^R, k_3^R)$ from b. From S it receives one authenticated message (x, y) and a plain message m_p. If R is able to verify (x, y) with K^R then it outputs $m_R = x - k_3^R$ otherwise it outputs $m_R = m_p$.

We now prove that this protocol is δ-reliable and ϵ-secure such that we can make ϵ and δ arbitrarily small by increasing the size of $\mathbb{F}$.

RELIABILITY: Suppose w.l.o.g. that B_2 is corrupt. At the end of the subprotocol P_F, if R outputs the message m' then $Pr[m_S = m'] \geq 1 - \frac{1}{|\mathbb{F}|}$, else $Pr[\mathcal{I}_R = B_2] \geq 1 - \frac{1}{|\mathbb{F}|}$. Now consider the execution of P_1. We initially assume that the instances of P_1, that are called inside P_1 recursively, finish successfully. In case of Construction (1), R simply receives m_S from node a. In case of Construction (2) since B_2 is corrupt, whatever S sends to R through the path p_2, that avoids B_2, reaches R with perfect reliability and secrecy. We also know that $Pr[K' = K \vee \mathcal{I}_S = B_2] \geq 1 - \frac{1}{|\mathbb{F}|}$, where K' are the keys S receives from b. If $K' = K$ then R will be able to verify (x, y) with the keys K that it receives from b and output $m_S = x - k_3$. Otherwise, when $\mathcal{I}_S = B_2$, S sends $(x, y) = (f_1, f_2) \in_R \mathbb{F}^2$ to R along with m_S. Therefore (x, y) will not verify with the keys K with probability at least $1 - \frac{1}{|\mathbb{F}|}$ and hence R is informed to output $m_p = m_S$. We can easily find the success probability as follows: Let Ev be the event that verification of (x, y) at R fails given that S had sent $(f_1, f_2) \in_R \mathbb{F}^2$.

$$Pr[m_R = m_S] \geq Pr[m' = m_S \vee \mathcal{I}_R = B_2] * Pr[K' = K \vee \mathcal{I}_S = B_2] * Pr[Ev]$$
$$\geq \left(1 - \frac{1}{|\mathbb{F}|}\right) * \left(1 - \frac{1}{|\mathbb{F}|}\right) * \left(1 - \frac{1}{|\mathbb{F}|}\right)$$
$$\geq \left(1 - \frac{3}{|\mathbb{F}|}\right)$$

Hence, the protocol is $\frac{3}{|\mathbb{F}|}$-reliable. This argument can be further extended to show that through this protocol even if S sends a set of messages M_S ($|M_S| > 1$), in parallel, the probability that R receives all of them reliably is still at least $1 - \frac{3}{|\mathbb{F}|}$. This can be shown by replacing single messages in the probability expressions by message sets and they shall be considered equal only when all the messages in them are equal. The main reason behind the error probability not increasing is that the fault knowledge ($\mathcal{I}_S$ or $\mathcal{I}_R$), once achieved, can be reused.

The above probabilities are conditioned on the fact that all the messages sent through instances of Protocol P_1 that are invoked recursively inside P_1 itself are received reliably. At most there can be t such recursive calls to the Protocol P_1, where $t = |\mathbb{V}|$, which are all $\frac{3}{|\mathbb{F}|}$-reliable. If we choose $\mathbb{F}$ such that $|\mathbb{F}| \geq 864 * 3t$, we get $\delta = \frac{3t}{|\mathbb{F}|} \leq \frac{1}{864}$.

SECRECY: Suppose w.l.o.g. that B_1 is corrupt. Adversary's view will only consist of the messages sent through the corrupt paths (that contain nodes from B_1). We already know that messages sent through $URMT_{FK}$ remain perfectly secret from the adversary. Hence we will only consider adversary's view as the messages sent by S to R along p_2, that is the path avoiding B_2 in protocol P_1. Now we prove using induction that messages sent from S to R using P_1 remain $\frac{1}{|\mathbb{F}|}$-secret under the assumption that messages sent by nodes already in $Z_1(R)$ remain $\frac{1}{|\mathbb{F}|}$-secret. In case of Construction (1), S simply sends m_S to a and since a was already in $Z_1(R)$, m_S remains $\frac{1}{|\mathbb{F}|}$-secret when it is sent from a to R. Now we discuss Construction (2). Take the case when adversary alters the keys sent by b to S through URMT$_{FK}$. With probability at least $1 - \frac{1}{|\mathbb{F}|}$, S will find out that B_2 is corrupt and in that case all the messages sent along path p_2 will be independent of m_S. But with probability at most $\frac{1}{|\mathbb{F}|}$, S may get the wrong fault information in which case it will send m_S in plaintext along p_2. In any case, the authenticated message (x, y) conveys no additional information about m_S to the adversary. Hence we consider the view of the adversary as the plain message m_p sent along p_2 and find the error in secrecy.

$$\forall m, r, Pr[adv(m, r) = m] = \frac{1}{|\mathbb{F}|} * 1 + (1 - \frac{1}{|\mathbb{F}|}) * \frac{1}{|\mathbb{F}|} = \frac{2}{|\mathbb{F}|} - \frac{1}{|\mathbb{F}|^2}$$

$$\forall m, m', r, s.t., m \neq m' Pr[adv(m, r) = m'] = (1 - \frac{1}{|\mathbb{F}|}) * \frac{1}{|\mathbb{F}|} = \frac{1}{|\mathbb{F}|} - \frac{1}{|\mathbb{F}|^2}$$

$$\Rightarrow \forall m, m', r \sum_c |Pr[adv(m, r) = c] - Pr[adv(m', r) = c]| \leq \frac{2}{|\mathbb{F}|}$$

where the sum is over all possible views of the adversary, i.e. $c \in \mathbb{F}$. Since the sum is bounded by $\frac{2}{|\mathbb{F}|}$, the protocol is $\frac{1}{|\mathbb{F}|}$-secret.

Now take the case when the adversary does not alter the keys sent by b to S. In that case, (x, y) and m_p sent along p_2 are independent of m_S as long as the keys K remain secret. Hence the secrecy of the protocol completely depends upon the secrecy of K which is sent to R by b. But we know that messages sent by b remain $\frac{1}{|\mathbb{F}|}$-secret and hence, the complete protocol is $\frac{1}{|\mathbb{F}|}$-secret. We already chose $\mathbb{F}$ such that $|\mathbb{F}| \geq 864 * 3t \geq 648$, therefore $\epsilon = \frac{1}{|\mathbb{F}|} \leq \frac{1}{648}$.

Thus we prove the sufficiency.

Necessity. It is obvious that $S \in Y(R)$ is necessary for (ϵ, δ)-SMT because it is necessary for URMT alone from S to R. For the same reason the two paths (not necessarily distinct) avoiding sets B_1 and B_2 respectively are also necessary for (ϵ, δ)-SMT . Now we show that $S \in Z_1(R)$ and $S \in Z_2(R)$ are necessary too. We prove the necessity of $S \in Z_1(R)$ and the proof for the latter is similar.

Lemma 6. $S \in Z_1(R)$ *is necessary for* (ϵ, δ)-*SMT from* S *to* R.

Proof. Let $S \notin Z_1$ (in this proof, we simply write Z_1 to denote $Z_1(R)$). We know that S has a path avoiding B_2 to R. Therefore the reason behind S not being in Z_1 is that there is no node in Z_1 that can do $URMT_{FK}$ to S. We now show that there does not exist any (ϵ, δ)-SMT protocol from S to R in that case. Suppose, for contradiction, that there exists such a protocol. We now divide the set of honest nodes *not* in Z_1 into the following sets:

- $X_R = \{x \mid \exists\, a \in Z_1 \text{ s.t. } a \text{ can do } URMT_{FK} \text{ to } x\}$
- $X_S = \{x \mid x \notin X_R\}$

From the definition of Z_1 and the above sets the following facts are clear: (i) X_S, X_R and Z_1 are disjoint and $X_S \cup X_R \cup Z_1 = \mathbb{V} \setminus (B_1 \cup B_2)$; (ii) $R \in Z_1$; (iii) $S \in X_S$; (iv) $\forall\, u \in Z_1 \cup X_R$, u cannot do $URMT_{FK}$ to any node in X_S; (v) $\forall x \in X_R$, any path from x to Z_1 will have to pass through some node in B_2 otherwise x would be in Z_1. Figure 5 describes the possible connections between the sets. A path p (of a particular kind) from a set H_1 to a set H_2 means that $\exists h_1 \in H_1, \exists h_2 \in H_2, s.t.$ there is a path p (of that kind) from h_1 to h_2. For

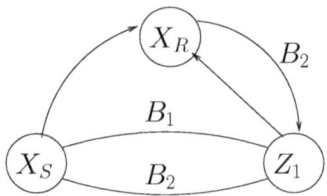

Fig. 5. Connections between the disjoint sets

example the edge from X_R to Z_1 labelled B_2 means that $\exists x \in X_R$, $\exists z \in Z_1$, s.t. there is a path from x to z that passes through some nodes in B_2. Paths with no labels are honest paths.

Note that, given the constraints, these are the best possible connections for the feasibility of the protocol in the graph. For instance there may or may not be an honest path from set X_S to X_R, but we have assumed there is. We shall now give an adversary strategy to prove the impossibility of (ϵ, δ)-SMT in the above graph which will imply that (ϵ, δ)-SMT will be impossible in all the other graphs where $S \notin Z_1$.

The adversary always corrupts one of $\{B_1, B_2\}$. We describe later how it chooses which set to corrupt. The corrupt set B_α behaves as follows:

- It does not send any messages to Z_1, X_R and $B_{\overline{\alpha}}$ and also ignores all the messages it receives from these sets. Here $\overline{\alpha} = 3 - \alpha$.
- It simulates a copy of each node in Z_1 and X_R. Call the simulated sets of nodes $\overline{Z_1}$ and $\overline{X_R}$ respectively. The simulation is carried out as described in [14].

Notice that since Z_1 and X_R can't do $URMT_{FK}$ to X_S, from Lemma 2 we know that the adversary will always be able to successfully simulate $\overline{Z_1}$ and $\overline{X_R}$ and thereby will be able to confuse X_S between the messages it receives from the "actual" and the "simulated" sets. Also note that "X_R can't do $URMT_{FK}$ to X_S" is independent of whether X_S has an honest path to X_R or not.

Observe that one of $\{B_1, B_2\}$ is always corrupt. Let B_α be the corrupt set. The "simulated" sets interact only with B_α and the "actual" sets interact only with $B_{\overline{\alpha}}$. In this way if M_R is the set of messages Z_1 intends to send to X_S, then X_S will receive M_R^1 from B_1 and M_R^2 from B_2.

Consider the case when B_2 is corrupt. In this case: (a) Z_1 will only receive messages from X_S sent along the path avoiding B_2, (b) Z_1 will not receive any message from X_R, (c) $Pr[M_R^1 = M_R] = 1$ and for $|M_R| \geq 1$, $Pr[M_R^2 = M_R] \leq \frac{1}{|\mathbb{F}|}$.

We now describe how the adversary chooses which set to corrupt. Consider the event E when X_S sends some set of messages M_S along the path containing B_1 (and avoiding B_2) such that m_S can be recovered by R from the knowledge of M_S and M_R^1 only, i.e. without the knowledge of M_R^2. For a given protocol, the adversary strategy depends on $Pr[E]$:

- Case 1: if $Pr[E] \leq \frac{1}{2}$, then corrupt B_2
- Case 2: if $Pr[E] > \frac{1}{2}$, then corrupt B_1.

It is easy to see that with such a strategy a (ϵ, δ)-SMT protocol will not exist with $\delta < \frac{1}{2}\left(1 - \frac{1}{|\mathbb{F}|}\right)$ and $\epsilon < \frac{1}{2}$ simultaneously which means that these error probabilities cannot be made arbitrarily small.

In Case 1, B_2 is corrupt and hence R receives messages only from X_S that were sent along the path containing B_1 (and avoiding B_2). Hence R can recover m_S if E happens. In addition to this, even if E does not happen, R may be able to recover the message m_S if B_2 simulates the sets on the message set M_R itself. This means that $Pr[m_R = m_S] \leq Pr[E] * Pr[M_R \neq M_R^2] + 1 * Pr[M_R = M_R^2] \leq \frac{1}{2}\left(1 + \frac{1}{|\mathbb{F}|}\right)$.[5] Therefore $\delta \geq \frac{1}{2}\left(1 - \frac{1}{|\mathbb{F}|}\right)$. In Case 2, B_1 is corrupt and hence if E happens B_1 will always be able to recover m_S from M_S if it knows M_R^1. Since M_R^1 was the set of messages on which it simulated the copy of Z_1, it knows M_R^1. Therefore in this case, since $Pr[E] > \frac{1}{2}$, it gets the message with probability $> \frac{1}{2}$, i.e. $\epsilon > \frac{1}{2}$.

This completes the proof of necessity.   □

Combining the result of Theorem 3 and Theorem 4 we can now give the Main Theorem of the paper that gives the complete characterization of directed networks in which (ϵ, δ)-SMT is possible.

Theorem 5. *In a directed network $\mathcal{N} = (\mathbb{V}, \mathcal{E})$, (ϵ, δ)-SMT from S to R tolerating $\mathbb{A}$ is possible if and only if for every $\mathcal{A} = \{B_1, B_2\}$ where $\mathcal{A} \subseteq \overline{\mathbb{A}}$, we have $S \in Y(R) \cap Z_1(R) \cap Z_2(R)$ where $Y(R)$, $Z_1(R)$ and $Z_2(R)$ are defined for a particular $\{B_1, B_2\}$ as described in Section 3 and Section 4.1.*

Proof of the theorem is immediate from Theorem 3 and Theorem 4.

We can now see that (ϵ, δ)-SMT, tolerating $\mathbb{A} = \{\{b_1\}, \{b_2\}\}$, is possible over the network $\mathcal{G}$ in Figure 1 with the help of the above theorem. Notice that there is only one 2-sized subset of $\mathbb{A}$ that needs to be considered, which is $\mathbb{A}$ itself.

We construct sets $Y(R)$, $Z_1(R)$ and $Z_2(R)$ for $B_1 = \{b_1\}$ and $B_2 = \{b_2\}$. S is added to $Y(R)$ through the following steps: w is first added to $Y(R)$ through Construction 2, v is then added through Construction 1, u is then added through Construction 2, and finally, S is added through Construction 1. Hence $S \in Y(R)$. We can follow similar steps to show $R \in Y(S)$. Now, since S has a path to R avoiding b_2 and $R \in Y(S)$, $S \in Z_1(R)$. Similarly, $S \in Z_2(R)$, which further implies that $S \in Y(R) \cap Z_1(R) \cap Z_2(R)$. Thus, (ϵ, δ)-SMT is possible from S to R.

5   Concluding Remarks

From the above characterization it follows that URMT between two nodes u and v in both the directions is necessary and sufficient for (ϵ, δ)-SMT between them. URMT between u and v implies that for any given adversary structure $\mathcal{A} = \{B_1, B_2\}$ $(\mathcal{A} \subseteq \overline{\mathbb{A}})$, the following holds:

[5] If $|M_R| = 0$ then $Pr[m_R = m_S] \leq Pr[E]$.

1. $v \in Y(u)$ and $u \in Y(v)$
2. u has path p_1 and p_2 to v with p_α avoiding nodes from B_α
3. v has paths q_1 and q_2 to u with q_α avoiding nodes from B_α.

(1) and (2) $\Rightarrow u \in Y(v) \cap Z_1(v) \cap Z_2(v)$; (1) and (3) $\Rightarrow v \in Y(u) \cap Z_1(u) \cap Z_2(u)$. Therefore (ϵ, δ)-SMT between u and v is possible in both directions.

This is in line with the existing results in literature, e.g. in both directed and undirected graphs, Perfectly Reliable Message Transmission (PRMT) between two nodes in both directions implies Perfectly Secure Message Transmission (PSMT) between them.

We leave it as an open problem to devise worst case efficient protocols or to characterize graphs over which efficient protocols for (ϵ, δ)-SMT exist.

Acknowledgements. We would like to thank the anonymous referees for their extensive and detailed comments on our writing and technical contents.

References

[1] Ben-Or, M., Goldwasser, S., Wigderson, A.: Completeness Theorems for Non-cryptographic Fault-tolerant Distributed Computation. In: Proceedings of the 20th Symposium on Theory of Computing (STOC), pp. 1–10. ACM Press, New York (1988)

[2] Chaum, D., Crepeau, C., Damgard, I.: Multi-party Unconditionally Secure Protocols. In: Proceedings of 20th Symposium on Theory of Computing (STOC), pp. 11–19. ACM Press, New York (1988)

[3] Desmedt, Y.G., Wang, Y.: Perfectly secure message transmission revisited. In: Knudsen, L.R. (ed.) EUROCRYPT 2002. LNCS, vol. 2332, pp. 502–517. Springer, Heidelberg (2002)

[4] Franklin, M.K., Wright, R.N.: Secure communication in minimal connectivity models. J. Cryptology 13(1), 9–30 (2000)

[5] Goldreich, O., Micali, S., Wigderson, A.: How to Play any Mental Game. In: Proceedings of the 19th Symposium on Theory of Computing (STOC), pp. 218–229. ACM Press, New York (1987)

[6] Hirt, M., Maurer, U.: Complete Characterization of Adversaries Tolerable in Secure Multi-party Computation. In: Proceedings of the 16th Symposium on Principles of Distributed Computing (PODC), pp. 25–34. ACM Press, New York (1997)

[7] Kumar, M.V.N.A., Goundan, P.R., Srinathan, K., Pandu Rangan, C.: On perfectly secure communication over arbitrary networks. In: Proceedings of the 21st Symposium on Principles of Distributed Computing (PODC), pp. 193–202. ACM Press, Monterey (2002)

[8] Lamport, L., Shostak, R., Pease, M.: The byzantine generals problem. ACM Trans. Program. Lang. Syst. 4(3), 382–401 (1982)

[9] Patra, A., Shankar, B., Choudhary, A., Srinathan, K., Rangan, C.P.: Perfectly secure message transmission in directed networks tolerating threshold and non threshold adversary. In: Bao, F., Ling, S., Okamoto, T., Wang, H., Xing, C. (eds.) CANS 2007. LNCS, vol. 4856, pp. 80–101. Springer, Heidelberg (2007)

[10] Rabin, T., Ben-Or, M.: Verifiable Secret Sharing and Multiparty Protocols with Honest Majority. In: Proceedings of the 21st Symposium on Theory of Computing (STOC), pp. 73–85. ACM Press, New York (1989)
[11] Rabin, T., Ben-Or, M.: Verifiable secret sharing and multiparty protocols with honest majority. In: STOC 1989: Proceedings of the Twenty-First Annual ACM Symposium on Theory of Computing, pp. 73–85. ACM, New York (1989)
[12] Shankar, B., Gopal, P., Srinathan, K., Pandu Rangan, C.: Unconditionally reliable message transmission in directed networks. In: SODA 2008: Proceedings of the Nineteenth Annual ACM-SIAM Symposium on Discrete Algorithms, pp. 1048–1055. Society for Industrial and Applied Mathematics, Philadelphia (2008)
[13] Srinathan, K., Patra, A., Choudhary, A., Pandu Rangan, C.: Unconditionally secure message transmission in arbitrary directed synchronous networks tolerating generalized mixed adversary. In: ASIACCS 2009: Proceedings of the 4th International Symposium on Information, Computer, and Communications Security, pp. 171–182. ACM, New York (2009)
[14] Srinathan, K., Pandu Rangan, C.: Possibility and complexity of probabilistic reliable communications in directed networks. In: Proceedings of 25th ACM Symposium on Principles of Distributed Computing, PODC 2006 (2006)
[15] Yang, Q., Desmedt, Y.: Cryptanalysis of secure message transmission protocols with feedback. In: Kurosawa, K. (ed.) Information Theoretic Security. LNCS, vol. 5973, pp. 159–176. Springer, Heidelberg (2010)

A Appendix

A.1 Proof of Lemma 1

We give a proof by induction on the iteration at which a node is added. We denote by Π_v the URMT_{FK} protocol which is run in the network to enable v to send a message to u.

Base Step: The first node added to $Y(u)$ is u which can obviously send any message reliably and securely to itself. Hence, Π_u is trivial.

Induction Step: Assume that $k-1$ nodes $v_1, v_2, \ldots, v_{k-1}$ ($v_1 = u$) have been added to $Y(u)$ in that order. At the k-th iteration, node v_k is added. Let m_k be the message v_k intends to send. Protocol Π_{v_k} proceeds as follows. If v_k was added to $Y(u)$ by:

- Construction (1), then there exists a node $v_i \in Y(u)$ ($1 \leq i \leq k-1$) s.t. v_k has an honest path p to v_i. First, v_k sends message m_k to v_i along path p, which v_i receives reliably and securely. Now, protocol Π_{v_i} is run on message m_k in the network. As Π_{v_i} is a URMT_{FK} protocol with perfect secrecy, so is Π_{v_k}.
- Construction (2), then there exist two nodes $v_i, v_j \in Y(u)$ ($1 \leq i,j \leq k-1$) s.t. v_i has an honest path p_1 to v_k and v_k has a path p_2 passing through at most one of B_1 and B_2 to v_j. Let p_2 pass through B_α. Protocol Π_{v_k} proceeds in the following sequence of steps:
  1. Node v_i chooses three random keys $k_1, k_2, k_3 \in_R \mathbb{F}$ and sends them along path p_1 to v_k which v_k receives reliably and securely.
  2. Node v_k sends $\zeta(m_k, k_1, k_2, k_3)$ to v_j along p_2.

3. Let v_j receive (f_1, f_2) along p_2. If v_j does not receive two field elements along p_2, it picks two elements $f_1, f_2 \in_R \mathbb{F}$ on its own[6]. Now, protocol Π_{v_j} is run twice in the network, first on message f_1, then on message f_2.
4. Protocol Π_{v_i} is run thrice in the network, first on message k_1, then on message k_2 and then on k_3.

Since both Π_{v_j} and Π_{v_i} are URMT$_{FK}$ protocols with perfect security, any tampering of the messages sent through either of them is detected with probability at least $(1 - \frac{1}{|\mathbb{F}|})$. If there is no tampering of the message sent through these protocols then u receives f_1, f_2 and keys k_1, k_2, k_3 reliably and securely. Therefore u will be able to recover the message m_k or detect any tampering by B_α ($\alpha \in \{1, 2\}$) on path p_2 with at least $(1 - \frac{1}{|\mathbb{F}|})$ probability (due to the property of the authentication code). Hence, Π_{v_k} is a URMT$_{FK}$ protocol. Also, since adversary does not know k_1, k_2 and k_3, it gets no information about m from $\zeta(m, k_1, k_2, k_3)$.

A.2 Proof of Lemma 3

Each one of protocols $\Pi_{i,j}$, $\Pi_{j,k}$ and $\Pi_{k,i}$ are (ϵ, δ)-SMT protocols. Let us suppose w.l.o.g. that B_i is corrupt. It means that protocols $\Pi_{i,j}$ and $\Pi_{k,i}$ will be δ-reliable and ϵ-secret. Therefore, with probability at least $(1 - \delta)^{10}$, R will receive the following 10 elements sent through $\Pi_{i,j}$ and $\Pi_{k,i}$ reliably: $\zeta(m_S, K_2)$, K_3, $\zeta(m_S, K_3)$ and K_2.[7] In that case protocols $\Pi_{i,j}$ and $\Pi_{k,i}$ will be consistent with each other and $m_R = x_2^{i,j} - k_{23}'$ will be equal to m_S if R chooses α to be i. But α can have other possible values also. The corrupt set B_i can read and alter all the messages that are sent through the protocol $\Pi_{j,k}$. Suppose, in Phase 3, it modifies K_1 to K_1' such that a different message, $m' \neq m_S$, is recovered when $\zeta(m_S, K_1)$ is unlocked using K_1'. Then it also must modify at least one of $\zeta(m_S, K_2)$ (in Phase 2) and $\zeta(m_S, K_3)$ (in Phase 3) such that the verification passes and the message recovered is m'. But the probability that both these verifications fail (if altered) is at least $(1 - \frac{1}{|\mathbb{F}|})^2$, since adversary does not know the keys K_2 and K_3 during Phase 1 and 2 (this is why it is crucial that Phase 3 begins only after the completion of Phases 1 and 2). Hence the probability that R chooses i as α, given that it received the 10 elements reliably, is at least $(1 - \frac{1}{|\mathbb{F}|})^2$.

$$\Rightarrow Pr[m_R = m_S] \geq (1 - \delta)^{10} * (1 - \frac{1}{|\mathbb{F}|})^2$$

$$\Rightarrow Pr[m_R = m_S] \geq (1 - \delta)^{12}, \text{ choose } \mathbb{F} \text{ such that } \delta \geq \frac{1}{|\mathbb{F}|}$$

$$\Rightarrow Pr[m_R = m_S] \geq 1 - 12\delta, \text{ since } \delta \leq \frac{1}{864}$$

---

[6] This is an attempt to inform R that path p_2 (and thus, B_α) is corrupt.
[7] Recall that $\zeta(m_S, K)$ consists of 2 field elements and K consists of 3 field elements for any $K \in \{K_1, K_2\}$.

Note that there is another way in which B_i can always pass the verifications, i.e. by not altering any messages. But it won't affect this probability because in that case m_R will always be equal to m_S no matter what value of α is chosen. Hence the protocol $\Pi_{i,j,k}$ is (12δ)-reliable.

A.3   Proof of Lemma 4

Suppose w.l.o.g. that B_i is corrupt. Therefore $\Pi_{j,k}$ will fail completely and hence $\zeta(m_S, K_2)$, $\zeta(m_S, K_3)$ and K_1 will be revealed to the adversary. But we see that these messages convey no information about m_S to the adversary because of the following reasons:

- due to the property of ζ function if K is not known to the adversary then $\zeta(m_S, K)$ is independent of m_S.
- since K_1 was randomly chosen by S it has no relation with the message m_S.

Now notice that among all the messages sent to R through the protocols $\Pi_{i,j}$ and $\Pi_{k,i}$ only six contain "useful" information for the adversary viz.: $\zeta(m_S, K_1)$ and k_{33} sent through $\Pi_{i,j}$ and $\zeta(m_S, K_1)$ and k_{23} sent through $\Pi_{k,i}$. $\zeta(m_S, K_2)$ and $\zeta(m_S, K_3)$ are not useful because they are already revealed to the adversary. Only the third element of the keys K_2 and K_3, i.e. k_{23} and k_{33}, are useful because if they are known, even if adversary knows the other two elements it gains no extra information about the message m_S. Also, without the third element the other two elements give absolutely no information about m_S. For example, even if adversary knows $\zeta(m_S, K_2)$, k_{21} and k_{22} it has no information about m_S. On the other hand if it knows $\zeta(m_S, K_2)$ and k_{23}, it knows m_S completely.

Therefore there are 6 elements sent through $\Pi_{i,j}$ and $\Pi_{k,i}$ that need to be kept secret from the adversary. Let $\{a_i \mid 1 \leq i \leq 6\}$ be the variables representing these six elements. It can be clearly seen that if any a_i is revealed to the adversary, m_S will be revealed. For example, if the first element of $\zeta(m_S, K_1)$, i.e. $m_S + k_{13}$ sent through $\Pi_{i,j}$ is revealed then it can find out m_S since it already knows k_{13}. Similarly, it can find out m_S using any of the other 5 "useful" elements. In other words once $\zeta(m_S, K_2)$, $\zeta(m_S, K_3)$ and K_1 are revealed to the adversary (that means once they are fixed), for a given message m_S the values of all the a_i's are fixed. Also, we send all these elements through some ϵ-secret protocol. Suppose protocol P_i was used to send a_i. To find the secrecy factor of the entire protocol $\Pi'_{i,j,k}$ we look at it as a series of 6 protocols $(P_1, P_2, ..., P_6)$. Therefore, we need to find an upper bound on the expression

$$X = \sum_c |Pr[adv(m_0, r) = c] - Pr[adv(m_1, r) = c]|, \forall m_0, m_1 \in \mathbb{F}, \forall r$$

where r denotes all the coin tosses of the adversary in the six executions combined, i.e. $r = (r_1, r_2, \ldots r_6)$. The sum is over all possible views of the adversary for the execution of the six protocols. In other words $c \in \mathbb{C} = C_1 \times C_2 \cdots \times C_6$ where C_i is the set of all possible views of the adversary for an execution of protocol P_i.

We now define the following notation for readability. $p_i(m, r, c)$ is the probability that adversary's view is c when the message sent was m and its coin tosses were r in an execution of P_i. Notice that these probabilities are over the coin tosses of honest players and hence all the six p_i's are independent of each other.

Let a_i^b be the value fixed for a_i when $m = m_b$, $b \in \{1, 2\}$. Hence we can rewrite the expression X as:

$$X = \sum_{(c_1, c_2, \ldots c_6) \in \mathbb{C}} | \prod_{i=1}^{6} p_i(a_i^0, r_i, c_i) - \prod_{i=1}^{6} p_i(a_i^1, r_i, c_i)|$$

Now we list out some properties of $p_i(m, c, r)$ which will help us in evaluating the above expression:

- $\forall m, r, \sum_{c \in C_i} p_i(m, r, c) = 1$ where $1 \leq i \leq 6$.

- $\forall m_1, m_2, r, \sum_{c \in C_i} |p_i(m_1, r, c) - p_i(m_2, r, c)| \leq 2\epsilon$ since all the protocols are ϵ-secure.

Using the result of Lemma 7 it can be easily shown that $X \leq 12.\epsilon$. Hence the protocol $\Pi'_{i,j,k}$ is (6ϵ)-secure.

Corollary 1. *If an ϵ-secret protocol is repeated k number of times then the error in secrecy increases at most by a factor of k. (In that case all the useful elements, a_i's are m itself).*

Lemma 7. *Given n pairs of vectors u_i and v_i of size l_i, i.e. $u_i = (u_{i1}, u_{i2}, \ldots u_{il_i})$ and $v_i = (v_{i1}, v_{i2}, \ldots v_{il_i})$, $i \in \{1, 2, \ldots, n\}$. Also given that $\forall i \in \{1, 2, \ldots, n\}$:*

1. $\sum_{j=1}^{l_i} u_{ij} \leq 1$ and $\sum_{j=1}^{l_i} v_{ij} \leq 1$

2. $\sum_{j=1}^{l_i} |u_{ij} - v_{ij}| \leq 2\epsilon$

Then $\sum_{k_1, k_2, \ldots k_n} | \prod_{i=1}^{n} u_{ik_i} - \prod_{i=1}^{n} v_{ik_i}| \leq 2n.\epsilon$, where k_i varies from 1 to l_i.

Proof (By Induction). Let T_n denote the sum in the expression and let $P(n)$ denote the above inequality. In other words:

$$P(n) \Rightarrow (T_n \leq 2n.\epsilon)$$

We know that $P(1)$ is true since it is given that $\sum_{k_1=1}^{l_1} |u_{1k_1} - v_{1k_1}| \leq 2\epsilon$. Suppose $P(n-1)$ is true. Therefore we have: $T_{n-1} \leq 2(n-1).\epsilon$.

Now,

$$T_n = \sum_{k_1,k_2,\ldots k_n} |\prod_{i=1}^{n} u_{ik_i} - \prod_{i=1}^{n} v_{ik_i}|$$

$$\Rightarrow T_n = \sum_{k_1,k_2,\ldots k_n} |\left(\prod_{i=1}^{n-1} u_{ik_i} - \prod_{i=1}^{n-1} v_{ik_i}\right).u_{nk_n} + \left(\prod_{i=1}^{n-1} v_{ik_i}\right)(u_{nk_n} - v_{nk_n})|$$

$$\Rightarrow T_n \le \sum_{k_1,k_2,\ldots k_n} |\left(\prod_{i=1}^{n-1} u_{ik_i} - \prod_{i=1}^{n-1} v_{ik_i}\right).u_{nk_n}| + \sum_{k_1,k_2,\ldots k_n} |\left(\prod_{i=1}^{n-1} v_{ik_i}\right)(u_{nk_n} - v_{nk_n})|$$

$$\Rightarrow T_n \le T_{n-1}.1 + 1.2\epsilon$$

$$\Rightarrow T_n \le 2(n-1).\epsilon + 2\epsilon$$

$$\Rightarrow T_n \le 2n.\epsilon$$

$\square$

Quantum-Resilient Randomness Extraction
(Invited Talk)

Renato Renner

ETH Zurich, 8093 Zurich, Switzerland
renner@phys.ethz.ch
http://www.itp.phys.ethz.ch/people/renner/

Abstract. Randomness extraction is the art of distilling almost perfectly random bits from an entropy source. Since the source can generally be considered as one that emits classical data, randomness extraction is usually analyzed within the framework of classical probability theory. However, it has been realized recently that this classical treatment is limited: it does not cover situations where the source—while still emitting classical data—is correlated to quantum side information. Here, we review some recent work that overcomes this limitation.

1 Randomness Extraction

Let X be a value from a set $\mathcal{X}$ and let E be a system that is correlated to X. *Randomness extraction* is concerned with the task of computing a bitstring $Z \in \{0,1\}^\ell$, by applying a function f to X, such that $Z = f(X)$ is virtually uniformly distributed and independent of E. By a suitable choice of f, this task can be achieved provided that X is sufficiently random given E. More precisely, the requirement is that ℓ (the size of Z) is slightly smaller than the min-entropy $H_{\min}(X|E)$ (see below for a definition) of the source, X, conditioned on the side information, E.

2 Applications

Randomness extraction is relevant in a variety of applications. One of them is "recycling" of randomness [17]. Consider a probabilistic computation which, in each run i, requires ℓ uniformly random bits, Z_i, as input and produces an output, O_i, of length k. Assume furthermore that we wish to run this algorithm N times, producing a sequence of outputs $O_1, \ldots, O_N$. Doing this in a naive way would require us to generate $N\ell$ random bits, which may be expensive. However, if $k < \ell$, there is a more resource-saving method to produce the sequence of outputs $O_1, \ldots, O_N$. Observe that the randomness Z_i used for the ith run must be independent of the previous outputs $O_1, \ldots, O_{i-1}$. This randomness can be obtained by recycling the previous input, Z_{i-1}. For this, one simply appends to Z_{i-1} a fresh random string of length k, resulting in an $(\ell + k)$-bit string,

S. Fehr (Ed.): ICITS 2011, LNCS 6673, pp. 52–57, 2011.

denoted X_i. A simple argument[1] shows that its entropy, $H_{\min}(X_i|O_1,\ldots,O_{i-1})$, is at least ℓ. Hence, by applying an appropriate randomness extraction function to X_i, we can distill a string Z_i of (almost) ℓ uniformly random bits. This procedure uses in each round only k fresh random bits (except in the first, where ℓ bits are needed). The total consumption of randomness is thus (roughly) $\ell + (N-1)k < N\ell$.

Another application of random extractors is situated in the area of cryptography. Here, a typical scenario is that honest parties have access to randomness, X, about which an adversary has partial information, E. For example, in a key distribution scheme, X may be a raw key generated by two parties communicating over an insecure communication channel, and E is the information that an adversary may have gained by a wiretapping attack. Randomness extraction can then be used as *privacy amplification* [3,2]. That is, the honest parties generate a key which is secure (i.e., uniformly distributed and independent of E) by applying an appropriate function to X.

3   Classical versus Quantum Side Information

In the standard literature on randomness extraction [20], the side information, E, is (often implicitly) assumed to be classical—or is not even modeled explicitly. Indeed, if E is classical, then it is sufficient to consider the distribution $P_{X|E=e}$ of the entropy source, X, conditioned on any possible value $E = e$ that the side information can take. If the distribution $P_{Z|E=e}$ of the output $Z = f(X)$ is uniform conditioned on any $E = e$, then Z is automatically independent of E.

This reasoning no longer applies to the more general situation where the side information, E, is represented by the state of a quantum system. For example, E may be in a pure state, ψ_E^x, for any possible value $X = x$, where the different states ψ_E^x are not perfectly distinguishable. In this case, "conditioning" on the side information E, as in the classical case described above, is no longer possible (see [13] for an example). And indeed, as we shall see below, an extractor that is sound if the side information is classical may not necessarily be resilient in the presence of quantum side information.

The two applications sketched above are examples where a quantum-mechanical treatment of side-information (and therefore the use of quantum-resilient extractors) may be necessary. In the first, this is for instance the case if we apply the randomness recycling procedure to a probabilistic algorithm that prepares a quantum system (in this case, O_i would correspond to the quantum system prepared in the ith round). Similarly, the adversary occurring in the cryptographic example may make use of quantum devices to store the information she has gained during an eavesdropping attack (see, e.g., [18,1,7,12]).

---

[1] Assume (by induction) that Z_{i-1} is independent of all previous outputs. We then have $H_{\min}(Z_{i-1}|O_1,\ldots,O_{i-2}) = \ell$. Since conditioning on the k-bit output O_{i-1} can reduce the min-entropy by at most k, we have $H_{\min}(Z_{i-1}|O_1,\ldots,O_{i-2},O_{i-1}) \geq \ell-k$. The claim then follows because adding k fresh bits will raise the entropy by k.

4   Quantum-Resilient Extractors—Technical Definition

In the following, we state the technical definition for an extractor to be resilient in the presence of quantum side information [19,5]. The definition follows the "classical" definition of extractors. The idea is that the extractor is supposed to generate a uniform output whenever the min-entropy of the input, X, is sufficiently large. However, in contrast to the classical case, the min-entropy is measured relative to quantum side information [18,14].

Definition 1. *Let ρ_{XE} be a cq-state.[2] The* min-entropy *of X conditioned on E (evaluated for $\rho = \rho_{XE}$) is defined as*

$$H_{\min}(X|E)_\rho := -\log_2 p_{\text{guess}}(X|E)$$

where $p_{\text{guess}}(X|E)$ is the average probability of guessing the value of X correctly using an optimal strategy with access to E.

Let $\{f_s\}_{s\in\mathcal{S}}$ be a family of functions from $\mathcal{X}$ to the set of ℓ-bit strings $\{0,1\}^\ell$. The index $s \in \mathcal{S}$ is called *seed*.[3]

Definition 2. *The family $\{f_s\}_{s\in\mathcal{S}}$ is a (k,ε)-strong quantum-resilient extractor if for all cq-states ρ_{XE} with $H_{\min}(X|E)_\rho \geq k$ we have*

$$\left\langle \left\| \rho_{f_s(X)E} - \tau_X \otimes \rho_E \right\|_1 \right\rangle_s \leq \varepsilon$$

where τ_X is the state corresponding to a uniformly distributed X, and where $\langle\cdot\rangle_s$ denotes the expectation value over a uniform choice of the seed $s \in \mathcal{S}$.[4]

We note that the "classical" definition of extractors is retrieved (see [12] or [5] for details) if the system E is replaced by a purely classical value (or omitted completely). In particular, any (k,ε)-strong quantum-resilient extractor is automatically a (k,ε)-strong extractor in the classical sense.

However, the converse is not true. As shown in [9], it is possible to construct strong extractors (in the classical sense) which are not quantum-resilient. This result implies that separate proofs are required for the individual known extractor constructions in order to show that they can be used in the presence of quantum side information. In the following section, we summarize some recent results in this direction.

---

[2] A *classical-quantum-state* (or cq-state) is a bipartite density operator ρ_{XE} describing the joint state of a classical value X and a quantum system E. Formally, it has the form $\rho_{XE} = \sum_x p_x |x\rangle\langle x| \otimes \rho_E^x$, where p_x is the probability distribution of the values X and ρ_E^x is the state of E conditioned on $X = x$.

[3] In the classical literature on randomness extraction, the seed is usually considered as an input to the extractor function.

[4] More generally, one may assign probabilities p_s to each element in $\{f_s\}_{s\in\mathcal{S}}$ and define extractors with respect to a seed chosen according to this probability distribution.

5 Specific Constructions of Randomness Extractors

The following table summarizes some of the extractor constructions for which resilience against quantum side information has been proved. For example, the first line refers to extractors defined as two-universal families of functions [4,26]. These extractors extract essentially the entire min-entropy, i.e., they are (k, ε)-strong quantum resilient extractors for any $k \geq \ell + 2\log_2(1/\varepsilon)$, where ℓ is the output length.[5]

	resilience	
	classical	quantum
two-universal hashing	[10,2]	[11,19]
almost two-universal hashing	[21]	[23]
δ-biased masking	[16]	[8]
sample-then-extract	[25]	[12]
Trevisan's extractor	[24]	[22,6,5]

While the results on the right hand side of this table have all been proved separately, it would be desirable to have techniques that enable a more generic proof of the quantum-resilience of the classical extractor constructions. Recently, some promising results of this type have been obtained (for example, a proof that any one-bit strong extractor is automatically resilient against quantum side information [15]). Nevertheless, the construction and analysis of randomness extraction in the general case (where side-information is not guaranteed to be classical) is still a widely open research field.

Acknowledgments. This presentation is based on work with Robert König and Ueli Maurer [11,19,12], with Christian Schaffner, Adam Smith, and Marco Tomamichel [23], and with Anindya De, Christopher Portmann, and Thomas Vidick [5]. I would like to thank these collaborators.

References

1. Ben-Aroya, A., Regev, O., de Wolf, R.: A hypercontractive inequality for matrix-valued functions with applications to quantum computing and LDCs. In: Proceedings of the 49th Annual IEEE Symposium on Foundations of Computer Science, FOCS 2008, pp. 477–486 (2008)
2. Bennett, C.H., Brassard, G., Crépeau, C., Maurer, U.: Generalized privacy amplification. IEEE Transaction on Information Theory 41(6), 1915–1923 (1995)
3. Bennett, C.H., Brassard, G., Robert, J.-M.: Privacy amplification by public discussion. SIAM Journal on Computing 17(2), 210–229 (1988)

---

[5] This is essentially optimal, because the min-entropy of the output of a function can never be larger than the min-entropy of its input.

4. Carter, J.L., Wegman, M.N.: Universal classes of hash functions. Journal of Computer and System Sciences 18, 143–154 (1979)
5. De, A., Portmann, C., Vidick, T., Renner, R.: Trevisan's extractor in the presence of quantum side information. arXiv:0912.5514 (2009)
6. De, A., Vidick, T.: Near-optimal extractors against quantum storage. In: Proceedings of the 42nd Annual ACM Symposium on Theory of Computing, STOC 2010, pp. 161–170 (2010)
7. Desrosiers, S.P., Dupuis, F.: Quantum entropic security and approximate quantum encryption. IEEE Transactions on Information Theory, 3455–3464 (2010)
8. Fehr, S., Schaffner, C.: Randomness extraction via δ-biased masking in the presence of a quantum attacker. In: Canetti, R. (ed.) TCC 2008. LNCS, vol. 4948, pp. 465–481. Springer, Heidelberg (2008)
9. Gavinsky, D., Kempe, J., Kerenidis, I., Raz, R., de Wolf, R.: Exponential separations for one-way quantum communication complexity, with applications to cryptography. In: Proceeding of the 39th STOC (2007)
10. Impagliazzo, R., Levin, L.A., Luby, M.: Pseudo-random generation from one-way functions (extended abstract). In: Proceedings of the Twenty-First Annual ACM Symposium on Theory of Computing, pp. 12–24 (1989)
11. König, R., Maurer, U., Renner, R.: On the power of quantum memory. IEEE Transactions on Information Theory 51(7), 2391–2401 (2005)
12. König, R., Renner, R.: Sampling of min-entropy relative to quantum knowledge. IEEE Transactions on Information Theory (to appear, 2011); preprint: arXiv:0712.4291
13. König, R., Renner, R., Bariska, A., Maurer, U.: Small accessible quantum information does not imply security. Phys. Rev. Lett. 98, 140502 (2007)
14. König, R., Renner, R., Schaffner, C.: The operational meaning of min- and max-entropy. IEEE Transactions on Information Theory 55, 4337–4347 (2009)
15. König, R., Terhal, B.: The bounded storage model in the presence of a quantum adversary. IEEE Transactions on Information Theory, 749–762 (2008)
16. Naor, J., Naor, M.: Small-bias probability spaces: efficient constructions and applications. In: Proceedings of the 22nd Annual ACM Symposium on Theory of Computing (STOC), pp. 213–223 (1990)
17. Nisan, N., Zuckerman, D.: Randomness is linear in space. Journal of Computer and System Sciences 52, 43–52 (1996); A preliminary version appeared at STOC 1993
18. Renner, R.: Security of Quantum Key Distribution. PhD thesis, Swiss Federal Institute of Technology (ETH) Zurich (2005), Available at arXiv:quant-ph/0512258
19. Renner, R., König, R.: Universally composable privacy amplification against quantum adversaries. In: Kilian, J. (ed.) TCC 2005. LNCS, vol. 3378, pp. 407–425. Springer, Heidelberg (2005)
20. Shaltiel, R.: Recent developments in explicit constructions of extractors. Bulletin of the EATCS 77, 67–95 (2002)
21. Stinson, D.R.: Universal hash families and the leftover hash lemma, and applications to cryptography and computing. J. Combin. Math. Combin. Comput. (2002)
22. Ta-Shma, A.: Short seed extractors against quantum storage. In: Proceedings of the 41st Annual ACM Symposium on Theory of Computing, STOC 2009, pp. 401–408 (2009)

23. Tomamichel, M., Schaffner, C., Smith, A., Renner, R.: Leftover hashing against quantum side information. IEEE Transactions on Information Theory (to appear, 2011); preprint: arXiv:1002.2436
24. Trevisan, L.: Extractors and pseudorandom generators. Journal of the ACM 48, 860–879 (2001)
25. Vadhan, S.P.: On constructing locally computable extractors and cryptosystems in the bounded storage model. In: Boneh, D. (ed.) CRYPTO 2003. LNCS, vol. 2729, pp. 61–77. Springer, Heidelberg (2003)
26. Wegman, M.N., Carter, J.L.: New hash functions and their use in authentication and set equality. Journal of Computer and System Sciences 22, 265–279 (1981)

Homogeneous Faults, Colored Edge Graphs, and Cover Free Families

Yongge Wang[1] and Yvo Desmedt[2]

[1] University of North Carolina at Charlotte, USA
yonwang@uncc.edu
[2] University College London, UK
y.desmedt@cs.ucl.ac.uk

Abstract. In this paper, we use the concept of colored edge graphs to model homogeneous faults in networks. We then use this model to study the minimum connectivity (and design) requirements of networks for being robust against homogeneous faults within certain thresholds. In particular, necessary and sufficient conditions for most interesting cases are obtained. For example, we will study the following cases: (1) the number of colors (or the number of non-homogeneous network device types) is one more than the homogeneous fault threshold; (2) there is only one homogeneous fault (i.e., only one color could fail); and (3) the number of non-homogeneous network device types is less than five.

1 Background and Colored Edge Graph

In network communications, the communication could fail if some nodes or some edges are broken. Though the failure of a modem could be considered the failure of a node, we can model this scenario also as the failure of the communication link (the edge) attached to this modem. Thus it is sufficient to consider edge failures in communication networks. It is also important to note that several nodes (or edges) in a network could fail at the same time. For example, all brand X routers in a network could fail at the same time due to a platform dependent computer worm (virus) attack. In order to design survivable communication networks, it is essential to consider this kind of homogeneous faults for networks. Existing works on network quality of services have not addressed this issue in detail and there is no existing model to study network reliability in this aspect. In this paper, we use the colored edge graphs which could be used to model homogeneous faults in networks. The model is then used to optimize the design of survivable networks and to study the minimum connectivity (and design) requirements of networks for being robust against homogeneous faults within certain thresholds.

Definition 1. *A colored edge graph is a tuple $G(V, E, C, f)$, with V the node set, E the edge set, C the color set, and f a map from E onto C. The structure*

$$\mathcal{Z}_{C,t} = \{Z : Z \subseteq E \text{ and } |f(Z)| \leq t\}.$$

is called a t-color adversary structure. Let $A, B \in V$ be distinct nodes of G. A, B are called $(t + 1)$-color connected for $t \geq 1$ if for any color set $C_t \subseteq C$ of size t,

S. Fehr (Ed.): ICITS 2011, LNCS 6673, pp. 58–72, 2011.

there is a path p from A to B in G such that the edges on p do not contain any color in C_t. A colored edge graph G is $(t+1)$-color connected if and only if for any two nodes A and B in G, they are $(t+1)$-color connected.

The interpretation of the above definition is as follows. In a network, if two edges have the same color, then they could fail at the same time. This may happen when the two edges are designed with same technologies (e.g., with same operating systems, with same application software, with same hardware, or with same hardware and software). If a colored edge network is $(t+1)$-color connected, then the network communication is robust against the failure of edges of any t colors (that is, the adversary may tear down any t types of devices).

In practice, one communication link may be attached to different brands of network devices (e.g., routers, modems) on both sides. For this case, the edge can have two different colors. If any of these colors is broken, the edge is broken. Thus from a reliability viewpoint, if one designs networks with two colors on the same edge, the same reliability/security can be obtained by having only one color on each edge. In the following discussion, we will only consider the case with one color on each edge. Meanwhile, multiple edges between two nodes are not allowed either.

We are interested in the following practical questions. For a given number n of nodes in V (i.e., the number of network nodes), a given number m of the colors (e.g., the number of network device types), and a given number t, how can we design a $(t+1)$-color connected colored edge graph $G(V, E)$ with minimum number λ of edges? In another word, how can we use minimum resources (e.g., communication links) to design a network that will keep working even if t types of devices in the network fail?

For practical network designs, one needs first to have an estimate on the number of homogeneous faults. For example, the number t of brands of routers that could fail at the same time. Then it is sufficient to design a $(t+1)$-color connected network with $m = t+1$ colors (e.g., with $t+1$ different brands of routers). Necessary and sufficient conditions for this kind of network design will be obtained in this paper.

Another important issue that should be taken into consideration in practical network designs is that the number m of colors (e.g., the number of brands for routers) is quite small. For example, m is normally less than five. Necessary and sufficient conditions for network designs with $m \leq 5$ and with optimized resources will be obtained in this paper. Note that for cases with small m, we may have $m > t+1$.

The outline of the paper is as follows. Section 3 describes the necessary and sufficient conditions for the case of $m = t+1$ without optimizing the number of edges in the networks. Section 4 gives a necessary condition for colored edge networks in terms of optimized number of edges. Section 5 shows that the necessary conditions in Section 4 are also sufficient for the most important three cases: (1) $m = t+1$; (2) $t = 1$; and (3) $m \leq 5$. Section 6 shows that it is **coNP**-hard to determine whether a given colored edge graph is $(t+1)$-connected.

2   Related Works

Though colored-edge graph is a new concept which we used to model network survivability issues, there are related research topics in this field. For example, edge-disjoint (colorful) spanning trees have been extensively studied in the literature (see, e.g., [1]). These results are mainly related to our discussion in the next section for the case of $m = t + 1$. A colored edge graph G is *proper* if whenever two edges share an end point they carry different colors. A spanning tree for a colored edge graph is called colorful if no two of its edges have the same color. Two spanning trees of a graph are edge disjoint if they do not share common edges. For a non-negative integer s, let K_s denote the complete graph on s vertices. A classical result from Euler (see [1]) shows that the edges of K_{2n} can be partitioned into n isomorphic spanning trees (paths, for example) and each of these spanning trees can easily be made colorful, but the resulting edge colored graph usually fails to be proper.

   Though it is important to design colored edge graphs with required security parameters, for several scenarios it is also important to calculate the robustness of a given colored edge graphs. Roskind and Tarjan [7] designed a greedy algorithm to find $(t+1)$-edge disjoint spanning trees in a given graph. This is related to the questions $(t + 1)$-color connectivity for the case of $m = t + 1$. We are not aware of any approximate algorithms for deciding $(t + 1)$-color connectivity of a given colored edge graph. Indeed, we will show that this problem is **coNP**-hard.

3   Necessary and Sufficient Conditions for Special Cases

In this section, we show necessary and sufficient conditions for some special cases.

Lemma 1. *A colored edge graph $G(V, E, C, f)$ is $(t + 1)$-color connected if and only if, for all $i_1, i_2, \ldots, i_{m-t} \le m$, $(V, E_{i_1} \cup E_{i_2} \cup \cdots \cup E_{i_{m-t}})$ is a connected graph, where $E_1, E_2, \ldots, E_m$ is a partition of E under the m different colors.*

As we have mentioned in the previous section, the classical result from Euler shows that K_{2n} can be partitioned into n spanning trees. Thus, by Lemma 1, we have the following theorem.

Theorem 1. *(Euler) For $n = 2m$, there is a coloration $G(V, E, C, f)$ of K_n such that G is $(m - 1)$-color connected.*

In the following, we extend Theorem 1 to the general case of $n \ge 2m$.

Lemma 2. *For $n \ge 2m$ and $m \ge 2$, there exists a graph $G(V, E)$ with $|V| = n, |E| = m(n-1)$, and $E = E_1 \cup E_2 \cup \cdots \cup E_m$ such that the following conditions are satisfied:*

1. *$G(V, E_i)$ is a connected graph for all $0 < i \le m$;*
2. *$E_i \cap E_j = \emptyset$ for all $i, j \le m$.*

Proof. We prove the Lemma by induction on n and m. For $n = 2$ and $m = 1$, the Lemma holds obviously. Assume that the Lemma holds for $n_0 = 2m_0$.

In the following, we show that the Lemma holds for $n = n_0 + 1, m = m_0$ and for $n = n_0 + 2, m = m_0 + 1$. Let $G(V_0, E_0)$ be the graph with $|V_0| = n_0, |E_0| = m_0(n_0 - 1)$, and $E_0 = E_1^0 \cup E_2^0 \cup \cdots \cup E_{m_0}^0$ such that the conditions in the Lemma are satisfied:

For the case of $n = n_0 + 1$ and $m = m_0$, let $V = V_0 \cup \{u\}$ where u is a new node that is not in V_0, and let $E_1 = E_1^0 \cup \{(u, u_1)\}$, $E_2 = E_2^0 \cup \{(u, u_2)\}$, ..., $E_{m_0} = E_{m_0}^0 \cup \{(u, u_{m_0})\}$ where $u_1, u_2, \ldots, u_{m_0}$ are distinct nodes from V_0. It is straightforward to show that $|V| = n, |E| = m(n - 1)$, $G(V, E_i)$ is a connected graph, and $E_i \cap E_j = \emptyset$ for all $i, j \leq m$. Thus the Lemma holds for this case.

For the case of $n = n_0 + 2$ and $m = m_0 + 1$, let $V = V_0 \cup \{u, v\}$ where u, v are new nodes that are not in V_0, and define $E_1, \ldots, E_m$ as follows.

1. Set $E_m = \emptyset$ and $U = \emptyset$, where U is a temporary variable.
2. Define E_1:
   (a) Select an edge $(v_1, v_2) \in E_1^0$.
   (b) Let $E_1 = \left(E_1^0 \setminus \{(v_1, v_2)\}\right) \bigcup \{(v_1, u), (u, v), (v, v_2)\}$.
   (c) Let $E_m = E_m \cup \{(v, v_1), (v_1, v_2), (v_2, u)\}$ and $U = U \cup \{v_1, v_2\}$.
3. Define E_i for $2 \leq i \leq m_0$:
   (a) Select $v_{2i-1}, v_{2i} \notin U$.
   (b) Let $E_i = E_i^0 \cup \{(u, v_{2i-1}), (v, v_{2i})\}$.
   (c) Let $E_m = E_m \cup \{(v, v_{2i-1}), (u, v_{2i})\}$ and $U = U \cup \{v_{2i-1}, v_{2i}\}$.

It is straightforward to show that $|V| = n, |E_i| = (n - 1)$ (thus $|E| = m(n - 1)$), $G(V, E_i)$ is a connected graph, and $E_i \cap E_j = \emptyset$ for all $i, j \leq m$. This completes the proof of the Lemma.   Q.E.D.

Theorem 2. *Given n, m, t with $m = t + 1$, there exists a $(t + 1)$-color connected colored edge graph $G(V, E, C, f)$ with $|V| = n$ and $|C| = m$ if and only if $n \geq 2m$.*

Proof. By Lemma 1, a $(t + 1)$-color connected colored edge graph $G(V, E, C, f)$ with $|V| = n$ and $|C| = m = t + 1$ contains at least $m(n - 1)$ edges. Meanwhile, $G(V, E, C, f)$ contains at most $n(n - 1)/2$ edges. Thus for $n < 2m$, we have $n(n - 1)/2 < m(n - 1)$. In another word, for $n < 2m$, there is no $(t + 1)$-color connected colored edge graph $G(V, E, C, f)$ with $|V| = n$ and $|C| = m = t + 1$. Now the theorem follows from Lemmas 1 and 2.   Q.E.D.

4 Necessary Conditions for General Cases

First we note that for a colored edge graph G to be $(t + 1)$-color connected, each node must have a degree of at least $t + 1$. Thus the total degree of an n-node graph should be at least $n(t + 1)$. This implies the following lemma.

Lemma 3. *For $m \geq t + 1 > 1$, and a $(t + 1)$-color connected colored edge graph $G(V, E, C, f)$ with $|V| = n$, $|E| = \lambda$, and $|C| = m$, we have $2\lambda \geq (t + 1)n$.*

In the following, we use cover free family concepts to study the necessary conditions for colored edge graphs connectivity.

Definition 2. *Let X be a finite set with $|X| = \lambda$ and $\mathcal{F}$ be a set of mutually disjoint subsets of X with $|\mathcal{F}| = m$. Then $(X, \mathcal{F})$ is called a (λ, m)-partition of X if $X = \bigcup_{P \in \mathcal{F}} P$. Let n, t be positive integers. An (λ, m)-partition $(X, \mathcal{F})$ is called a $(t; n-1)$-cover free family (or $(t; n-1)$-CFF(λ, m)) if, for any t elements $B_1, \ldots, B_t \in \mathcal{F}$, we have that*

$$\left| X \setminus \left(\bigcup_{i=1}^{t} B_i \right) \right| \geq n - 1 \qquad \left(\text{or} \left| \bigcap_{i=1}^{t} (X \setminus B_i) \right| \geq n - 1 \right)$$

It should be noted that our above definition of cover-free family is different from the generalized cover-free family definition for set systems in the literature. In [8], a set system $(X, \mathcal{F})$ is called a $(w, t; n-1)$-cover free family if for any w blocks $A_1, \ldots, A_w \in \mathcal{F}$ and any t blocks $B_1, \ldots, B_t \in \mathcal{F}$, one has $\left| (\cap_{j=1}^{w} A_j) \setminus (\cup_{i=1}^{t} B_i) \right| \geq n - 1$. Specifically, there are two major differences between our (λ, m)-partition system and the set systems in the literature[1].

1. For a set system $(X, \mathcal{F})$, $\mathcal{F}$ may contain repeated elements.
2. For a set system $(X, \mathcal{F})$, the elements in $\mathcal{F}$ are not necessarily mutually disjoint.

It is straightforward to show that a colored edge graph G is $(t+1)$-color connected if and only if for any color set $C_t \subseteq C$ of size t, after the removal of edges in G with colors in C_t, G remains connected. Assume that G contains n nodes. Then a necessary condition for connectivity is that G contains at least $n-1$ edges. From this discussion, we get the following lemma.

Lemma 4. *For a colored edge graph $G(V, E, C, f)$, with $|V| = n$, $|E| = \lambda$, $|C| = m$, a necessary condition for $G(V, E, C, f)$ to be $(t+1)$-color connected is that the (λ, m)-partition $(X, \mathcal{F})$ is a $(t; n-1)$-CFF(λ, m) with $X = E$ and $\mathcal{F} = \{E_c : c \in C\}$ where $E_c = \{e : f(e) = c, e \in E\}$.*

In the following, we analyze lower bounds for the number λ of edges for the existence of a $(t; n-1)$-CFF(λ, m). For a set partition $(X, \mathcal{F})$ and a positive integer t, let

$$\mu(X, \mathcal{F}; t) = \min \left\{ \left| X \setminus \left(\bigcup_{i=1}^{t} B_i \right) \right| : B_1, \ldots, B_t \in \mathcal{F} \right\}$$

It is straightforward to see that a (λ, m)-partition $(X, \mathcal{F})$ is a $(t; n-1)$-CFF(λ, m) if and only if $\mu(X, \mathcal{F}; t) \geq n - 1$.

Given positive integers λ, m, t, let

$$\mu(\lambda, m; t) = \max \{\mu(X, \mathcal{F}; t) : (X, \mathcal{F}) \text{ is a } (\lambda, m)\text{-partition}\}$$

From the above discussion and Lemma 3, we have the following theorem.

---

[1] The first author of this paper would like to thank Prof. Doug Stinson for pointing this out to the author.

Theorem 3. *Let λ, m, t be given positive integers. $\mu(\lambda, m; t) \geq n - 1$ and $2\lambda \geq (t+1)n$ are necessary conditions for the existence of a $(t+1)$-color connected colored edge graph $G(V, E, C, f)$, with $|V| = n$, $|E| = \lambda$, $|C| = m$.*

Theorem 4. *Let λ, m, t be given positive integers. Then we have*

$$\mu(\lambda, m; t) = \begin{cases} (m-t) \cdot \lfloor \frac{\lambda}{n} \rfloor & \text{if } t \geq \lambda - \lfloor \frac{\lambda}{m} \rfloor \cdot m \\ (m-t) \cdot \lfloor \frac{\lambda}{m} \rfloor + (\lambda - \lfloor \frac{\lambda}{m} \rfloor \cdot m - t) & \text{otherwise} \end{cases}$$

Proof. For a given (λ, m)-partition $(X, \mathcal{F})$, let $B_1, \ldots, B_m$ be an enumeration of elements in $\mathcal{F}$ such that $|B_i| \leq |B_{i+1}|$ for all $i < m$. It is straightforward to show that $\mu(X, \mathcal{F}; t) = \sum_{i=1}^{m-t} |B_i|$. Thus $\mu(\lambda, m; t)$ takes the maximum value if $\sum_{i=1}^{m-t} |B_i|$ is maximized. It is straightforward to show that this value is maximized when the (λ, m)-partition $(X, \mathcal{F})$ satisfies the following conditions:

1. $|B_i| = \lfloor \frac{\lambda}{m} \rfloor$ for $i \leq m - (\lambda - \lfloor \frac{\lambda}{m} \rfloor \cdot m)$, and
2. $|B_i| = \lfloor \frac{\lambda}{m} \rfloor + 1$ for $m \geq i > m - (\lambda - \lfloor \frac{\lambda}{m} \rfloor \cdot m)$.

The theorem follows from the above discussion. Q.E.D.

Example 1. For $n = 7, \lambda = 10, m = 5$, and $t = 2$, we have $\mu(10, 5; 2) = 6 = n - 1$. However, $2\lambda = 20 < (t+1)n = 21$. This shows that the condition $2\lambda \geq (t+1)n$ in Theorem 3 is not redundant.

Example 2. There are no $(t+1)$-color connected colored edge graph $G(V, E, C, f)$ for the following special cases:

1. $m = 2, t = 1, n = 3$.
2. $m = 4, t = 2, n = 4$.
3. $m = 3, t = 2, n \leq 5$.

Proof. Before we consider the specific cases, we observe that, when m and t are fixed, the function μ is nondecreasing when λ increases.

1. In this case, the maximum value that λ could take is 3. Thus $\mu(3, 2; 1) = 1 < n - 1 = 2$. That is, there is no $(1; 2)$-CFF$(3, 2)$, which implies the claim. Note that this result also follows from Theorem 2.

2. In this case, the maximum value that λ could take is 6. Thus $\mu(6, 4; 2) = 2 < n - 1 = 3$.

3. We only show this for the case $m = 3, t = 2, n = 5$. In this case, the maximum value that λ could take is 10. Thus $\mu(10, 3; 2) = 3 < n - 1 = 4$. Note that this result also follows from Theorem 2. Q.E.D

The following theorem is a variant of Theorem 3.

Theorem 5. *For $m - 1 > t > 0$, a necessary condition for the existence of a $(t+1)$-color connected colored edge graph $G(V, E, C, f)$ with $|V| = n$, $|E| = \lambda$, and $|C| = m$ is that $2\lambda \geq (t+1)n$ and the following conditions are satisfied:*

- *If $n = (m-t)k$ for some integer $k > 0$, then $\lambda \geq mk - 1$.*
- *If $n = (m-t)k + 1$ for some integer $k > 0$, then $\lambda \geq mk$.*
- *If $n = (m-t)k + 2$ for some integer $k > 0$, then $\lambda \geq mk + t + 1$.*
- ......
- *If $n = (m-t)k + m - t - 1$ for some integer $k > 0$, then $\lambda \geq mk + m - 2$.*

Proof. For $m > t + 1$, by Theorem 4, we have

$$
\mu(\lambda, m; t) = \begin{cases}
(m-t)k' & \text{if } \lambda = mk' + i \text{ for } 0 \leq i \leq t \\
(m-t)k' + 1 & \text{if } \lambda = mk' + t + 1 \\
\cdots\cdots \\
(m-t)k' + m - t - 1 & \text{if } \lambda = mk' + m - 1
\end{cases}
$$

Thus the necessary condition $\mu(\lambda, m; t) \geq n - 1$ in Theorem 3 can be interpreted as the following conditions:

$$
k' \geq \begin{cases}
\frac{n-1}{m-t} & \text{if } \lambda = mk' + i \text{ for } 0 \leq i \leq t \\
\frac{n-2}{m-t} & \text{if } \lambda = mk' + t + 1 \\
\cdots\cdots \\
\frac{n-m+t}{m-t} & \text{if } \lambda = mk' + m - 1
\end{cases}
$$

In aother word, for a $(t+1)$-color connected colored edge graph $G(V, E, C, f)$, the following $m - t$ conditions (the disjunction not conjunction) are satisfied:

- $|V| = n, |E| \geq m \left\lceil \frac{n-1}{m-t} \right\rceil$, and $|C| = m$.
- $|V| = n, |E| \geq m \left\lceil \frac{n-2}{m-t} \right\rceil + t + 1$, and $|C| = m$.
- ......
- $|V| = n, |E| \geq m \left\lceil \frac{n-m+t}{m-t} \right\rceil + m - 1$, and $|C| = m$.

By distinguishing the cases for $n = (m-t)k$, $n = (m-t)k + 1$, $\cdots$, and $n = (m-t)k + m - t - 1$, and by reorganizing above lines, these necessary conditions can be interpreted as the following $m - t$ conditions:

- $n = (m-t)k$ and $\lambda \geq mk - 1$ for some $k > 0$. Note that this follows from the last line of the above conditions (one can surely take other lines, but then the value of λ would be larger). This comment applies to following cases also.
- $n = (m-t)k + 1$ and $\lambda \geq mk$ for some $k > 0$.
- $n = (m-t)k + 2$ and $\lambda \geq mk + t + 1$ for some $k > 0$.
- ......
- $n = (m-t)k + m - t - 1$ and $\lambda \geq mk + m - 2$ for some $k > 0$.   Q.E.D.

5   Necessary and Sufficient Conditions for Practical Cases (with Small m and t)

Generally we are interested in the question whether the necessary condition in Theorems 3 and 5 are also sufficient. In the following, we show that this is true for several important practical cases.

Theorem 6. *The necessary condition in Theorem 3 is sufficient for the case of* $m = t + 1$.

Proof. Since $\lambda - \lfloor \frac{\lambda}{m} \rfloor \cdot m$ is the remainder of λ divided by m, we trivially have $t = m - 1 \geq \lambda - \lfloor \frac{\lambda}{m} \rfloor \cdot m$. Now assume that $m > \frac{n}{2}$. By Theorem 4, we have $\mu(\lambda, m; t) = \lfloor \frac{\lambda}{m} \rfloor \leq \lfloor \frac{n(n-1)}{2m} \rfloor < n - 1$. The rest follows from Theorem 2. Q.E.D.

Before we show that the necessary conditions in Theorems 3 and 5 are sufficient for the case of $t = 1$, we first present two lemmas whose proofs are straightforward.

Lemma 5. *For* $n = m = \lambda \geq 3$ *and* $t = 1$, *the following m-node circle graph is* $(1 + 1)$-color connected:

$$\{(v_1, v_2), (v_2, v_3), \ldots, (v_m, v_1)\}$$

with $f(v_i, v_{i+1}) = c_i$ *for* $i < m$ *and* $f(v_m, v_1) = c_m$.

Lemma 6. *For* $t = 1$, $m \geq 3$, *and* $m < n \leq 2m - 2$, *the* $(1+1)$-color connected *graph in Figure 1 has the edges:*

$$\{(v_1, v_2), (v_2, v_3), \ldots, (v_m, v_1)\} \cup \{(v_m, v_{m+1}), (v_{m+1}, v_{m+2}), \ldots, (v_n, v_1)\}$$

and colors defined by the following map:

$$
\begin{aligned}
f(v_i, v_{i+1}) &= c_i & \text{for } 1 \leq i \leq m - 1 \\
f(v_m, v_1) &= c_m \\
f(v_{m+i-1}, v_{m+i}) &= c_i & \text{for } 1 \leq i \leq n - m \\
f((v_n, v_1)) &= c_{n-m+1}
\end{aligned}
$$

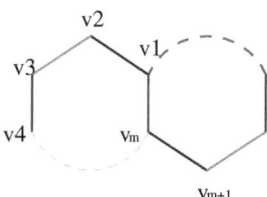

Fig. 1. For Lemma 6

Before we show that the necessary condition in Theorem 3 is also sufficient for the case of $t = 1$, we first prove this for $m = 3$.

Theorem 7. *The necessary condition in Theorem 3 is sufficient for the case of* $m = 3$ *and* $t = 1$.

Proof. For $m = 3$ and $t = 1$, we have

$$\mu(\lambda, m; t) = \begin{cases} 2k' & \text{if } \lambda = 3k' \text{ or } \lambda = 3k' + 1 \\ 2k' + 1 & \text{if } \lambda = 3k' + 2 \end{cases}$$

By the condition $\mu(\lambda, m; t) \geq n - 1$, the necessary condition is converted to the following conditions:

$$k' \geq \begin{cases} \frac{n-1}{2} & \text{if } \lambda = 3k' \text{ or } \lambda = 3k' + 1 \\ \frac{n-2}{2} & \text{if } \lambda = 3k' + 2 \end{cases}$$

Thus in order to prove the theorem, it is sufficient to construct $(1+1)$-color connected colored edge graph $G(V, E, C, f)$ for each of the following two conditions:

- $|V| = n, |E| = 3 \left\lceil \frac{n-1}{2} \right\rceil$, and $|C| = 3$.
- $|V| = n, |E| = 3 \left\lceil \frac{n-2}{2} \right\rceil + 2$, and $|C| = 3$.

By distinguishing the cases for $n = 2k$ and $n = 2k+1$, it is sufficient to construct the required colored edge graph for each of the following two conditions:

- $n = 2k$, $\lambda = 3k - 1$, and $m = 3$.
- $n = 2k + 1$, $\lambda = 3k$, and $m = 3$.

For the case of $n = 2k$, let

$$\begin{aligned} V &= \{v_1, \cdots, v_{2k}\}, \\ E_1 &= \{(v_1, v_{2i}) : 1 \leq i < k\} \\ E_2 &= \{(v_1, v_{2i+1}) : 1 \leq i < k\} \cup \{(v_1, v_{2k})\} \\ E_3 &= \{(v_{2i}, v_{2i+1}) : 1 \leq i < k)\} \cup \{(v_2, v_{2k})\} \\ E &= E_1 \cup E_2 \cup E_3 \end{aligned}$$

For each $e \in E_i$ ($i \leq 3$), let $f(e) = c_i$. Then it is straightforward to check that the colored edge graph $G(V, E, C, f)$ is $(1+1)$-color connected, $|V| = n$, and $|E| = 3k - 1$.

For the case of $n = 2k + 1$, let

$$\begin{aligned} V &= \{v_1, \cdots, v_{2k+1}\}, \\ E_1 &= \{(v_1, v_{2i}) : 1 \leq i \leq k\} \\ E_2 &= \{(v_1, v_{2i+1}) : 1 \leq i \leq k\} \\ E_3 &= \{(v_{2i}, v_{2i+1}) : 1 \leq i \leq k)\} \\ E &= E_1 \cup E_2 \cup E_3 \end{aligned}$$

For each $e \in E_i$ ($i \leq 3$), let $f(e) = c_i$. Then it is straightforward to check that the colored edge graph $G(V, E, C, f)$ is $(1+1)$-color connected, $|V| = n$, and $|E| = 3k - 1$,   Q.E.D.

Corollary 1. *For $m = 3$, $t = 1$, and $n, \lambda > 0$, there exists an $(1+1)$-color connected colored edge graph $G(V, E, C, f)$ with $|V| = n$ and $|E| = \lambda$ if and only if $\lambda \geq \min \left\{ 3 \left\lceil \frac{n-1}{2} \right\rceil, 3 \left\lceil \frac{n-2}{2} \right\rceil + 2 \right\}$.*

Now let us prove the theorem for the general case of $t = 1$.

Theorem 8. *The necessary conditions in Theorems 3 and 5 are sufficient for the case of $t = 1$.*

Proof. For the case of $m = 2$ and $t = 1$, it follows from Theorem 6. Now assume that $m > 2$ and $t = 1$. In this special case, the necessary conditions in Theorem 5 is as follows:

- $n = (m-1)k$ and $\lambda \geq mk - 1$ for some $k > 0$.
- $n = (m-1)k + 1$ and $\lambda \geq mk$ for some $k > 0$.
- $n = (m-1)k + 2$ and $\lambda \geq mk + 2$ for some $k > 0$.
- $\ldots\ldots$
- $n = (m-1)k + m - 2$ and $\lambda \geq mk + m - 2$ for some $k > 0$.

In the following we first show that the condition "$n = (m-1)k + 1$ and $\lambda \geq km$" is sufficient. Let the graph in Figure 2a be defined as follows:

$$
\begin{aligned}
V &= \{v_0, v_1 \cdots, v_{(m-1)k}\}, \\
E_1 &= \{(v_0, v_{(m-1)i+1}) : 0 \leq i \leq k-1\} \\
E_j &= \{(v_{(m-1)i+j-1}, v_{(m-1)i+j}) : 0 \leq i \leq k-1\} \text{ for } 2 \leq j \leq m-1 \\
E_m &= \{(v_{(m-1)i}, v_0) : 1 \leq i \leq k\} \\
E &= E_1 \cup E_2 \cup \cdots \cup E_m
\end{aligned}
$$

For each $e \in E_j$ with $i \leq m$, let $f(e) = c_j$. Then it is straightforward to check that the colored edge graph $G(V, E, C, f)$ is $(1+1)$-color connected, $|V| = (m-1)k + 1$, and $|E| = mk$.

Now we show that the condition "$n = (m-1)k + j$ and $\lambda \geq km + j$ for $2 \leq j \leq m-1$" is sufficient. Let $G(V, E, C, f)$ be the colored edge graph that we have just constructed with $|V| = (m-1)k + 1$, and $|E| = mk$.

Let $V' = V \cup \{v_{(m-1)k+1}, \ldots, v_{(m-1)k+j-1}\}$. Define a new colored edge graph $G(V', E', C, f')$ (see Figure 2b) by attaching the following edges to the m-node circle $\{(v_0, v_1), (v_1, v_2), \ldots, (v_{m-1}, v_0)\}$:

$$
\{(v_{m-1}, v_{(m-1)k+1}), (v_{(m-1)k+1}, v_{(m-1)k+2}), \ldots, (v_{(m-1)k+j-1}, v_0)\}
$$

The colors for the new edges are defined by letting $f'(v_{(m-1)k+i}, v_{(m-1)k+i+1}) = c_{i+1}$ for $0 \leq i \leq j-2$ and $f'(v_{(m-1)k+j-1}, v_0) = c_j$. It is straightforward to check that $G(V', E', C, f')$ is $(1+1)$-color connected, $|V| = (m-1)k + j$, and $|E| = mk + j$.   Q.E.D.

Corollary 2. *For $t = 1$ and $m, n, \lambda > 1$, there exists an $(1+1)$-color connected colored edge graph $G(V, E, C, f)$ with $|V| = n$ and $|E| = \lambda$ if and only if*

$$
\lambda \geq \min\left\{ m\left\lceil \frac{n-1}{m-1} \right\rceil, m\left\lceil \frac{n-2}{m-1} \right\rceil + 2, \ldots, m\left\lceil \frac{n-m+1}{m-1} \right\rceil + m - 1 \right\}.
$$

Proof. It follows from the proof of Theorem 8.   Q.E.D.

Theorem 9. *The conditions in Theorems 3 and 5 are sufficient for the case of $m = 4, t = 2$.*

Proof. It is sufficient to show that both of the conditions "$n = (m-t)k + 1$ and $\lambda \geq km$" and "$n = (m-t)k + 2$ and $\lambda \geq mk + t + 1$" are sufficient (note that $m = 4$

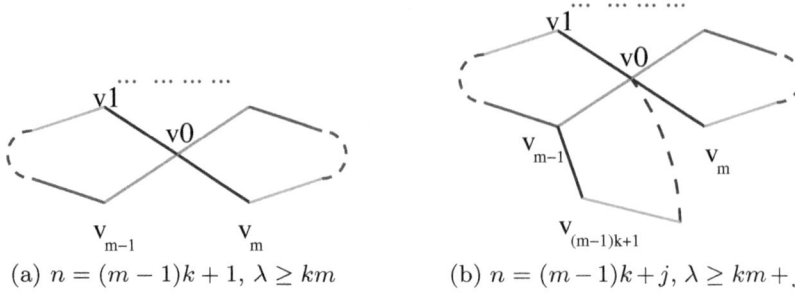

(a) $n = (m-1)k+1, \lambda \geq km$ (b) $n = (m-1)k+j, \lambda \geq km+j$

Fig. 2. Figures for Theorem 8

and $t = 2$). In the following we first show that the condition "$n = (m-t)k+1$ and $\lambda \geq km$" is sufficient by induction on k.

For the case of $k = 2$, we have $n = 5, \lambda = 8, m = 4$, and $t = 2$. Let the graph G_1 in Figure 3a be defined as

$$G_1 = \{(v_1, v_2)_1, (v_2, v_3)_2, (v_3, v_4)_1, (v_4, v_5)_3, (v_5, v_1)_2, (v_1, v_3)_3, (v_1, v_4)_4, (v_2, v_5)_4\}$$

where $(v, v')_i$ means that the edge (v, v') takes color c_i. It is straightforward to check that G_1 is $(2+1)$-color connected.

For the case of $k = 3$, we have $n = 7, \lambda = 12, m = 4$, and $t = 2$. Let the graph G_2 in Figure 3b be defined as

$$\{(v_1, v_2)_1, (v_2, v_3)_2, (v_4, v_5)_3, (v_5, v_1)_2, (v_1, v_3)_3, (v_1, v_4)_4,$$
$$(v_2, v_5)_4, (v_3, v_6)_1, (v_6, v_7)_3, (v_7, v_4)_1, (v_4, v_6)_4, (v_3, v_7)_2\}$$

where $(v, v')_i$ means that the edge (v, v') takes color c_i. It is straightforward to check that G_2 is $(2+1)$-color connected.

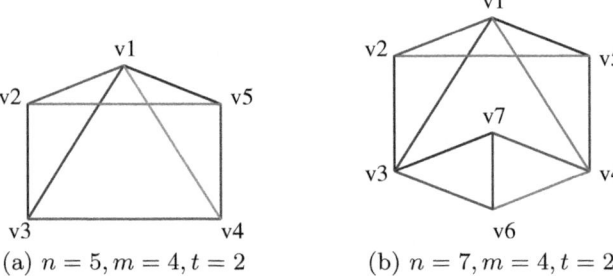

(a) $n = 5, m = 4, t = 2$ (b) $n = 7, m = 4, t = 2$

Fig. 3. Figures for Theorem 9

Now for $k = 2r$ ($r \geq 2$), we have $n = (m-t)k+1 = 4r+1$ and $\lambda = km = 8r$. If we glue the v_1 node of r copies of G_1, we get a $(t+1)$-color connected colored graph G with $n = 4r+1$ and $\lambda = 8r$. Thus the condition for the case of $k = 2r$ holds.

For $k = 2r+1$ $(r \geq 2)$, we have $n = (m-t)k+1 = 4r+3$ and $\lambda = km = 8r+4$. If we glue the v_1 node of $r-1$ copies of G_1 and one copy of G_2, we get a $(t+1)$-color connected colored graph G with $n = 4(r-1)+1+6 = 4r+3$ and $\lambda = 8(r-1)+12 = 8r+4$. Thus the condition for the case of $k = 2r+1$ holds. This completes the induction.

For the condition "$n = (m-t)k+2$ and $\lambda \geq mk+t+1$", one can add one node to the graph for the case "$n = (m-t)k+1$ and $\lambda \geq km$" with 3 edges (with distinct colors) to any three nodes. The resulting graph meets the requirements.   Q.E.D.

Theorem 9 could be extended to the case of $m = 5$ and $t = 3$.

Theorem 10. *The conditions in Theorems 3 and 5 are sufficient for the case of $m = 5$ and $t = 3$.*

Proof. It is sufficient to show that both of the conditions "$n = (m-t)k+1$ and $\lambda \geq km$" and "$n = (m-t)k+2$ and $\lambda \geq mk+t+1$" are sufficient (note that $m-t = 2$). In the following we first show that the condition "$n = 2k+1$ and $\lambda \geq km$" is sufficient by induction on k and m.

For $m = 5$ and $k = 2$, we have $n = 5, \lambda = 10$. The graph in Figure 4a shows that the condition is sufficient also. For the case of $k = 3$, we have $n = 7, \lambda = 15$. The graph in Figure 4b shows that the condition is sufficient also.

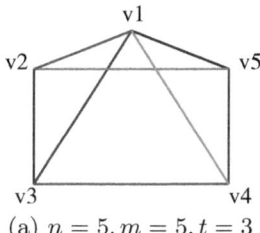 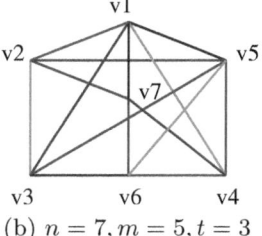

(a) $n = 5, m = 5, t = 3$ (b) $n = 7, m = 5, t = 3$

Fig. 4. Figures for Theorem 10

For $k = 2r$ $(r \geq 2)$, the condition becomes $n = (m-t)k+1 = 4r+1$ and $\lambda = km = 10r$. If we glue the v_1 node of r copies of $G_{5,1}$, we get a $(t+1)$-color connected colored graph G with $n = 4r+1$ and $\lambda = 10r$. Thus the condition for the case of $k = 2r$ holds.

For $k = 2r+1$ $(r \geq 2)$, the condition becomes $n = (m-t)k+1 = 4r+3$ and $\lambda = km = 10r+5$. If we glue the v_1 node of $r-1$ copies of $G_{5,1}$ and one copy of $G_{5,2}$, we get a $(t+1)$-color connected colored graph G with $n = 4(r-1)+1+6 = 4r+3$ and $\lambda = 10(r-1)+15 = 10r+5$. Thus the condition for the case of $k = 2r+1$ holds. This completes the induction.

For the condition "$n = (m-t)k+2$ and $\lambda \geq mk+t+1$", we have $n = 2k+2$ and $\lambda \geq 5k+4$. We can add one node to the graph for the case "$n = (m-t)k+1$ and $\lambda \geq km$" with 4 edges (with distinct colors) to any four nodes. The resulting graph meets the requirements.   Q.E.D.

Open Questions: We showed in this section that the conditions in Theorems 3 and 5 are sufficient for practical cases. It would be interesting to show that these conditions are also sufficient for general cases. We leave this as an open question.

6   Hardness Results

We have given necessary and sufficient conditions for $(t + 1)$-color connected colored edge graphs. Sometimes, it is also important to determine whether a given graph is $(t + 1)$-color connected. Unfortunately, the following Theorem shows that the problem ceConnect is **coNP**-complete. The ceConnect problem is defined as follows.

INSTANCE: A colored edge graph $G = G(V, E, C, f)$, two nodes $A, B \in V$, and a positive integer $t \le |C|$.
QUESTION: Are A and B t-color connected?
    Before we prove the hardness result, we first introduce the concept of color separator. For a colored edge graph $G = G(V, E, C, f)$, a color separator for two nodes A and B of the graph G is a color set $C' \subseteq C$ such that the removal of all edges with colors in C' from the graph G will disconnect A and B. It is straightforward to observe that A and B are $(t + 1)$-color connected if and only there is no t-size color separator for A and B.

Theorem 11. *The problem ceConnect is **coNP**-complete.*

Proof. It is straightforward to show that the problem is in **coNP**. Thus it is sufficient to show that it is **coNP**-hard. The reduction is from the Vertex Cover problem. The VC problem is as follows (definition taken from [6]):

INSTANCE: A graph $G = (V, E)$ and a positive integer $t \le |V|$.
QUESTION: Is there a vertex cover of size t or less for G, that is, a subset $V' \subseteq V$ such that $|V'| \le t$ and, for each edge $(u, v) \in E$, at least one of u and v belongs to V'?

For a given instance $G = (V, E)$ of VC, we construct a colored edge graph $G_c = (V_c, E_c, f, C)$ as follows. First assume that the vertex set V is ordered as in $V = \{v_1, \ldots, v_n\}$. Let

$$
\begin{aligned}
V_c &= \{A, B\} \bigcup \{e_{(v_i, v_j)} : (v_i, v_j) \in E \text{ and } i < j\} \\
E_c &= \{(A, e_{(v_i, v_j)}), (e_{(v_i, v_j)}, B) : (v_i, v_j) \in E\} \\
C &= \{c_v : v \in V\} \\
f &= \{f(A, e_{(v_i, v_j)}) = c_{v_i}, f(e_{(v_i, v_j)}, B) = c_{v_j} : (v_i, v_j) \in E, i < j\}
\end{aligned}
$$

In the following, we show that there is a vertex cover of size t in G if and only if there is a t-color edge separator for G_c.
    Without loss of generality, assume that $V' = \{v'_1, \ldots, v'_k\}$ is a vertex cover for G. Then it is straightforward to show that $C' = \{c_{v'_i} : v'_i \in V'\}$ is a color separator for G_c since each incoming path for B in G_c contains two colors corresponding to one edge (v_i, v_j) in G.

For the other direction, assume that $C' = \{c_{v_i'} : i = 1, \ldots, t\}$ is a t-color separator for G_c. Let $V' = \{v_i' : c_{v_i'} \in C'\}$. By the fact that C' is a color separator for G_c, for each edge $(v_i, v_j) \in E$ in G, the path $(A, e_{(v_i, v_j)}, B)$ in G_c contains at least one color from C'. Since this path contains only two colors c_{v_i} and c_{v_j}, we know that v_i or v_j or both belong to V'. In another word, V' is a t-size vertex cover for G. This completes the proof of the Theorem.   Q.E.D.

7 Disjunct Systems

We conclude our paper with some observations on the relationship between disjunct system and cover free families.

Incidence matrix is usually used to describe set systems. Let $(X, \mathcal{F})$ be a (λ, m)-partition of X with $X = \{x_1, \ldots, x_\lambda\}$ and $\mathcal{F} = \{B_1, \ldots, B_m\}$. Then the incidence matrix of $(X, \mathcal{F})$ is the $\lambda \times m$ matrix $(a_{i,j})$ where $a_{i,j} = 1$ if $x_i \in B_j$ and $a_{i,j} = 0$ otherwise. If A is an incidence matrix of a set system, then A^T (the transpose of A) is an extended incidence matrix of a disjunct system. Note that by extended incidence matrix, we mean that, after consolidating repeated columns of the matrix we get the incident matrix of a disjunct system.

Definition 3. *Let Y be a set of m elements, and $\mathcal{B}$ be a set of λ subsets of Y. Then the set system $(Y, \mathcal{B})$ is called a $(t; n - 1)$-disjunct system (or $(t; n - 1)$-DS(m, λ)) if for any $P \subseteq Y$ such that $|P| \leq t$, there exist at least $n - 1$ blocks $B \in \mathcal{B}$ such that $P \cap B = \emptyset$.*

Theorem 12. *1. If there exists a $(t; n - 1)$-CFF(λ, m) then there exists a $(t; n' - 1)$-DS(m, λ') for some $1 < n' \leq n$ and $\lambda' \leq \lambda$.*
  2. If there exists a $(t; n - 1)$-DS(m, λ), then there exists a $(t; n - 1)$-CFF(λ', m) for some $0 < \lambda' \leq \lambda$.

Proof. Assume that $(X, \mathcal{F})$ is a $(t; n - 1)$-CFF(λ, m) with incidence matrix A. Let $Y = \mathcal{F}$ and $\mathcal{B} = \{[x] : x \in X\}$ where $[x] = \{P : x \in P \text{ and } P \in \mathcal{F}\}$. In the following, we show that $(Y, \mathcal{B})$ is a $(t; n' - 1)$-DS(m, λ') with extended incidence matrix A^T for some $1 < n' \leq n$ and $\lambda' \leq \lambda$. By the fact that $(X, \mathcal{F})$ is a $(t; n - 1)$-CFF(λ, m), for any $P = \{B_1, \ldots, B_t\} \subseteq Y$, there exist distinct $x_1, \ldots, x_{n-1} \in X \setminus (\cup_{i=1}^t B_i)$. That is, for any $i \leq n - 1$ and $j \leq t$, we have $x_i \notin B_j$ which means $B_j \notin [x_i]$. Thus $P \cap [x_i] = \emptyset$ for all $i \leq n - 1$. Note that for $i \neq j$, we may have $[x_i] = [x_j]$. Thus the above arguments only guarantee that there exists $n' > 1$ such that $(Y, \mathcal{B})$ is a $(t; n' - 1)$-DS(m, λ').

For the other direction, assume that $(Y, \mathcal{B})$ is a $(t; n - 1)$-DS(m, λ) with incidence matrix A. Let $X = \mathcal{B}$ and $\mathcal{F} = \{[y] : y \in Y\}$ where $[y] = \{P : y \in P \text{ and } P \in \mathcal{B}\}$. In the following, we show that $(X, \mathcal{F})$ is a $(t, n - 1)$-CFF(λ, m) with incidence matrix A^T. For any t blocks $[y_1], \ldots, [y_t] \in \mathcal{F}$, let $P = \{y_1, \ldots, y_t\}$. By the fact that $(Y, \mathcal{B})$ is a $(t, n - 1)$-DS(m, λ), there exist distinct blocks $B_1, \ldots, B_{n-1} \in \mathcal{B}$ such that $P \cap B_i = \emptyset$. That is, for each $i \leq t$ and $j \leq n - 1$, we have $y_i \notin B_j$ which means $B_j \notin [y_i]$. Thus $\{B_1, \ldots, B_{n-1}\} \in X \setminus (\cup_{i=1}^t [y_t])$. It follows that $(X, \mathcal{F})$ is a $(t, n - 1)$-CFF(λ, m).   Q.E.D.

Acknowledgement

The first author of this paper would like to thank Prof. Doug Stinson and Prof. Ruizhong Wei for some discussions on generalized cover-free families.

References

1. Constantine, G.: Colorful isomorphic spanning trees in complete graphs. Annals of Combinatorics 9, 163–167 (2005)
2. Desmedt, Y., Wang, Y.: Perfectly Secure Message Transmission Revisited. In: Knudsen, L.R. (ed.) EUROCRYPT 2002. LNCS, vol. 2332, pp. 502–517. Springer, Heidelberg (2002)
3. Desmedt, Y., Wang, Y., Burmester, M.: A complete characterization of tolerable adversary structures for secure point-to-point transmissions without feedback. In: Deng, X., Du, D.-Z. (eds.) ISAAC 2005. LNCS, vol. 3827, pp. 277–287. Springer, Heidelberg (2005)
4. Desmedt, Y.G., Wang, Y., Safavi-Naini, R., Wang, H.: Radio networks with reliable communication. In: Wang, L. (ed.) COCOON 2005. LNCS, vol. 3595, pp. 156–166. Springer, Heidelberg (2005)
5. Engel, K.: Interval packing and covering in the boolean lattice. Combin. Probab. Comput. 5, 373–384 (1995)
6. Garey, M.R., Johnson, D.S.: Computers and Intractability: A Guide to the Theory of NP-Completeness. W. H. Freeman and Company, San Francisco (1979)
7. Roskind, J., Tarjan, R.: A note on finding minimum-cost edge-disjoint spanning trees. Math. Oper. Res. 10, 701–708 (1985)
8. Stinson, D., Wei, R.: Generalized cover-free families. Discrete Math. 279, 463–477 (2004)
9. Wang, Y., Desmedt, Y.: Secure communication in multicast channels. Journal of Cryptology 14(2), 121–135 (2001)

On Information Theoretic Security: Mathematical Models and Techniques

(Invited Talk)

Imre Csiszár

Rényi Insitute of Mathematics, Hungarian Academy of Sciences,
P.O. Box 127, H1364 Budapest,
Hungary

Abstract. Some key results about information theoretic secrecy will be surveyed, both for scenarios without and with public communication. Attention is focused on fundamental limits, and on the underlying proof techniques. This talk is based on the chapter on information theoretic security of the book [5].

Keywords: Common randomness, correlated sources, memoryless channel, extractor, privacy amplification, public discussion, secrecy capacity, security index.

1   Introduction

Following Shannon [13] though not directly his terminology, a random variable (RV) K with range $\mathcal{K} = \{1, \dots, k\}$ represents $\log_2 k$ secret bits within threshold $\varepsilon \geq 0$, secret from an adversary whose knowledge is represented by a RV Z, if the *security index*

$$S(K|Z) = \log_2 k - H(K) + I(K \wedge Z) = \log_2 k - H(K|Z)$$

does not exceed ε. A RV with small security index is a good *encryption key*: If a $\mathcal{K}$-valued message M, independent of (K, Z), is encrypted as $C = M + K$ $(\mathrm{mod}\, k)$, the amount of information available about M to a cryptanalyst knowing Z and the cryptogram C is bounded as $I(M \wedge C, Z) \leq S(K|Z)$. In particular, perfect secrecy is guaranteed if $S(K|Z) = 0$.

We shall consider models involving sequences of RVs of length $n \to \infty$, and address the problem of *secrecy capacity*, the asymptotically largest rate $\frac{1}{n} \log_2 k_n$ at which two or more parties can obtain secret bits within threshold ε_n. In early works only $\varepsilon_n/n \to 0$ was required. Maurer [11] argued for requiring $\varepsilon_n \to 0$. Under general conditions, the weak and strong security requirements lead to the same secrecy capacity [12], and so does the still stronger one that $\varepsilon_n \to 0$ exponentially fast [5].

S. Fehr (Ed.): ICITS 2011, LNCS 6673, pp. 73–75, 2011.

2   Some Important Models

Wyner [14] recognized that secure transmission over an insecure channel does not necessarily need encryption. His *wiretap channel* consists of two DMCs with common input, and reliable transmission of messages to the receiver at output 1 is required, keeping them secret from the other receiver. Secrecy capacity was determined under a degradedness condition on the channels. The more general *broadcast channel with confidential messages* [4] models scenarios where, in addition to confidential messages to receiver 1, common messages have to be reliably sent to both receivers, and there are also messages of a third kind merely reqired to be decodable at output 1. The region of achievable rate triples for this model, for any pair of underlying DMCs, was determined in [4]. Recently, that result was generalized to so-called *cognitive interference channels* [9].

Another kind of models [3], [10] addresses generating a secret key for two or more parties with the help of (restricted or unrestricted) public discussion over a noiseless channel, using as main resource either correlated sources or a DMC with multiple outputs. In source models, the parties (and the eavesdropper) observe outputs of one component source, each; in channel models one party controls the DMC inputs, the others observe one output, each. The eavesdropper has full access to the public communication of the parties but (in models reviewed here) she cannot interfere with it. For two-party models (of both kinds), secrecy capacity has been determined under some conditions [10], [1], but remains unknown in general. The mathematically simpler case when the eavesdropper lacks private knowledge has been solved for both kinds of models and any number of parties [6], [7]. Recent progress on the general problem, including multi-party models, has been reported in [8].

3   Proof Techniques

Achievability results (lower bounds to secrecy capacity) are typically proved considering protocols of the following kind. First, non-secret *common randomness* (CR) is generated for the involved parties, using standard techniqes of multiuser information theory, such as random binning and superposition coding. Then *privacy amplification* is employed, which means taking a suitable function of the CR which maps this CR into a RV K that has range $\{1, \ldots, k_n\}$, k_n as desired, such that K has small security index relative to the eavesdropper's knowledge. The existence of such function, called (deterministic) *extractor*, can be proved via random selection [2]. Instead of deterministic extractors, *seeded extractors* can also be used [12].

Converse results (upper bounds to secrecy capacity) are typically proved by judicious manipulations of information measures, a technique standard in information theory, though sometimes tedious. One identity of [4] has turned out remarkably useful in this context.

Acknowledgements. This work has been supported by the Hungarian National Foundation for Scientific Research, Grant OTKA 76088.

References

1. Ahlswede, R., Csiszár, I.: Common Randomness in Information Theory and Cryptography. Part 1, Secret Sharing. IEEE Trans. Inform. Theory 39, 1121–1132 (1993)
2. Ahlswede, R., Csiszár, I.: Common Randomness in Information Theory and Cryptography. Part 2, CR Capacity. IEEE Trans. Inform. Theory 44, 225–240 (1998)
3. Bennett, C.H., Brassard, G., Robert, J.-M.: Privacy Amplification by Public Discussion. SIAM J. Comput. 17, 210–229 (1988)
4. Csiszár, I., Körner, J.: Broadcast Channels with Confidential Messages. IEEE Trans. Inform. Theory 24, 339–348 (1978)
5. Csiszár, I., Körner, J.: Information Theory: Coding Theorems for Discrete Memoryless Systems, 2nd edn. Cambridge University Press, Cambridge (2011)
6. Csiszár, I., Narayan, P.: The Secret Key Capacity for Multiple Terminals. IEEE Trans. Inform. Theory 50, 3047–3061 (2004)
7. Csiszár, I., Narayan, P.: Secrecy Capacities for Multiterminal Channel Models. IEEE Trans. Inform. Theory 54, 2437–2452 (2008)
8. Gohari, A.A., Anantharam, V.: Information-Theoretic Key Agreement of Multiple Terminals, Parts I-II. IEEE Trans. Inform. Theory 56, 3973–3996, 3997–4010 (2010)
9. Liang, Y., Somekh-Baruch, A., Poor, V., Shamai, S., Verdú, S.: Capacity of Cognitive Interference Channels With and Without Secrecy. IEEE Trans. Inform. Theory 55, 619–694 (2009)
10. Maurer, U.M.: Secret Key Agreement by Public Discussion from Common Information. IEEE Trans. Inform. Theory 39, 733–743 (1993)
11. Maurer, U.M.: The Strong Secret Key of Discrete Random Triples. In: Blahut, R.E., Costello, J., Maurer, U., Mittelholzer, T. (eds.) Communication and Cryptography - Two Sides of One Tapestry, pp. 271–285. Kluwer, Dordrecht (1994)
12. Maurer, U.M., Wolf, S.: Information-Theoretic Key Agreement: From Weak to Strong Secrecy for Free. In: Preneel, B. (ed.) EUROCRYPT 2000. LNCS, vol. 1807, pp. 351–368. Springer, Heidelberg (2000)
13. Shannon, C.E.: Communication Theory of Secrecy Systems. Bell Syst. Tech. J. 28, 656–715 (1949)
14. Wyner, A.D.: The Wiretap Channel. Bell Syst. Tech. J. 54, 1355–1387 (1975)

Common Randomness and Secret Key Capacities of Two-Way Channels

Hadi Ahmadi and Reihaneh Safavi-Naini

Department of Computer Science, University of Calgary, Canada
{hahmadi,rei}@ucalgary.ca

Abstract. Common Randomness Generation (CRG) and Secret Key Establishment (SKE) are fundamental primitives in information theory and cryptography. We study these two problems over the two-way communication channel model, introduced by Shannon. In this model, the common randomness (CK) capacity is defined as the maximum number of random bits per channel use that the two parties can generate. The secret key (SK) capacity is defined similarly when the random bits are also required to be secure against a passive adversary. We provide lower bounds on the two capacities. These lower bounds are tighter than those one might derive based on the previously known results. We prove our lower bounds by proposing a two-round, two-level coding construction over the two-way channel. We show that the lower bound on the common randomness capacity can also be achieved using a simple interactive channel coding (ICC) method. We furthermore provide upper bounds on these capacities and show that the lower and the upper bounds coincide when the two-way channel consists of two independent (physically degraded) one-way channels. We apply the results to the case where the channels are binary symmetric.

Keywords: Two-way channel, wiretap channel, common randomness capacity, secret key capacity.

1 Introduction

The *two-way discrete memoryless channel* (TWDMC) setup was initially proposed as a communication model by Shannon [23], where he studied the problem of *reliable message transmission* (RMT) between two parties, here referred to as Alice and Bob. Shannon's work brought about the foundation of multi-user information theory and attracted much attention in theory and practice. The TWDMC setup is a general two-party communication model, where in each communication round both parties, simultaneously, provide inputs to the channel, and receive their corresponding outputs as (possibly probabilistic) functions of the two inputs. In each channel use, a TWDMC receives the inputs X_A and X_B from Alice and Bob and returns to them the outputs Y_A and Y_B, respectively. The channel is specified by the conditional distribution $P_{Y_A,Y_B|X_A,X_B}$. In Reliable Message Transmission (RMT) using a TWDMC, Alice and Bob want

S. Fehr (Ed.): ICITS 2011, LNCS 6673, pp. 76–93, 2011.
© Springer-Verlag Berlin Heidelberg 2011

to reliably send messages to each other. The reliable message (RM) rate R_{AB} from Alice to Bob is *achievable* if Alice can send nR_{AB} bits of message reliably to Bob in n channel uses; in analogy, an achievable RM rate R_{BA} from Bob to Alice is defined. Accordingly, a pair (R_{AB}, R_{BA}) is achievable if the two rates can be achieved using the TWDMC at the same time. The *RM capacity region* is the set of all achievable pairs. An extension of RMT in the above setup when the two-way channel leaks information to a passive adversary, Eve, is called *secure message transmission* (SMT) over a *two-way discrete memoryless wiretap channel* (TWDMWC) [26]. The *secure message (SM) capacity region* for this problem is defined analogously to that of RMT, except that the messages are required to be both reliable and secure.

This paper considers two other well-studied problems, for the first time, in the above setups. The first problem is *common randomness generation* (CRG) over a TWDMC, where Alice and Bob aim at calculating a shared random variable. The common randomness (CR) rate R_{cr} is called achievable if the parties can generate nR_{cr} shared random bits in n channel uses, and the *CR capacity* is the highest achievable CR rate. The second problem is *secret key establishment* (SKE) over a TWDMWC, where Alice and Bob aim at calculating a shared random variable that is unknown to the adversary, Eve. This problem can be seen as an extension of CRG when the two-way channel leaks information to Eve and the parties want their shared randomness to be secure from her. The *Secret Key (SK) capacity* is defined similarly to the CR capacity with the extra requirement that the randomness must satisfy reliability and security, both. This immediately induces the following question.

Question 1. *What is the CR/SK capacity of a two-way channel?*

We remark that the two problems of RMT and CRG over TWDMCs are different in general: An RMT protocol is used to deliver given messages reliably to their destinations, while a CRG protocol produces shared randomness. However, when the parties have free access to independent sources of randomness (also assumed in this paper), any RMT protocol can be used to achieve CRG, by Alice and Bob generating their random variables and sending them to each other reliably. A similar argument holds to relate SMT and SKE. As a consequence, an achievable pair (R_{AB}, R_{BA}) for RMT/SMT results in an achievable rate $R_{AB} + R_{BA}$ for CRG/SKE. This leads to the following natural question.

Question 2. *Can the CR/SK capacity be obtained from the RM/SM capacity region by maximizing $R_{AB} + R_{BA}$ over all choices of (R_{AB}, R_{BA})?*

Certainly, this maximization suggests a lower bound on the CR/SK capacity; nevertheless, this *trivial lower bound* may not be tight since the shared randomness could also be generated as a result of interaction between the two parties.

1.1 Our Work

We give general descriptions of multi-round CRG and SKE protocols in the above setups and formally define the CR and the SK capacities. We first use the previous results on RMT and SMT, esp., those in [23, 26], to derive "trivial lower bounds" on the CR and the SK capacities. Next, we prove that the trivial bounds cannot be tight by giving a two-way channel example, where one bit of common randomness (or secret key) per channel use is achievable while the trivial bound is zero. We prove better lower bounds on the capacities by a two-round construction that uses a two-level coding method, i.e., applying two sequential encoding functions to a message. We also prove that the lower bound on the CR capacity can be achieved using the two-round, but one-level, *interactive channel coding* (ICC) method introduced in [5].

We also prove upper bounds on the capacities. We show that the two bounds on the CR capacity coincide if the two-way channel consists of two independent one-way channels in both directions, and the two bounds on the SK capacity coincide if these one-way (wiretap) channels are "physically degraded". The bounds proved in this paper are expressed by single-letter formulas, i.e., they can easily be derived from the channel probability distribution.

1.2   Related Work

We first provide a selected summary of the literature on reliable/secure message transmission as related problems, and then discuss the work in the area of CRG and SKE. The systematic study of reliable message transmission over noisy channels is due to Shannon [22]. The problem has since been extended to many other communication setups; see, e.g., [12]. In [23], Shannon introduced the two-way channel setup as a general two-party communication model, and proved inner and outer bounds on the RM capacity region. In general, an inner bound contains a subset of the achievable pairs of RM rates (R_{AB}, R_{BA}), whereas an outer bound is a superset of the set of all these pairs. The bounds in [23] were later improved in [14, 28]; yet, due to the gap between the two bounds, finding the capacity region in this setup is an open problem.

Transmission of secure messages over noisy channels was first considered by Wyner [27]. SMT over special cases of two-way wiretap channels was investigated by Tekin and Yener [25, 26], where inner bounds on the SM capacity region were derived. The bounds were improved in [15, 13, 19] using feedback and key exchange mechanisms as techniques to increase achievable rates.

The problem of common randomness generation (CRG) has been studied in various setups, e.g., CRG over noiseless channels using correlated randomness [2] or CRG over noisy channels [24], where the authors derived expressions for the CR capacity. Determining the CR capacity is important due to the role of common randomness in building two-party randomized protocols that, compared to deterministic protocols, have higher computation and communication efficiencies. Examples of such applications appear in random coding over arbitrarily varying channels (AVC) [10], identification over noisy channels [3], and oblivious transfer and bit commitment schemes [21].

The CRG problem when the communication is over a hostile environment turns into the fundamental problem of secret key establishment (SKE) in cryptography: Alice and Bob want to share a common key about which an adversary,

Eve, should be uncertain. The problem has been studied in numerous setups including noiseless public channels and noisy broadcast channels. The results on "secure transmission" over one-way wiretap channels [27, 9] imply the possibility of SKE when Eve's wiretapping channel is noisier than the channel between Alice and Bob. Maurer [17], concurrently with Ahlswede and Csiszár [1], showed that by assuming an additional two-way noiseless public discussion channel SKE may be possible even when Eve's wiretapping channel is less noisy. Noiseless channels in practice are realized from physical noisy channels using error correcting codes. Noting that this approach does not always lead to the highest achievable secret key rates, recent work studied SKE in setups that replace the above public discussion channel with other resources, e.g., a wiretap noisy channel in the opposite direction [4] or correlated sources of randomness [16, 20].

1.3   Discussion

The two-way (wiretap) channel setup naturally captures a communication environment between two parties with no prior correlated information. The channel combines the inputs that the two parties provide and returns to each of them a noisy version of this combination; it may also leak a noisy version to an eavesdropper in the environment. Examples of such a communication scenario are mobile ad hoc networks and wireless sensor networks. We note that noiseless public channel, one-way wiretap channel, or a pair of independent wiretap channels, studied in [24, 17, 9], are special cases of the general two-way (wiretap) channel setup. None of these settings, however, can model combination of two inputs that are transmitted simultaneously over the channel.

To prove lower bounds on the CR/SK capacities, we use random coding arguments that only show the existence of CRG/SKE constructions, which can achieve the lower bounds. One can, however, design practical constructions by using concrete primitives in the CRG/SKE protocols, proposed in this paper. An example of such approaches to construct concrete protocols is the work in [7] that proposes a practical wireless key establishment scheme based on the theoretical results of [27, 17].

1.4   Notation

We use calligraphic letters ($\mathcal{X}$), uppercase letters (X), and lowercase letters (x) to denote finite alphabets, random variables (RVs), and their realizations over sets, respectively. $X^n = (X_1, X_2, \ldots, X_n) \in \mathcal{X}^n$ denotes a random sequence of length n (n-sequence) in $\mathcal{X}^n$. To save space, we may use bold $\mathbf{X}$ and $\mathbf{x}$ to denote a random sequence and its realization. For the RVs X, Y, and Z, we use $X \leftrightarrow Y \leftrightarrow Z$ to denote a Markov chain. '$||$' denotes concatenation of sequences. For a value x, we use $[x]_+$ to show $\max\{0, x\}$ and, for $0 \leq p \leq 1$, $h(p) = -p \log p - (1-p) \log(1-p)$ denotes the binary entropy function. Hereafter, we use the terms CRG and SKE specifically for the two-way (wiretap) channel setup.

1.5   Paper Organization

Section 2 describes the two-way channel model, related problems, and current results. Section 3 summarizes our main results in the paper, including lower and upper bounds and their coincidence. In Section 4, we briefly present our CRG and SKE constructions that achieve the lower bounds on the CR and the SK capacities. Section 5 applies the lower bound results to the case of two-way binary channels. We conclude the paper in Section 6.

2   Model and Definitions

2.1   CRG in the TWDMC Setup

Alice and Bob are connected by a Two-Way Discrete Memoryless Channel (TWDMC) that is denoted by $(X_A, X_B) \to (Y_A, Y_B)$ and specified by the conditional distribution $P_{Y_A,Y_B|X_A,X_B}$ over the finite sets $\mathcal{X}_A, \mathcal{X}_B, \mathcal{Y}_A, \mathcal{Y}_B$ (see Fig. 1). We assume each party has free access to an independent random source.

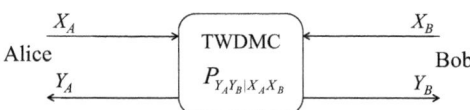

Fig. 1. Two-way discrete memoryless channel (TWDMC)

In general, a CRG protocol in the TWDMC setup consists of a certain number of communication rounds, denoted by t. In each round, $1 \leq r \leq t$, Alice and Bob send the n_r-sequences $\mathbf{X}_A^{:r}$ and $\mathbf{X}_B^{:r}$, and receive the n_r-sequences $\mathbf{Y}_A^{:r}$ and $\mathbf{Y}_B^{:r}$, respectively. The sequence $\mathbf{X}_A^{:r}$ (resp. $\mathbf{X}_B^{:r}$), for round r, is determined as a function of some independent, local randomness and the view of Alice (resp. Bob) at the end of round $r - 1$, denoted by $V_A^{:r-1}$ (resp. $V_B^{:r-1}$). View of a party consists of the set of their communicated (sent and received) sequences, i.e.,

$$V_A^{:r-1} = ||_{i=1}^{r-1} \left(\mathbf{X}_A^{:i} || \mathbf{Y}_A^{:i} \right), \qquad V_B^{:r-1} = ||_{i=1}^{r-1} \left(\mathbf{X}_B^{:i} || \mathbf{Y}_B^{:i} \right). \qquad (1)$$

Eventually, Alice uses $V_A^{:t}$ to calculate $S_A \in \mathcal{S}$ and Bob uses $V_B^{:t}$ to calculate $S_B \in \mathcal{S}$. The total number of channel uses is calculated as

$$n = \sum_{r=1}^{t} n_r. \qquad (2)$$

Definition 1. *For $R_{cr} \geq 0$ and $0 \leq \delta \leq 1$, the CRG protocol Π in the TWDMC setup is (R_{cr}, δ)-reliable if there exists an RV $S \in \mathcal{S}$ such that*

$$\frac{H(S)}{n} > R_{cr} - \delta, \qquad (3)$$

$$\Pr(S_A = S_B = S) > 1 - \delta. \qquad (4)$$

Definition 2. *The* common randomness (CR) *rate* $R_{cr} \geq 0$ *is achievable if, for an arbitrarily small* $\delta > 0$, *there exists an* (R_{cr}, δ)-*reliable CRG protocol. The CR capacity,* C_{cr}^{TWDMC}, *is the highest achievable CR rate.*

2.2 SKE in the TWDMWC Setup

As indicated in Fig. 2, Alice and Bob are connected by the Two-Way Discrete Memoryless Wiretap Channel (TWDMWC) $(X_A, X_B) \rightarrow (Y_A, Y_B, Z)$ that receives inputs from Alice and Bob and returns outputs to Alice, Bob, and the adversary, Eve, respectively. The channel is specified by the conditional distribution $P_{Y_A, Y_B, Z|X_A, X_B}$ over the finite sets $\mathcal{X}_A, \mathcal{X}_B, \mathcal{Y}_A, \mathcal{Y}_B, \mathcal{Z}$. Again, the parties have free access to independent sources.

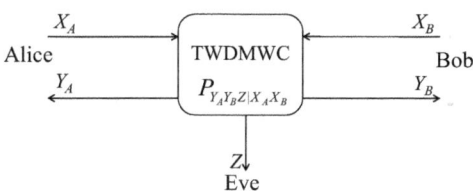

Fig. 2. Two-way discrete memoryless wiretap channel (TWDMWC)

A general t-round SKE protocol in this setup is described analogously to a general CRG protocol except that, in each round r, Eve receives an n_r-sequence $\mathbf{Z}^{:r}$ and her view at the end of this round is written as

$$V_E^{:r} = ||_{i=1}^r \mathbf{Z}^{:i}. \tag{5}$$

Eve's view at the end of the protocol is $View_E = V_E^{:t}$.

Definition 3. *For* $R_{sk} \geq 0$ *and* $0 \leq \delta \leq 1$, *the SKE protocol* Π *in the TWDMWC setup is* (R_{sk}, δ)-*secure if there exists an RV* $S \in \mathcal{S}$ *such that*

$$\frac{H(S)}{n} > R_{sk} - \delta, \tag{6}$$

$$\Pr(S_A = S_B = S) > 1 - \delta, \tag{7}$$

$$\frac{H(S|View_E)}{H(S)} > 1 - \delta. \tag{8}$$

Definition 4. *The* secret key (SK) *rate* $R_{sk} \geq 0$ *is achievable if, for an arbitrarily small* $\delta > 0$, *there exists an* (R_{sk}, δ)-*secure SKE protocol. The SK capacity,* C_{sk}^{TWDMWC}, *is the highest achievable SK rate.*

Remark 1. The above definition of SK capacity follows those in [27, 9, 17, 16]. This definition is referred to as *the weak SK capacity* as it requires Eve's uncertainty rate about the secret key (8) to be negligible, whereas the "strong"

SK capacity [18] requires Eve's total uncertainty to be negligible, i.e., requiring $H(S|View_E) > H(S) - \delta$. It is shown [18] that, for the setups in [27, 9, 17], the weak definition can be replaced by the strong definition without sacrificing the SK capacity. This result can also be extended to the TWDMBC setup by modifying the proof in [18]. This is left as future work.

2.3   Known Results on Two-Way Channels

Shannon's work [23] on reliable message transmission (RMT) over TWDMCs proved the following inner bound, G_I, and outer bound, G_O, on the RM capacity region of the channel $(X_A, X_B) \to (Y_A, Y_B)$. Letting $P = P_{X_A, X_B, Y_A, Y_B}$,

$$\mathcal{R}(P) = \{(R_{AB}, R_{BA}) : R_{AB} \leq I(X_A; Y_B|X_B),\ R_{BA} \leq I(X_B; Y_A|X_A)\},$$

$$G_I = \bigcup_{P_{X_A, X_B} = P_{X_A} \cdot P_{X_B}} \mathcal{R}(P), \qquad G_O = \bigcup_{P_{X_A, X_B}} \mathcal{R}(P), \qquad (9)$$

where, by $\cup$, we mean the convex closure of the union of $\mathcal{R}(P)$'s. The bound on R_{AB} (if maximized w.r.t. P_{X_A, X_B}) somehow reflects the capacity of the one-way channel $X_A \to Y_B$ from Alice to Bob when X_B is known to Bob; similarly, one can interpret the bound on R_{BA}. The two inner and outer bounds in (9) have been later discussed and slightly improved e.g., in [28, 11, 14].

Tekin and Yener [25, 26] considered secure message transmission (SMT) over Gaussian and binary two-way wiretap channels, and proved the following inner bound on the SM capacity region. Letting $P = P_{X_A, X_B, Y_A, Y_B, Z}$,

$$G_{s,I} = \bigcup_{P_{X_A, X_B} = P_{X_A} \cdot P_{X_B}} \mathcal{R}_s(P), \text{ where } \mathcal{R}_s(P) = \{\ (R_{s,AB}, R_{s,BA}) \text{ s.t.}$$

$$R_{s,AB} \leq [I(X_A; Y_B|X_B) - I(X_A; Z)]_+,\quad R_{s,BA} \leq [I(X_B; Y_A|X_A) - I(X_B; Z)]_+,\quad \text{and}$$

$$R_{s,AB} + R_{s,BA} \leq [I(X_A; Y_B|X_B) + I(X_B; Y_A|X_A) - I(X_A, X_B; Z)]_+\ \}. \qquad (10)$$

The bound on $R_{s,AB}$ (if maximized w.r.t. P_{X_A, X_B}) shows the SM capacity of the channel $X_A \to (Y_A, Z)$ when X_B is known to Bob; similar is the bound on R_{BA}. The inner bound (10) has been improved in [15, 13, 19] using techniques such as feedback and key exchange mechanisms in addition to cooperative jamming.

2.4   Two-Way Channels with Independent Components

A special class of TWDMCs includes those which consist of two independent DMCs in the two directions, i.e.,

$$P_{Y_A, Y_B|X_A, X_B} = P_{Y_B|X_A} \cdot P_{Y_A|X_B}.$$

We refer to this class as *2DMC*. The CRG problem in this setup when Alice and Bob have "limited" access to independent sources of randomness has been considered in [24], where a single letter formula for the capacity was determined.

Likewise, 2DMWCs refer to a class of TWDMWCs that consist of two independent DMWCs in opposite directions: A TWDMWC $(X_A, X_B) \to (Y_A, Y_B, Z)$ is a 2DMWC when

$$Z = (Z_1, Z_2), \quad \text{and} \quad P_{Y_A, Y_B, Z | X_A, X_B} = P_{Y_B, Z_1 | X_A} \cdot P_{Y_A, Z_2 | X_B}.$$

The SKE problem in this setup has been recently studied in [4], where lower and upper bounds on the SK capacity were provided and were shown to coincide when each DMWC is physically degraded. Informally, in a physically degraded DMWC, one of the receivers always receives a noisy version (though a noisy channel) of what the other receiver receives. This can be modeled using a Markov chain. e.g., the Markov chain $X \leftrightarrow Y \leftrightarrow Z$ indicates a degraded channel where Y is a noisy version of the input X and Z (as a noisy version of Y) is a noisier version of X. This Markov chain implies $I(X; Z|Y) = 0$.

Definition 5. *The DMWC $X \to (Y, Z)$ is called* obversely degraded *if $X \leftrightarrow Y \leftrightarrow Z$ forms a Markov chain. It is called* reversely degraded *if $X \leftrightarrow Z \leftrightarrow Y$ forms a Markov chain. The DMWC is called* physically degraded *if we can write $X = [X_O, X_R]$, $Y = [Y_O, Y_R]$, and $Z = [Z_O, Z_R]$, such that*

$$Z_O \leftrightarrow Y_O \leftrightarrow X_O \leftrightarrow X_R \leftrightarrow Z_R \leftrightarrow Y_R.$$

In this paper, we verify our results on SKE in the TWDMWC setup by simplifying them for the case of 2DMWCs with degraded components and seeing whether our results are consistent with the results in [4]. Here, we only consider obversely degraded channels; nonetheless, the results of this verification can be easily extended to the general physically degraded DMWCs, as defined above.

3   Statement of the Main Results

3.1   Trivial Lower Bounds and a TWDMC Example

From (9) and (10), we can derive trivial lower bounds on the CR and the SK capacities, respectively. Again, note that if (R_{AB}, R_{BA}) is an achievable RM/SM rate, then $R_{AB} + R_{BA}$ is an achievable CR/SK rate. As a consequence, the two following expressions respectively give trivial lower bounds on the CR capacity, C_{cr}^{TWDMC}, and the SK capacity, C_{sk}^{TWDMWC}.

$$C_{cr}^{TWDMC} \geq \max_{P_{X_A, X_B} = P_{X_A} \cdot P_{X_B}} [I(X_A; Y_B | X_B) + I(X_B; Y_A | X_A)], \tag{11}$$

$$C_{sk}^{TWDMWC} \geq \max_{P_{X_A, X_B} = P_{X_A} \cdot P_{X_B}} [[I(X_A; Y_B | X_B) - I(X_A; Z)]_+$$
$$+ [I(X_B; Y_A | X_A) - I(X_B; Z)]_+]. \tag{12}$$

One may ask whether the above trivial lower bounds cannot be improved or, more generally, whether the RM/SM capacity region specifies a tight lower bound on the CR/SK capacity, by maximizing $R_{AB} + R_{BA}$ over all choices of achievable pairs. We give a negative answer to this question using the following simple example. Consider the TWDMC shown in Fig. 3 which is a modified version of Shannon's modulo-two additive two-way channel example [23, Fig. 4], where there exists a binary symmetric channel (BSC) with bit error probability $\frac{1}{2}$, right after the XOR operand. In this example, the channel outputs are independent of the inputs; hence, little chance of reliable message transmission. This implies that no pair of rates except $(R_{AB} = 0, R_{BA} = 0)$ is achievable; in this case, the inner bound in (9) is tight and represents the capacity region.

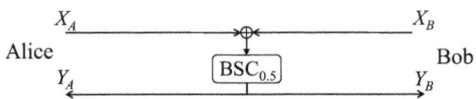

Fig. 3. A TWDMC example

Using (11), which is obtained from (9), we derive a "zero" lower bound on the CR capacity. However, this lower bound is not tight since Alice and Bob can share one random bit $(Y_A = Y_B)$ each time they use the channel. The key observation is that the common randomness is a function of channel noise and the parties' inputs, and it does not need to be selected a priori by the parties. Since RMT and CRG in TWDMC are viewed respectively as special cases of SMT and SKE in TWDMWC, the above example also lets us conclude that the SM capacity region of a TWDMWC does not necessarily give a tight lower bound on the SK capacity in general.

3.2   Common Randomness Capacity

We provide lower and upper bounds on the CR capacity in the TWDMC setup, present give our informal interpretation of the expressions. Let the RVs X_A, Y_A, X_B, and Y_B correspond to the channel probability distribution $P_{Y_A,Y_B|X_A,X_B}$. Let U_A and U_B be RVs from arbitrary sets $\mathcal{U}_A$ and $\mathcal{U}_B$ that satisfy the Markov chain

$$U_A \leftrightarrow (X_A, Y_A) \leftrightarrow (X_B, Y_B) \leftrightarrow U_B.$$

Theorem 1. *The CR capacity in the TWDMC setup is lower bounded as*

$$C_{cr}^{TWDMC} \geq \max_{n_1,n_2,P_{U_A,X_A}P_{U_B,X_B}} \Big[$$

$$\frac{n_1[I(U_A;X_B,Y_B)+I(U_B;X_A,Y_A|U_A)]+n_2[I(X_A;Y_B,X_B)+I(X_B;Y_A,X_A)]}{n_1+n_2}, \quad (13)$$

$$s.t. \quad P_{X_A,X_B} = P_{X_A}.P_{X_B}, \quad (14)$$

$$n_1 I(U_A; X_A, Y_A|X_B, Y_B) < n_2 I(X_A; X_B, Y_B), \quad (15)$$

$$n_1 I(U_B; X_B, Y_B|X_A, Y_A) < n_2 I(X_B; X_A, Y_A)\Big]. \quad (16)$$

Proof. See Section 4.1 and [6, Appendix A].

Remark 2. Since X_A and X_B are independent, the second term can also be written as $n_2[I(X_B; Y_A|X_A) + I(X_A; Y_B|X_B)]$; hence, when $n_1 = 0$ the argument equals that of (11). This shows that the new lower bound is greater than or equal to the trivial lower bound in (11).

Remark 3. The above lower bound is achieved using a two-round coding construction. Informally, he first term of (13), $n_1[I(U_A; X_B, Y_B) + I(U_B; X_A, Y_A|U_A)]$, shows the amount of raw (uncoded) correlated information that is provided in the first communication round with n_1 channel uses. This information is obtained based on the inputs and the outputs of the channel. The second term $n_2[I(X_B; Y_A, X_A) + I(X_A; Y_B, X_B)]$ indicates the amount of correlated information, provided in the second communication round, following the coding construction. This information equals the sum of the RM rates of the channel in both directions (i.e., the bounds on R_{AB} and R_{BA} in (9)). The conditions (15) and (16) mean that the amount of confusion (uncertainty) about the transmitted information in the first round can not be more than the capability of the channel for reliable transmission in the second round.

Theorem 2. *The CR capacity in the TWDMC setup is upper bounded as*

$$C_{cr}^{TWDMC} \leq \max_{P_{X_A, X_B}} [I(X_B; Y_A|X_A) + I(X_A; Y_B|X_B) + I(Y_A; Y_B|X_A, X_B)]. \quad (17)$$

Proof. See [6, Appendix B].

Remark 4. The first two terms of (17) are the same as those of (9) for the RM capacity region. The third term, however, is due to the exclusive property of CRG that the common randomness may be obtained from the correlated information between the outputs. This again articulates the essential difference between the two problems in the TWDMC setup.

Theorems 1 and 2 are proved as special cases of Theorems 4 and 5 (in the sequel), respectively [6]. The proof for the lower bound [6, Appendix A] is based on a two-round SKE protocol that uses a two-level coding construction. Although the proposed construction is convenient for the lower bound proof, it will be of practical significance to construct a simpler protocol that achieves the same lower bound. This motivated us to propose a new CRG protocol that achieves the lower bound (13). The protocol uses Interactive Channel Coding (ICC) [5] that is an extension of systematic channel coding to a two-round protocol. The messages in the two-round ICC are essentially parts of a codeword from a systematic channel code, split into two parts: one obtained in the first round and one sent in the second round. In a systematic code, each codeword consists of a message (information sequence), followed by a parity-check sequence. Bipartite systematic codes generalize this definition by allowing the two (information and parity-check) parts to come from (possibly) different alphabets.

Definition 6. *A* (bipartite) systematic channel code, *with encoding alphabets* $(\mathcal{T}, \mathcal{U})$ *and decoding alphabets* $(\mathcal{V}, \mathcal{W})$, *is a pair of encoding/decoding functions* (Enc/Dec), *where*

- $Enc : \mathcal{T}^{n_1} \times \mathcal{U}^{n_{2,i}} \to \mathcal{V}^{n_1} \times \mathcal{W}^{n_2}$ *deterministically maps* $(t^{n_1} || u^{n_{2,i}})$ *(as the information sequence) to a sequence* $(t^{n_1} || u^{n_2})$, *such that* $(u^{n_2} = u^{n_{2,i}} || u^{n_{2,p}})$ *and* $n_2 = n_{2,i} + n_{2,p}$; *we call* $u^{n_{2,p}}$ *the parity check sequence.*
- $Dec : \mathcal{V}^{n_1} \times \mathcal{W}^{n_2} \to \mathcal{T}^{n_1} \times \mathcal{U}^{n_{2,i}}$ *assigns a guess sequence* $(\hat{t}^{n_1} || \hat{u}^{n_{2,i}})$ *to each input* $(v^{n_1} || w^{n_2})$.

The ICC method has been proposed in [5] and was shown to be useful in achieving the lower bound on the SK capacity of a 2DMWC under certain conditions [5].

Theorem 3. *The lower bound (13) on the CR capacity can be achieved using the one-level interactive channel coding method.*

Proof. See Section 4.2 and [6, Appendix C].

In the following, we consider the 2DMC setup as described in Section 2.4, and show that the lower and the upper bounds on the CR capacity coincide for this class of TWDMCs. We note that the CR capacity (18) matches the result in [24], on CRG over 2DMCs, when there is no limit on the available independent randomness.

Proposition 1. *When the TWDMC consists of two independent DMCs in the two directions (called a 2DMC as in Section 2.4), the two bounds coincide and the CR capacity equals*

$$C_{cr}^{2DMC} = \max_{P_{X_A}, P_{X_B}} \{ I(X_A; Y_B) + I(X_B; Y_A) \}. \tag{18}$$

Proof. See [6, Appendix D].

Proposition 1 implies that, in the 2DMC setup, the RM capacity region, e.g., obtained from the results of [23] (see (9)), can be used to obtain the CR capacity (i.e., a tight lower bound), by solving the sum maximization problem.

3.3   Secret Key Capacity

We provide lower and upper bounds on the SK capacity in the TWDMWC setup. These bounds are generalizations of the bounds, given in Section 3.2, to the cases when the communication is eavesdropped by Eve. Let the RVs X_A, Y_A, X_B, Y_B, and Z correspond to the channel probability distribution $P_{Y_A, Y_B, Z | X_A, X_B}$ and let $U_A, W_{1A}, W_{2A}, U_B, W_{1B}$, and W_{2B} be RVs from arbitrary sets $\mathcal{U}_A, \mathcal{W}_{1A}, \mathcal{W}_{2A}, \mathcal{U}_B, \mathcal{W}_{1B}$, and $\mathcal{W}_{2B}$, respectively, such that the following Markov chains hold:

$$U_A \leftrightarrow (X_A, Y_A) \leftrightarrow (X_B, Y_B) \leftrightarrow U_B, \tag{19}$$

$$W_{2A} \leftrightarrow W_{1A} \leftrightarrow X_A \leftrightarrow (X_B, Y_A, Y_B, Z), \tag{20}$$

$$W_{2B} \leftrightarrow W_{1B} \leftrightarrow X_B \leftrightarrow (X_A, Y_A, Y_B, Z). \tag{21}$$

Theorem 4. *The SK capacity in the TWDMWC setup is lower bounded as*

$$C_{sk}^{TWDMWC} \geq \max_{n_1,n_2,P_{W_{2A},W_{1A},U_A,X_A}P_{W_{2B},W_{1B},U_B,X_B}} [\frac{1}{n_1 + n_2}$$

$$(n_1[I(U_A; X_B, Y_B) + I(U_B; X_A, Y_A|U_A) - I(U_A, U_B; Z)] + n_2[I(W_{1A}; X_B, Y_B|W_{2A})$$

$$+I(W_{1B}; X_A, Y_A|W_{2B}) - I(W_{1A}, W_{1B}; Z|W_{2A}, W_{2B})]_+), \qquad (22)$$

s.t.
$$P_{X_A,X_B} = P_{X_A}.P_{X_B}, $$

$$n_1 I(U_A; X_A, Y_A|X_B, Y_B) < n_2 I(W_{1A}; X_B, Y_B), \qquad (23)$$

$$n_1 I(U_B; X_B, Y_B|X_A, Y_A) < n_2 I(W_{1B}; X_A, Y_A)]. \qquad (24)$$

Proof. See Section 4.1 and [6, Appendix A].

The terms in (22) can be interpreted in analogy to the argument following (13), adding that the shared information is required to remain secure from Eve. Informally, the terms $n_1 I(U_A, U_B; Z)$ and $n_2 I(W_{1A}, W_{1B}; Z|W_{2A}, W_{2B})$ show the amount of leakage of shared randomness in the first and the second rounds, respectively.

The upper bound on the SK capacity is provided in the following. Let Q be an RV from an arbitrary set $\mathcal{Q}$ that satisfies the Markov chain

$$Q \leftrightarrow (X_A, X_B) \leftrightarrow (Y_A, Y_B, Z).$$

Theorem 5. *The SK capacity in the TWDMWC setup, C_{sk}^{TWDMWC}, is upper bounded as*

$$C_{sk}^{TWDMWC} \leq \max_{P_{Q,X_A,X_B}} [I(X_A; Y_B|X_B, Z) + I(X_B; Y_A|X_A, Z)$$

$$+ I(Y_A; Y_B|X_A, X_B, Z) + I(X_A; X_B|Z, Q) - I(X_A; X_B|Q)]. \qquad (25)$$

Proof. See [6, Appendix B].

The following proposition states that if the TWDMWC consists of two independent DMWCs with degraded channels (see Section 2.4), then the lower and the upper bounds coincide and the SK capacity is achieved by a one-round protocol. In [4], SKE over 2DMWCs has been considered in the half-duplex communication model where the two forward and backward channels could be used for different number of times. The following special case of TWDMWC, however, complies a full-duplex communication model where the channels are used together and the number of channel uses must be the same for the two channels. The results in [4] are consistent to those in Proposition 2, assuming the full-duplex communication model.

Proposition 2. *When the 2DMWC consists of degraded DMWCs $X_A \leftrightarrow Y_B \leftrightarrow Z_1$ and $X_B \leftrightarrow Y_A \leftrightarrow Z_2$ (as in Definition 5), the lower bound coincides with the upper bound, and the SK capacity equals*

$$C_{sk}^{2DMWC} = \max_{P_{X_A},P_{X_B}} \{I(X_A; Y_B|Z_1) + I(X_B; Y_A|Z_2)\}. \qquad (26)$$

Furthermore, the SK capacity is achieved by a one-round protocol.

Proof. See [6, Appendix D].

4   CRG/SKE Protocol Outline

In this section, we present a brief explanation of the protocols that achieve the lower bounds on the CR and the SK capacities. For the complete structure of these protocols, we refer to the full version of the paper in [6].

4.1   The Two-Round CRG/SKE Protocol (Theorems 1 and 4)

For simplicity, we give an outline of the SKE protocol in the following special case: $W_{1A} = X_A$, $W_{1B} = X_B$, $W_{2A} = W_{2B} = 0$, and the two conditions in (23) and (24) hold with almost equality. We note that this protocol can be also used to generate common randomness with rates up to the lower bound (13) when there is no adversary, equivalently when $Z = 0$. Let n_1, n_2, P_{U_A, X_A}, and P_{U_B, X_B} be those that maximize the right side of (22), which is written as

$$R_{sk} = \tfrac{1}{n_1+n_2}(\ n_1[I(U_A; X_B, Y_B) + I(U_B; X_A, Y_A|U_A) - I(U_A, U_B; Z)]$$
$$+ n_2[I(X_A; X_B, Y_B) + I(X_B; X_A, Y_A) - I(X_A, X_B; Z)]_+). \quad (27)$$

Define

$$\eta_{a,f} \approx n_1 I(U_A; X_A, Y_A), \qquad \eta_{a,t} \approx n_2 I(X_A; X_B, Y_B) \qquad\qquad (28)$$
$$\eta_{b,f} \approx n_1 I(U_B; X_B, Y_B), \qquad \eta_{b,t} \approx n_2 I(X_B; X_A, Y_A), \qquad\qquad (29)$$
$$\eta \approx n_1 I(U_A, U_B; X_A, Y_A, X_B, Y_B), \qquad \kappa = (n_1 + n_2)R_{sk}, \qquad \gamma = \eta - \kappa. \quad (30)$$

- Let $\mathcal{U}_{A,\epsilon}^{n_1}$ (resp. $\mathcal{U}_{B,\epsilon}^{n_1}$) be obtained by randomly and independently choosing $2^{\eta_{a,f}}$ (resp. $2^{\eta_{b,f}}$) typical sequences from $\mathcal{U}_A^{n_1}$ (resp. $\mathcal{U}_B^{n_1}$).
- Let $\{\mathcal{U}_{A,\epsilon,i}^{n_1}\}_{i=1}^{2^{\eta_{a,t}}}$ be a partition of $\mathcal{U}_{A,\epsilon}^{n_1}$ into $2^{\eta_{a,t}}$ equal-sized parts. Define the function $\mathsf{t}_A : \mathcal{U}_{A,\epsilon}^{n_1} \to \mathcal{T}_A = \{1, 2, \ldots, 2^{\eta_{a,t}}\}$ such that, for any input in $\mathcal{U}_{A,\epsilon,i}^{n_1}$, it outputs i. Similarly define the partition $\{\mathcal{U}_{i,B,\epsilon}^{n_1}\}_{i=1}^{2^{\eta_{b,t}}}$ and the function t_B.
- Let $\{\mathcal{K}_s\}_{s=1}^{2^{\kappa}}$ be a partition of $\mathcal{U}_{A,\epsilon}^{n_1} \times \mathcal{U}_{B,\epsilon}^{n_1}$ into equal-sized parts of size 2^{γ}. Define the key derivation function $\phi : \mathcal{U}_{A,\epsilon}^{n_1} \times \mathcal{U}_{B,\epsilon}^{n_1} \to \{1, 2, \ldots, 2^{\kappa}\}$ such that, for any input in $\mathcal{K}_s$, it outputs s.

The protocol proceeds in two rounds. In round 1, Alice and Bob send i.i.d. n_1-sequences $\mathbf{X}_A^{:1}$ and $\mathbf{X}_B^{:1}$ according to P_{X_A} and P_{X_B}, and receive the n_1-sequences $\mathbf{Y}_A^{:1}$ and $\mathbf{Y}_B^{:1}$, respectively, while Eve receives $\mathbf{Z}^{:1}$. Alice searches in $\mathcal{U}_{A,\epsilon}^{n_1}$ to find a sequence $U_A^{n_1}$ that is jointly typical to $(\mathbf{X}_A^{:1}, \mathbf{Y}_A^{:1})$ w.r.t. $P_{(X_A, Y_A), U_A}$. Similarly, Bob searches for a sequence $U_B^{n_1}$ that is jointly typical to $(\mathbf{X}_B^{:1}, \mathbf{Y}_B^{:1})$ w.r.t. $P_{(X_B, Y_B), U_B}$. Now, $(U_A^{n_1}, U_B^{n_1})$ represents the common randomness that needs to be made reliable in the second round.

In round 2, Alice computes $T_A = \mathsf{t}_A(U_A^{n_1})$, which can help Bob decode his $(\mathbf{X}_B^{:1}, \mathbf{Y}_B^{:1})$ to $U_A^{n_1}$. Bob also computes $T_B = \mathsf{t}_B(U_B^{n_1})$. Alice and Bob encode T_A and T_B to n_2-sequences $\mathbf{X}_A^{:2} = Enc(T_A)$ and $\mathbf{X}_B^{:2} = Enc(T_B)$ and send them over the channel. The parties and Eve receive $\mathbf{Y}_A^{:2}$, $\mathbf{Y}_B^{:2}$, and $\mathbf{Z}^{:2}$, respectively. Alice first decodes $(\mathbf{X}_A^{:2}, \mathbf{Y}_A^{:2})$ to $\hat{T}_B \approx T_B$, and uses this for decoding $(\mathbf{X}_A^{:1}, \mathbf{Y}_A^{:1})$ to $\hat{U}_B^{n_1} \approx U_B^{n_1}$. The decoding function relies on the jointly-typical decoding technique for long sequences (see, e.g., [8, Chapter 8]). Similarly Bob finds $\hat{T}_A \approx T_A$

and then $\hat{U}_A^{n_1} \approx U_A^{n_1}$. Now, the parties have a reliable common randomness, but it is not perfectly secure against Eve. To derive a secret key, the parties compute $\phi(U_A^{n_1}, U_B^{n_1})$. The rest of the proof is to show that there exist encoding/decoding functions and a key derivation function for the above construction with parameters (28)-(30), such that the protocol achieves the lower bound (22) and satisfies reliability and secrecy requirements (7) and (8) for an arbitrarily small $\delta > 0$.

4.2 The CRG Construction Using the ICC Method (Theorem 3)

Again for simplicity, let the two conditions in (15) and (16) hold with almost equality. Also let n_1, n_2, P_{X_A}, and P_{X_B} be those that maximize the right side of (13). The protocol has two rounds. The first round is the same as that in Section 4.1, and so the common randomness is defined to be $(U_A^{n_1}, U_B^{n_1})$. However, the second round differs as follows.

Alice and Bob use their systematic coding functions to encode $(U_A^{n_1}, \mathbf{X}_A^{:2}) = Enc(U_A^{n_1})$ and $(U_B^{n_1}, \mathbf{X}_B^{:2}) = Enc(U_B^{n_1})$, respectively. Next, they send the parity-check sequences $\mathbf{X}_A^{:2}$ and $\mathbf{X}_B^{:2}$, and receive $\mathbf{Y}_A^{:2}$ and $\mathbf{Y}_B^{:2}$. Using the bipartite jointly typical decoding method (see [6, Appendix C]), Alice decodes $(\mathbf{X}_A^{:1}, \mathbf{Y}_A^{:1}, \mathbf{X}_A^{:2}, \mathbf{Y}_A^{:2})$ to $\hat{U}_B^{n_1} \approx U_B^{n_1}$, and Bob decodes $(\mathbf{X}_B^{:1}, \mathbf{Y}_B^{:1}, \mathbf{X}_B^{:2}, \mathbf{Y}_B^{:2})$ to $\hat{U}_A^{n_1} \approx U_A^{n_1}$. Overall, the common randomness is $S = (U_A^{n_1}, U_B^{n_1})$: Alice obtains $S_A = (U_A^{n_1}, \hat{U}_B^{n_1})$, and Bob obtains $S_B = (\hat{U}_A^{n_1}, U_B^{n_1})$. In [6, Appendix C], we show that the rate achieved by this construction matches the lower bound in (13) and the protocol satisfies the reliability requirement (4) for an arbitrarily small $\delta > 0$.

5 Achievable Rates over Two-Way Binary Channel

Consider the Two-Way Binary Wiretap Channel (TWBWC) setup in Fig. 4. In this model, the two input bits X_A and X_B are XORed (added modulo two): Alice and Bob receive noisy versions of the XORed bit through independent BSCs, with noises N_{rA} and N_{rB}, respectively, where $\Pr(N_{rA} = 1) = p_{r_a}$ and $\Pr(N_{rB} = 1) = p_{r_b}$; Eve also receives a noisy version through an eavesdropping channel with noise N_E, where $\Pr(N_E = 1) = p_e$. One can relate the channel output bits to the input bits as

$$Y_A = X_A + X_B + N_{rA}, \tag{31}$$

$$Y_B = X_A + X_B + N_{rB}, \tag{32}$$

$$Z = X_A + X_B + N_E, \tag{33}$$

where $+$ indicates modulo-two addition.

In this section, we study the behavior of the lower bounds, proved in Section 3, for the case of binary channels and compare them to the trivial lower bounds that are obtained based on the previous work on message transmission. Since the CRG problem can be viewed as a spacial case of SKE, where Eve receives no information about the transmitted sequences (i.e., when $p_e = 0.5$), we only

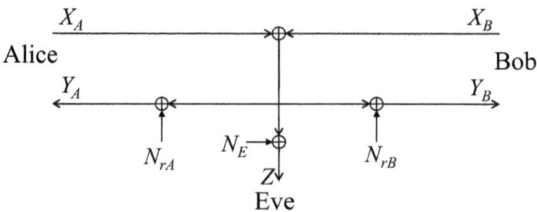

Fig. 4. Two-way binary wiretap channel

focus on the SKE problem. Throughout, for two real values $0 \le x, y \le 1$, we use $x \star y$ to denote the error probability in the cascade of two BSCs with error probabilities x and y, i.e., $x \star y = x + y - 2xy$.

We use Theorem 4 to obtain a lower bound, $Lbound_N$, on the SK capacity in the above model.

Lemma 1. *The SK capacity in the TWBWC setup is lower bounded as*

$$C_{sk}^{TWBWC} \ge Lbound_N \overset{\triangle}{=} \max_{0 \le p_1, p_2 \le 1} [\mu L_1 + (1-\mu)[L_2]_+], \tag{34}$$

where

$$L_1 = 1 + h(p_1 \star p_2 \star p_{r_a} \star p_{r_b} \star p_e) - h(p_1 \star p_{r_a}) - h(p_2 \star p_{r_b}), \tag{35}$$

$$L_2 = 1 + h(p_1 \star p_2 \star p_e) - h(p_1 \star p_{r_a}) - h(p_2 \star p_{r_b}), \tag{36}$$

$$\mu = \min\left\{ \frac{1 - h(p_1 \star p_{r_a})}{1 - h(p_2 \star p_{r_b}) + h(p_1 \star p_{r_a})}, \frac{1 - h(p_2 \star p_{r_b})}{1 - h(p_1 \star p_{r_a}) + h(p_2 \star p_{r_b})} \right\}; \tag{37}$$

furthermore,

$$Lbound_N \ge \max_{0 \le p_1, p_2 \le 1} [L_2]_+. \tag{38}$$

Proof. See [6, Appendix F]. ∎

Remark 5. In the sequel, we show that the lower bound (34) dominates the trivial lower bound, achieved from the previous work. Nevertheless, the lower bound (34) is not the highest rate one can obtain from the results of Theorem 4; in other words, one may use the result of Theorem 4 to derive a tighter lower bound in the TWBWC model. This is left as future work.

Secure message transmission in the above TWBWC model has been considered in [25, 13]. We choose to study the results in [13], which provide a strictly larger achievable rate region for secure message transmission. The achievable rate region in [13] is given as follows:

$$G_{s,I} = \text{convex hull of } \{(R_{s,AB}, R_{s,BA}), \text{ s.t. } \exists 0 \le p_1, p_2 \le 1:$$
$$R_{s,AB} \le 1 - h(p_2 \star p_{r_b}), \quad R_{s,BA} \le 1 - h(p_1 \star p_{r_a}),$$
$$R_{s,AB} + R_{s,BA} \le [1 + h(p_1 \star p_2 \star p_e) - h(p_1 \star p_{r_a}) - h(p_2 \star p_{r_b})]_+\}. \tag{39}$$

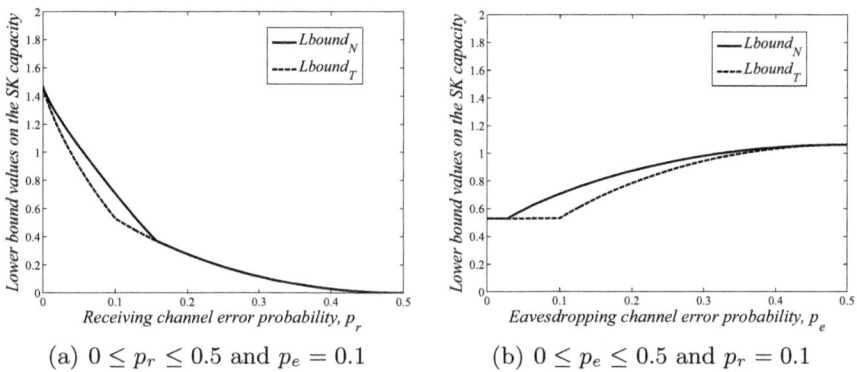

(a) $0 \le p_r \le 0.5$ and $p_e = 0.1$ (b) $0 \le p_e \le 0.5$ and $p_r = 0.1$

Fig. 5. Comparison of the lower bound values with respect to the error probabilities

This implies the following lower bound on the SK capacity.

$$
\begin{aligned}
Lbound_T &= \max_{(R_{s,AB}, R_{s,BA}) \in G_{s,I}} [R_{s,AB} + R_{s,BA}] \\
&= \max_{0 \le p_1, p_2 \le 1} [1 + h(p_1 \star p_2 \star p_e) - h(p_1 \star p_{r_b}) - h(p_2 \star p_{r_a})]_+ \\
&= \max_{0 \le p_1, p_2 \le 1} [L_2]_+,
\end{aligned}
\tag{40}
$$

where the last equality follows from (36). Comparing (38) and (40) leads to the following corollary.

Corollary 1. *The lower bound (34), proved in this paper, is always greater than or equal to the trivial lower bound (40), i.e.,*

$$
Lbound_N \ge Lbound_T.
\tag{41}
$$

To better understand the gap between the two lower bounds in inequality (41), we evaluate these two quantities with respect to different choices of channel error probabilities in Fig. 5, where the two bounds are indicated by dashed and solid lines, respectively. For simplicity, we assume that the receiving channel noise for Alice and Bob is the same, i.e., $p_{r_a} = p_{r_b} = p_r$. Fig. 5(a) compares the two lower bound values with respect to p_r when $p_e = 0.1$. Observe the non-zero gap between $Lbound_N$ and $Lbound_T$ for receiving channel noise $p_r < 0.15$. This confirms that the lower bounds proved in this paper strictly dominate those which can be obtained using the previous results on secure message transmission. Fig. 5(b) compares the bound values as functions of p_e when $p_r = 0.1$. It shows the gap between the two bounds expect for much small or much large values of the eavesdropping channel error probability p_e.

6   Conclusion

We considered the two-way channel setup and studied the problems of common randomness generation and secret key establishment for the first time in this setup. We discussed the relation between the above problems and reliable/secure message transmission over two-way channels, which are previously studied in the literature. We defined the common randomness and the secret key capacities and derived trivial lower bounds on these capacities based on the previously known results. Next, we showed that these trivial lower bounds can be improved by proposing two-round protocols that can achieve higher rates of common randomness/secret key. We applied the results to the case of two-way binary channels, where we showed the gap between the trivial lower bounds and those derived in this paper. We also proved upper bounds on the capacities and discussed the cases that the lower and the upper bounds coincide. It has not been shown whether any of the bounds are tight in general, or more specifically, whether one can improve the bounds by allowing more rounds of interaction. These open questions proffer directions to future work.

References

1. Ahlswede, R., Csiszár, I.: Common randomness in information theory and cryptography. Part I: secret sharing. IEEE Transactions on Information Theory 39, 1121–1132 (1993)
2. Ahlswede, R., Csiszár, I.: Common randomness in information theory and cryptography. Part II: CR capacity. IEEE Transactions on Information Theory 44, 225–240 (1998)
3. Ahlswede, R., Dueck, G.: Identification via channels. IEEE Transactions on Information Theory 35, 15–29 (1989)
4. Ahmadi, H., Safavi-Naini, R.: Secret key establishment over a pair of independent broadcast channels. In: International Symposium Information Theory and its Application, pp. 185–190 (2010)
5. Ahmadi, H., Safavi-Naini, R.: New results on key establishment over a pair of independent broadcast channels. In: International Symposium Information Theory and its Application, pp. 191–196 (2010)
6. Ahmadi, H., Safavi-Naini, R.: Common Randomness and Secret Key Capacities of Two-way Channels. Technical Report, Cryptology ePrint archive (2011)
7. Bloch, M., Barros, J., Rodrigues, M.R.D., McLaughlin, S.W.: Wireless Information Theoretic Security. IEEE Transactions on Information Theory 54, 2515–2534 (2008)
8. Cover, T.M., Thomas, J.A.: Elements of Information Theory, 2nd edn. Wiley-IEEE (2006)
9. Csiszár, I., Körner, J.: Broadcast channels with confidential messages. IEEE Transactions on Information Theory 24, 339–348 (1978)
10. Csiszár, I., Narayan, P.: The capacity of the arbitrarily varying channel revisited: positivity, constraints. IEEE Transactions on Information Theory 34, 181–193 (1988)
11. Dueck, G.: The capacity region of the two-way channel can exceed the inner bound. Information and Control 40, 258–266 (1979)
12. El Gamal, A., Cover, T.: Multiple User Information Theory. Proceedings of IEEE 68, 1466–1483 (1980)
13. El Gamal, A., Koyluoglu, O.O., Youssef, M., El Gamal, H.: The two way wiretap channel: theory and practice, Available on the arXiv preprint server, arXiv:1006.0778v1 (2010)

14. Han, T.S.: A general coding scheme for the two-way channel. IEEE Transactions on Information Theory 30, 35–44 (1984)
15. He, X., Yener, A.: The role of feedback in two-way secure communications, Available on the arXiv preprint server, arXiv:0911.4432v1 (2009)
16. Khisti, A., Diggavi, S., Wornell, G.: Secret key generation with correlated sources and noisy channels. In: IEEE International Symposium Information Theory (ISIT), pp. 1005–1009 (2008)
17. Maurer, U.: Secret key agreement by public discussion from common information. IEEE Transactions on Information Theory 39, 733–742 (1993)
18. Maurer, U., Wolf, S.: Information-theoretic key agreement: from weak to strong secrecy for free. In: Preneel, B. (ed.) EUROCRYPT 2000. LNCS, vol. 1807, pp. 351–351. Springer, Heidelberg (2000)
19. Pierrot, A.J., Bloch, M.R.: Strongly secure communications over the two-Way wire-tap channel, Available on the arXiv preprint server, arXiv:1010.0177v1 (2010)
20. Prabhakaran, V., Eswaran, K., Ramchandran, K.: Secrecy via sources and channels - a secret key - secret message rate trade-off region. In: IEEE International Symposium Information Theory (ISIT), pp. 1010–1014 (2008)
21. Rivest, R.L.: Unconditionally secure commitment and oblivious transfer schemes using private channels and a trusted initializer (1999), Available online at http://theory.lcs.mit.edu/~rivest/Rivest-commitment.pdf
22. Shannon, C.E.: A mathematical theory of communication. Bell System Technical Journal 27, 379–423, 623–656 (1948)
23. Shannon, C.E.: Two-way communication channels. In: 4th Berkeley Symposium on Mathematical Statistics and Probability, vol. 1, pp. 611–644 (1961)
24. Venkatesan, S., Anantharam, V.: The common randomness capacity of a pair of independent discrete memoryless channels. IEEE Transactions on Information Theory 44, 215–224 (1998)
25. Tekin, E., Yener, A.: Achievable rates for two-way wire-tap channels. In: IEEE International Symposium on Information Theory (ISIT), pp. 941–945 (2007)
26. Tekin, E., Yener, A.: The general Gaussian multiple access channel and two-way wire-tap channels: achievable rates and cooperative jamming. IEEE Transactions on Information Theory 54, 2735–2751 (2008)
27. Wyner, A.D.: The wire-tap channel. Bell System Technical Journal 54, 1355–1367 (1975)
28. Zheng, Z., Berger, T., Schalkwijk, J.P.M.: New outer bounds to capacity region of two-way channels. IEEE Transaction Information Theory 32, 383–386 (1986)

LT-Codes and Phase Transitions for Mutual Information
(Invited Talk)

Amin Shokrollahi

EPFL, Lausanne, Switzerland
amin.shokrollahi@epfl.ch

1 Introduction and Problem Formulation

The last two decades have witnessed a full revival of graph based codes. The advent of Turbo codes [1] in the early 1990's, the revival of Gallager's LDPC codes in the 1990's [12,11,7,8], and a decade long research on their properties [16] have brought fundamental changes to coding theory in general, and to the practical design of codes in particular. Today, a number of international standards such as DVB-S2, ITU-T G.hn, or 10 GBase-T use LDPC codes for the transmission of signals.

A different class of graph based codes, called Fountain codes, was stipulated in [2] to solve many of the problems associated with the delivery of data on unreliable networks. The first efficient version of these codes, called LT-codes [10] was invented by Luby and put into effective use in the company "Digital Fountain." LT-codes were extended in [17] to Raptor codes, a class of fountain codes with linear time encoding and decoding complexity. LT- and Raptor codes have been quite successful in the sense that they have been incorporated into a number of standards (such as 3GPP, IETF, OMA, BMCO, DVB-IPDC, DVB-IPTV, MPE IFEC, etc) that govern various aspects of data transmission on unreliable networks.

Despite the success of graph based codes, it is still unknown whether it is possible to design graph based codes that achieve the capacity of an arbitrary binary memoryless symmetric channel using a computationally efficient decoder. In fact, the only channel for which this is known to be true is the binary erasure channel [9,6,17]. In all other cases, the algorithms that are used for decoding are either too complex to execute (for example, when they are ML-based), or too complex to analyze (for example the belief-propagation algorithm [16]), or too simple to get us close to the capacity (such as various flavors of Gallager's algorithms A and B [16]).

This extended abstract reports on a different approach towards solving this problem which generates questions of interest in their own right. We formulate this approach using LT-codes, as these codes seem to be to ones most amenable to our particular method. An LT-code is given by two parameters (k, Ω) wherein k is a positive integer, and Ω is a probability distribution on $\mathbb{F}_2^k$, wherein Ω_d is the probability of the integer d. An LT-code produces for a given vector $(x_1, \ldots, x_k)$

S. Fehr (Ed.): ICITS 2011, LNCS 6673, pp. 94–99, 2011.

of k symbols a potentially limitless stream of output symbols; for each such output symbol an integer d is chosen according to the probability distribution Ω, and then d distinct input symbols are chosen uniformly at random. These symbols are added together to form the output symbol which is transmitted on the channel. We always assume that output symbols are equipped with an indication of which input symbols were chosen to create its value.

The decoding problem is now as follows: given that we have collected n output symbols, infer the values of the k input symbols from the values of the received n output symbols, and the knowledge of the underlying channel. Typically, the inference needs to be done using an efficient algorithm, i.e., an algorithm that runs in time polynomial in the number k of the input symbols.

This problem is entirely solved when the channel is the erasure channel [6,17]. In this case, it is possible to recover the k input symbols from the n output symbols with high probability for values of n that are as close to k as desired.

When the channel $\mathcal{C}$ is a memoryless binary symmetric channel which is not the erasure channel, then it is unknown whether for any k there is a degree distribution Ω^k such that for any given $\epsilon > 0$ the k input bits can be recovered from $n = k(1 + \epsilon)/\mathrm{Cap}(\mathcal{C})$ output bits using an efficient decoder (such as the belief-propagation decoder) when k is large enough. Here, $\mathrm{Cap}(\mathcal{C})$ denotes the capacity of the channel $\mathcal{C}$. If such a sequence of degree distributions exists, and if the sequence has a limit Ω (which means that Ω is a degree distribution and $\Omega_d^k \to \Omega_d$ as $k \to \infty$ for all d), then we call the limiting degree distribution Ω "capacity-achieving." When $\mathcal{C}$ is the erasure channel, it is known [6,17] that the sequence $(1/2, 1/6, \ldots, 1/(d(d-1)), \ldots)$ is capacity-achieving.

Though capacity-achieving distributions are not known (and are not even known to exist) for channels other than the erasure channel, we know that [3]: (1) Ω_1^k, the probability of the number 1 under the distribution Ω^k, should converge to 0, as k converges to infinity, and (2) Ω_2^k should converge to $\Pi(\mathcal{C})/2$, where $\Pi(\mathcal{C})$ is a certain parameter associated to the channel $\mathcal{C}$ which will be described in more detail below. This means that in a capacity achieving distribution for the channel $\mathcal{C}$ we have $\Omega_1 = 0$ and $\Omega_2 = \Pi(\mathcal{C})/2$. The other probabilities of a capacity-achieving distribution are, as of yet, unknown.

In this paper, we will discuss a related problem and mention some of the work that has been done in this direction. We will take a reverse approach, and ask for a degree distribution that satisfies an information theoretic extremal condition. Our approach is based on the following simple fact: if x denotes the vector of k input symbols, and y denotes any subset of ℓ output symbols where $\ell \leq k/\mathrm{Cap}(\mathcal{C}) + o(k)$, and the code operates close to the capacity of the channel, then $I(x; y)$ is necessarily equal to $\ell \mathrm{Cap}(\mathcal{C}) + o(k)$.

To make the discussion more precise, let x be a uniform random variable over $\mathbb{F}_2^k$ (denoting the source), and y denote the random variable describing the received bits. Our final goal is to find a degree distribution $\Omega_2, \Omega_3, \ldots$ with the following property: given k input bits, and n output bits, let y_d denote the vector of output bits of degree d, and $|y_d|$ denote the length of this vector. Then we want the following to be true

$$I(x; y_2) = |y_2|\text{Cap}(\mathcal{C}) + o(k)$$
$$I(x; y_2, y_3) = (|y_2| + |y_3|)\text{Cap}(\mathcal{C}) + o(k)$$

$$\vdots \quad \vdots$$

We now formulate a series of conjectures which, if true, will provide a set of "degrees" $\Omega_2, \Omega_3, \ldots$ which *may* be capacity-achieving. They are, however, interesting in their own right due to their extremality properties. To formulate the conjectures, we need one more piece of notation. Let f and g be real functions defined on the set of natural numbers. We say that $f \ll g$ if $g(n)/f(n)$ converges to a number $\mu > 1$ when n goes to infinity. We say that $f \preceq g$ if $f(n)/g(n)$ converges to a number $\mu \le 1$ as n goes to infinity.

Conjecture 1. For all $d \ge 2$ there is $\tau_d > 0$ depending on the channel $\mathcal{C}$ such that $I(x; y_d) = |y_d|\text{Cap}(\mathcal{C}) + o(k)$ if $|y_d| \preceq \tau_d k$. If $|y_d| \gg \tau_d k$, then there is $\epsilon > 0$ depending on $\mathcal{C}$ and on $|y_d$ such that $I(x; y_d) < (|y_d| - \epsilon k)\text{Cap}(\mathcal{C})$.

Conjecture 2. There are positive real numbers $\theta_2, \theta_3, \ldots$ depending on the channel $\mathcal{C}$ such that for all $d \ge 2$ if $|y_i| \preceq \theta_i k$ for $i = 2, \ldots, k$, then

$$I(x; y_2, y_3, \ldots, y_{d-1}, y_d) = (|y_2| + \cdots + |y_d|)\text{Cap}(\mathcal{C}) + o(k).$$

If, however, there is i such that $|y_i| \gg \theta_i k$, then there exists $\epsilon > 0$ depending on the channel and on $|y_2|, \ldots, |y_d|$ such that

$$I(x; y_2, y_3, \ldots, y_{d-1}, y_d) \le (|y_2| + \cdots + |y_d| - \epsilon k)\text{Cap}(\mathcal{C}).$$

Conjecture 3. The sequence $\theta_2, \theta_3, \ldots$ of the previous conjecture has the property that $\theta_2 + \theta_3 + \cdots = 1$. Hence, it is a degree distribution on the set $\{2, 3, \ldots\}$.

Conjecture 4. The sequence $\theta_2, \theta_3, \ldots$ of the previous conjecture is a capacity-achieving sequence for the channel $\mathcal{C}$.

2   The Trivial Channel

Consider the case where the channel $\mathcal{C}$ is trivial, i.e., sends the bits across without introducing any errors. In this case, the mutual information between the source x and the received bits y becomes the rank of the matrix describing the dependency of y on x. This matrix is a random variable, and we can talk about its expected rank. Even in this case the conjectures above are nontrivial to prove, since the expected rank of random matrices is not easy to compute when the probability distribution on the matrix is not uniform.

Nevertheless, [15] manages to prove all the above conjectures for this case.

Theorem 1. (1) *[15, Theorem 2] If $\mathcal{C}$ is the trivial channel, then τ_d in Conjecture 1 exists, and their value is equal to the smallest root of $z(1 - \ln(z)) - \frac{1-z}{d}\ln(z) - 1$ in the half open interval $(0, 1]$.*

(2) *[15, Example 3] If $\mathcal{C}$ is the trivial channel, then the sequence $\theta_2, \theta_3, \dots$ of Conjecture 2 exists and is equal to*

$$\theta_2 = \frac{1}{2}, \theta_3 = \frac{1}{6}, \dots, \theta_d = \frac{1}{d(d-1)}, \dots$$

(3) *(Trivial consequence of part (2)) Conjecture 3 is true for the trivial channel.*
(4) *[6,17] Conjecture 4 is true for the trivial channel.*

The proof of parts (1) and (2) above uses the theory of EXIT functions [13].

3   The Case $d = 2$

Much of the motivation for that above conjectures comes from their proofs for the trivial channel, and for the case $d = 2$. In the latter case, we have the following result [3].

Theorem 2. *Let $\mathcal{C}$ be a binary input memoryless symmetric channel, and let g be the pdf of its LLR. Further, let $\mathrm{E}(\mathcal{C}) := \int_{-\infty}^{\infty} \tanh(x/2)g(x)\mathrm{d}x$, and $\Pi(\mathcal{C}) := \mathrm{Cap}(\mathcal{C})/\mathrm{E}(\mathcal{C})$. Conjecture 1 above is true for $d = 2$, and the value of τ_2 equals*

$$\tau_2 = \frac{\Pi(\mathcal{C})}{2}.$$

The value of τ_2 can be calculated for different channels using numerical approximations of closed form expressions. For example, if $\mathcal{C}$ is the trivial channel (or an erasure channel), then $\tau_2 = 1/2$. If $\mathcal{C}$ is the binary symmetric channel with probability p, then $\tau_2 = (1 - h(p))/2(1 - 2p)^2$, where $h(p)$ is the binary entropy function. If $\mathcal{C}$ is the additive white Gaussian noise channel with variance σ^2, then

$$\tau_2 = \frac{1 - \dfrac{1}{\sqrt{2\pi m}} \displaystyle\int_{-\infty}^{\infty} \log_2(1 + e^{-x}) e^{-\frac{(x-m)^2}{4m}} \mathrm{d}x}{\dfrac{1}{\sqrt{\pi m}} \displaystyle\int_{-\infty}^{\infty} \tanh(x/2) e^{-\frac{(x-m)^2}{4m}} \mathrm{d}x},$$

where $m = 2/\sigma^2$.

4   The General Case

Little progress has been made so far towards proving the general case of the above conjectures. A partial step towards proving Conjecture 1 has been undertaken in [5]. Though we cannot prove that the numbers τ_d even exist (when $d \geq 3$) we can find lower bounds for these numbers, at least for the case of binary symmetric channels. More precisely, we have the following.

Theorem 3. *[5, Theorem 5] Let $\mathcal{C}$ be the binary symmetric channel with probability p, and let $d \geq 3$. Define*

$$f(\lambda) := \frac{ed}{\lambda \tanh(\lambda)} \cosh(\lambda)^{d/\lambda \tanh(\lambda)} \left(\frac{\tanh(\lambda)}{e} \right)^d (1 - 2p)^2,$$

$$g(\lambda, \phi) := \cosh(\lambda) \left(\frac{\tanh(\lambda)}{e} \right)^{\lambda \tanh(\lambda)} \left(\frac{d\phi}{d\phi - \lambda \tanh(\lambda)} \right)^{\phi}$$
$$\cdot \left(\frac{d\phi - \lambda \tanh(\lambda)}{\lambda \tanh(\lambda)} (1 - 2p)^2 \right)^{\lambda \tanh(\lambda)/d},$$

and

$$u(\phi) = \frac{1}{2} \left\{ 1 - \left(\frac{1 + e^{-2\phi d}}{2} \right)^{\left(1 - \frac{1}{\phi} \right)} \right\}.$$

Let $1/t_0$ be the maximum of $f(\lambda)$ in the interval $(0, \infty)$, and let t_1 be the largest positive value of ϕ such that $g(\lambda, \phi) \leq 1$ for all λ with $\lambda \tanh(\lambda) \leq d\phi$. Also, let t_2 be the maximum value of $\phi \geq 0$ such that $u(\phi) < p$. Then, provided τ_d exists, we have $\tau_d \geq \min\left(\max(t_0, t_1), t_2 \right)$.

The proof of this theorem uses a result that is interesting in its own right. To bound the mutual information of x and y, we need to calculate the expected entropy of y, where expectation is over the choices of the random variable y. Using a Hadamard Transform [5, Theorem 4], the entropy of y is connected to the weight distribution of a particular code. The expected weight distribution can be effectively calculated using the methods outlined in [4, Sect. 3.6].

The bound of the previous theorem is probably very far from the correct value of τ_d. For example, we would expect this bound to go to $1/(1 - h(p))$ when d becomes large. However, numerical calculations suggest otherwise. In fact, when p is close to 0.5, the product of the bound of the previous theorem and $(1 - h(p))$ is around 0.5 [5, Table II].

The proofs of the above conjectures in the general case thus remains elusive. They are most probably not of the same level of difficulty, though. For example, it is possible that one can prove the existence (but not necessarily the values) of the numbers τ_d and θ_d using general principles; once the existence of these numbers is shown, it is probably not too hard to show Conjecture 3. Conjecture 4 is, however, most probably of a different caliber.

A sort of "converse" to the information theoretic approach of this work has been accomplished in [14] where lower bounds are obtained for the entropy of the transmitted message conditional to the received message, i.e., upper bounds on the mutual information $I(x; y)$. These upper bounds are conjecturally sharp, and hence would provide candidate values for the numbers τ_d, and θ_d. This is work in progress, and corresponding results will be reported elsewhere.

References

1. Berrou, C., Glavieux, A., Thitimajshima, P.: Near Shannon limit error-correcting coding and decoding. In: Proceedings of ICC 1993, Geneva, Switzerland, pp. 1064–1070 (May 1993)
2. Byers, J., Luby, M., Mitzenmacher, M., Rege, A.: A digital fountain approach to reliable distribution of bulk data. In: proceedings of ACM SIGCOMM 1988 (1998)
3. Etesami, O., Shokrollahi, A.: Raptor codes on binary memoryless symmetric channels. IEEE Trans. Inform. Theory 52(5), 2033–2051 (2006)
4. Kolchin, V.: Random Graphs. Encyclopedia of Mathematics and its Applications, vol. 53. Cambridge University Press, Cambridge (1999)
5. Kumar, K., Pakzad, P., Salavati, A., Shokrollahi, A.: Phase transitions for mutual information. In: 2010 6th International Symposium on Turbo Codes and Iterative Information Processing (ISTC), pp. 137–141 (2010)
6. Luby, M.: LT-codes. In: Proceedings of the 43rd Annual IEEE Symposium on the Foundations of Computer Science (FOCS), pp. 271–280 (2002)
7. Luby, M., Mitzenmacher, M., Shokrollahi, A., Spielman, D.: Analysis of low density codes and improved designs using irregular graphs. In: Proceedings of the 30th Annual ACM Symposium on Theory of Computing, pp. 249–258 (1998)
8. Luby, M., Mitzenmacher, M., Shokrollahi, A., Spielman, D.: Improved low-density parity-check codes using irregular graphs and belief propagation. In: Proceedings 1998 IEEE International Symposium on Information Theory, p. 117 (1998)
9. Luby, M., Mitzenmacher, M., Shokrollahi, A., Spielman, D.: Efficient erasure correcting codes. IEEE Trans. Inform. Theory 47, 569–584 (2001)
10. Luby, M.G.: Lt codes. In: Proceedings of 43rd IEEE Symposium Foundations of Computer Science, p. 10 (2002)
11. MacKay, D.: Good error-correcting codes based on very sparse matrices. IEEE Trans. Inform. Theory 45, 399–431 (1999)
12. MacKay, D., Neal, R.: Good codes based on very sparse matrices. In: Boyd, C. (ed.) Cryptography and Coding 1995. LNCS, vol. 1025, pp. 100–111. Springer, Heidelberg (1995)
13. Measson, C., Montanari, A., Urbanke, R.: Maxwell Construction: The Hidden Bridge Between Iterativew and Maximum a Posteriori Decoding. IEEE Transansactions on Information Theory 54(12), 5277–5307 (2008)
14. Montanari, A.: Tight bounds for ldpc and ldgm codes under map decoding. IEEE Transactions on Information Theory 51(9), 3221–3246 (2005)
15. Pakzad, P., Shokrollahi, A.: EXIT functions for LT and raptor codes, and asymptotic ranks of random matrices. In: Proc. of the IEEE International Symposium on Information Theory (ISIT), 2007, pp. 411–415 (June 2007)
16. Richardson, T., Urbanke, R.: Modern Coding Theory. Cambridge University Press, Cambridge (2008)
17. Shokrollahi, A.: Raptor codes. IEEE Trans. Inform. Theory 52(6), 2551–2567 (2006)

Unconditionally Secure Signature Schemes Revisited

Colleen M. Swanson and Douglas R. Stinson*

David R. Cheriton School of Computer Science
University of Waterloo
Waterloo, Ontario, Canada N2L 3G1
{c2swanso,dstinson}@uwaterloo.ca

Abstract. Unconditionally secure signature (USS) schemes provide the
ability to electronically sign documents without the reliance on computational assumptions needed in traditional digital signatures. Unlike digital
signatures, USS schemes require both different signing and different verification algorithms for each user in the system. Thus, any viable security
definition for a USS scheme must carefully treat the subject of what constitutes a valid signature. That is, it is important to distinguish between
signatures that are created using a user's signing algorithm and signatures that may satisfy one or more user verification algorithms. Moreover,
given that each verifier has his own distinct verification algorithm, a USS
scheme must necessarily handle the event of a disagreement. In this paper, we present a new security model for USS schemes that incorporates
these notions, as well as give a formal treatment of dispute resolution
and the trust assumptions required. We provide formal definitions of
non-repudiation and transferability in the context of dispute resolution,
and give sufficient conditions for a USS scheme to satisfy these properties. Finally, we present the results of an analysis of Hanaoka et al.'s
construction in our security model.

1   Introduction

Unconditionally secure signature (USS) schemes provide the ability to electronically sign documents without the reliance on computational assumptions needed
in traditional digital signatures. That is, USS schemes are the analogue of digital
signatures in the unconditionally secure cryptographic setting. The construction
of such schemes is interesting not only from a theoretical perspective, but also
from the viewpoint of ensuring security of information in the long term or designing schemes that are viable in a post-quantum world.

Unlike digital signatures, USS schemes require both different signing and different verification algorithms for each user in the system. Thus, any viable security definition for a USS scheme must carefully treat the subject of what
constitutes a valid signature. That is, it is important to distinguish between signatures that are created using a user's signing algorithm and signatures that may

---

* Research supported by NSERC grant 203114-06.

S. Fehr (Ed.): ICITS 2011, LNCS 6673, pp. 100–116, 2011.

satisfy one or more user verification algorithms. Current research [5,6,10,12,7] has proposed various models for unconditionally secure signature schemes, but these models do not fully treat the implications of having multiple verification algorithms or analyze the need for (and trust questions associated with) having a dispute resolution mechanism. We address both of these issues in this paper.

Historically, there have been several attempts to create unconditionally secure constructions that satisfy security properties required for digital signatures, including non-repudiation, transferability, and unforgeability. Chaum and Roijakkers [2] introduced unconditionally secure signatures, proposing an interactive scheme that does not have transferability. Another approach to creating unconditionally secure signatures has been to enhance existing unconditionally secure message authentication codes (MACs), making these codes more robust in a signature setting. MACs clearly do not provide non-repudiation, as the sender and receiver compute authentication tags using the same algorithm. In addition, the need for a designated sender and receiver further limits the applicability of such schemes to a general signature setting.

Much research has been devoted to the removal of the standard MAC trust assumptions, in which both sender and receiver are assumed to be honest. In A^2-codes [13,14,8], the sender and receiver may be dishonest, but there is a trusted arbiter to resolve disputes; in A^3-codes [1,3,9], the arbiter is no longer trusted prior to dispute resolution, but is trusted to make an honest decision in event of a disagreement. Johansson [9] used A^3-codes to improve the construction of Chaum and Roijakkers by making it non-interactive, but the signatures produced by the scheme are not transferable, as the use of a designated receiver limits the verification of the signature to those who have the appropriate key. Multi-receiver authentication codes (MRAs) [4] and multi-receiver authentication codes with dynamic sender (DMRAs) [11] use a broadcast setting to relax the requirement for designation of receivers, and also, in the latter case, senders. These codes are not appropriate outside of a broadcast setting, however, as neither non-repudiation nor transferability are satisfied.

Unsurprisingly, the first security models for unconditionally secure signature schemes, including Johansson [9] and Hanaoka et al. [5,6], drew upon the standard MAC security models. Shikata et al. [12] introduced a model using notions from public-key cryptography, which was also adopted in the work by Hara et al. [7] on blind signatures. Safavi-Naini et al. [10] presented a MAC-based model meant to encompass the notions developed by Shikata et al. In this work, we present a new security model. Our model is more general than the MAC-based models of Hanaoka et al. [5,6] and Safavi-Naini et al. [10] and covers the attacks described in these works. Like that of Shikata et al. [12], our work is based on security notions from traditional public-key signature systems. However, our model differs from those in the existing literature in its careful treatment of the concept of a "valid" signature. Our aim is to provide a rigorous and natural security model that covers all reasonable attacks.

In addition, we analyze a construction of Hanaoka et al. [5] in our model and provide the security results. We remark that while Hanaoka et al. make claims about the security of this construction in their model, they do not provide an analysis. In fact, security proofs are not provided for most of the constructions given in existing research. Thus, we feel it is useful to include the results of our analysis of a basic unconditionally secure signature construction in our security model; a proof of security appears in the full version of our paper [15].

Our basic notion of security is easily extendable to a system with dispute resolution, which we argue is a necessary component of any USS scheme. Furthermore, our treatment of dispute resolution allows us to give formal definitions of non-repudiation and transferability. We show that a USS scheme that satisfies our unforgeability definition and has an appropriate dispute resolution method also satisfies non-repudiation and transferability, both of which are required properties for any reasonable signature scheme. Finally, we define various dispute resolution methods and examine the amount of trust each requires.

An outline of our paper is as follows. In Section 2, we give a basic definition of a USS scheme, before moving to an informal treatment of the desired security properties. We then define a formal security model in Section 3. We formally discuss dispute resolution in Section 4 and give examples of dispute resolution methods in Section 5. In Section 6, we compare our work with that of previous literature. Finally, we analyze the construction of Hanaoka et al. [5] in Section 7 and give some concluding remarks in Section 8.

2   Preliminaries

We require the following definitions.

Definition 2.1. *An unconditionally secure signature scheme (or USS scheme) Π consists of a tuple $(\mathcal{U}, X, \Sigma, \mathsf{Gen}, \mathsf{Sign}, \mathsf{Vrfy})$ satisfying the following:*

- *The set $\mathcal{U} = \{U_1, \ldots U_n\}$ consists of possible users, X is a finite set of possible messages, and Σ is a finite set of possible signatures.*
- *The* key-generation algorithm Gen *takes as input a security parameter 1^k and outputs the signing algorithm Sign and the verification algorithm Vrfy. The parameter k is relevant to the overall security of the scheme, as discussed later.*
- *The* signing algorithm $\mathsf{Sign}: \mathcal{X} \times \mathcal{U} \to \Sigma$ *takes a message $x \in \mathcal{X}$ and a signer $U_i \in \mathcal{U}$ as input, and outputs a signature $\sigma \in \Sigma$. For each $U_i \in \mathcal{U}$, we let Sign_i denote the algorithm $\mathsf{Sign}(\cdot, U_i)$.*
- *The* verification algorithm $\mathsf{Vrfy}: \mathcal{X} \times \Sigma \times \mathcal{U} \times \mathcal{U} \to \{True, False\}$ *takes as input a message $x \in \mathcal{X}$, a signature $\sigma \in \Sigma$, a signer $U_i \in \mathcal{U}$, and a verifier $U_j \in \mathcal{U}$, and outputs either True or False. For each user U_j, we let Vrfy_j denote the algorithm $\mathsf{Vrfy}(\cdot, \cdot, \cdot, U_j)$.*

It is required that, for every k, for every pair $(\mathsf{Sign}, \mathsf{Vrfy})$ output by $\mathsf{Gen}(1^k)$, for every pair $U_i, U_j \in \mathcal{U}$, and for every $x \in \mathcal{X}$, it holds that

$$\mathsf{Vrfy}_j(x, \mathsf{Sign}_i(x), U_i) = True.$$

Remark 2.1. We are treating *deterministic* signature schemes only, in the sense that Sign and Vrfy are deterministic, although the above definition can easily be extended to the randomized setting.

We now define the concepts of authentic, acceptable, and fraudulent signatures. Distinguishing these three concepts is one of the main themes of this paper.

Definition 2.2. *A signature $\sigma \in \Sigma$ on a message $x \in \mathcal{X}$ is i-authentic if $\sigma =$* Sign$_i(x)$.

Definition 2.3. *A signature $\sigma \in \Sigma$ on a message $x \in \mathcal{X}$ is (i,j)-acceptable if* Vrfy$_j(x, \sigma, U_i) = True$.

Definition 2.4. *A signature $\sigma \in \Sigma$ on a message $x \in \mathcal{X}$ is (i,j)-fraudulent if σ is (i,j)-acceptable but not i-authentic.*

2.1   Security Notions

Informally, a secure signature scheme should satisfy the following three properties:

1. *Unforgeability*: Except with negligible probability, it should not be possible for an adversary to create a "valid" signature.
2. *Non-repudiation*: Except with negligible probability, a signer should be unable to repudiate a legitimate signature that he has created.
3. *Transferability*: If a verifier accepts a signature, he can be confident that any other verifier will also accept it.

One objective of this paper is to formalize these notions in the unconditionally secure setting; we provide precise definitions in Sections 3 and 4. In contrast to the usual public-key setting, the requirements of non-repudiation and transferability are not guaranteed in a USS scheme that satisfies the above intuitive notion of unforgeability. For "ordinary" digital signatures, non-repudiation is a consequence of unforgeability: a signature is considered "valid" if it passes a verification test, and it should be impossible for anyone to create such a signature without knowledge of the secret signing algorithm. Thus, assuming the signing algorithm is not known to some third party, the signer cannot create a signature and later repudiate it. Transferability of digital signatures is guaranteed since there is a single, public verification algorithm.

In USS schemes, the concept of a "valid" signature requires clarification. A verifier is always capable of finding a signature that passes his own, secret verification test, so we cannot define the validity of a signature based on whether it passes a given user's verification algorithm. Indeed, there must be signatures that pass a given user's verification algorithm but that could not have been created with the signer's signing algorithm; otherwise the scheme will not satisfy unforgeability. Similarly, each verifier's verification algorithm must be different, or a given verifier will be able to present a signature acceptable to any verifier who possesses the same algorithm. A "valid" signature, then, must be created using the signer's signing algorithm, and it should be impossible for anyone to create a signature that *appears* valid to other, non-colluding users, or the scheme will not have the properties of unforgeability, non-repudiation, and transferability. In particular, we have the following observations.

Theorem 2.1. *A necessary condition for a USS scheme to satisfy unforgeability is the existence of (i,j)-fraudulent signatures for $i \neq j$.*

Proof. A verifier U_j can always use his verification algorithm to create an (i,j)-acceptable signature for any $i \neq j$. If there are no (i,j)-fraudulent signatures, then all signatures produced in this fashion must be i-authentic, and therefore they are successful forgeries.   □

Theorem 2.2. *A USS scheme must satisfy $\mathsf{Vrfy}_j(\cdot,\cdot,\cdot) \neq \mathsf{Vrfy}_\ell(\cdot,\cdot,\cdot)$ for $j \neq \ell$.*

Proof. Suppose that $\mathsf{Vrfy}_j(\cdot,\cdot,\cdot) = \mathsf{Vrfy}_\ell(\cdot,\cdot,\cdot)$ where $j \neq \ell$. Clearly U_j can create an (i,j)-acceptable signed message, (x,σ). Because $\mathsf{Vrfy}_j(\cdot,\cdot,\cdot) = \mathsf{Vrfy}_\ell(\cdot,\cdot,\cdot)$, it follows immediately that (x,σ) is (i,ℓ)-acceptable. This implies that the user U_ℓ will accept (x,σ) as a valid signature, but (x,σ) was not created by U_i.   □

3   Formal Security Model

We now develop a formal security model for USS schemes. Our security definition is comparable to the notion of signatures secure against existential forgery under adaptive chosen message attacks in the case of public-key signature schemes. However, our definition takes into account the peculiarities of the unconditional security setting, in particular the existence of (and need for) fraudulent signatures and multiple verification algorithms.

We specify two types of existential forgery. In our setting, an "existential" forgery is either an (i,j)-fraudulent signature created without the help of the verifier U_j, or an i-authentic signature created without the help of the signer U_i. If a USS scheme is secure, then both of these types of forgeries should be infeasible for an adversary to create.

We need the following oracles:

- The $\mathsf{Sign}_\ell^{\mathcal{O}}(\cdot)$ *oracle*; this oracle takes as input a message x and outputs an ℓ-authentic signature for the message x.
- The $\mathsf{Vrfy}_\ell^{\mathcal{O}}(\cdot,\cdot,\cdot)$ *oracle*; this oracle takes as input a signature pair (x,σ) and a signer U_i, and runs user U_ℓ's verification algorithm on input (x,σ,U_i), outputting *True* or *False*.

Definition 3.1. *Let $\Pi = (\mathcal{U}, X, \Sigma, \mathsf{Gen}, \mathsf{Sign}, \mathsf{Vrfy})$ be a USS scheme with security parameter 1^k, let the set $C \subseteq \mathcal{U}$ be a coalition of at most t users, and let ψ_S and ψ_V be positive integers. We define the following signature game* $\mathrm{Sig\text{-}forge}_{C,\Pi}(k)$ *with target signer U_i and verifier U_j:*

1. $\mathsf{Gen}(1^k)$ is run to obtain the pair $(\mathsf{Sign}, \mathsf{Vrfy})$.

2. *The coalition C is given bounded access to the oracles $\mathsf{Sign}_\ell^{\mathcal{O}}(\cdot)$ and $\mathsf{Vrfy}_\ell^{\mathcal{O}}(\cdot,\cdot,U_i)$ for ℓ satisfying $U_\ell \notin C$. In particular, C is allowed a total of ψ_S and ψ_V queries to the $\mathsf{Sign}^{\mathcal{O}}$ and $\mathsf{Vrfy}^{\mathcal{O}}$ oracles, respectively. It should be noted that C has unlimited access to the signing and verification algorithms of any $U_\ell \in C$. We let $\mathcal{Q}$ denote the set of messages that the coalition submitted as queries to the oracles $\mathsf{Sign}_i^{\mathcal{O}}(\cdot)$. Note that $\mathcal{Q}$ does not contain messages submitted as queries to $\mathsf{Sign}_\ell^{\mathcal{O}}(\cdot)$ for $\ell \neq i$.*
3. *The coalition C outputs a signature pair (x,σ) satisfying $x \notin \mathcal{Q}$.*
4. *The output of the game is defined to be 1 if and only if one of the following conditions is met:*
   (a) *$U_j \notin C$ and σ is an (i,j)-fraudulent signature on x; or*
   (b) *$U_i \notin C$ and σ is an i-authentic signature on x.*

Definition 3.2. *Let $\Pi = (\mathcal{U}, X, \Sigma, \mathsf{Gen}, \mathsf{Sign}, \mathsf{Vrfy})$ be a USS scheme with security parameter 1^k and let $\epsilon(k)$ be a negligible function of k. We say Π is $(t, \psi_S, \psi_V, \epsilon)$-unforgeable if for all coalitions C of at most t possibly colluding users, and all choices of target signer U_i and verifier U_j,*

$$\Pr[\text{Sig-forge}_{C,\Pi}(k) = 1] \leq \epsilon(k).$$

Remark 3.1. Another option is to include a $\mathsf{Fraud}_{(i,j)}^{\mathcal{O}}(\cdot)$ *oracle*; this oracle takes as input a message x and outputs an (i,j)-fraudulent signature on x. Providing certain (i,j)-fraudulent signatures to the adversary could only increase his chances of ultimately constructing a new (i,j)-fraudulent signature. Thus this would constitute a stronger security model than the one we consider. On the other hand, it is hard to envisage a scenario where an adversary would have this kind of additional information about a verifier whom the adversary is attempting to deceive. Therefore we do not include the $\mathsf{Fraud}^{\mathcal{O}}$ oracle in our basic model of USS schemes. However, it would be straightforward to modify our model to include these oracles, if desired.

Remark 3.2. We can also define the notion of *strongly unforgeable* USS schemes by appropriately redefining the set $\mathcal{Q}$ of Definition 3.1. That is, we let $\mathcal{Q}$ contain signature pairs of the form (x,σ), where the message x was submitted as a query to the given oracles and the signature σ was the oracle response, and require that the submitted signature pair $(x,\sigma) \notin \mathcal{Q}$.

We observe that a scheme meeting the unforgeability requirement of Definition 3.2 satisfies our intuitive notions of non-repudiation and transferability. We explain these relationships in the following observations, noting that formal definitions of non-repudiation and transferability are intrinsically linked to the dispute resolution process, and so will be provided later, in Section 4. We formalize these observations in Theorems 4.1 and 4.2.

Observation 3.1 *A $(t, \psi_S, \psi_V, \epsilon)$-unforgeable USS scheme Π provides non-repudiation.*

Proof. Suppose that Π is $(t, \psi_S, \psi_V, \epsilon)$-unforgeable. Then U_i cannot repudiate a given i-authentic signature σ, as Definition 3.2 guarantees that σ can be created without U_i only with negligible probability (as Condition 4b of Definition 3.1 holds only with negligible probability). Thus U_i cannot claim that other users may have created σ. The other possibility for a signer U_i to repudiate a signature on a message given to U_j is if the signature is (i, j)-fraudulent. Definition 3.2 also implies that U_i cannot create an (i, j)-fraudulent signature (even with the help of $t - 1$ other users not including U_j) except with negligible probability, as Condition 4a of Definition 3.1 is assumed to not hold (except with negligible probability). ☐

Observation 3.2 *A $(t, \psi_S, \psi_V, \epsilon)$-unforgeable USS scheme Π provides transferability.*

Proof. In order for a signature σ to be non-transferable from U_j to U_ℓ, σ would have to be (i, j)-acceptable, but not (i, ℓ)-acceptable, where $j \neq \ell$. If σ were i-authentic, it would also be (i, ℓ)-acceptable. Therefore σ must be (i, j)-fraudulent. However, Definition 3.2 implies an (i, j)-fraudulent signature cannot be created without the assistance of U_j, except with negligible probability. ☐

From the point of view of a verifier, a scheme meeting Definition 3.2 gives reasonable assurance of the validity of a received signature. If a verifier U_j receives a signature pair (x, σ) purportedly from U_i, then U_j will accept the signature so long as σ is (i, j)-acceptable for the message x. In this case, there are only two possibilities: either σ is i-authentic or (i, j)-fraudulent for the message x. If σ is i-authentic, then a coalition that does not include the signer U_i has only a negligible probability of creating σ by Condition 4b of Definition 3.1. If σ is (i, j)-fraudulent, then Condition 4a of Definition 3.1 guarantees that a coalition that does not include U_j cannot create σ, except with negligible probability.

4   Dispute Resolution

Given that each verifier has his own distinct verification algorithm, a USS scheme must necessarily handle the event of a disagreement. That is, since there is no public verification method as in traditional digital signatures, a USS scheme must have a mechanism to determine the authenticity of a signature when some subset of users disagree whether a given signature should be accepted. In particular, dispute resolution is necessary to convince an outsider of the authenticity of a disputed signature. In traditional digital signatures, there are no outsiders to the scheme, in the sense that everyone has access to the public verification method. In our setting, however, the number of participants (and thereby access to verification algorithms) is limited. Dispute resolution is a method that effectively deals with need for resolution of disagreements in, for example, a court setting. Typically, dispute resolution involves all the users voting on the validity of a signature, or alternatively, a trusted arbiter stating whether a signature is valid.

We now incorporate a mechanism for dispute resolution into the basic USS scheme defined in Section 2. We first consider the requirements of a dispute resolution system. With a definition of dispute resolution in place, we can formally define non-repudiation and transferability and give sufficient conditions for a USS scheme to satisfy these properties.

Ideally, the dispute resolution process validates a signature if and only if the signature is authentic, i.e., the signature was produced by the signer. This leads to the following definitions.

Definition 4.1. *A dispute resolution method $\mathcal{DR}$ for a USS scheme Π is a procedure invoked when a user U_ℓ questions the validity of a given signature (x, σ), purportedly signed by U_i. Here U_ℓ may be any user in $\mathcal{U}$, including U_i. The procedure $\mathcal{DR}$ consists of an algorithm* DR *that takes as input a signature pair (x, σ) and a signer U_i, and outputs a value in $\{valid, invalid\}$, together with the following rules:*

1. *If* DR *outputs valid, then (x, σ) must be accepted as an i-authentic signature on x by all users.*
2. *If* DR *outputs invalid, then (x, σ) must be rejected by all users.*

We remark that the algorithm DR *may have access to additional (secret) scheme information, as specified by the particular dispute resolution method.*

The following definitions formalize the notion of utility of a given $\mathcal{DR}$.

Definition 4.2. Soundness. *Let Π be a USS scheme and let $\mathcal{DR}$ be a dispute resolution method for Π. We say $\mathcal{DR}$ is* sound *if, whenever σ is not an i-authentic signature on x, then* $DR((x, \sigma), U_i)$ *outputs invalid.*

Definition 4.3. Completeness. *Let Π be a USS scheme and let $\mathcal{DR}$ be a dispute resolution method for Π. We say $\mathcal{DR}$ is* complete *if, whenever σ is an i-authentic signature on x, then* $DR((x, \sigma), U_i)$ *outputs valid.*

Definition 4.4. Correctness. *Let Π be a USS scheme and let $\mathcal{DR}$ be a dispute resolution method for Π. If $\mathcal{DR}$ is both sound and complete, we say $\mathcal{DR}$ is* correct.

With the addition of a dispute resolution method $\mathcal{DR}$, we adjust the unforgeability requirement of a USS scheme by requiring $\mathcal{DR}$ to be sound. Similarly, we require $\mathcal{DR}$ to be performed honestly, in the sense that the adversary is not allowed to modify the algorithm DR or its outputs, as this is a necessary condition for a $\mathcal{DR}$ to be sound (or, in fact, complete). In particular, we recognize a new type of forgery introduced by the dispute resolution process, which necessitates the soundness property of $\mathcal{DR}$:

Definition 4.5. *Let Π be a USS scheme and let $\mathcal{DR}$ be a dispute resolution method for Π. We say a signature σ on a message x is an* arbiter-enabled forgery *for signer U_i if σ is not i-authentic, but* $DR((x, \sigma), U_i)$ *outputs valid.*

This leads to the following new definition of unforgeability:

Definition 4.6. *Let Π be a USS scheme and let $\mathcal{DR}$ be a dispute resolution method for Π. We say Π is $\mathcal{DR}$-unforgeable with parameters $(t, \psi_S, \psi_V, \epsilon)$ if Π is $(t, \psi_S, \psi_V, \epsilon)$-unforgeable (as in Definition 3.2) and the dispute resolution method $\mathcal{DR}$ is sound.*

We now move to a discussion of the properties of non-repudiation and transferability. As previously mentioned, both of these properties are intrinsically linked to the dispute resolution method. That is, the outcome of the dispute resolution method determines the success or failure of these attacks. In particular, we show that completeness is required to achieve both non-repudiation and transferability.

We remark that in order for the dispute resolution method to be invoked in the first place, there must be disagreement as to the validity of a given signature σ. In a repudiation attack, the dispute resolution method is necessarily invoked, as the attack relies on the signer U_i giving a *seemingly* valid signature σ to the verifier U_j and then later denying the validity of σ. Similarly, for a transferability attack, a signature σ that appears valid to U_j is transferred to and rejected by another user U_ℓ, so the dispute resolution method is again invoked. We now provide formal definitions of these two attacks.

Definition 4.7. *Let $\Pi = (\mathcal{U}, X, \Sigma, \mathsf{Gen}, \mathsf{Sign}, \mathsf{Vrfy})$ be a USS scheme with security parameter 1^k and let $\mathcal{DR}$ be a dispute resolution method for Π. Let the set $C \subseteq \mathcal{U}$ be a coalition of at most t users, and let ψ_S and ψ_V be positive integers. We define the following* signature game Repudiation$_{C,\Pi}(k)$ *with signer $U_i \in C$ and target verifier U_j satisfying $U_j \notin C$:*

1. $\mathsf{Gen}(1^k)$ *is run to obtain the pair $(\mathsf{Sign}, \mathsf{Vrfy})$.*
2. *The coalition C is given bounded access to the oracles $\mathsf{Sign}_\ell^{\mathcal{O}}(\cdot)$ and $\mathsf{Vrfy}_\ell^{\mathcal{O}}(\cdot, \cdot, U_i)$ for ℓ satisfying $U_\ell \notin C$. In particular, C is allowed a total of ψ_S and ψ_V queries to the $\mathsf{Sign}^{\mathcal{O}}$ and $\mathsf{Vrfy}^{\mathcal{O}}$ oracles, respectively. It should be noted that C has unlimited access to the signing and verification algorithms of any $U_\ell \in C$.*
3. *The coalition C outputs a signature pair (x, σ).*
4. *The output of the game is defined to be 1 if and only if the following conditions are met:*
   (a) σ *is (i, j)-acceptable, and*
   (b) *the dispute resolution method $\mathcal{DR}$ rejects σ as invalid.*

Definition 4.8. *Let $\Pi = (\mathcal{U}, X, \Sigma, \mathsf{Gen}, \mathsf{Sign}, \mathsf{Vrfy})$ be a USS scheme with security parameter 1^k and let $\mathcal{DR}$ be a dispute resolution method for Π. Let $\epsilon(k)$ be a negligible function of k. We say the combined scheme $(\Pi, \mathcal{DR})$ satisfies* non-repudiation *with parameters $(t, \psi_S, \psi_V, \epsilon)$ if for all coalitions C of at most t possibly colluding users, and for all choices of signer U_i and target verifier U_j,*

$$\Pr[\text{Repudiation}_{C,\Pi}(k) = 1] \leq \epsilon(k).$$

Theorem 4.1. *Let Π be a $(t, \psi_S, \psi_V, \epsilon)$-unforgeable USS scheme and let $\mathcal{DR}$ be a complete dispute resolution method for Π. Then $(\Pi, \mathcal{DR})$ provides non-repudiation, provided that $\mathcal{DR}$ is performed honestly.*

Proof. Assume Π does not provide non-repudiation; that is, the game Repudiation$_{C,\Pi}(k)$ outputs 1 with non-negligible probability. Suppose Repudiation$_{C,\Pi}(k)$ with signer U_i and target verifier U_j outputs 1. Then C has created an (i, j)-acceptable signature pair (x, σ), such that the dispute resolution method rejects σ as invalid.

Now, σ is either i-authentic or (i, j)-fraudulent. If σ is (i, j)-fraudulent, then Condition 4a of Definition 3.1 holds, so the output of Sig-forge$_{C,\Pi}(k)$ with target signer U_i and verifier U_j is 1. That is, Π is not $(t, \psi_S, \psi_V, \epsilon)$-unforgeable. If σ is i-authentic, then the dispute resolution method rejected an i-authentic signature and is therefore not complete. □

Definition 4.9. *Let $\Pi = (\mathcal{U}, X, \Sigma, \mathsf{Gen}, \mathsf{Sign}, \mathsf{Vrfy})$ be a USS scheme with security parameter 1^k and let $\mathcal{DR}$ be a dispute resolution method for Π. Let the set $C \subseteq \mathcal{U}$ be a coalition of at most t users, and let ψ_S and ψ_V be positive integers. We define the following signature game Non-transfer$_{C,\Pi}(k)$ with signer U_i and target verifier U_j, where $U_j \notin C$:*

1. $\mathsf{Gen}(1^k)$ *is run to obtain the pair* $(\mathsf{Sign}, \mathsf{Vrfy})$.
2. *The coalition C is given bounded access to the oracles $\mathsf{Sign}_\ell^{\mathcal{O}}(\cdot)$ and $\mathsf{Vrfy}_\ell^{\mathcal{O}}(\cdot, \cdot, U_i)$ for ℓ satisfying $U_\ell \notin C$. In particular, C is allowed a total of ψ_S and ψ_V queries to the $\mathsf{Sign}^{\mathcal{O}}$ and $\mathsf{Vrfy}^{\mathcal{O}}$ oracles, respectively. It should be noted that C has unlimited access to the signing and verification algorithms of any $U_\ell \in C$. We let $\mathcal{Q}$ denote the set of messages that the coalition submitted as queries to the oracle $\mathsf{Sign}_i^{\mathcal{O}}(\cdot)$. Note that $\mathcal{Q}$ does not contain messages submitted as queries to $\mathsf{Sign}_\ell^{\mathcal{O}}(\cdot)$ for $\ell \neq i$.*
3. *The coalition C outputs a signature pair (x, σ) satisfying $x \notin \mathcal{Q}$.*
4. *The output of the game is defined to be 1 if and only if the following conditions are met:*
   (a) *σ is (i, j)-acceptable but not (i, ℓ)-acceptable for some verifier $U_\ell \notin C$; or σ is (i, j)-acceptable and some verifier $U_\ell \in C$ invokes the dispute resolution method $\mathcal{DR}$ (regardless of whether σ is (i, ℓ)-acceptable).*
   (b) *the dispute resolution method $\mathcal{DR}$ rejects σ as invalid.*

Definition 4.10. *Let $\Pi = (\mathcal{U}, X, \Sigma, \mathsf{Gen}, \mathsf{Sign}, \mathsf{Vrfy})$ be a USS scheme with security parameter 1^k and let $\mathcal{DR}$ be a dispute resolution method for Π. Let $\epsilon(k)$ be a negligible function of k. We say the combined scheme $(\Pi, \mathcal{DR})$ satisfies transferability with parameters $(t, \psi_S, \psi_V, \epsilon)$ if for all choices of signer U_i and target verifier U_j,*
$$\Pr[\text{Non-transfer}_{C,\Pi}(k) = 1] \leq \epsilon(k).$$

Theorem 4.2. *Let Π be a $(t, \psi_S, \psi_V, \epsilon)$-unforgeable USS scheme and let $\mathcal{DR}$ be a complete dispute resolution method for Π. Then $(\Pi, \mathcal{DR})$ provides transferability, provided that $\mathcal{DR}$ is performed honestly.*

Proof. Suppose Π does not provide transferability, and assume the game Non-transfer$_{C,\Pi}(k)$ outputs 1, with signer U_i and target verifier $U_j \notin C$. Then C output a signature pair (x, σ) such that $x \notin \mathcal{Q}$, σ is (i, j)-acceptable, and the dispute resolution method rejected σ as invalid.

Now, if σ is not (i, ℓ)-acceptable for some U_ℓ, then σ must be (i, j)-fraudulent. This implies that Condition 4a of Definition 3.1 is met. That is, the output of Sig-forge$_{C,\Pi}(k)$ with target signer U_i and verifier U_j is 1, so Π is not $(t, \psi_S, \psi_V, \epsilon)$-unforgeable.

If σ is not (i, j)-fraudulent (and therefore i-authentic), then the dispute resolution method rejected an i-authentic signature and is therefore not complete. $\square$

Together, Definition 4.6 and Theorems 4.1 and 4.2 outline requirements for a USS scheme Π and a dispute resolution method $\mathcal{DR}$ to satisfy the desired properties of unforgeability, non-repudiation, and transferability. In particular, Π must be $(t, \psi_S, \psi_V, \epsilon)$-unforgeable and $\mathcal{DR}$ must be correct (under the assumption that the adversary is not allowed to modify the algorithm DR).

5   Some Examples of Dispute Resolution Processes

We define three dispute resolution methods and examine the level of trust required in each scheme.

Definition 5.1. *We have the following dispute resolution methods, assuming a disputed signature σ on message x with signer U_i:*

- Omniscient Arbiter (OA) Dispute Resolution: *Designate an arbiter equipped with all of the USS scheme set-up information. The signature σ is considered valid if the arbiter, using his knowledge of all the signing and verification algorithms, accepts the signature as authentic.*
- Verifier-equivalent Arbiter (VEA) Dispute Resolution: *Designate an arbiter equipped with his or her own verification algorithm, Vrfy$_A$, (i.e., the arbiter will be termed a glorified verifier). The arbiter tests the authenticity of the signature σ by running Vrfy$_A(x, \sigma, U_i)$; the signature is considered valid if Vrfy$_A(x, \sigma, U_i)$ outputs True.*
- Majority Vote (MV) Dispute Resolution: *Resolve disputes by having the verifiers vote on the validity of the signature σ. Each verifier is responsible for running his verification algorithm on (x, σ, U_i) and casting a valid vote if the verification algorithm outputs True and an invalid vote otherwise. The signature is considered valid if a predefined threshold of valid votes are cast; here we consider the case of a majority threshold and assume all verifiers vote.*

However we choose to define the dispute resolution method, it is necessary to determine the amount of trust placed in the arbiter(s) and incorporate this notion into the security model. In particular, we must consider the correctness of these dispute resolution methods.

In the case of OA dispute resolution, we must completely trust the arbiter, as he has all the necessary information to sign and verify documents on behalf of other users. That is, a USS scheme Π with OA dispute resolution clearly cannot satisfy Definition 4.6 unless the arbiter is honest. Moreover, provided that the arbiter is honest, this dispute resolution method is both sound and complete, as the arbiter will be able to determine the authenticity of a given signature and behave appropriately.

In MV and VEA dispute resolution, we can once again achieve correctness by assuming the complete honesty of a majority of verifiers or, respectively, the arbiter. Achieving soundness and completeness is not as clear if we weaken this trust requirement, however. Suppose we establish VEA dispute resolution and we allow the arbiter to be a colluding member of a given coalition; we will argue that soundness is no longer guaranteed.

In the typical VEA setup of current literature [7,10,12], the arbiter is assumed to be a glorified verifier, with the same type of keying information as an arbitrary verifier. The arbiter is assumed to follow the rules of the dispute resolution method honestly and is otherwise treated as a normal verifier in the context of the security model, i.e., he is allowed to be dishonest otherwise. We refer to this set of trust assumptions as *standard trust assumptions*.

We argue that the arbiter's distinct role in the dispute resolution method necessitates a more careful study of the arbiter, and that treating the arbiter as a normal verifier in the context of the security model is insufficient. While certainly an arbiter that is dishonest during dispute resolution can cause a fraudulent signature to be deemed valid, we cannot allow the arbiter to be dishonest before dispute resolution either, contrary to the claims of [10,12]. The case of MV may be viewed as a generalized version of VEA dispute resolution and the security results are similar.

In the following theorem, we demonstrate the existence of an arbiter-enabled forgery in the VEA and MV dispute resolution methods, if we assume that the arbiter(s) may be dishonest prior to dispute resolution. Thus these methods do not achieve soundness under the standard trust assumptions.

Theorem 5.1. *Let Π be a USS scheme and let $\mathcal{DR}$ be a VEA (respectively, MV) dispute resolution method for Π. Suppose Π is $\mathcal{DR}$-unforgeable. Then the arbiter $\mathcal{A}$ is not a member of C (respectively, a majority of verifiers are not in C).*

Proof. In both cases, we assume the dispute resolution process itself is performed honestly, as otherwise Π clearly fails to have sound dispute resolution. (For MV dispute resolution, it suffices to assume the dispute resolution process is performed honestly by a majority of the verifiers.)

We proceed with VEA dispute resolution. By definition, any $(i, \mathcal{A})$-acceptable signature will be accepted by the dispute resolution method as a signature from U_i. In particular, this implies any $(i, \mathcal{A})$-fraudulent signature will be accepted by the dispute resolution method. For any message x, if $\mathcal{A} \in C$, then C can create a signature σ on x that is $(i, \mathcal{A})$-fraudulent. This signature σ is not i-authentic, but would be accepted by the dispute resolution method, thereby violating soundness.

Similarly, in the case of MV dispute resolution, a group C of dishonest verifiers can, for any message x, create a signature σ on x such that σ is (i, ℓ)-fraudulent for any $U_\ell \in C$. If C contains a majority of verifiers, the signature σ would pass the dispute resolution process and be declared a valid signature from U_i, thereby violating soundness. □

Theorem 5.1 indicates that a cheating arbiter $\mathcal{A}$ (respectively, a collusion of a majority of verifiers) can successfully forge an (i, j)-fraudulent signature that will be accepted by the dispute resolution method for any cooperating user U_j. Hence, VEA and MV dispute resolution do not protect the signer against dishonest arbiters, since arbiter-enabled forgeries exist.

We remark that completeness in the VEA and MV methods is guaranteed, provided that the dispute resolution process itself is performed honestly. Thus, by Theorem 4.1, a $(t, \psi_S, \psi_V, \epsilon)$-USS scheme Π with VEA or MV dispute resolution provides non-repudiation under the standard trust assumptions. Transferability, as noted in Theorem 4.2, also follows under the standard trust assumptions.

That is, the VEA and MV methods do not require trust in the arbiter(s) prior to dispute resolution in order to achieve non-repudiation and transferability. As seen above, however, the VEA and MV methods do require the arbiter(s) to be honest prior to dispute resolution in order to achieve soundness. In this sense, we see that VEA and MV dispute resolution provide similar *verifier* security to trusted OA dispute resolution, but fail to provide similar *signer* security.

6   Comparison with Existing Models

Our model differs from those in the existing literature in its careful treatment of i-authentic and (i, j)-fraudulent signatures. In comparison to other works, our approach is most similar to that of Shikata et al. [12], whose model is also designed as an extension of traditional public-key signature security notions. We compare our model with [12] in Section 6.1.

The Hara et al. [7] model for unconditionally secure blind signatures is essentially the same as the Shikata et al. model with an added blindness condition. Hara et al. separate the unforgeability definition of [12] into a weaker notion of unforgeability and an additional non-repudiation requirement. The non-repudiation requirement actually treats more cases than a simple non-repudiation attack (as the success of the attack is not dependent on dispute resolution), so the reason for this separation is unclear. The authors of [7] also allow the signer to be the target verifier, which was not explicitly allowed in the Shikata et al. model, and so add a separate unforgeability definition for this case.

The models of Hanaoka et al. [5,6] and Safavi-Naini et al. [10] are based on security notions from message authentication codes (MACs). Hanaoka et al. treat only a limited attack scenario (which is covered by our model), including *impersonation*, *substitution*, and *transfer with a trap*, and do not include a verification oracle. Safavi-Naini et al. treat a similar range of attacks as our model, specified through *denial*, *spoofing*, and *framing* attacks, and allow both signature and verification oracles. It is unclear whether Safavi-Naini et al. meant to ensure strong unforgeability, as the relationship between successful forgeries and oracle queries is unspecified. Furthermore, our model is more concise, as the denial attack covers a signer trying to repudiate a signature, whereas we show that it is unnecessary to treat non-repudiation as a separate part of an unforgeability definition. In addition, not all attack scenarios included in our definition are covered by the Safavi-Naini et al. model. For instance, the attack consisting of signer $U_i \in C$ with target verifier U_j, where C creates an (i,j)-fraudulent signature, is not considered. The Safavi-Naini et al. model considers this scenario only in the case where an arbiter is involved and rejects the signature (i.e. a denial attack). In certain applications (e.g., e-cash) we do not want the signer to be able to create an (i,j)-fraudulent signature, regardless of whether a dispute resolution mechanism is invoked.

6.1   Comparison with the Model of Shikata et al.

In this section, we discuss several aspects of the model of Shikata et al. [12] and how our approach differs from theirs.

1. The model in [12] is limited to a single-signer scenario. We consider a more general model in which any participant can be a signer.
2. In Definition 2 of [12], a signed message (x, σ) is defined to be *valid* if it was created using the signer's signing algorithm. Then, in their "Requirement 1," which includes notions for verifiability, dispute resolution, and unforgeability, it is stated that (x, σ) is valid if and only if U_j's verification algorithm outputs *True* when given (x, σ) as input. This requirement is problematic, since U_j can use knowledge of his verification algorithm to find a pair (x, σ) that has output *True*; such a pair is then "valid." However, this means that a receiver can create valid signatures, and consequently the signature scheme does not provide unforgeability. Shikata et al. relax this condition in Requirement 2 by allowing a small error probability that an "invalid" signature will be accepted by a given verifier. However, this does not rectify the aforementioned problem, as the probability space in this definition is unspecified.
3. The definitions of *existential forgery* and *existential acceptance forgery* (Definitions 3 and 4, respectively) are rather complicated. It seems that the notion of "existential forgery" corresponds to our definition of an *i-authentic signature*. The coalition that creates this signature should not include U_i. The notion of "existential acceptance forgery" apparently is dependent upon the coalition that creates it. If U_i is in the coalition, then an existential acceptance forgery would most naturally coincide with our definition of an (i,j)-*fraudulent signature*. If U_i is not in the coalition, then it would more likely mean an (i,j)-*acceptable signature*. In each case, the coalition creating

the signature should not include U_j. These definitions are a bit confusing, and we believe that the concepts of authentic, acceptable, and fraudulent signatures are helpful in phrasing clear and concise definitions.

4. In Theorem 2 of [12], it is stated without proof that a signature scheme that is "existentially acceptance unforgeable" is necessarily "existentially unforgeable." Roughly speaking, this is logically equivalent to the statement that an adversary that can create an existential forgery can also create an existential acceptance forgery. This statement seems rather obvious, but we need to also consider the coalitions that are creating these signatures. The adversary creating the existential forgery (i.e., an i-authentic signature) could be any coalition C that does not include U_i. An i-authentic signature is an existential acceptance forgery for any user $U_j \notin C \cup \{U_i\}$. However, a problem arises if C consists of all users except for U_i. In this situation, an i-authentic signature created by C is not an existential acceptance forgery for any user. This situation is not accounted for in Theorem 2 of [12].

5. Notwithstanding the previous points, the definition of "strong security" in [12] (Definition 9) is very similar to our properties 4a and 4b of Definition 3.1, except that Definition 9 only covers existential acceptance forgeries. In order to compare our model with [12], we consider the following three attack scenarios, where U_i denotes the signer and U_j denotes a verifier:

case A. Neither U_i nor U_j is in the coalition C, and C creates an (i,j)-fraudulent signature.

case B. U_i is not in the coalition C, and C creates an i-authentic signature.

case C. $U_i \in C$, $U_j \notin C$, and C creates an (i,j)-fraudulent signature.

In our security definition (Definition 3.1), property 4a is equivalent to the union of case A and case C, and property 4b is equivalent to case B. Now, Definition 9 in [12] considers two attacks: property 1) is the union of cases A and B, but does not include the case where there is no target verifier, as discussed in the previous point; and property 2) is case C.

6. Finally, we give a more complete treatment of dispute resolution than is presented in [12].

7   Construction

Current literature favors constructions using multivariate polynomials. We consider the security of the construction from Hanaoka et al. [5] in our security model.

7.1   General Scheme Outline

Key Pair Generation. Let $\mathbb{F}_q$ be a finite field with q elements such that $q \geq n$. The TA picks $v_1, \ldots, v_n \in \mathbb{F}_q^\omega$ uniformly at random for users $U_1, \ldots U_n$, respectively. For technical reasons, we assume the n elements $v_1, \ldots v_n \in \mathbb{F}_q^\omega$ satisfy the additional property that for any subset of size $\omega + 1$, the corresponding subset of size $\omega + 1$ formed from the new vectors $[1, v_1], \ldots, [1, v_n] \in \mathbb{F}_q^{\omega+1}$ is a linearly independent set.

The TA constructs the polynomial $F(x, y_1, \ldots, y_\omega, z)$ as

$$F(x, y_1, \ldots, y_\omega, z) = \sum_{i=0}^{n-1} \sum_{k=0}^{\psi} a_{i0k} x^i z^k + \sum_{i=0}^{n-1} \sum_{j=1}^{\omega} \sum_{k=0}^{\psi} a_{ijk} x^i y_j z^k,$$

where the coefficients $a_{ijk} \in \mathbb{F}_q$ are chosen uniformly at random.

For each user U_ζ for $1 \leq \zeta \leq n$, the TA computes the signing key $s_\zeta(y_1, \ldots, y_\omega, z) = F(U_\zeta, y_1, \ldots, y_\omega, z)$ and the verification key $\tilde{v}_\zeta(x, z) = F(x, v_\zeta, z)$. It is assumed the TA can communicate with the users via secure channels and deletes the information afterwards.

Signature Generation and Verification. For a message $m \in \mathbb{F}_q$, U_ζ generates a signature σ by

$$\sigma(y_1, \ldots, y_\omega) = s_\zeta(y_1, \ldots, y_\omega, m).$$

To verify a signature pair (m, σ) from U_ζ, a user U_ν checks that

$$\sigma(v_\nu) = \tilde{v}_\nu(U_\zeta, m).$$

7.2   Security Results

We consider the game $\text{Sig-forge}_{C,\Pi}(k)$ and calculate the probability that the output is 1. In particular, we consider the probability that the coalition C produces a signature pair (x, σ) satisfying Conditions 4a and 4b of Definition 3.1 separately. Here we set $t = \omega$ and $\psi_S = (n - \omega)\psi$, where ψ is the total number of $\text{Sign}_\ell^{\mathcal{O}}$ oracle queries for each user $U_\ell \notin C$. That is, we allow C to have at most ω members and to have access to ψ sample signatures from each user $U_\ell \notin C$. In addition, C has access to ψ_F $\text{Vrfy}^{\mathcal{O}}$ queries.

The proof for the following result appears in the full version of our paper [15].

Theorem 7.1. *Under the above assumptions, C outputs a signature pair (x, σ) in the game $\text{Sig-forge}_{C,\Pi}(k)$ of Definition 3.1 satisfying Condition 4a with probability at most $\frac{1}{q - \psi_F - 1}$ and Condition 4b with probability at most $\frac{1}{q - \psi_F}$.*

8   Conclusion

We have presented a new security model for unconditionally secure signature schemes, one which fully treats the implications of having multiple verification algorithms. In particular, we have given a formal discussion of dispute resolution, a necessary component of any USS scheme, and analyzed the effect of dispute resolution on unforgeability. We have provided formal definitions of non-repudiation and transferability, and given sufficient conditions for a USS scheme to satisfy these properties. Moreover, we have analyzed the trust assumptions required in typical examples of dispute resolution. Finally, we have given the results of an analysis of Hanaoka et al.'s construction [5] in our security model.

References

1. Brickell, E., Stinson, D.: Authentication Codes with Multiple Arbiters. In: Günther, C.G. (ed.) EUROCRYPT 1988. LNCS, vol. 330, pp. 51–55. Springer, Heidelberg (1988)
2. Chaum, D., Roijakkers, S.: Unconditionally Secure Digital Signatures. In: Menezes, A., Vanstone, S.A. (eds.) CRYPTO 1990. LNCS, vol. 537, pp. 206–214. Springer, Heidelberg (1991)
3. Desmedt, Y., Yung, M.: Arbitrated Unconditionally Secure Authentication Can Be Unconditionally Protected against Arbiter's Attacks. In: Menezes, A., Vanstone, S.A. (eds.) CRYPTO 1990. LNCS, vol. 537, pp. 177–188. Springer, Heidelberg (1991)
4. Desmedt, Y., Frankl, Y., Yung, M.: Multi-receiver / Multi-sender Network Security: Efficient Authenticated Multicast / Feedback. In: INFOCOM 1992, pp. 2045–2054 (1992)
5. Hanaoka, G., Shikata, J., Zheng, Y., Imai, H.: Unconditionally Secure Digital Signature Schemes Admitting Transferability. In: Okamoto, T. (ed.) ASIACRYPT 2000. LNCS, vol. 1976, pp. 130–142. Springer, Heidelberg (2000)
6. Hanaoka, G., Shikata, J., Zheng, Y., Imai, H.: Efficient and Unconditionally Secure Digital Signatures and a Security Analysis of a Multireceiver Authentication Code. In: Naccache, D., Paillier, P. (eds.) PKC 2002. LNCS, vol. 2274, pp. 64–79. Springer, Heidelberg (2002)
7. Hara, Y., Seito, T., Shikata, J., Matsumoto, T.: Unconditionally Secure Blind Signatures. In: Desmedt, Y. (ed.) ICITS 2007. LNCS, vol. 4883, pp. 23–43. Springer, Heidelberg (2009)
8. Johansson, T.: On the Construction of Perfect Authentication Codes that Permit Arbitration. In: Stinson, D.R. (ed.) CRYPTO 1993. LNCS, vol. 773, pp. 343–354. Springer, Heidelberg (1994)
9. Johansson, T.: Further Results on Asymmetric Authentication Schemes. Information and Computation 151, 100–133 (1999)
10. Safavi–Naini, R., McAven, L., Yung, M.: General Group Authentication Codes and Their Relation to "Unconditionally-Secure Signatures". In: Bao, F., Deng, R., Zhou, J. (eds.) PKC 2004. LNCS, vol. 2947, pp. 231–247. Springer, Heidelberg (2004)
11. Safavi-Naini, R., Wang, H.: Broadcast Authentication in Group Communication. In: Lam, K.-Y., Okamoto, E., Xing, C. (eds.) ASIACRYPT 1999. LNCS, vol. 1716, pp. 399–412. Springer, Heidelberg (1999)
12. Shikata, J., Hanaoka, G., Zheng, Y., Imai, H.: Security Notions for Unconditionally Secure Signature Schemes. In: Knudsen, L.R. (ed.) EUROCRYPT 2002. LNCS, vol. 2332, pp. 434–449. Springer, Heidelberg (2002)
13. Simmons, G.: Message Authentication with Arbitration of Transmitter/Receiver Disputes. In: Price, W.L., Chaum, D. (eds.) EUROCRYPT 1987. LNCS, vol. 304, pp. 151–165. Springer, Heidelberg (1988)
14. Simmons, G.: A Cartesian Product Construction for Unconditionally Secure Authentication Codes that Permit Arbitration. J. Cryptology 2, 77–104 (1990)
15. Swanson, C., Stinson, D.: Unconditionally Secure Signature Schemes Revisited. Full version to appear in IACR eprint archive http://eprint.iacr.org/

Bell Inequalities: What Do We Know about Them and Why Should Cryptographers Care?⋆
(Invited Talk)

Ronald de Wolf

CWI and University of Amsterdam, The Netherlands

Abstract. Bell inequalities are linear constraints on the set of output-probabilities of multi-player protocols that are satisfied by all classical (i.e., local realist) protocols, but that can be violated by quantum protocols using entanglement. This talk will survey the history and present state of knowledge regarding such inequalities, with a view to their application in (quantum) cryptography.

1 Entanglement

One of the most striking features of quantum mechanics is the fact that *entangled* particles exhibit correlations that cannot be reproduced or explained by classical physics (i.e., by "local hidden-variable theories"). This was first discovered by Bell [1] in response to Einstein-Podolsky-Rosen's challenge to the completeness of quantum mechanics [2]. Experimental realization of such correlations is the strongest proof we have that nature does not behave according to classical physics—one of the deepest and most puzzling results to have come out of all of science. Many such experiments have been done. All behave in accordance with quantum predictions, though so far none has closed all "loopholes" that would allow some (usually very contrived) classical explanation of the observations based on imperfect behavior of, for instance, the photon detectors used.

2 Bell Inequalities

We will restrict attention to two-player scenarios. For our purposes, it is convenient to cast Bell inequalities as statements about two-player *games*. In such a game G, the two players (call them Alice and Bob) receive inputs x and y, respectively, distributed according to some known joint probability distribution π. Alice and Bob produce outputs a and b, respectively, and there is a predicate V (possibly randomized) to determine whether an output pair a, b wins the game given input pair x, y.

A protocol describes what Alice and Bob do given their respective inputs. The players are assumed to be spatially separated and hence cannot communicate

---

⋆ Supported by a Vidi grant from NWO, and EU-grant QCS.

during the course of the game. Classical players can start the game with shared randomness, while quantum players can start with a shared entangled state, for instance some EPR pairs. The protocol determines, for each input pair x, y, a probability distribution $P(ab|xy)$ on the various possible output pairs. We will use P to denote both a protocol and its associated set of output distributions. The *winning probability* of a protocol P is

$$w(P, G) = \sum_{x,y,a,b} \pi(x, y) P(ab|xy) V(ab|xy).$$

A *Bell inequality* is the statement that $w(P, G) \leq w$ for all classical protocols P. The tightest possible Bell inequality for the game G has of course $w = \max_{\text{classical } P} w(P, G)$. A quantum protocol whose output probabilities satisfy $W(P, G) > w$, is said to *violate* this Bell inequality—it achieves something that no classical protocol can achieve.

Most of the talk will survey the main things we know about Bell inequalities:

- Even one or a few EPR pairs can already give substantial Bell inequality violations, for instance in the CHSH game [3] and the magic square game [4].
- For XOR games, where a and b are one bit each, and the winning predicate depends only on the XOR $a \oplus b$, the maximal Bell inequality violation is bounded by a constant independent of how much entanglement the quantum players use [5]. This is a consequence of Grothendieck's inequality.
- With non-binary outputs and large entangled states, the Bell inequality violation can be unbounded for games that are not XOR-games. In particular, there exists a game where each player has n possible outputs, the best classical winning probability is roughly $1/n$, and the best quantum winning probability is roughly $1/(\log n)^2$, achieved using a maximally entangled state of local dimension n [6]. Such a separation is close to best-possible when measured in terms of the local dimension of the entangled state [7], as well as the number of outputs per player [8].
- There are games where maximally entangled states (e.g., arbitrarily many EPR pairs) do not yield any advantage over classical protocols, while some specific non-maximally entangled state gives huge advantage [8,9]. This refutes the intuition that maximally entangled states are somehow the "best" or "strongest" entangled states in our scenario.

3   Cryptography

Entanglement often plays a destructive role in quantum cryptography. For instance it can be used to break all quantum protocols for *bit commitment* [10,11], even ones that were earlier claimed to be perfectly secure [12] (and which indeed are secure in the absence of entanglement). A more recent example is the use of entanglement to break all possible schemes for *position-based cryptography* [13].

However, there are also some positive uses of entanglement (and Bell inequalities) in cryptography. For example, Ekert's scheme [14] distributes EPR pairs between Alice and Bob, and then tests a random subset of them to ensure that Alice and Bob really share states that are sufficiently close to EPR pairs (i.e., that the eavesdropper hasn't tampered with them too much). One way to test this is by implementing a Bell inequality violation: for example if Alice and Bob do not share close-to-perfect EPR pairs, then they won't be able to maximally violate the CHSH inequality. Once this test is passed, the shared EPR pairs can be measured to yield shared random bits that are unknown to the eavesdropper. Other applications of Bell inequalities are device-independent cryptography [15] (where Alice and Bob don't trust their own measuring devices), testing the dimension of Hilbert spaces [16], and the analysis of parallel repetition.

References

1. Bell, J.S.: On the Einstein-Podolsky-Rosen paradox. Physics 1, 195–200 (1964)
2. Einstein, A., Podolsky, B., Rosen, N.: Can quantum-mechanical description of physical reality be considered complete? Physical Review 47, 777–780 (1935)
3. Clauser, J.F., Horne, M.A., Shimony, A., Holt, R.A.: Proposed experiment to test local hidden-variable theories. Physical Review Letters 23(15), 880–884 (1969)
4. Aravind, P.K.: A simple demonstration of Bell theorem involving two observers and no probabilities or inequalities. quant-ph/0206070 (2002)
5. Cleve, R., Høyer, P., Toner, B., Watrous, J.: Consequences and limits of nonlocal strategies. In: Proceedings of 19th IEEE CCC, pp. 236–249 (2004)
6. Buhrman, H., Regev, O., Scarpa, G., de Wolf, R.: Near-optimal and explicit Bell inequality violations. In: Proceedings of 26th IEEE CCC (2011); quant-ph/0608146
7. Junge, M., Palazuelos, C., Pérez-García, D., Villanueva, I., Wolf, M.: Unbounded violations of bipartite Bell inequalities via Operator Space theory. Communications in Mathematical Physics 300(3), 715–739 (2010); Shorter version appeared in PRL 104:170405
8. Junge, M., Palazuelos, C.: Large violation of Bell inequalities with low entanglement. Communications in Mathematical Physics (2010)
9. Regev, O.: Bell violations through independent bases games. arXiv:1101.0576 (January 3, 2011)
10. Mayers, D.: Unconditionally secure quantum bit commitment is impossible. Physical Review Letters 78, 3414–3417 (1997); quant-ph/9605044
11. Lo, H.K., Chau, H.F.: Is quantum bit commitment really possible? Physical Review Letters 78, 3410 (1997); quant-ph/9603004
12. Brassard, G., Crépeau, C., Jozsa, R., Langlois, D.: A quantum bit commitment scheme provably unbreakable by both parties. In: Proceedings of 34th IEEE FOCS, pp. 362–371 (1993)
13. Buhrman, H., Chandran, N., Fehr, S., Gelles, R., Goyal, V., Ostrovsky, R., Schaffner, C.: Position-based quantum cryptography: Impossibility and constructions. arXiv:1009.2490 (September 13, 2010)
14. Ekert, A.: Quantum cryptography based on Bell's theorem. Physical Review Letters 67, 661–663 (1991)
15. Acin, A., Brunner, N., Gisin, N., Massar, S., Pironio, S., Scarani, V.: Device-independent security of quantum cryptography against collective attacks. Physical Review Letters 98, 230501 (2008)
16. Brunner, N., Pironio, S., Acin, A., Gisin, N., Méthot, A., Scarani, V.: Testing the dimension of Hilbert spaces. Physical Review Letters 100(21), 210503 (2008)

Efficient Reductions for Non-signaling Cryptographic Primitives

Nico Döttling, Daniel Kraschewski, and Jörn Müller-Quade

Institute of Cryptography and Security, Faculty of Informatics,
Karlsruhe Institute of Technology, Germany
{doettling,kraschewski,mueller-quade}@kit.edu

Abstract. Tamper-proof devices, especially *one-time memories* (OTMs), are very powerful primitives. They can, e.g., implement one-time programs, i.e. circuits that can be evaluated only once. Furthermore they exhibit a non-signaling nature: The issuer of the device cannot tell whether the receiver interacted with the device. However, due to this non-signaling property, it is non-trivial to obtain protocols with a clear defined end from such devices. The main contribution of this paper is a significant improvement of previous reductions from oblivious transfer to OTMs. The most extreme primitive with respect to non-signaling is the so called *non-local box* (NL-Box), where neither the sender nor the receiver get to know if the respective other party has interacted with the NL-Box. We show that OTMs can securely be implemented from NL-Boxes. To the best of our knowledge this is the first protocol to cancel the non-signaling property of an NL-Box for *exactly one* party.

Keywords: Statistical Security, Efficient Reductions, One-Time Memories, Non-local Boxes.

1 Introduction

Tamper-proof hardware tokens, in particular *one-time memories* (OTMs), have turned out as very useful primitives in cryptography, as they allow for information-theoretically secure protocols that are universally composable. Beyond that, they can be employed for one-time programs, i.e. circuits that can be evaluated only once. An interesting feature of such hardware tokens is that the hardware vendor is completely oblivious of when the receiver of a token interacts with it. Following terms of quantum physics, we say that OTMs are "non-signaling" for the sender. However, this property is a mixed blessing. Sophisticated protocol techniques are needed, when one wants to implement functionalities with well-defined end for all participants.

In this paper we contribute a significant improvement on previous reducibility results between OTMs (which can be seen as a non-signaling version of oblivious transfer that does not let the sender learn when the receiver did input his choice bit) and Ext-OTMs (which additionally output an auxiliary string that may serve as a proof that the receiver has interacted with the hardware token). The new protocol has a linear complexity and hence is asymptotically optimal.

S. Fehr (Ed.): ICITS 2011, LNCS 6673, pp. 120–137, 2011.

Another non-signaling primitive we study are *non-local boxes* (NL-Boxes). These are a concept from physics which in an abstract way captures the properties of entanglement and local measurements[1]. Due to the non-signaling condition of local measurements *neither* party can be sure that the other party already provided input to the NL-Box. As mentioned above, this necessitates sophisticated protocol techniques, when one wants to implement functionalities with well-defined end from NL-Boxes. We show how an ideal OTM-functionality can be reduced to NL-Boxes. To the best of our knowledge we provide the first protocol that abrogates the non-signaling property of an NL-Box for *exactly one* party, while non-signaling is still granted for the other party.

1.1 Related Work

Recently, [GKR08] introduced the notion of one-time programs. Such programs can be executed only on one single input, which is chosen at runtime. The non-interactivity of one-time programs is attained by the use of *one-time memory* devices (OTMs). The intuition behind such an OTM is a hardware token with two values stored on it, such that after one value has been read out the other one becomes unaccessible. Hence OTMs are somehow a natural non-interactive variant of $\binom{2}{1}$-OT [EGL85]: While in the OT-functionality the sender gets informed whether the receiver provided his choice bit to the primitive or not, OTMs do not provide any well defined moment of protocol termination to the sender. In [GIS+10] it was shown that a protocol from [BCS96], which implements String-OT from Bit-OT in a non-interactive way, can be adapted to implement String-OTMs from Bit-OTMs. Another contribution of [GIS+10] is the construction of so-called Ext-OTMs, which comprise the same functionality as OTMs, but additionally take an auxiliary input string from the sender and output this string upon input of the receiver's choice bit. Ext-OTMs are of particular interest, as the receiver now can easily prove (by announcing the auxiliary string) that his input is fixed.

In [WW05] *non-local boxes* (NL-Boxes), a somewhat artificial primitive arising from the study of non-locality in quantum systems [PR94], were used to construct a non-interactive protocol for OT. NL-Boxes are two-party primitives that take input $x, y \in \{0, 1\}$ and produce random output $a, b \in \{0, 1\}$ with $x \wedge y = a \oplus b$, where (x, a) is Alice's input-output tuple and (y, b) is Bob's input-output tuple. A crucial feature is that NL-Boxes are non-signaling: Whenever a party provides its input bit, the according output bit is generated immediately. So NL-Boxes go a step further than OTMs in matters of keeping secret the moment of protocol termination.

It was noticed by [BCU+06] and independently by [SGP06] that the protocol for OT from NL-Boxes in [WW05] is not composable unless the protocol parties are notified about the NL-Box inputs of each other, what would be a direct contradiction to the non-signaling property. Still, [BCU+06] provided an

---

[1] Actually, NL-Boxes are an over-idealization, which cannot be implemented by quantum measurements [PR94].

alternative protocol for OT from NL-Boxes. This protocol ensures that no party can delay its input beyond the moment of the other party's output, but needs several rounds of interaction between the sender and the receiver of the OT.

1.2   Our Contribution

We give a new construction for Ext-OTMs from OTMs, which is more efficient than that of [GIS+10]. Thereby we achieve asymptotic efficient String-OT from Bit-OTMs (via Ext-OTMs), using only a linear number (in the string length) of Bit-OTMs. This can be considered an optimal result, as String-OT obviously cannot be implemented from a sub-linear number of Bit-OTMs. In contrast, the original construction of [GIS+10] has a polynomial reduction factor of much higher degree. Additionally, by similar techniques we implement OTMs from NL-Boxes. To the best of our knowledge we give the first protocol for OTMs from NL-Boxes in the literature. We also argue that NL-Boxes cannot be implemented from OTMs, which in turn cannot be implemented from OT. Conclusively, this provides a strict hierarchy of NL-Boxes, OTMs and OT.

For our reduction of Ext-OTM to OTM we develop a new information-theoretic tool, which we call (C, ρ)-All-Or-Nothing matrices and that might be of independent interest. These matrices are an advancement over the zizag matrices introduced in [BCS96], as they can be used to disguise random codewords from linear codes instead of only random bit-strings. We also show that (C, ρ)-All-Or-Nothing matrices can be generated probabilistically, using a very simple and efficient algorithm.

2   Preliminaries

2.1   Framework

We state and prove our results in the Universal-Composability (UC) framework of [Can01]. In this framework security is defined by comparison of an *ideal model* and a *real model*. The protocol of interest is running in the latter, where an adversary $\mathcal{A}$ coordinates the behavior of all corrupted parties. In the ideal model, which is secure by definition, an ideal functionality $\mathcal{F}$ implements the desired protocol task and a simulator $\mathcal{S}$ tries to mimic the actions of $\mathcal{A}$. An environment $\mathcal{Z}$ is plugged either to the ideal or the real model and has to guess, which model it is actually plugged to. When $\mathcal{Z}$ cannot distinguish between ideal and real model, the protocol is considered secure.

2.2   Linear Codes

For our constructions, we need certain results from coding theory. Specifically, there exists an explicit family of binary linear codes $\{C_n\}$ of constant rate R arbitrarily close to 1 that can efficiently correct an α-fraction of errors, for a constant $\alpha > 0$ [SS96, Zém01]. Moreover, for all constants $l_0 \in \mathbb{N}$ and $0 < R < 1$, there exists an explicit family of linear codes $\{C_n\}$ over $\mathbb{F}_{2^l}$ with $l > l_0$, such that $\{C_n\}$ has rate $\geq R$ and it can efficiently correct an α-fraction of errors for a constant α [GI05]. Such a code can also efficiently correct at least an α-fraction of erasures for trivial reasons.

2.3   Notations

We will use the notation $[n] = \{1, \ldots, n\}$. We will generally identify bits $b \in \{0, 1\}$ with elements of the finite field $\mathbb{F}_2$, thus we will use $+$ instead of $\oplus$ and $\cdot$ instead of $\wedge$. If $I \subseteq [n]$ and $x \in \mathbb{F}_q^n$, we will use the notation x_I for the vector $(x_i)_{i \in I} \in \mathbb{F}_q^{|I|}$. Similarly, if $M \in \mathbb{F}_q^{n \times m}$, M_I denotes the matrix that consists of the rows of M whose index is in I. For two strings s_1 and s_2, we denote the concatenation of s_1 and s_2 by $s_1 \| s_2$.

3   One-Time-Memories and Non-local Boxes

We say that a cryptographic primitive $\mathcal{F}$ is signaling for a party P_i, if P_i is notified each time another party provides input to $\mathcal{F}$. The well-known Oblivious Transfer (OT) [Rab81, EGL85] (Figure 1) obviously enjoys this feature. On the other hand, we shall call primitives that lack this feature non-signaling for P_i.

Functionality $\mathcal{F}^{\mathrm{OT}}$

Parametrized by a parameter l.

Send Upon receiving a message $(\mathbf{send}, \mathrm{sid}, P_i, P_j, (s^{(0)}, s^{(1)}))$ with $(s^{(0)}, s^{(1)}) \in \{0, 1\}^l \times \{0, 1\}^l$ from party P_i, go to state **ready** and store $(s^{(0)}, s^{(1)})$. Send $(\mathbf{ready}, \mathrm{sid}, P_i, P_j)$ to party P_j.

Choice Upon receiving a message $(\mathbf{choice}, \mathrm{sid}, P_i, P_j, x)$ with $x \in \{0, 1\}$ from P_j, check if current state is **ready**. If so, send $(\mathbf{out}, \mathrm{sid}, P_i, P_j, s^{(x)})$ to P_j and send $(\mathbf{notify}, \mathrm{sid}, P_i, P_j)$ to P_i. Go to state **dead**.

Fig. 1. The Oblivious-Transfer Functionality

One-Time-Memories (OTM) [GKR08, GIS⁺10] (Figure 2) are cryptographic primitives that model tamper-proof memory devices, in which a sender can store two strings and send the device to a receiver. In their functionality, OTMs resemble OT-primitive, with just a slight difference.

An l-Bit-String-OTM stores 2 strings $s^{(0)}$ and $s^{(1)}$ of length l. When queried with a choice-bit x, the OTM outputs $s^{(x)}$ and erases its contents. Unlike OT, for which interactive protocols exist, OTM does not notify its sender that it is being queried by the receiver. Thus, OTM is a non-signaling primitive for the sender. Moreover, OTMs are unrevocable, as we think of the hardware device locally present at the receiver. Once sent by its sender, the receiver can choose to provide its input to the primitive arbitrarily late.

OTMs were introduced by [GKR08] to implement a cryptographic primitive called *one-time programs* (OTPs). The OTP functionality takes a function description from its sender and allows its receiver to evaluate this function on exactly one input. Moreover, the receiver's query is non-signaling for the sender. The construction of [GKR08] is non-interactive, but it assumes that the sender of the OTP is trusted and it relies on additional computational assumptions.

Functionality $\mathcal{F}^{\mathrm{OTM}}$

Parametrized by a parameter l.

Creation Upon receiving a message (create,sid,P_i,P_j,($s^{(0)}, s^{(1)}$)) with ($s^{(0)}, s^{(1)}$) $\in$ $\{0, 1\}^l \times \{0, 1\}^l$ from party P_i, go to state **ready** and store ($s^{(0)}, s^{(1)}$). Send (ready,sid,P_i,P_j) to party P_j.

Choice Upon receiving a message (choice,sid,P_i,P_j,x) with $x \in \{0, 1\}$ from P_j, check if current state is **ready**. If so, send (out,sid,P_i,P_j,$s^{(x)}$) to P_j and go to state **dead**.

Fig. 2. The One-Time-Memory Functionality

Subsequently, [GIS+10] showed that *trusted* one-time programs can be implemented using Bit-OTMs alone (Bit-OTMs store strings of length 1). A trusted one-time program is guaranteed to compute a predefined function of the untrusted sender's secret input and the receiver's input. Moreover, the construction of [GIS+10] is unconditionally secure and non-interactive. An important building-block in [GIS+10] is the Extended-One-Time-Memory (Ext-OTM) functionality (Figure 3). Ext-OTM comprises the same functionality as OTM, but it takes, additionally to the strings $s^{(0)}$ and $s^{(1)}$, an auxiliary input string r from its sender. When queried by the receiver with a choice-bit x, it outputs $(s^{(x)}, r)$. An important property of this primitive is that the string r, which the receiver gets, is independent of his choice-bit x. The reduction of Ext-OTM to OTM given in [GIS+10] is non-trivial. The trivial approach of using a single OTM with sender-input $((s^{(0)}, r), (s^{(1)}, r))$ is insecure, as a corrupted sender is not bound to use the same r for both inputs.

[GIS+10] gives a very simple implementation of OT from Ext-OTM. The sender chooses an auxiliary string r of length n (statistical security parameter) uniformly at random and inputs $((s^{(0)}, s^{(1)}), r)$ into Ext-OTM. To prove that he has already queried Ext-OTM, the receiver sends r to the sender. A cheating receiver has only negligible chance of guessing r correctly, thus this protocol securely implements OT. Hence, the signaling property of OT is enforced by sending the auxiliary string r.

While OTMs are non-signaling only for its sender, there are two-party primitives that are non-signaling for both parties. The Non-local Box (NL-Box) primitive [PR94, WW05] falls in this category (Figure 4). An NL-Box has the following

---

Functionality $\mathcal{F}^{\text{Ext}-\text{OTM}}$

Parametrized by parameters l and m.

Creation   Upon receiving a message $(\texttt{create},\text{sid},P_i,P_j,((s^{(0)},s^{(1)}),r))$ with $(s^{(0)},s^{(1)}) \in \{0,1\}^l \times \{0,1\}^l$ and $r \in \{0,1\}^m$ from party P_i, go to state **ready** and store $(s^{(0)},s^{(0)})$ and r. Send $(\texttt{ready},\text{sid},P_i,P_j)$ to party P_j.

Choice Upon receiving a message $(\texttt{choice},\text{sid},P_i,P_j,x)$ with $x \in \{0,1\}$ from P_j, check if current state is **ready**. If so, send $(\texttt{out},\text{sid},P_i,P_j,(s^{(x)},r))$ to P_j and go to state **dead**.

Fig. 3. The Extended One-Time-Memory Functionality

functionality. It takes an input $x \in \mathbb{F}_2$ from a party Alice and immediately outputs a random value $a \in \mathbb{F}_2$ to her. It also takes an input $y \in \mathbb{F}_2$ from Bob and immediately outputs a random value b to him. Alice and Bob may query the NL-Box at an arbitrary time and are oblivious to each others queries, due to the non-signaling property. However, after both of them have queried the NL-Box the identity $x \cdot y = a + b$ holds, thus their respective outputs are random shares of $x \cdot y$. So NL-Boxes compute a shared-AND-function, which takes two inputs x and y and outputs shares of their product. As the shares are random, they reveal no information about the other party's input nor if the other party has provided its input yet. [WW05] noted that OT can be implemented using a trusted shared-AND primitive that is signaling for both parties. [BCU+06] gave an interactive protocol that realizes OT from NL-Boxes (which are non-signaling).

Functionality: $\mathcal{F}^{\text{NL}}$

Initialization Set a state $S := \emptyset$. Create variables a, b, x and y. Send **ready** to P_A and P_B.

Choice phase of P_A Upon receiving a message $(\texttt{choice},\text{sid},P_A,x)$ from a party P_A, check if $P_A \in S$. If so, do nothing. Otherwise, if $S = \emptyset$ store x, choose a uniformly at random, store a, set $S := \{P_A\}$ and send $(\texttt{result},\text{sid},P_A,a)$ to P_A. If $S \neq \emptyset$, set $a = y \cdot x + b$, $S := S \cup \{P_A\}$ and send $(\texttt{result},\text{sid},P_A,a)$ to P_A. The output to P_A is immediate.

Choice phase of P_B Upon receiving a message $(\texttt{choice},\text{sid},P_B,y)$ from a party P_B, check if $P_B \in S$. If so, do nothing. Otherwise, if $S = \emptyset$ store y, choose b uniformly at random, store b, set $S := \{P_B\}$ and send $(\texttt{result},\text{sid},P_B,b)$ to P_B. If $S \neq \emptyset$, set $b = y \cdot x + a$, $S := S \cup \{P_B\}$ and send $(\texttt{result},\text{sid},P_B,b)$ to P_B. The output to P_B is immediate.

Fig. 4. The NL-Box functionality

4   Impossible Reductions

In this Section we show that OTMs cannot be implemented from OT and that NL-Boxes cannot be implemented from OTMs, even if OTMs in both directions are granted.

Lemma 1. *There is no UC-secure protocol for OTMs in the $\mathcal{F}^{OT}$-hybrid model.*

Proof. Note that, once an OTM token has arrived at the reveiver party, all communication between the token and the receiver party is immediate. In contrast, all communication in the $\mathcal{F}^{OT}$-hybrid model is scheduled by the adversary; this especially holds for all messages from and to the granted $\mathcal{F}^{OT}$ functionalities. Now let us consider a hypothetical protocol for OTM in the $\mathcal{F}^{OT}$-hybrid model. First we show that upon input of his choice bit x an honest OTM receiver must not send any message to the OTM sender or any of the granted $\mathcal{F}^{OT}$ functionalities. This holds true, as otherwise the adversary would be activated between input of x and output of $s^{(x)}$, either for scheduling an $\mathcal{F}^{OT}$ output or for scheduling a regular message. However, this enables the adversary to send an arbitrary message to the environment, while the receiver party has already got input, but did not produce output yet. This cannot be simulated in the ideal model, as there the receiver's output is immediate. But now we have a contradiction. If the reciever, upon getting his input, can compute his output without any further interaction, then this means that he can compute $s^{(0)}$ as well as $s^{(1)}$. Thus, there is no UC-secure reduction of OTMs to OT.

Lemma 2. *There is no UC-secure protocol for NL-Boxes in the $\mathcal{F}^{OTM}$-hybrid model.*

Proof. Note that NL-Box outputs always are immediate. Hence, analogously to our argumentation above, in a hypothetical NL-Box protocol in the $\mathcal{F}^{OTM}$-hybrid model each party must be able to perform its choice phase only by local computation (including some interaction with previously received OTM tokens). However, this would lead to a hidden variable model for NL-Boxes, but such a hidden variable model is impossible. If x, y are the NL-Box inputs and the random variables a, b are the random NL-Box outputs, then in case of $x = y = 1$ the distribution of a must be close to $1 - b$; in all other cases the distribution of a must be close to b. As this case differentiation obviously cannot be obtained from local computations of the participants, we can conclude that NL-Boxes cannot be implemented from OTMs in a UC-secure manner.

5   All-Or-Nothing Disclosure of Secrets

In this Section we give a brief introduction of zigzag matrices and define a new type of All-Or-Nothing matrices that we call (C, ρ)-AON matrices. Zigzag matrices were originally defined in [BCS96] in order to give a perfectly secure implementation of String-OT from Bit-OT.

Definition 1. *A matrix $M \in \mathbb{F}_q^{m \times n}$, where $n > m$ is a zigzag matrix, if and only if for every subset $I \subseteq [n]$ at least one of the matrices $M_I^T, M_{[n] \setminus I}^T$ has full rank. In other words, if V is the set of columns of M, then for every subset $W \subseteq V$, at least one of the sets $W, V \setminus W$ has full rank.*

[BCS96] gives probabilistic and deterministic constructions for zigzag matrices in $\mathbb{F}_q^{m \times (1+\alpha)m}$ for some constant $\alpha > 0$. The purpose of zigzag matrices is reducing String-OT to Bit-OT by the following simple, perfectly secure, universally composable protocol (See Figure 5).

Protocol: String-OT from Bit-OT

Let $M \in \mathbb{F}_2^{m \times n}$ be a zigzag matrix.

Send phase Let $s^{(0)}, s^{(1)} \in \mathbb{F}_2^m$ be Alice's String-OT input.

- **(Alice)** Choose $v^{(0)}, v^{(1)} \in \mathbb{F}_2^n$ uniformly at random such that $s^{(0)} = Mv^{(0)}$ and $s^{(1)} = Mv^{(1)}$. Instantiate n Bit-OTs $OT_1, \ldots, OT_n$. For $i = 1, \ldots, n$, input $(v_i^{(0)}, v_i^{(1)})$ into OT_i.

Choice phase Let $x \in \{0,1\}$ be Bob's Choice-Bit.

- **(Bob)** For $i = 1, \ldots, n$, input x into OT_i and let v_i be the according OT-output. Set $v = (v_1, \ldots, v_n)$ and $s = M \cdot v$. Output s.

Fig. 5. String-OT from Bit-OT

The security-proof for a corrupted sender is trivial. For a corrupted receiver, it is sufficient to note the following. Let $I_0 \subseteq [m]$ and $I_1 = [m] \setminus I_0$. If for $i \in I_0$ Bob queries OT_i with choice-bit 0 and for $i \in I_1$ with choice-bit 1, then $M_{I_0}^T$ or $M_{I_1}^T$ has full rank, which means that s_1 or s_0 could be equivoked to any value. This construction has an interesting feature: It is completely non-interactive. As noted in [GIS+10], it can thus be used to reduce String-OTM to Bit-OTM.

In our construction, we will require the vectors $v^{(0)}$ and $v^{(1)}$ to be codewords from an error-correcting code C. However, in this case the above protocol will not be secure anymore in general. The reason for this is that codewords contain redundancy. More specifically, if $M \in \mathbb{F}_q^{m \times n}$ is a zigzag matrix, then we can always find a code $C \subseteq \mathbb{F}_q^n$ such that for every codeword $c \in C$, the first component s_1 of $s = M \cdot c$ can always be learned from a single component c_i of c. Let, for instance h^T be the first row of M and let $e \in \mathbb{F}_2^n$ be the 1-st unit vector ($e_i = 1$ for $i = 1$, otherwise $e_i = 0$). We now choose the code C so that $(h - e)^T$ is a row of the parity-check matrix H of C. But then, for every codeword $c \in C$ it holds that $s_1 = h^T c = (h - e)^T c + e^T c = e^T c = c_1$. Thus the first component of $s = M \cdot c$ is always identical to the first component of c.

To fix this issue, we have to replace the zigzag matrices by matrices that allow all-or-nothing disclosure of codewords from a code C. We will call those matrices (C, ρ)-All-Or-Nothing (AON) matrices.

Definition 2. *Let $C \subseteq \mathbb{F}_q^n$ be a linear code of rate R. Let $0 < \rho < R$. We call $M \in \mathbb{F}_q^{m \times n}$ a (C, ρ)-AON matrix, if for any subset $I \subseteq [n]$ with $|I| < \rho n$, any $y \in \mathbb{F}_q^m$ and any codeword $c \in C$, there exists a codeword $c' \in C$, such that $Mc' = y$ and $c_I = c'_I$.*

The idea behind this definition is that any codeword c, of which no more than ρn components are known to an adversary, can be equivoked to a codeword c', which maps to a desired value under the AON-matrix M. If we choose $\rho > \frac{1}{2}$, (C, ρ)-AON matrices enjoy similar properties as zigzag matrices, as for each decomposition $I \dot{\cup} \bar{I} = [n]$ either $|I| \geq \rho n$ or $\bar{I} \geq \rho n$. The following theorem states that, given a family of linear codes $\{C_n\}$ over $\mathbb{F}_q$, there always exists an (C_n, ρ)-AON matrix $M \in \mathbb{F}_q^{\gamma n \times n}$, for a certain choice of the parameters γ and ρ and sufficiently large n. Let $H(\cdot)$ denote the binary entropy-function.

Theorem 1. *Let $\{C_n\}$ with $C_n \subseteq \mathbb{F}_q^n$ be a family of linear codes of rate R. If $\frac{H(\rho)}{\log(q)} + \rho + \gamma < R$, then, for all sufficiently large n, there exists a (C_n, ρ)-AON matrix $M_n \in \mathbb{F}_q^{\gamma n \times n}$. Moreover, if $\frac{H(\rho)}{\log(q)} + \rho + \gamma = R - \epsilon$ for some $\epsilon > 0$, then such M_n can be generated probabilistically. The probability of generating a matrix that does not suffice the (C_n, ρ)-AON property is asymptotically less than $q^{-\epsilon n}$.*

For the proof see Appendix Section A. In the context of String-OTMs, we can use AON-matrices to force a corrupted receiver to open more than ρn single OTMs before he can even learn a single bit of the output. In the UC-scenario, this means that a simulator can always equivoke a String-OTM output as long as the adversary has queried less than ρn OTMs, which we will take advantage of in our protocol construction in the next Section.

Finally, we remark that (C, ρ)-AON matrices are related to ramp-secret-sharing-schemes [CDG+05, CC06, CCG+07]. In fact, if $C \subseteq \mathbb{F}_q^n$ is a linear code with minimum-distance d, then C together with a (C, ρ)-AON matrix $M \in \mathbb{F}_q^{\gamma n \times n}$ yield a linear ramp secret-sharing scheme with ρn-privacy, $n-d+1$-reconstruction (as each codeword $c \in C$ is uniquely determined by any set of $n - d + 1$ of its components) and rate γ. The secret-sharing-scheme obtained in this manner inherits the specific properties of the code C, like efficient error-correction.

6   Implementing String Ext-OTM from OTM Efficiently

In this Section, we will describe our protocol that efficiently implements an $O(n)$-Bit-String-Ext-OTM from $O(n)$ Bit-OTMs. Before we give a formal description of the protocol, we shall briefly develop the ideas behind it. The first idea was using n 2-Bit-String-OTMs, such that Alice's input to OTM$_i$ has the form $(r_i||s_i^{(0)}, r_i||s_i^{(1)})$, where the r_i are the bits of the string r and $s_i^{(0)}$, $s_i^{(1)}$ are the bits of the strings $s^{(0)}$ and $s^{(1)}$. Thereafter, the receiver has to apply a zigzag matrix M to his output $s^{(x)}$ so that we can ensure that he only learns one string. However, there is an obvious problem. A corrupted sender may input different

$r^{(0)}$ and $r^{(1)}$ for choice bit 0 and 1, thus the string r would depend on the receiver's choice bit. To avoid this problem, Bob has to be able to check if both strings, $r^{(0)}$ and $r^{(1)}$ are the same. To do so, we will encode the string r as a codeword c of an error-correcting code C_n of rate R_1 that can correct an α-fraction of errors. We further encode the strings $s^{(0)}$ and $s^{(1)}$ as codewords d_0 and d_1 of an erasure-correcting code D_n of rate R_2 and relative minimum-distance δ.

In the choice phase, Bob will choose a small random set of indices $I \subseteq [n]$, on which he will check the codeword c for consistency. He needs to perform this consistency check on the vector $\tilde{c}$ he receives to make sure $c^{(0)}$ and $c^{(1)}$ were almost (up to a small Hamming-distance) identical. He will query OTM_i for $i \in I$ with random choice-bits u_i, while he will query all OTM_i for $i \in [n]\backslash I$ with his choice-bit x. Bob runs the error-correction algorithm of C_n on $\tilde{c}$. If the error-correction fails, Bob aborts the protocol. Otherwise the error-correction returns a decomposition $\tilde{c} = \bar{c} + e$, for a codeword $\bar{c} \in C_n$ and an error-vector e. If an error occurred on support I, thus if $e_I \neq 0$, Bob aborts the protocol. The idea behind this check-step is the following. If a corrupted sender inputs two different vectors $c^{(0)} \neq c^{(1)}$ that are not both in a small hamming-ball around a common codeword c, then Bob will find an error on support I with high probability and abort. We remark that simpler abort-criteria for Bob lead to insecure protocols. If, for instance, Bob's abort-criterion was to abort if $\tilde{c}$ contains an error in an arbitrary position (not just on I), then Bob's abort behavior clearly depends on his choice-bit x. A corrupted Alice could exploit this by choosing $c^{(0)}$ as a codeword and $c^{(1)}$ as a non-codeword, such that Bob would, with high probability, abort if his choice-bit is 1.

We still need to deal with the problem that Bob will have incomplete information about his desired output $d^{(x)}$. As OTM_i has been queried with a uniformly random choice-bit u_i for $i \in I$, Bob will observe some erasures on the support I in his desired output $d^{(x)}$. For simplicity, we consider all components of $d^{(x)}$ on support I to be erased. However, those erasures can be corrected using the erasure-correction algorithm of D_n. If the erasure-correction fails, which can happen if $d^{(x)}$ contains errors on support $[n]\backslash I$, then Bob will set $d^{(x)} = 0$.

This protocol is secure against a corrupted sender, however, we can not yet simulate this protocol for a corrupted receiver. A corrupted receiver may learn single bits of c, $d^{(0)}$ or $d^{(1)}$ "prematurely", that is before his choice-bit x is determined. Thus a simulator would have to know some bits of c before extracting the choice-bit x. This is where the (C, ρ)-AON matrices come into play. We will not use the zigzag matrix anymore to process $d^{(x)}$ to $s^{(x)}$. Instead, the protocol will require two AON-matrices, one to process the codeword c and one to process the codeword $d^{(x)}$. The choice of the constants for the AON matrices requires some care, so we will explain it in detail. Let $|I| = \beta n$, for some constant β. Let $M_1 \in \mathbb{F}_q^{\gamma_1 n \times n}$ be a (C_n, ρ_1)-AON matrix and let $M_2 \in \mathbb{F}_q^{\gamma_2 n \times n}$ be a (D_n, ρ_2)-matrix. We will now derive the constraints by which the constants have to be chosen. As long as the receiver has opened less than $\rho_2 n$ OTMs with a choice-bit $x \in \{0, 1\}$, he has no information about $s^{(x)} = \hat{s}^{(x)} + M_2 \cdot d^{(x)}$, or that is to say, a simulator can still equivoke the output. Thus the receiver is committed to a choice-bit $x \in \{0, 1\}$ after opening $2(1 - \rho_2)n$ OTMs, as either at least $(1 - \rho_2)n$ of them were queried with choice bit $x = 0$ or at least $(1 - \rho_2)n$ were queried with choice-bit $x = 1$. This means that we have to be able to equivoke the codeword c until at least $2(1 - \rho_2)n$ OTMs in $[n]$ have been queried, which means that we have to choose ρ_1 according to

$$\rho_1 n > 2(1 - \rho_2)n \Leftrightarrow \rho_2 > 1 - \frac{\rho_1}{2}. \tag{1}$$

Moreover, we have to choose $\beta < \delta$, as Bob needs to be able to correct the erasures that arise from randomly checking OTMs on support I.

We will now show that these constraints on the constants can always be met. For sake of simplicity, we will choose $D_n = C_n$, as any error-correcting code is also a erasure-correcting code. This choice also allows us to set $M = M_1 = M_2$, and therefore $\rho = \rho_1 = \rho_2$. Thus, (1) becomes $\rho > \frac{2}{3}$. Now fix a $\frac{2}{3} < \rho < 1$. We can always find constants q, $\gamma > 0$ and $\epsilon > 0$, such that $r = \frac{H(\rho)}{\log(q)} + \rho + \gamma < 1 - \epsilon$. Moreover, there exists a family C_n of linear codes of length n, that has rate $R > r$, an alphabet-size $2^l = q$, relative minimum-distance δ that can correct an α-fraction of error [GI05]. Finally we can fix a constant $\beta > 0$ with $\beta < \frac{\alpha}{2}$ and $\beta < \rho$. As the choice of C_n involves choosing the order $q = 2^l$ of the field $\mathbb{F}_q$ to be a large constant, we need to use $2l$-Bit-String-OTMs for $\text{OTM}_1, \ldots, \text{OTM}_n$. Each of those $2l$-Bit-String-OTMs can be efficiently realized using a constant number of Bit-OTMs with the construction of [BCS96] using intersecting codes. We thus implement a γln-String Ext-OTM with auxiliary string of length γln, using a total of σln Bit-OTMs. Here, σl is the number of Bit-OTMs required to construct an l-Bit-String-OTM by one of the constructions given in [BCS96]. This concludes the informal description of the protocol, the full description is given in Figure 6. For the proof of UC-security of the Ext-OTM from OTM protocol, see the full version of this paper.

7   Implementing OTM from NL-Boxes

In this Section, we will show that some of the same techniques as used in Section 6 can be used to implement OTMs from NL-Boxes. The starting-point for this protocol-construction is noting that the functionalities NL-Boxes and OT/OTM are closely related [WW05, BCU+06]. More precisely, consider the following simple protocol that implements a Bit-OTM from a single NL-Box, given that the sender Alice is honest. If $(s^{(0)}, s^{(1)}) \in \mathbb{F}_2 \times \mathbb{F}_2$ is Alice's input, she inputs $s^{(0)} + s^{(1)}$ into the NL-Box and receives a share a. Alice then sends $\hat{s} = a + s^{(0)}$ to Bob, what concludes the send phase. In his choice phase, Bob inputs his choice-bit x into the NL-Box and receives a share b. Bob then sets $s^{(x)} = \hat{s} + b$ to be his output. It holds that $s^{(x)} = \hat{s} + b = s^{(0)} + a + b = s^{(0)} + (s^{(0)} + s^{(1)})x$, thus this protocol correctly implements an OTM. [BCU+06, SGP06] pointed out a problem if Alice is corrupted: Alice does not provide input but sends a random $\hat{s}$ to Bob. Bob will then receive a random $s^{(x)}$, but Alice will be able to adaptively

---

Protocol: Ext-OTM from OTM

Let $n \in \mathbb{N}$ be the security parameter and let $C_n \subseteq \mathbb{F}_{2^l}^n$ be a linear code of rate R, relative minimum-distance δ that can correct an α-fraction of errors.

Send phase: (**Alice**) Let $(s^{(0)}, s^{(1)}) \in \mathbb{F}_{2^l}^{\gamma n} \times \mathbb{F}_{2^l}^{\gamma n}$ and $r \in \mathbb{F}_{2^l}^{\gamma n}$ be Alice's Ext-OTM input.

  – Generate a (C_n, ρ)-AON matrix $M \in \mathbb{F}_{2^l}^{\gamma n \times n}$.
  – Choose three codewords $c, d^{(0)}, d^{(1)} \in C_n$ uniformly at random. Set $\hat{s}^{(0)} = s^{(0)} - Md^{(0)}$, $\hat{s}^{(1)} = s^{(1)} - Md^{(1)}$ and $\hat{r} = r - Mc$.
  – Instantiate n $2l$-bit OTMs $\mathrm{OTM}_1, \ldots, \mathrm{OTM}_n$ and input $(c_i||d_i^{(0)}, c_i||d_i^{(1)})$ into OTM_i for $i = 1, \ldots, n$. Send M, $\hat{s}^{(0)}$, $\hat{s}^{(1)}$ and $\hat{r}$ to Bob.

Choice phase: (**Bob**) Let $x \in \{0, 1\}$ be Bob's choice bit.

  – Wait until the **ready**-message has been received from all of $\mathrm{OTM}_1, \ldots, \mathrm{OTM}_n$.
  – Choose a set $I \subseteq [n]$ with $|I| = \beta n$ uniformly at random.
  – For $i \in [n]\backslash I$, set $y_i = x$. For $i \in I$, choose y_i uniformly at random. Input y_i into OTM_i for $i = 1, \ldots, n$. Let $\tilde{c}_i || d_i$ be the output of OTM_i. Set $\tilde{c} = (\tilde{c}_1, \ldots, \tilde{c}_n)$. Set $\tilde{d}$ such that $\tilde{d}_i = \bot$ for $i \in I$ and $\tilde{d}_i = d_i$ for $i \in [n]\backslash I$.
  – Run the decoding-algorithm of C_n on $\tilde{c}$. Abort if the decoding fails. Let $\tilde{c} = \bar{c} + e$, for a $\bar{c} \in C_n$ and an error-vector e, be the decomposition returned by the decoding algorithm. Abort if $e_I \neq 0$. Otherwise set $r = \hat{r} + M \cdot \bar{c}$
  – Run the erasure-correction algorithm of C_n on $\tilde{d}$. If the erasure-correction fails, set $s = 0$. Otherwise, if $\bar{d} \in C_n$ is the output of the erasure-correction, set $s = \hat{s}^{(x)} + M \cdot \bar{d}$.
  – Output (s, r)

Fig. 6. Ext-OTM from OTM

change $s^{(1-x)}$ (the value Bob did not query). This can lead to problems, for instance when implementing commitments [EGL85] with OTM. We thus need to enforce that Alice provides inputs to her NL-Boxes, which we will obtain in a similar fashion as in Protocol Ext-OTM from OTM.

We will now explain our protocol that implements the OTM primitive from NL-Boxes. It will have an interactive send phase and a non-interactive choice phase. Let $C_n \subseteq \mathbb{F}_2^n$ be a code from a family of binary linear codes of rate R that can correct an α-fraction of errors and let $\beta > 0$ be a constant such that $\beta < \frac{\alpha}{2}$ and $\beta < \frac{R}{2}$. The protocol will make use of $3n$ NL-Boxes $\mathrm{NL}_1^{(1)}, \mathrm{NL}_1^{(2)}, \mathrm{NL}_1^{(3)}, \ldots,$ $\mathrm{NL}_n^{(1)}, \mathrm{NL}_n^{(2)}, \mathrm{NL}_n^{(3)}$. In a nutshell, for indices $i = 1, \ldots, n$, we will use an "*entanglement*" of $\mathrm{NL}_i^{(1)}$ and $\mathrm{NL}_i^{(2)}$, to transfer the bits c_i of a codeword $c \in C_n$ from Bob to Alice. For indices i in a subset $\bar{I} \subseteq [n]$ we will use an "*entanglement*" of $\mathrm{NL}_i^{(2)}$ and $\mathrm{NL}_i^{(3)}$ to implement an OTM from Alice to Bob. Alice will have to query both $\mathrm{NL}_i^{(1)}$ and $\mathrm{NL}_i^{(2)}$ to learn the code-bit c_i and she will be committed to an input once she has queried a $NL^{(2)}_{i_0}$ with $i_0 \in \bar{I}$ with an input x_{i_0}. If Alice inputs an $x' \neq x_{i_0}$ into one of $NL^{(2)}_i$ and $NL^{(3)}_i$ for $i \in \bar{I}$, Bob's output will be random. In order to learn the codeword c with sufficiently high probability, Alice has to query such an $NL^{(2)}_{i_0}$. Thus Alice can prove to Bob that she has fixed her input by sending c to Bob. To make sure that c does not contain information about Alice's input, we will use error-correction.

The protocol starts with an initialization phase. First, the parties instantiate $3n$ NL-Boxes $NL^{(1)}_1, NL^{(2)}_1, NL^{(3)}_1 \ldots, NL^{(1)}_n, NL^{(2)}_n, NL^{(3)}_n$ between them. Bob now chooses a codeword $c \in C_n$ uniformly at random. For $i = 1, \ldots, n$, Bob chooses a random bit u_i and inputs u_i into $NL^{(1)}_i$ and $NL^{(2)}_i$, let $b^{(1)}_i$ and $b^{(2)}_i$ be Bob's according outputs. Set $\hat{c} = (c_1 + b^{(1)}_1 + b^{(2)}_1, \ldots, c_n + b^{(1)}_n + b^{(2)}_n)$. Bob now sends $\hat{c}$ to Alice. The idea about this is the following. $\hat{c}$ is a *double-encryption* of c. In order to decrypt a bit $\hat{c}_i$ to c_i, Alice needs to query $NL^{(1)}_i$ and $NL^{(2)}_i$ with some choice-bit x_i, to get the shares $a^{(1)}_i$ and $a^{(2)}_i$. Assume Alice queries $NL^{(1)}_i$ with x_i and $NL^{(2)}_i$ with x'_i. Let Alice's outputs of $NL^{(1)}_i$ and $NL^{(1)}_i$ be $a^{(1)}_i$ and $a^{(2)}_i$. Then it holds that $\hat{c} + a^{(1)}_i + a^{(2)}_i = c_i + b^{(1)}_i + b^{(2)}_i + a^{(1)}_i + a^{(2)}_i = c_i + x_i u_i + x'_i u_i$. Thus, if $x_i = x'_i$ then $\hat{c}_i$ decrypts to c_i, otherwise $\hat{c}_i$ decrypts to a random value $c_i + u_i$. We have thus forced the receiver Alice to provide input to the $NL^{(2)}_i$ in order to learn the codeword c.

We will now continue describing the protocol. Upon receiving $\hat{c}$ from Bob, Alice chooses a set $I \subseteq [n]$ with $|I| = \beta n$ uniformly at random. Let $s^{(0)}, s^{(1)} \in \mathbb{F}_2$ be Alice's input. For $i \in I$, Alice chooses x_i uniformly at random, for $i \in \bar{I}$ she sets $x_i = s^{(0)} + s^{(1)}$. For $i = 1, \ldots, n$ Alice inputs x_i into $NL^{(1)}_i$, $NL^{(2)}_i$ and $NL^{(3)}_i$. Let $a^{(1)}_i$, $a^{(2)}_i$ and $a^{(3)}_i$ be her according outputs. As discussed, she computes $\tilde{c} = (\hat{c}_1 + a^{(1)}_1 + a^{(2)}_1, \ldots, \hat{c}_n + a^{(1)}_n + a^{(2)}_n)$. To make sure that the codeword she will send to Bob is independent of the x_i, Alice now runs the error-correction algorithm of C_n on $\tilde{c}$ and aborts if the error-correction fails. If not, let $\tilde{c} = \bar{c} + e$ for a codeword $\bar{c} \in C_n$ and an error-vector e. If $e_I \neq 0$ Alice aborts. This means, if Alice finds that Bob tried to cheat her on a randomly chosen check-set I, Alice decides to abort. Otherwise she computes $\hat{s} = s^{(0)} + \sum_{i \in \bar{I}}(a^{(2)}_i + a^{(3)}_i)$ and sends $(I, \bar{c}, \hat{s})$ to Bob. If $\bar{c} \neq c$, Bob aborts. This concludes the send phase.

We will now describe Bob's choice phase. Let $y \in \mathbb{F}_2$ be Bob's choice-bit. Bob chooses input bits $y_i \in \mathbb{F}_2$ for $i \in \bar{I} = [n] \setminus I$ uniformly at random such that $\sum_{i \in \bar{I}} y_i = y$ and inputs $y_i + u_i$ into $NL^{(3)}_i$, for $i \in \bar{I}$. Let $b^{(3)}_i$, for $i \in \bar{I}$, be the according outputs. Bob computes $s^{(y)} = \hat{s} + \sum_{i \in \bar{I}}(b^{(2)}_i + b^{(3)}_i)$ and creates output $s^{(y)}$. This concludes the description of the protocol. The formal description is given in Figure 7.

We will now briefly sketch why Alice is committed to a fixed input, once she has sent $\hat{s}$ and queried an NL-Box $NL^{(2)}_{i_0}$ with index $i_0 \in \bar{I}$. Assume that Alice has queried some of the $NL^{(2)}_i$ or $NL^{(3)}_i$ with x_{i_0}, and others with $x' \neq x_{i_0}$. Let $J^{(2)} \subseteq \bar{I}$ be the set of indices such that Alice has input x_{i_0} into $NL^{(2)}_j$ (for $j \in J^{(2)}$) and, analogously, $J^{(3)} \subseteq \bar{I}$ be the set of indices such that Alice has

---

Protocol: OTM from NL

Let $n \in \mathbb{N}$ be the security parameter and let $C_n \subseteq \mathbb{F}_2^n$ be a binary linear code of rate R that can correct an α-fraction of errors.

Send Phase: Let $(s^{(0)}, s^{(1)}) \in \mathbb{F}_2 \times \mathbb{F}_2$ Alice's OTM input.

1. Instantiate $3n$ NL-Boxes $\mathrm{NL}_1^{(1)}, \mathrm{NL}_1^{(2)}, \mathrm{NL}_1^{(3)} \ldots, \mathrm{NL}_n^{(1)}, \mathrm{NL}_n^{(2)}, \mathrm{NL}_n^{(3)}$ between Alice and Bob.
2. (**Bob**) Choose a codeword $c \in C_n$ uniformly at random. For $i = 1, \ldots, n$ choose $u_i \in \mathbb{F}_2$ uniformly at random and input u_i into $\mathrm{NL}_i^{(1)}$ and $\mathrm{NL}_i^{(2)}$. Let $b_i^{(1)}$ and $b_i^{(2)}$ be the according outputs. Set $v = (b_1^{(1)} + b_1^{(2)}, \ldots, b_n^{(1)} + b_n^{(2)})$, $\hat{c} = c + v$. Send $\hat{c}$ to Alice.
3. (**Alice**) Choose a set $I \subseteq [n]$ with $|I| = \beta n$ uniformly at random. For $i \in I$, choose x_i uniformly at random, for $i \in \bar{I}$, set $x_i = s^{(0)} + s^{(1)}$. For $i = 1, \ldots, n$, input x_i into $\mathrm{NL}_i^{(1)}, \mathrm{NL}_i^{(2)}, \mathrm{NL}_i^{(3)}$ and let $a_i^{(1)}, a_i^{(2)}$ and $a_i^{(3)}$ be the according outputs. Set $w = (a_1^{(1)} + a_1^{(2)}, \ldots, a_n^{(1)} + a_n^{(2)})$ and compute $\tilde{c} = \hat{c} + w$. Run the error-correction algorithm of C_n on $\tilde{c}$ and abort if it fails. Otherwise, let $\tilde{c} = \bar{c} + e$ for a codeword $\bar{c} \in C_n$ and an error-vector e. Abort if $e_I \neq 0$. Otherwise set $\hat{s} = s^{(0)} + \sum_{i \in \bar{I}} a_{2,i}$. Send is $(I, \bar{c}, \hat{s})$.
4. (**Bob**) Abort if $\bar{c} \neq c$.

Choice Phase: (**Bob**) Let $y \in \mathbb{F}_2$ be Bob's choice-bit.

– For $i \in \bar{I}$, choose y_i uniformly at random such that $\sum_{i \in \bar{I}} y_i = y$. For $i \in \bar{I}$, input $y_i + u_i$ into $\mathrm{NL}_i^{(3)}$ and let $b_i^{(3)}$ be the according output. Set $s^{(y)} = \hat{s} + \sum_{i \in \bar{I}} (b_i^{(2)} + b_i^{(3)})$ and output $s^{(y)}$.

Fig. 7. OTM from NL

input x_{i_0} into $\mathrm{NL}_j^{(3)}$ (for $j \in J^{(3)}$). Then, the $s^{(y)}$ that Bob observes will have the form

$$s^{(y)} = \hat{s} + \sum_{i \in \bar{I}} (b_i^{(2)} + b_i^{(3)}) = s^{(0)} + \sum_{i \in \bar{I}} (a_i^{(2)} + a_i^{(3)} + b_i^{(2)} + b_i^{(3)})$$

$$= s^{(0)} + x_{i_0} \left(\sum_{j \in J^{(2)}} u_j + \sum_{j \in J^{(3)}} (u_j + y_j) \right) + x' \left(\sum_{j \in \bar{I} \backslash J^{(2)}} u_j + \sum_{j \in \bar{I} \backslash J^{(3)}} (u_j + y_j) \right)$$

$$= s^{(0)} + u^*$$

for a random u^*. The value u^* is random (from Alice's view) because it holds that either $x_{i_0} = 1$ or $x' = 1$ and the u_j, $u_j + y_j$ are $2n-1$-wise independent (they are only restricted by $\sum_{i \in \bar{I}} y_i = y$), i.e. the bracket terms each are uniformly random. Thus, the only effect of retaining some of her NL-Box inputs is that she learns her own (fixed) input either delayed or not at all. The correctness of the protocol can be seen as follows. We have

$$s^{(y)} = \hat{s} + \sum_{i\in\bar{I}}(b_i^{(2)} + b_i^{(3)}) = s^{(0)} + \sum_{i\in\bar{I}}(a_i^{(2)} + a_i^{(3)} + b_i^{(2)} + b_i^{(3)})$$

$$= s^{(0)} + \sum_{i\in\bar{I}}(x_i u_i + x_i(u_i + y_i)) = s^{(0)} + (s^{(0)} + s^{(1)})\sum_{i\in\bar{I}} y_i$$

$$= s^{(0)} + (s^{(0)} + s^{(1)})y,$$

thus Protocol OTM from NL correctly implements the OTM-functionality. For the proof of UC-security of the OTM from NL-Box protocol, see the full version of this paper.

8   Conclusion

In this paper we have provided a new construction for Ext-OTM from String-OTM. As String-OTM has recently been shown linear-rate reducible to Bit-OTM, our construction yields Ext-OTM from Bit-OTM with linear rate, what is asymptotically optimal. Furthermore, we gave a protocol for Bit-OTM from NL-Boxes, which uses similar techniques. To the best of our knowledge this is the first protocol that reliably cancels the non-signaling property of an NL-Box for exactly one party. However, when implementing String-OTMs from NL-Boxes using our constructions, one ends up with an overall reduction factor which is super-linear. So there still is some potential for optimization.

As a vital tool for our reduction of Ext-OTM to String-OTM we developed a new All-or-Nothing technique to hide random codewords of linear codes. In particular, we defined (C,ρ)-AON matrices $M \in \mathbb{F}_q^{\gamma n\times n}$ that allow to arbitrarily equivoke Mc for every codeword c, even if any ρn components of c are already public. We showed that such matrices can be constructed probabilistically by a very simple and efficient algorithm. We consider it an interesting problem, whether there is a deterministic construction of (C,ρ)-AON matrices $M \in \mathbb{F}_q^{\gamma n\times n}$ for a linear code C of constant rate R that can efficiently corrects an α-fraction of errors. If such a construction is possible for $\rho > \frac{2}{3}$ and arbitrary rate R, then the protocol in Figure 6 can be made perfectly secure against a corrupted receiver.

Acknowledgments. We would like to thank the anonymous reviewers of IC-ITS 2011 for their helpful comments. This work was in part supported by IBM Research & Development Germany within the HomER-project.

References

[BCS96]   Brassard, G., Crépeau, C., Santha, M.: Oblivious transfers and intersecting codes. IEEE Transactions on Information Theory 42(6), 1769–1780 (1996)

[BCU+06]   Buhrman, H., Christandl, M., Unger, F., Wehner, S., Winter, A.: Implications of superstrong nonlocality for cryptography. Proceedings of The Royal Society A 462, 1919–1932 (2006)

[Can01]   Canetti, R.: Universally composable security: A new paradigm for cryptographic protocols. In: FOCS, pp. 136–145 (2001)

[CC06]   Chen, H., Cramer, R.: Algebraic geometric secret sharing schemes and secure multi-party computations over small fields. In: Dwork, C. (ed.) CRYPTO 2006. LNCS, vol. 4117, pp. 521–536. Springer, Heidelberg (2006)

[CCG+07]   Chen, H., Cramer, R., Goldwasser, S., de Haan, R., Vaikuntanathan, V.: Secure computation from random error correcting codes. In: Naor, M. (ed.) EUROCRYPT 2007. LNCS, vol. 4515, pp. 291–310. Springer, Heidelberg (2007)

[CDG+05]   Cramer, R., Daza, V., Gracia, I., Urroz, J.J., Leander, G., Martí-Farré, J., Padró, C.: On codes, matroids and secure multi-party computation from linear secret sharing schemes. In: Shoup, V. (ed.) CRYPTO 2005. LNCS, vol. 3621, pp. 327–343. Springer, Heidelberg (2005)

[EGL85]   Even, S., Goldreich, O., Lempel, A.: A randomized protocol for signing contracts. Commun. ACM 28(6), 637–647 (1985), doi:10.1145/3812.3818

[GI05]   Guruswami, V., Indyk, P.: Linear time encodable/decodable codes with nearoptimal rate. IEEE Transactions on Information Theory 51, 3393–3400 (2005)

[GIS+10]   Goyal, V., Ishai, Y., Sahai, A., Venkatesan, R., Wadia, A.: Founding cryptography on tamper-proof hardware tokens. In: Micciancio, D. (ed.) TCC 2010. LNCS, vol. 5978, pp. 308–326. Springer, Heidelberg (2010)

[GKR08]   Goldwasser, S., Kalai, Y.T., Rothblum, G.N.: One-time programs. In: Wagner, D. (ed.) CRYPTO 2008. LNCS, vol. 5157, pp. 39–56. Springer, Heidelberg (2008)

[PR94]   Popescu, S., Rohrlich, D.: Quantum nonlocality as an axiom. Foundations of Physics 24(3), 379–385 (1994)

[Rab81]   Rabin, M.O.: How to exchange secrets by oblivious transfer. technical report tr-81. Technical report, Aiken Computation Laboratory, Harvard University (1981)

[SGP06]   Short, A.J., Gisin, N., Popescu, S.: The physics of no-bit-commitment: Generalized quantum non-locality versus oblivious transfer. Quantum Information Processing 5(2), 131–138 (2006)

[SS96]   Sipser, M., Spielman, D.A.: Expander codes. IEEE Transactions on Information Theory 42, 1710–1722 (1996)

[WW05]   Wolf, S., Wullschleger, J.: Oblivious transfer and quantum non-locality. In: Proceedings of International Symposium on Information Theory, ISIT 2005, pp. 1745–1748 (September 2005)

[Zém01]   Zémor, G.: On expander codes. IEEE Transactions on Information Theory 47(2), 835–837 (2001)

Appendix

A   Existence and Generation of (C, ρ)-AON Matrices

Here, we will prove that, given a family of linear codes $\{C_n\}$ over $\mathbb{F}_q$, there always exists an (C_n, ρ)-AON matrix $M \in \mathbb{F}_q^{\gamma n \times n}$, for a certain choice of the parameters γ and ρ and sufficiently large n. We will also show that such (C_n, ρ)-AON matrices can be generated probabilistically. We will first prove a technical lemma for our theorem.

Lemma 3. *Let* $M \in \mathbb{F}_q^{m \times n}$ *be a random matrix that is uniformly distributed. Let* $B \in \mathbb{F}_q^{n \times k}$, *where* $k \leq n$, *be a full rank matrix. Then the random matrix* $M' = M \cdot B$ *is uniformly distributed in* $\mathbb{F}_q^{m \times k}$.

Proof. The i-th row of M assigns how to linearly combine the i-th row of M' from the rows of B, thus the rows of M' are statistically independent of each other. Further, since the rows of B contain a basis of $\mathbb{F}_q^{1 \times k}$, each row of M' is uniformly random.

We will now state and prove our main theorem about (C, ρ)-AON-matrices. $H(\cdot)$ denotes the binary entropy-function.

Theorem 1. *Let* $\{C_n\}$ *with* $C_n \subseteq \mathbb{F}_q^n$ *be a family of linear codes of rate R. If* $\frac{H(\rho)}{\log(q)} + \rho + \gamma < R$, *then, for all sufficiently large n, there exists a (C_n, ρ)-AON matrix* $M_n \in \mathbb{F}_q^{\gamma n \times n}$. *Moreover, if* $\frac{H(\rho)}{\log(q)} + \rho + \gamma = R - \epsilon$ *for some $\epsilon > 0$, then such M_n can be generated probabilistically. The probability of generating a matrix that does not suffice the (C_n, ρ)-AON property is asymptotically less than $q^{-\epsilon n}$.*

Proof. Let the code C_n be given by a generator-matrix G in systematic form, thus the first Rn components of a codeword is its corresponding information-word. Let P be a matrix that projects $\mathbb{F}_q^n$ to $\mathbb{F}_q^{Rn}$ by dropping all but the first Rn components of a vector, thus $P \cdot G = \mathbf{1}$, where $\mathbf{1} \in \mathbb{F}_q^{Rn \times Rn}$ is the identity matrix. For a subset $I \subseteq [n]$ with $|I| < \rho n$ let $V_I = \ker(G_I) = \{s \in \mathbb{F}_q^{Rn} | G_I s = 0\}$. V_I has a dimension greater than or equal $(R - \rho)n$, as the linear equation-system $G_I s = 0$ puts at most $|I| < \rho n$ linear constraints on $s \in \mathbb{F}_q^{Rn}$. Let $B_I \in \mathbb{F}_q^{Rn \times m}$ be the basis-matrix for a canonical basis of V_I, where $m = \dim(V_I) \geq (R - \rho)n$.

In the first step of the proof we will show the following. The matrix $M = W \cdot P$, where W is an arbitrary $\mathbb{F}_q^{\gamma n \times Rn}$ matrix, is a (C_n, ρ)-AON matrix, if and only if for every $I \subseteq [n]$ with $|I| < \rho n$ the matrix $W' = W \cdot B_I$ has full rank. In the second step we will show that if the matrix W is chosen uniformly at random, this condition is met with high probability, given that n is sufficiently large.

Assume now that for every subset $I \subseteq [n]$ with $|I| < \rho n$ the matrix $W' = W \cdot B_I$ has full rank. Fix such an I, a codeword $c \in C_n$ and a vector $y \in \mathbb{F}_q^{\gamma n}$. We have to find a codeword $c' \in C$, such that $Mc' = y$ and $c_I = c'_I$. The information-words $s \in \mathbb{F}_q^{Rn}$ that are consistent with the partial codeword c_I are characterized by $G_I s = c_I$. Thus, the s consistent with c_I form an affine space $A_I = \{s \in \mathbb{F}_q^{Rn} | G_I s = c_I\}$. As A_I is an affine space, it can be represented by $A_I = p + \ker(G_I) = p + V_I$, where $p \in \mathbb{F}_q^{Rn}$ is a reference point. As the matrix $W \cdot B_I \in \mathbb{F}_q^{\gamma n \times m}$ has full rank and $m > \gamma n$ (as $m \geq (R - \rho)n > \gamma n + \frac{H(\rho)}{\log(q)} n > \gamma n$), we find a $t \in \mathbb{F}_q^m$ such that $y - Wp = WB_I t$, thus $y = W(p + B_I t)$. Let $s' := p + B_I \cdot t \in A_I$ and $c' = G \cdot s'$. It holds that $c'_I = G_I \cdot s' = c_I$ as $s' \in A_I$. We further have $Mc' = W \cdot Pc' = WPGs' = Ws' = y$. Thus M is an (C_n, ρ)-AON matrix.

Conversely fix $c = 0$, then the (C_n, ρ)-AON property states that for every $I \subseteq [n]$ with $|I| < \rho n$ and every $y \in \mathbb{F}_q^{\gamma n}$ there exists an $s' \in V_I$ (as $G_I s' = c_I = 0$)

such that $y = MGs' = Ws'$. As $s' \in V_I$ can be written as $s' = B_I t$, we have that for every $y \in \mathbb{F}_q^{\gamma n}$ there exists a $t \in \mathbb{F}_q^m$ such that $y = W B_I t$, but this is equivalent to $W B_I$ having full rank.

We will now show that, if $W \in \mathbb{F}_q^{\gamma n \times Rn}$ is chosen uniformly at random, the probability that there exists an $I \subseteq [n]$ with $|I| < \rho n$ such that $W' = W B_I$ is rank-deficient is negligible in n. We will first analyze the probability that W' is rank-deficient for a fixed $I \subseteq [n]$ with $|I| < \rho n$. As B_I is a basis-matrix and thus has full rank and W is a matrix chosen uniformly at random, Lemma 3 states that $W' \in \mathbb{F}_q^{\gamma n \times m}$ is also a uniformly random matrix. Thus $\Pr_W[\operatorname{rank}(W B_I) < \gamma n] = \Pr_{W'}[\operatorname{rank}(W') < \gamma n]$. The probability that a uniformly chosen matrix $W' \in \mathbb{F}_q^{\gamma n \times m}$, with $m > \gamma n$, has full rank is

$$\Pr_{W'}[\operatorname{rank}(W') = \gamma n] = \prod_{i=0}^{\gamma n - 1} \frac{q^m - q^i}{q^m} \geq 1 - \sum_{i=0}^{\gamma n - 1} q^{i-m} = 1 - \frac{q^{\gamma n} - 1}{q^m(q-1)} > 1 - q^{\gamma n - m}.$$

Consequently,

$$\Pr_{W'}[\operatorname{rank}(W') < \gamma n] < q^{\gamma n - m} \leq q^{n(\rho + \gamma - R)}$$

as $m \geq (R - \rho)n$. We can now use the union-bound to get an upper bound for the probability that there exists such an I such that $\operatorname{rank}(W B_I) < \gamma n$.

$$\Pr_W[\exists I \subseteq [n], |I| < \rho n : \operatorname{rank}(W B_I) < \gamma n] \leq \binom{n}{\rho n} \Pr_{W'}[\operatorname{rank}(W') < \gamma n]$$

$$\leq 2^{nH(\rho)} \cdot q^{n(\rho + \gamma - R)}$$

$$= q^{n\left(\frac{H(\rho)}{\log(q)} + \rho + \gamma - R\right)}$$

Now let $\frac{H(\rho)}{\log(q)} + \rho + \gamma - R < -\epsilon$ for a constant $\epsilon > 0$. Then

$$\Pr_W[\exists I \subseteq [n], |I| < \rho n : \operatorname{rank}(W B_I) < \gamma n] < q^{-\epsilon n}$$

Thus the probability that $M = W \cdot P$ is not a (C_n, ρ)-AON matrix is negligible in n.

Some Notions of Entropy for Cryptography
(Invited Talk)

Leonid Reyzin

Boston University Computer Science
111 Cummington St., Boston, MA 02215, USA
http://www.cs.bu.edu/~reyzin

Abstract. This paper presents a brief and (necessarily) incomplete survey of some notions of entropy that have been recently used in the analysis of cryptographic constructions. It focuses on min-entropy and its extensions to the cases when the adversary has correlated information and/or is computationally bounded. It also presents results that can be used to bound such entropy and apply it to the analysis of cryptographic constructions.

1 Information-Theoretic Case

In many contexts, particularly in security-related ones, the ability to guess the value of a random variable (in a single attempt) is an important measures of the variable's quality. This ability is captured by the following notion.

Definition 1. *A random variable X has **min-entropy** k, denoted $H_\infty(X) = k$, if*

$$\max_x \Pr[X = x] = 2^{-k}.$$

Randomness extractors were defined to work with any distribution that has min-entropy [NZ96]. Moreover, strong extractors (whose outputs are nearly uniform even the presence of the seed) produce outputs that have, with high probability over the choice of seed, almost maximal min-entropy.

Lemma 1 ([CKOR10]). *If $\mathsf{Ext} : N \times I \to \{0,1\}^\ell$ is a (k, ε)-strong extractor with inputs from a set N and seeds from a distribution I, and X is a random variable taking values in N with $\mathbf{H}_\infty(X) \geq k$, then $\mathbf{H}_\infty(\mathsf{Ext}(X; i)) \geq \ell - 1$ with probability at least $1 - 2^\ell \varepsilon$ over the choice of the seed i.*

A less demanding notion is sometimes more suitable and allows for better analysis of constructions, because one can "pretend" to work with a very close distribution Y that has more min-entropy:

Definition 2 ([RW04]). *A random variable X has ε-**smooth min-entropy** k if $\max_{Y: \mathbf{SD}(X,Y) \leq \varepsilon} \mathbf{H}_\infty(Y) = k$ (here, $\mathbf{SD}(X, Y)$ is the usual statistical distance, defined as $\max_T \Pr[X \in T] - \Pr[Y \in T]$).*

S. Fehr (Ed.): ICITS 2011, LNCS 6673, pp. 138–142, 2011.

Quite often, the adversary has some additional information Z that is correlated with X. Conditional min-entropy $\mathbf{H}_\infty(X|Z)$ is defined in [RW05] as $-\log\max_{x,z}\Pr(X = x \mid Z = z) = \min_z \mathbf{H}_\infty(X \mid Z = z)$ (an ε-smooth version is also defined in [RW05, Section 1.3] by eliminating bad portions of (X, Z) that occur with probability at most ε). Again, a less restrictive notion is sometimes more suitable (a comparison of the notions is given in [DORS08, Appendix B]):

Definition 3 ([DORS08, Section 2.4]). *Let (X, Z) be a pair of random variables. The* **average min-entropy** *of X conditioned on Z is*

$$\tilde{H}_\infty(X|Z) \stackrel{\text{def}}{=} -\log \mathop{\mathbf{E}}_{z \leftarrow Z} \max_x \Pr[X = x|Z = z] = -\log[\mathop{\mathbf{E}}_{z \leftarrow Z}(2^{-H_\infty(X|Z=z)})].$$

Average min-entropy, like min-entropy, is simply the logarithm of the probability that the adversary (this time, given the value of Z) will guess the value of X in a single attempt.

Average min-entropy exhibits some properties that agree with our intuition: conditioning on Z that has b bits of information reduces the entropy of X by at most b.

Lemma 2 ([DORS08, Lemma 2.2b]). $\tilde{\mathbf{H}}_\infty(X \mid Z) \geq \mathbf{H}_\infty(X, Z) - b$, *where 2^b is the number of elements in Z (more generally, $\tilde{\mathbf{H}}_\infty(X \mid Z_1, Z_2) \geq \tilde{\mathbf{H}}_\infty(X, Z_1 \mid Z_2) - b$, where 2^b is the number of elements in Z_2).*

Randomness extractors, which were originally analyzed for distribution of min-entropy, can also be used on distributions that have average min-entropy [DORS08, Section 2.5] (in some cases even without any additional loss in parameters); moreover, extracted outputs themselves will have average min-entropy. A (k, ε)-average-case extractor is defined as a function that takes in a sample from a distribution X such that $\tilde{\mathbf{H}}_\infty(X \mid Z) \geq k$ and a random seed, and produces an output that is ε-close to uniform even in the presence of the correlated value from Z and the seed.

Lemma 3 ([KR09, Lemma 1]). *If $\mathsf{Ext} : N \times I \to \{0, 1\}^\ell$ is a (k, ε)-average-case extractor with inputs from a set N and seeds from a distribution I, and (X, Z) is a pair of random variables with X taking values in N and $\tilde{\mathbf{H}}_\infty(X|Z) \geq k$, then $\tilde{\mathbf{H}}_\infty(\mathsf{Ext}(X; I) \mid Z, I) \geq \min\left(\ell, \log\frac{1}{\varepsilon}\right) - 1$.*

Average min-entropy often allows for simpler statements and analyses; for example, the security of information-theoretic MACs with nonuniform keys can be analyzed using the average min-entropy of the keys (see [KR09, Proposition 1]). However, average min-entropy can be converted to min-entropy when needed.

Lemma 4 ([DORS08, Lemma 2.2a]). *For any $\delta > 0$, $\mathbf{H}_\infty(X|Z = z)$ is at least $\tilde{\mathbf{H}}_\infty(X|Z) - \log(1/\delta)$ with probability at least $1 - \delta$ over the choice of z.*

This style of analysis—using average min-entropy wherever possible and converting it to min-entropy when needed—was used, for example, in [KR09], [CKOR10], to analyze complex interactive protocols involving extractors and MACs.

2   Computational Case

It is natural to say that if a distribution cannot be distinguished by a resource-bounded adversary from one that has entropy, then it has computational entropy. For example, pseudorandom distributions have this property.

Definition 4 ([HILL99, BSW03]). *A distribution X has* **HILL entropy** *at least k, denoted by $H_{\varepsilon,s}^{\mathsf{HILL}}(X) \geq k$, if there exists a distribution Y such that $H_\infty(Y) \geq k$ and no circuit of size s can distinguish X and Y with advantage more than ε.*

(Here and below, unless otherwise specified, distinguishers are randomized and output a single bit.)

A conditional notion can be defined similarly.

Definition 5 ([HLR07, Section 2]). *X has* **conditional HILL entropy** *at least k conditioned on Z, denoted $H_{\varepsilon,s}^{\mathsf{HILL}}(X|Z) \geq k$, if there exists a collection of distributions Y_z (for $z \in Z$) giving rise to a joint distribution (Y, Z), such that the average min-entropy $\tilde{H}_\infty(Y|Z) \geq k$ and no circuit of size s can distinguish (X, Z) and (Y, Z) with advantage more than ε.*

However, there are many variations of the computational definitions, and which one is "right" is unclear. For example, [GW11, Lemma 3.1] allow one to change not only X, but also Z, as long as the change is computationally indistinguishable.

As another example, [BSW03], following [Yao82], proposed an alternative way to measure computational entropy: by measuring compressibility of the string by efficient algorithms. It was further converted to conditional entropy in [HLR07].

Definition 6 ([HLR07, Section 2]). *X has* **Yao entropy** *at least k conditioned on Z, denoted by $H_{\varepsilon,s}^{\mathsf{Yao}}(X|Z) \geq k$, if for every pair of circuits c, d of total size s with the outputs of c having length ℓ,*

$$\Pr_{(x,z)\leftarrow(X,Z)}[d(c(x,z),z) = x] \leq 2^{\ell-k} + \varepsilon.$$

It was shown in [HLR07, Theorem 4] that the two notions (which are equivalent in the information-theoretic case) are actually different in the computational setting: Yao entropy may be higher than HILL (but never lower), and measuring Yao entropy rather than HILL entropy may allow one to extract more pseudorandom bits from a distribution.

Another seemingly natural computational analog of min-entropy is "unpredictability" entropy, because it also measures the chances of correctly guessing X in a single try.

Definition 7 ([HLR07, Section 5]). *X has* **unpredictability entropy** *at least k conditioned on Z, denoted by $H_{\varepsilon,s}^{\mathsf{unp}}(X|Z) \geq k$, if there exists a collection of distributions Y_z (for $z \in Z$), giving rise to a joint distribution (Y, Z), such* *that no circuit of size s can distinguish* (X, Z) *and* (Y, Z) *with advantage more than ε, and for all circuits C of size s,*

$$\Pr[C(Z) = Y] \leq 2^{-k}.$$

As shown in [HLR07, Section 5], unpredictability entropy can be higher than HILL entropy but never higher than Yao entropy. We know that extractors work with conditional HILL entropy to produce pseudorandom outputs; some extractors ("reconstructive" ones) also work with conditional compressibility and unpredictability entropies.

Understanding how conditioning on information leakage Z impacts the entropy of X is particularly difficult. It would be highly desirable to have an analog of the simple statement of Lemma 2 to simplify the analysis of protocols in a variety of scenarios, particularly in leakage-resilient cryptography. The following result, for both average-case and worst-case entropy, is relatively simple to state. However, it is for a notion of entropy that is a lot less natural: Metric* entropy, which differs from HILL entropy in two respects: there can be a different distribution Y for each distinguishing circuit of size s, and the circuit, instead outputting 1 with some probability p and 0 with probability $1 - p$, deterministically outputs a value p in the interval $[0, 1]$.

Theorem 1 ([FR11]). *Define P_z as $\Pr[Z = z]$. Assume Z has 2^b elements. Then*

$$H^{\mathtt{Metric}^*}_{\varepsilon/P_z, s'}(X|Z = z) \geq H^{\mathtt{Metric}^*}_{\varepsilon, s}(X) - \log 1/P_z$$

and

$$H^{\mathtt{Metric}^*}_{\varepsilon 2^b, s'}(X|Z) \geq H^{\mathtt{Metric}^*}_{\varepsilon, s}(X) - b,$$

where $s' \approx s$.

A weaker version of this statement appeared in [DP08]. Fortunately, Metric* entropy can be converted, with some relatively small loss in s and ε, to HILL entropy ([BSW03, Theorem 5.2],[FR11]). A similar statement, but with the conversion to HILL entropy already performed, appeared in [RTTV08].

An alternative statement, in which the circuit size (rather than the distinguishability ε) loses a factor polynomial in 2^b, is implied by [GW11, Lemma 3.1] and Lemma 2. Again, the statement is not with respect to HILL conditional entropy of Definition 5, but rather with respect to a relaxed notion that I will denote here HILL-relaxed. It is the same as conditional HILL, except we are allowed to change not just X, but the entire pair (X, Z) to an indistinguishable pair (Y, W).

Theorem 2 ([GW11]). *Define P_z as $\Pr[Z = z]$. Assume elements of Z are length-b bit strings (or, more generally, can be enumerated in time $\mathrm{poly}(2^b)$). Then*

$$H^{\mathsf{HILL\text{-}relaxed}}_{2\varepsilon, s'/\mathrm{poly}(\varepsilon, 2^b)}(X|Z) \geq H^{\mathsf{HILL}}_{\varepsilon, s}(X) - b.$$

This theorem extends to the case when the initial entropy of X is *conditional* HILL-relaxed (conditioned on some Z_1), similarly to the more general case of Lemma 2.

References

[BSW03]   Barak, B., Shaltiel, R., Wigderson, A.: Computational Analogues of Entropy. In: Arora, S., Jansen, K., Rolim, J.D.P., Sahai, A. (eds.) RANDOM 2003 and APPROX 2003. LNCS, vol. 2764, pp. 200–215. Springer, Heidelberg (2003)

[CKOR10]   Chandran, N., Kanukurthi, B., Ostrovsky, R., Reyzin, L.: Privacy amplification with asymptotically optimal entropy loss. In: Schulman, L.J. (ed.) STOC, pp. 785–794. ACM Press, New York (2010), Full version available from http://www.cs.bu.edu/fac/reyzin/

[DORS08]   Dodis, Y., Ostrovsky, R., Reyzin, L., Smith, A.: Fuzzy extractors: How to generate strong keys from biometrics and other noisy data. SIAM Journal on Computing 38(1), 97–139 (2007); arXiv:cs/0602007

[DP08]   Dziembowski, S., Pietrzak, K.: Leakage-resilient cryptography. In: Ravi [Rav08], pp. 293–302 (2008)

[FR11]   Fuller, B., Reyzin, L.: Computational entropy and information leakage (2011), Available from http://www.cs.bu.edu/fac/reyzin

[GW11]   Gentry, C., Wichs, D.: Separating succinct non-interactive arguments from all falsifiable assumptions. In: Vadhan, S. (ed.) STOC. ACM, New York (2011)

[HILL99]   Hastad, J., Impagliazzo, R., Levin, L.A., Luby, M.: Construction of pseudorandom generator from any one-way function. SIAM Journal on Computing 28(4), 1364–1396 (1999)

[HLR07]   Hsiao, C.-Y., Lu, C.-J., Reyzin, L.: Conditional Computational Entropy, or Toward Separating Pseudoentropy from Compressibility. In: Naor, M. (ed.) EUROCRYPT 2007. LNCS, vol. 4515, pp. 169–186. Springer, Heidelberg (2007)

[KR09]   Kanukurthi, B., Reyzin, L.: Key Agreement from Close Secrets over Unsecured Channels. In: Joux, A. (ed.) EUROCRYPT 2009. LNCS, vol. 5479, pp. 206–223. Springer, Heidelberg (2009), Full version available at http://eprint.iacr.org/2008/494

[NZ96]   Nisan, N., Zuckerman, D.: Randomness is linear in space. Journal of Computer and System Sciences 52(1), 43–53 (1996)

[Rav08]   Ravi, R. (ed.): 49th Annual IEEE Symposium on Foundations of Computer Science, FOCS 2008, Philadelphia, PA, USA, October 25-28. IEEE Computer Society, Los Alamitos (2008)

[RTTV08]   Reingold, O., Trevisan, L., Tulsiani, M., Vadhan, S.P.: Dense subsets of pseudorandom sets. In: Ravi [Rav08], pp. 76–85 (2008)

[RW04]   Renner, R., Wolf, S.: Smooth Rényi entropy and applications. In: Proceedings of IEEE International Symposium on Information Theory, p. 233 (June 2004)

[RW05]   Renner, R.S., Wolf, S.: Simple and Tight Bounds for Information Reconciliation and Privacy Amplification. In: Roy, B. (ed.) ASIACRYPT 2005. LNCS, vol. 3788, pp. 199–216. Springer, Heidelberg (2005)

[Yao82]   Yao, A.C.: Theory and applications of trapdoor functions. In: 23rd Annual Symposium on Foundations of Computer Science, November 3-5, pp. 80–91. IEEE, Los Alamitos (1982)

The Round Complexity of Perfectly Secure General VSS

Ashish Choudhury[1,*], Kaoru Kurosawa[2], and Arpita Patra[3,**]

[1] Applied Statistics Unit
Indian Statistical Institute Kolkata India
partho_31@yahoo.co.in, partho31@gmail.com
[2] Department of Computer and Information Sciences
Ibaraki University, Hitachi Ibaraki, Japan
kurosawa@mx.ibaraki.ac.jp
[3] Department of Computer Science
Aarhus University Denmark
arpitapatra10@gmail.com, arpita@cs.au.dk

Abstract. The round complexity of verifiable secret sharing (VSS) schemes has been studied extensively for threshold adversaries. In particular, Fitzi et al. showed an efficient 3-round VSS for $n \geq 3t + 1$ [4], where an infinitely powerful adversary can corrupt t (or less) parties out of n parties. This paper shows that for non-threshold adversaries:

1. Two round perfectly secure VSS is possible if and only if the underlying adversary structure satisfies the $\mathcal{Q}^4$ condition;

2. Three round perfectly secure VSS is possible if and only if the underlying adversary structure satisfies the $\mathcal{Q}^3$ condition.

Further as a special case of our three round protocol, we can obtain a more efficient 3-round VSS than the VSS of Fitzi et al. for $n = 3t + 1$. More precisely, the communication complexity of the reconstruction phase is reduced from $\mathcal{O}(n^3)$ to $\mathcal{O}(n^2)$. We finally point out a flaw in the reconstruction phase of the VSS of Fitzi et al., and show how to fix it.

1 Introduction

Verifiable Secret Sharing (VSS) [2,1] is a two phase (sharing, reconstruction) protocol, carried out among n parties and is used as a fundamental building block in many distributed cryptographic protocols. VSS extends the notion of secret sharing [10] to the *active* corruption model. In VSS protocols, an *infinitely powerful malicious adversary* can corrupt not only some subset of parties but also the *dealer*, who shares the secret. Even then, a unique secret is reconstructed in the reconstruction phase no matter how the malicious parties behave.

* Financial Support from Department of Information Technology, Government of India Acknowledged.
** Financial Support from Center for Research in Foundations of Electronic Markets, Denmark Acknowledged.

S. Fehr (Ed.): ICITS 2011, LNCS 6673, pp. 143–162, 2011.
© Springer-Verlag Berlin Heidelberg 2011

Round complexity is one of the important complexity measures of any VSS protocol. Gennaro et al. [5] studied the round complexity of perfectly secure VSS, where they defined the round complexity of a VSS protocol as the number of *communication rounds* during the sharing phase. In their model, the n parties are pairwise connected by secure channels and a *common broadcast* channel is available, which allows any party to send some information identically to every other party. The adversary is characterized as a *threshold* adversary, who can corrupt any t parties. In such a model, Gennaro et al. showed the following:

1. Two round perfectly secure VSS is possible if and only if $n \geq 4t + 1$;
2. Three round perfectly secure VSS is possible if and only if $n \geq 3t + 1$.

Their 3-round VSS for $n \geq 3t + 1$ is *inefficient* while their 2-round VSS for $n \geq 4t + 1$ is efficient. A polynomial time, 3-round VSS for $n \geq 3t + 1$ was given by Fitzi et al. [4]. Later on, Katz et al. [7] improved the VSS of [4] in such a way that the broadcast channel is used for only one round during the sharing phase, whereas it is used for two rounds in [4].

1.1   Motivation of Our Work

Modeling the adversary by a threshold helps in easy characterization of the protocols and it also helps in analyzing the protocols. However, as mentioned in [6], modeling the (dis)trust in the network as a threshold adversary is not always appropriate because threshold protocol requires more *stringent* requirements than the reality. Let the set of n parties be denoted by $\mathcal{P} = \{P_1, \ldots, P_n\}$. Then a *non-threshold general adversary* $\mathcal{A}$ is characterized by an *adversary structure* Γ, which is a collection of the subsets of parties that the adversary $\mathcal{A}$ can *potentially* corrupt. That is, $\Gamma = \{B \subset \mathcal{P} \mid \mathcal{A} \text{ can corrupt } B\}$. Moreover, we assume that if $B \in \Gamma$ and if $B' \subset B$, then $B' \in \Gamma$.

Definition 1 ($\mathcal{Q}^k$ Condition [6]). *$\mathcal{A}$ satisfies $\mathcal{Q}^k$ condition with respect to $\mathcal{P}$, if there exists no k sets in Γ, which adds upto the whole set $\mathcal{P}$. That is:*

$$\forall B_1, \ldots, B_k \in \Gamma : B_1 \cup \ldots \cup B_k \neq \mathcal{P}.$$

Cramer et al. [3] showed a VSS for $\mathcal{Q}^3$ adversary structures by using a linear secret sharing scheme (LSSS). The VSS of [3] is *efficient* in the size of the underlying LSSS (see Sec. 2.2 for the definition of LSSS), but requires *more than seven rounds*. Maurer showed a *four round* VSS for $\mathcal{Q}^3$ adversary structures [9]. However, its computation and communication cost is *inefficient*[1].

In threshold settings, any $t + 1$ honest parties can reconstruct not only the secret s but also the randomness used by the dealer during the sharing phase. On the other hand, in non-threshold settings, an *access set* of parties can reconstruct *only* s, but not the randomness of the dealer in general. This is because the submatrix of the LSSS corresponding to an access set A is not necessarily of

---

[1] We can see that its round complexity can be reduced to three by using the technique from [5] for making pairwise consistency checks. Still it is very inefficient.

full rank (see Section 2 and in general [3] for more details). Due to this reason, a straightforward generalization of the techniques of [5,4] will not work in non-threshold settings. Indeed [3] introduces a *commitment transfer protocol* and a *commitment sharing protocol* to design VSS for $\mathcal{Q}^3$ adversary structures [3].

Though there exist VSS protocols tolerating general adversary, to the best of our knowledge, *nothing is known in the literature regarding the round complexity of VSS tolerating general adversary*. This motivates us to do the same.

1.2   Our Results

We generalize the results of [5] and show the following:

1. Two round perfectly secure VSS is possible iff $\mathcal{A}$ satisfies the $\mathcal{Q}^4$ condition;
2. Three round perfectly secure VSS is possible iff $\mathcal{A}$ satisfies the $\mathcal{Q}^3$ condition.

In our 2-round VSS, the communication cost is polynomial in the size of the underlying LSSS, and the computation cost is polynomial in the size of Γ. So if $|\Gamma|$ and size of the underlying LSSS is polynomial then our 2-round scheme is efficient. On the other hand, in our 3-round VSS, both the communication and communication cost are polynomial in the size of the underlying LSSS. Thus if the underlying LSSS is polynomial then our 3-round scheme is efficient. Further as a special case of our 3-round protocol, we can obtain a more efficient 3-round VSS than the VSS of Fitzi et al. for $n = 3t+1$. More precisely, the communication complexity of the reconstruction phase is reduced from $\mathcal{O}(n^3)$ to $\mathcal{O}(n^2)$.

Fitzi et al. [4] first designed a 3-round *weak secret sharing* (WSS) protocol. WSS is the same as VSS except for that a unique secret or $\perp$ must be reconstructed in the reconstruction phase (when the dealer is corrupted). Then they constructed their 3-round VSS by letting each party run the WSS as a dealer in parallel. Typically, a party participates in the reconstruction phase of his own WSS as like any other party and does not play any special role. On the other hand for constructing our VSS protocol, we first design a 3-round *weak commitment scheme* (WCS), and then replace the WSS with our WCS. An important difference now is that each party plays a special role in the reconstruction phase of his own WCS. It turns out that it is easier to construct a WCS than the WSS, and the efficiency is improved. Our WCS is also conceptually much simpler.

To design our 2-round VSS protocol, we generalize the techniques used in [5]. Notice that a straightforward generalization will not work, as the protocol of [5] uses the properties of Reed-Solomon codes [8]. To deal with this problem, we introduce the notion of $\mathcal{A}$-clique. Due to this, the resultant protocol performs computation which is polynomial in $|\Gamma|$. We finally point out a flaw in the reconstruction phase of the VSS of Fitzi et al., and show how to fix it.

2   Preliminaries

2.1   Secret Sharing Scheme

In a secret sharing scheme, a dealer $D \in \mathcal{P}$ distributes a secret $s \in \mathbb{F}$, where $\mathbb{F}$ is a finite field, to the parties in $\mathcal{P}$ in such a way that some subsets of the participants (called as access sets) can reconstruct s from their shares, while the other subsets of the participants (called forbidden sets) have no information about s from their shares. The family of access sets is called an *access structure*. Moreover, we assume that the access structure is *monotone* implying that if $A \in \Sigma$ and $A' \supseteq A$, then $A' \in \Sigma$. Corresponding to Σ, we have the *adversary structure* $\Gamma = \Sigma^c$, where c denotes the complement. The sets in Γ are called as forbidden sets. There exists a *computationally unbounded, adaptive, rushing* adversary $\mathcal{A}$, who can control any set in Γ. *However, it is assumed that D will not be under the control of $\mathcal{A}$ and every party under the control of $\mathcal{A}$ will follow the protocol instructions.*

2.2 Linear Secret Sharing Scheme (LSSS) [3]

A secret sharing scheme for any monotone access structure Σ can be realized by a LSSS [3] as follows: Let $\mathcal{M}$ be an $\ell \times e$ matrix over $\mathbb{F}$ and $\psi : \{1, \cdots, \ell\} \to \{1, \cdots, n\}$ be a labeling function, where $\ell \geq e$ and $\ell \geq n$.

Sharing algorithm:

1. To share a secret $s \in \mathbb{F}$, D first chooses a random vector $\boldsymbol{\rho} \in \mathbb{F}^{e-1}$ and compute a vector

$$\boldsymbol{v} = (v_1, \cdots, v_\ell)^T = \mathcal{M} \cdot \begin{pmatrix} s \\ \boldsymbol{\rho} \end{pmatrix}. \tag{1}$$

2. Let

$$\mathsf{LSSS}(s, \boldsymbol{\rho}) = (\mathsf{share}_1, \cdots, \mathsf{share}_n), \tag{2}$$

where $\mathsf{share}_i = \{v_j \mid \psi(j) = i\}$. Then D gives share_i to P_i as a share for s.

Reconstruction algorithm: A set of parties $A \in \Sigma$ can reconstruct s if and only if $(1, 0, \cdots, 0)$ is in the linear span of

$$\mathcal{M}_A = \{\mathbf{V}_j \mid \psi(j) \in A\},$$

where $\mathbf{V}_j$ denotes the jth row of $\mathcal{M}$. If this is indeed the case then there exists a *recombination vector* $\boldsymbol{\alpha}_A$, such that $\boldsymbol{\alpha}_A \cdot \mathcal{M}_A = (1, 0, \ldots, 0)$. Let $\boldsymbol{s}_A$ denote the set of shares corresponding to the parties in A. Then these parties can reconstruct s by computing $s = \langle \boldsymbol{\alpha}_A, \boldsymbol{s}_A^T \rangle$, where $\langle x, y \rangle$ denotes the *dot product* of x and y.

Definition 2 (Monotone Span Programme (MSP) [3]). *We say that the above $(\mathcal{M}, \psi)$ is a MSP which realizes Σ and the size of the MSP is ℓ.*

Theorem 1 ([3]). *The above algorithm constitutes a valid secret sharing scheme.*

Theorem 2 ([3]). *Two different secrets shared according to an MSP realizing Σ cannot have same shares corresponding to an access set.*

Notice that there may be more than one row of $\mathcal{M}$ assigned to a party P_i. However, as assumed in [3], for the ease of presentation, we assume that each P_i is assigned exactly one row in $\mathcal{M}$, namely $\mathbf{V}_i$. This is without loss of generality. Finally we use the following notation throughout our paper.

Notation 1. *Let $\mathcal{R}$ be any subset of $\mathcal{P}$ i.e $\mathcal{R} \subseteq \mathcal{P}$. Then $\mathcal{M}_\mathcal{R}$ denotes the matrix containing the rows of $\mathcal{M}$ corresponding to the parties in $\mathcal{R}$.*

2.3   Verifiable Secret Sharing (VSS)

In the definition of secret sharing (see Sec. 2.1), we assumed that $D \notin \mathcal{A}$ and the parties under the control of $\mathcal{A}$ *honestly* follows the protocol. However these are very restricting assumptions. A VSS scheme relaxes these assumptions. In a VSS protocol, $D \in \mathcal{P}$, holds a secret $s \in \mathbb{F}$. The protocol consists of a sharing phase and a reconstruction phase. During the protocol, a *computationally unbounded* adversary $\mathcal{A}$ can select any set $B \in \Gamma$ (possibly including D) for corruption. Moreover, the corrupted parties can behave in *any arbitrary manner*. Now we call the protocol a VSS protocol if it satisfies the following conditions:

1. **Secrecy:** If D is *honest*, then s will be information theoretically secure during the sharing phase.
2. **Correctness:** If D is *honest*, then the honest parties will output s at the end of the reconstruction phase, irrespective of the behavior of $\mathcal{A}$.
3. **Strong Commitment:** If D is *corrupted*, then at the end of the sharing phase there is a value $s^\star \in \mathbb{F}$, such that at the end of the reconstruction phase all honest parties will output $s^\star$, irrespective of the behavior of $\mathcal{A}$.

3   Two Round VSS Tolerating $\mathcal{Q}^4$ Adversary Structure

Let $\mathcal{A}$ be a non-threshold adversary, characterized by an adversary structure Γ, such that $\mathcal{A}$ satisfies the $\mathcal{Q}^4$ condition. Moreover let $\mathcal{M}$ be the $n \times e$ MSP realizing the corresponding access structure $\Sigma = \Gamma^c$. We then present a two round VSS protocol tolerating $\mathcal{A}$. Before presenting our protocol, we give the following definition:

Definition 3 ($\mathcal{A}$-clique). *Let $G = (V, E)$ be an undirected graph, where $V = \mathcal{P}$ and let C be a clique in G. Moreover, let V_C denote the vertices belonging to C. Then we say that C is an $\mathcal{A}$-clique in G if $V \setminus V_C \in \Gamma$. That is, the set $B = V \setminus V_C$ belongs to the adversary structure.*

Algorithm for Finding $\mathcal{A}$-clique: Let $\Gamma = \{B_1, \ldots, B_{|\Gamma|}\}$. For $i = 1, \ldots, \Gamma$, check whether the parties in $\mathcal{P} \setminus B_i$ form a clique in G, which requires *polynomial computation*. If yes, then the algorithm terminates and $\mathcal{P} \setminus B_i$ is the $\mathcal{A}$-clique. If there exists no $B_i \in \Gamma$ such that $\mathcal{P} \setminus B_i$ form a clique in G then there is no $\mathcal{A}$-clique. *This algorithm performs computation, which is polynomial in $|\Gamma|$.*

Our two round protocol is given in Fig. 1.

We now proceed to prove the properties of the protocol. In the proof, we will use the following notations:

– Let ShHo (resp. ShB) denote the set of honest (resp. corrupted) parties in Sh at the end of sharing phase when sharing phase is successful.
– Let ReHo (resp. ReB) denote the set of honest (resp. corrupted) parties in Rec.

Lemma 1. *An honest D will never be discarded during sharing phase.*

Sharing Phase

Round I:

1. D selects a random, symmetric $e \times e$ matrix R, such that $R[1,1] = s$.
2. D computes $u_i = \mathbf{V}_i \cdot R$ and sends u_i to P_i. The first entry of u_i, denoted by s_i, is referred as i^{th} share of s, given to P_i. Moreover, $\langle u_i, \mathbf{V}_j \rangle$, for $j = 1, \ldots, n$, is referred as j^{th} share-share of s_i, denoted by s_{ij}.
3. For $i = 1, \ldots, n - 1$, party P_i selects a random r_{ij} for every P_j, where $j > i$ and privately sends r_{ij} to P_j.

Round II:

1. For $i = 1, \ldots, n$, party P_i broadcasts the following, for each $j \neq i$:
   - $a_{ij} = r_{ij} + \langle u_i, \mathbf{V}_j \rangle = r_{ij} + s_{ij}$, if $j > i$;
   - $a_{ij} = r_{ji} + \langle u_i, \mathbf{V}_j \rangle = r_{ji} + s_{ij}$, if $j < i$;

Local Computation (By Each Party):

1. Construct an undirected graph G_{Sh} over $\mathcal{P}$, where there exists an edge (P_i, P_j), for $j > i$, if $a_{ij} = a_{ji}$. Notice that all honest parties will construct the *same* G_{Sh}.
2. If no $\mathcal{A}$-clique is present in G_{Sh} then the *sharing phase fails* and D is *discarded*. [a]
3. If there is an $\mathcal{A}$-clique in G_{Sh}, then *sharing phase succeeds*. Let Sh denote the parties in $\mathcal{A}$-clique and let Sh-Del $= \mathcal{P} \setminus$ Sh. Notice that all honest parties will find the *same* $\mathcal{A}$-clique and hence the same Sh.

Reconstruction Phase

Round I:

1. Each party $P_i \in$ Sh broadcasts u_i received from D. Let it be denoted by $\overline{u}_i$.

Local Computation (By Each Party):

1. Construct an undirected graph G_{Rec} over the set of parties in Sh, where there exists an edge (P_i, P_j), for $j > i$, if both $P_i, P_j \in$ Sh and $\langle \overline{u}_i, \mathbf{V}_j \rangle = \langle \overline{u}_j, \mathbf{V}_i \rangle$.
2. Find $\mathcal{A}$-clique (which is bound to exist) in G_{Rec}. Let Rec denote the parties in $\mathcal{A}$-clique and let Rec-Del $=$ Sh $\setminus$ Rec. Notice that all honest parties will find the *same* $\mathcal{A}$-clique and hence the set Rec.
3. Without loss of generality, let $P_1, \ldots, P_{|\mathsf{Rec}|}$ be the parties in Rec and let $\overline{s}_1, \ldots, \overline{s}_{|\mathsf{Rec}|}$ be the shares (the first entry of $\overline{u}_i$'s) revealed by these parties. Then reconstruct $\overline{s}$ by applying reconstruction algorithm of the LSSS to $\overline{s}_1, \ldots, \overline{s}_{|\mathsf{Rec}|}$ and terminate.

---

[a] Following the convention of [5,4,7], if D is discarded during the sharing phase, then some pre-defined value from $\mathbb{F}$ is taken as D's secret.

Fig. 1. Two Round VSS for Sharing a Secret s Tolerating $\mathcal{A}$

Proof: If D is honest, then $\langle u_i, \mathbf{V}_j \rangle = \langle u_j, \mathbf{V}_i \rangle$ and hence $a_{ij} = a_{ji}$ will hold for each honest P_i, P_j. So the set of honest parties will form an $\mathcal{A}$-clique in G_{Sh} and D will not be discarded. □

Lemma 2. *If the sharing phase succeeds, then ShHo is an access set. Moreover, $\langle u_i, \mathbf{V}_j \rangle = \langle u_j, \mathbf{V}_i \rangle$ will hold for each $P_i, P_j \in$ ShHo, where $i < j$.*

Proof. It is easy to see that $\mathsf{ShHo} \cup \mathsf{ShB} \cup \mathsf{Sh\text{-}Del} = \mathcal{P}$. If the sharing phase succeeds, then $\mathsf{Sh\text{-}Del} \in \Gamma$. Also $\mathsf{ShB} \in \Gamma$. Now if $\mathsf{ShHo} \in \Gamma$, then it implies that $\mathcal{A}$ does not satisfy $\mathcal{Q}^3$ (and hence $\mathcal{Q}^4$) condition, which is a contradiction. The second part of the lemma follows from the fact if $P_i, P_j \in \mathsf{ShHo}$, then $a_{ij} = a_{ji}$ and both P_i and P_j would have honestly used r_{ij}. $\qquad\square$

Lemma 3. *Without loss of generality, let* $\mathsf{ShHo} = \{P_1, \ldots, P_t\}$. *If the sharing phase succeeds, then there exists a vector* $\boldsymbol{x} = (s^\star, \boldsymbol{\rho})$, *for some* $\boldsymbol{\rho} \in \mathbb{F}^{e-1}$, *such that*

$$(s_1, \ldots, s_t)^T = \mathcal{M}_{ShHo} \cdot \boldsymbol{x}^T.$$

In other words, the shares of the parties in ShHo *will be valid shares of* $s^\star$, *such that D will be committed to $s^\star$. Moreover, if D is honest then $s^\star = s$.*

Proof. From the previous lemma, if the sharing phase succeeds, then for each $P_i, P_j \in \mathsf{ShHo}$, we have $s_{ij} = s_{ji}$. Let $S_{ShHo} = \{s_{ij}\}$ be the $t \times t$ symmetric matrix. Then S_{ShHo} can be expressed as

$$S_{ShHo} = \mathcal{M}_{ShHo} \cdot U_{ShHo} = U_{ShHo}^T \cdot \mathcal{M}_{HaHo}^T,$$

where $U_{ShHo} = [\boldsymbol{u_1}^T, \ldots, \boldsymbol{u_t}^T]$. Also from the previous lemma, ShHo is an access set. Therefore, there exists a recombination vector $\boldsymbol{\alpha}_{ShHo}$, such that $\boldsymbol{\alpha}_{ShHo} \cdot \mathcal{M}_{ShHo} = (1, 0, \ldots, 0)$. Hence,

$$\boldsymbol{\alpha}_{ShHo} \cdot S_{ShHo} = \boldsymbol{\alpha}_{ShHo} \cdot \mathcal{M}_{ShHo} \cdot U_{ShHo} = (1, 0, \ldots, 0) \cdot U_{ShHo} = (s_1, \ldots, s_t).$$

On the other hand,

$$\boldsymbol{\alpha}_{ShHo} \cdot S_{ShHo} = \boldsymbol{\alpha}_{ShHo} \cdot U_{ShHo}^T \cdot \mathcal{M}_{ShHo}^T = \boldsymbol{x} \cdot \mathcal{M}_{ShHo}^T,$$

where $\boldsymbol{x} = \boldsymbol{\alpha}_{ShHo} \cdot U_{ShHo}^T$. Therefore, $(s_1, \ldots, s_t) = \boldsymbol{x} \cdot \mathcal{M}_{ShHo}^T = \mathcal{M}_{ShHo} \cdot \boldsymbol{x}^T$.

If D is honest then $s^\star = s$. Because, in this case, $\boldsymbol{x} = \boldsymbol{\alpha}_{ShHo} \cdot U_{ShHo}^T = \boldsymbol{\alpha}_{ShHo} \cdot \mathcal{M}_{ShHo} \cdot R = (1, 0, \ldots, 0) \cdot R$, which is nothing but the first row of R. $\square$

Lemma 4. *If the sharing phase succeeds, then an $\mathcal{A}$-clique will be present in* G_{Rec}.

Proof. From Lemma 2, ShHo is an access set and for each $P_i, P_j \in \mathsf{ShHo}$, we have $\langle u_i, \mathbf{V}_j \rangle = \langle u_j, \mathbf{V}_i \rangle$. During the reconstruction phase, each $P_i, P_j \in \mathsf{ShHo}$ will correctly broadcast $\bar{u}_i = u_i$ and $\bar{u}_j = u_j$ respectively. So during the reconstruction phase also, $\langle u_i, \mathbf{V}_j \rangle = \langle u_j, \mathbf{V}_i \rangle$ will hold. Thus ShHo will always form an $\mathcal{A}$-clique in G_{Rec}. $\qquad\square$

Lemma 5. *If the sharing phase succeeds, then* ReHo *will be an access set. Moreover, the shares of the parties in* ReHo *will define the same secret* $s^\star$, *as committed by D to the parties in* ShHo *during the sharing phase.*

Proof. Notice that $\mathsf{ReHo} \cup \mathsf{ReB} \cup \mathsf{Rec\text{-}Del} \cup \mathsf{Sh\text{-}Del} = \mathcal{P}$. Now we know that $\mathsf{Sh\text{-}Del}, \mathsf{Rec\text{-}Del} \in \Gamma$. Also $\mathsf{ReB} \in \Gamma$. Now if $\mathsf{ReHo} \in \Gamma$, then it implies that $\mathcal{A}$ does not satisfy $\mathcal{Q}^4$ condition, which is a contradiction. The second part of the lemma follows from the fact that $\mathsf{ReHo} \subseteq \mathsf{ShHo}$. $\qquad\square$

Lemma 6. *During the reconstruction phase, every* $P_i \in$ Rec *will correctly disclose* s_i, *the* i^{th} *share of the secret* $s^\star$, *which is committed by* D *during the sharing phase to the parties in* ShHo.

Proof: The lemma holds trivially when $P_i \in$ Rec is *honest*. We now consider the case when $P_i \in$ Rec is *corrupted*. Before proceeding further, notice that P_i will have an edge with each of the parties in ReHo in graph G_{Rec}, since the set of parties in Rec forms a clique. This further implies that $\overline{u}_i$ disclosed by P_i satisfies $\langle \overline{u}_i, \mathbf{V}_j \rangle = \langle \overline{u}_j, \mathbf{V}_i \rangle$, for each $P_j \in$ ReHo. That is, $s_{ij} = s_{ji}$, for each $P_j \in$ ReHo. Also $\overline{u}_j = u_j$, for each $P_j \in$ ReHo. For simplicity assume that ShHo and ReHo contains the first t and y parties respectively, where $y \leq t$. Now from Lemma 3, we know that there exists $\boldsymbol{x} = (s^\star, \boldsymbol{\rho})$, such that

$$(s_1, \ldots, s_t)^T = \mathcal{M}_{ShHo} \cdot \boldsymbol{x}^T$$

Now following the notations as used in Lemma 3, we also have

$$(s_1, \ldots, s_y)^T = \mathcal{M}_{ReHo} \cdot \boldsymbol{x}^T$$

Now $(s_1, \ldots, s_y)^T = \mathcal{M}_{ReHo} \cdot \boldsymbol{x}^T$ implies that $\boldsymbol{x} \cdot \mathcal{M}_{ReHo}^T = \boldsymbol{\alpha}_{ReHo} \cdot U_{ReHo}^T \cdot \mathcal{M}_{ReHo}^T$. This is because $(s_1, \ldots, s_y)^T = \mathcal{M}_{ReHo} \cdot \boldsymbol{x}^T$ implies that

$$
\begin{aligned}
\boldsymbol{x} \cdot \mathcal{M}_{ReHo}^T &= (s_1, \ldots, s_y) \quad \text{(taking transpose on both sides)} \\
&= (1, 0, \ldots, 0) \cdot U_{ReHo} \\
&= \boldsymbol{\alpha}_{ReHo} \cdot \mathcal{M}_{ReHo} \cdot U_{ReHo} \\
&= \boldsymbol{\alpha}_{ReHo} \cdot U_{ReHo}^T \cdot \mathcal{M}_{ReHo}^T
\end{aligned}
$$

Here $\boldsymbol{\alpha}_{ReHo}$ is the recombination vector corresponding to the access set ReHo and $U_{ReHo} = [\boldsymbol{u}_1^T, \ldots, \boldsymbol{u}_y^T]$. Now we will show that $s_i = \overline{u}_{i1}$, as revealed by corrupted $P_i \in$ Rec is the ith share of $s^\star$. That is, $s_i = \boldsymbol{x} \cdot \mathbf{V}_i^T = \mathbf{V}_i \cdot \boldsymbol{x}^T$. Now notice that, $\boldsymbol{\alpha}_{ReHo} \cdot \mathcal{M}_{ReHo} = (1, 0, \ldots, 0)$. It is easy to see that

$$\boldsymbol{\alpha}_{ReHo} \cdot [s_{i1}, \ldots, s_{iy}]^T = \overline{u}_{i1} \tag{3}$$

Now we will show that following also is true:

$$\boldsymbol{\alpha}_{ReHo} \cdot [s_{1i}, \ldots, s_{yi}]^T = \boldsymbol{x} \cdot \mathbf{V}_i^T \tag{4}$$

We start with the known equation:

$$S_{ReHo} = U_{ReHo}^T \cdot \mathcal{M}_{ReHo}^T$$

Here $S_{ReHo} = \{s_{ij} : 1 \leq i, j \leq y\}$ is the symmetric matrix. Now pre-multiplying both the sides of above equation by $\boldsymbol{\alpha}_{ReHo}$, we get

$$\boldsymbol{\alpha}_{ReHo} \cdot S_{ReHo} = \boldsymbol{\alpha}_{ReHo} \cdot U_{ReHo}^T \cdot \mathcal{M}_{ReHo}^T$$

Now we know that $\boldsymbol{\alpha}_{ReHo} \cdot U_{ReHo}^T \cdot \mathcal{M}_{ReHo}^T = \boldsymbol{x} \cdot \mathcal{M}_{ReHo}^T$. So substituting in the above equation, we get

$$\boldsymbol{\alpha}_{ReHo} \cdot S_{ReHo} = \boldsymbol{x} \cdot \mathcal{M}_{ReHo}^T$$

Both the sides of the above equation turns out to be some row vector of equal length. Now concentrating on the value of the ith index of the row vectors in the above equation, we get $\boldsymbol{\alpha}_{ReHo} \cdot [s_{1i}, \ldots, s_{yi}]^T = \boldsymbol{x} \cdot \mathbf{V}_i^T$. Now as discussed above, $s_{ij} = s_{ji}$, for $j = 1, \ldots, y$. So left hand side of Eqn. 3 and Eqn. 4 are same. Thus s_i revealed by $P_i \in \mathsf{Rec}$ is the ith share of $s^\star$. $\qquad\square$

Now using the above lemmas, we prove the following theorem.

Theorem 3. *The protocol in Fig. 1 is a two round VSS scheme tolerating $\mathcal{A}$, satisfying the $\mathcal{Q}^4$ condition. The communication cost is polynomial in the size of $\mathcal{M}$, and the computation cost is polynomial in the size of Γ.*

PROOF: We only show that the protocol satisfies all the properties of VSS, as round, computation and communication complexity are easy to verify.

1. **Secrecy:** We have to only consider the case when D is honest. Let the adversary corrupt some $B \in \Gamma$. Then at the end of **Round I** of the sharing phase, adversary learns no information about s from their shares, as B is a non-access set. Let $i \notin B$ and $j \notin B$. Then at the end of **Round I** of the sharing phase, the adversary gains no information about r_{ij}. Hence at the end of **Round II**, adversary gains no information about u_i, as r_{ij} or r_{ji} works as the one-time pad. Thus, at the end of the sharing phase, s remains information theoretically secure (see [3] for complete details).

2. **Correctness:** We have to consider the case when D is honest. If D is honest then the sharing phase will succeed. Now the parties in ShHo is an access set and defines s. Moreover, correct share of s will be revealed by every P_i in Rec. These facts guarantee that by applying the reconstruction algorithm of the LSSS to the shares of the parties in Rec, s will be reconstructed correctly.

3. **Strong Commitment:** We have to consider the case when D is corrupted. The proof is very similar to the proof of correctness. In this case, the parties in ShHo is an access set and defines some secret $s^\star$, which is D's committed secret. Moreover, ReHo is an access set where $\mathsf{ReHo} \subseteq \mathsf{ShHo}$ and hence define the same secret $s^\star$. Furthermore, correct share of $s^\star$ will be revealed by every P_i in Rec. These facts guarantee that by applying the reconstruction algorithm of the LSSS to the shares of the parties in Rec, secret $s^\star$ will be reconstructed correctly and uniquely. $\qquad\square$

4   Three Round VSS Tolerating $\mathcal{Q}^3$ Adversary Structure

We first design a three round *weak commitment scheme* (WCS) protocol.

4.1   Three Round WCS Tolerating $\mathcal{Q}^3$ Adversary Structure

In a WCS, there exists a dealer $D \in \mathcal{P}$, who has a secret $s \in \mathbb{F}$, which he wants to commit to the parties in $\mathcal{P}$. The scheme consists of two phases as follows:

1. **Commit phase:** Initially, D has a secret s. At the end of the commit phase, either D is discarded (by all honest parties) or s is committed.

2. **Decommit phase:** If D is not discarded during the commit phase then:
   - D broadcasts (s, ρ), where ρ is the randomness used by D during the commit phase.
   - Each P_i broadcasts its view w_i of the commit phase.
   - Then a validity check function Valid is applied which outputs either *valid* or *invalid*.
   We say that s is accepted as *authentic* if

$$\mathsf{Valid}(s, \rho, w_1, \cdots, w_n) = \text{ valid}.$$

A protocol is a WCS scheme tolerating $\mathcal{A}$ if the following conditions are satisfied:

1. **Secrecy:** If D is *honest*, then $\mathcal{A}$ obtains no information about s during the commit phase.
2. **Correctness:** If D is *honest* then s will be accepted as authentic during the decommit phase.
3. **Weak Commitment:** If D is *corrupted* and not discarded during the commit phase, then there exists an $s^* \in \mathbb{F}$, such that D is committed to s^* during the commit phase. Moreover, if some s' is accepted as authentic during the decommit phase, then $s' = s^*$.

The *round complexity* of a WCS scheme is the number of communication rounds during the commit phase. We now present our three round WCS in Fig. 2.

We now show that the scheme presented in Fig. 2 is a valid WCS scheme, tolerating $\mathcal{A}$, provided $\mathcal{A}$ satisfies the $\mathcal{Q}^3$ condition. In the proofs, we use the following notations:

- Let HaHo (resp. HaB) denote the set of happy and honest (resp. happy and corrupted) parties at the end of commit phase if commit phase is successful.
- Let WCoHo (resp. WCoB) denote the set of honest (resp. corrupted) parties in $WCORE$ if decommit phase is successful.

Lemma 7. *If D is honest, then D will not be discarded during the commit phase. Moreover, s will be accepted as authentic during the decommit phase.*

Proof. By easy inspection we note that the set UnHappy contains only corrupted parties, when D is honest. Thus UnHappy $\in \Gamma$ and so the commit phase succeeds.

Now to show that s will be accepted as authentic during the decommit phase, we prove that $\mathcal{P} \setminus WCORE \in \Gamma$ during the decommit phase. To begin with, an honest D will correctly broadcast $\boldsymbol{x}' = \boldsymbol{x}$ and each honest P_i will correctly broadcast $s_i' = s_i$. Thus, all honest parties will be present in $WCORE$ and hence $\mathcal{P} \setminus WCORE$ will contain only corrupted parties. Hence $\mathcal{P} \setminus WCORE \in \Gamma$. Thus the decommit phase will also succeed and s will be accepted as authentic.   □

Lemma 8. *If the commit phase succeeds, then HaHo is an access set. Moreover, for each $P_i, P_j \in$ HaHo, where $i < j$, $\langle u_i, \mathbf{V}_j \rangle = \langle u_j, \mathbf{V}_i \rangle$.*

Proof. It is easy to see that HaHo $\cup$ HaB $\cup$ UnHappy $= \mathcal{P}$. If the commit phase succeeds, then UnHappy $\in \Gamma$. Also HaB $\in \Gamma$. This implies that HaHo $\notin \Gamma$, otherwise $\mathcal{A}$ does not satisfy $\mathcal{Q}^3$ condition, which is a contradiction. The second part follows from easy inspection.   □

Commit Phase

Round I:

1. D selects a random, symmetric $e \times e$ matrix R, such that $R[1,1] = s$. Let $\boldsymbol{x} = (s, \boldsymbol{\rho})$ be the first column (and row) of R.
2. D computes $u_i = \mathbf{V}_i \cdot R$ and privately sends u_i to party P_i. The first entry of u_i, denoted by s_i, is referred as the share of s, given to party P_i. Moreover, $\langle u_i, \mathbf{V}_j \rangle$ is referred as the jth share-share of s_i, denoted by s_{ij}.
3. Party P_i, for $i = 1, \ldots, n-1$, selects a random pad r_{ij}, for each $j > i$ and privately sends r_{ij} to party P_j.

Round II:

1. For $i = 1, \ldots, n$, party P_i broadcasts the following, for each $j \neq i$:
   - $a_{ij} = r_{ij} + \langle u_i, \mathbf{V}_j \rangle = r_{ij} + s_{ij}$, if $j > i$;
   - $a_{ij} = r_{ji} + \langle u_i, \mathbf{V}_j, \rangle = r_{ji} + s_{ij}$, if $j < i$;

Round III:

1. For each pair (i, j), such that $j > i$, if $a_{ij} \neq a_{ji}$, then
   - P_i broadcasts $\alpha_{ij} = \langle u_i, \mathbf{V}_j \rangle$;
   - P_j broadcasts $\beta_{ji} = \langle u_j, \mathbf{V}_i \rangle$;
   - D broadcasts $\gamma_{ij} = \langle u_i, \mathbf{V}_j \rangle = \langle u_j, \mathbf{V}_i \rangle$.
   Party P_i (P_j) is said to be *unhappy*, if the value broadcasted by him, mismatches the value broadcasted by D.

Local Computation (By Each Party):

1. Let UnHappy be the set of unhappy parties. If UnHappy $\in \Gamma$, then the commit phase succeeds. Otherwise, *commit phase fails* and D is discarded.

Decommit Phase

Round I:

1. D broadcasts the first row of R used by him during the sharing phase. Let it be denoted by $\boldsymbol{x}'$ and let s' be the first entry of $\boldsymbol{x}'$.
2. Each *happy* party P_i broadcasts the share received by him from D during the sharing phase. Let it be denoted by s_i'.

Local Computation (By Each Party):

1. Let $WCORE$ be the set of all such *happy* P_i's, such that $\boldsymbol{x}' \cdot \mathbf{V}_i^T = s_i'$. In other words, a happy $P_i \in WCORE$ if s_i' is a valid share of s' according to the LSSS.
2. If $\mathcal{P} \setminus WCORE \in \Gamma$, then *decommit succeeds* and so accept s' as authentic.
3. If $\mathcal{P} \setminus WCORE \notin \Gamma$, then *decommit fails* and so do not accept s' as authentic.

Fig. 2. Three Round WCS for Committing a Secret s

Lemma 9. *Without loss of generality, let* HaHo $= \{P_1, \ldots, P_t\}$. *If the commit phase succeeds, then there exists a vector* $\boldsymbol{x}^\star = (s^\star, \rho)$, *where* $\rho \in \mathbb{F}^{e-1}$ *such that*

$$(s_1, \ldots, s_t)^T = \mathcal{M}_{HaHo} \cdot \boldsymbol{x}^{\star T}.$$

In other words, D will commit the secret $s^\star$ to the parties in HaHo. Moreover, if D is honest then $x^\star = x$, where x is the first column of R used by D during the sharing phase and hence $s^\star = s$.

Proof: Follows using similar arguments as used in Lemma 3.   □

Lemma 10. *If the decommit phase succeeds, then WCoHo is an access set and $\langle u_i, \mathbf{V}_j \rangle = \langle u_j, \mathbf{V}_i \rangle$ for each $P_i, P_j \in$ WCoHo. Furthermore, the shares of the parties in WCoHo define the same secret as defined by shares of the parties in HaHo.*

Proof: Notice that WCoHo $\cup$ WCoB $\cup$ $(\mathcal{P} \setminus WCORE) = \mathcal{P}$. If the decommit phase succeeds, then $\mathcal{P} \setminus WCORE \in \Gamma$. Also, WCoB $\in \Gamma$. This implies that WCoHo $\notin \Gamma$, otherwise $\mathcal{A}$ does not satisfy the $\mathcal{Q}^3$ condition. The second and third part follows from Lemma 8 and the fact that WCoHo $\subseteq$ HaHo.   □

Theorem 4. *The protocol in Fig. 2 is a three round WCS scheme where the honest parties perform computation and communication, polynomial in $\mathcal{M}$.*

Proof: We only show that the protocol satisfies the properties of WCS scheme. The other properties follows easily from inspection.

1. **Secrecy:** Follows using similar arguments as used in our two round VSS.
2. **Correctness:** Follows from Lemma 7.
3. **Weak Commitment:** We have to consider the case when D is *corrupted*. If decommit phase fails, then it satisfies weak commitment. On the other hand, if decommit succeeds and s' is accepted as authentic then it implies that for each $P_i \in WCORE$, $x' \cdot \mathbf{V}_i^T = s'_i = \mathbf{V}_i \cdot x'^T$, where $x' = [s', \rho']$. This will also be true for each party in WCoHo. Without loss of generality, assume that the first y parties are present in WCoHo. The parties in WCoHo are honest implies $s_i = s'_i$ for $i = 1, \ldots, y$. Therefore we have $(s_1, \ldots, s_y)^T = \mathcal{M}_{WCoHo} \cdot x'^T$. Also from Lemma 9, we have $(s_1, \ldots, s_y)^T = \mathcal{M}_{WCoHo} \cdot x^{\star T}$, where $x^\star = [s^\star, \rho]$. Now this imply that $s' = s^\star$ because WCoHo is an access set and two different secrets cannot have same shares corresponding to an access set (see Theorem 2). Hence, the accepted secret s' is the same secret $s^\star$, as committed by D to WCoHo $\subseteq$ HaHo.   □

4.2 Three Round VSS Tolerating $\mathcal{Q}^3$ Adversary Structure

Now we design our three round VSS (given in Fig. 3) using our three round WCS as a black-box. We now prove the properties of the VSS protocol. For the proof, we use the following notations:

- Let ShHo (resp. ShB) denote the set of honest (resp. corrupted) parties in Sh at the end of sharing phase when the sharing phase is successful.
- ReHo (resp. ReB) denote the set of honest (resp. corrupted) parties in Rec.

Lemma 11. *If D is honest then the sharing phase will always succeed.*

Sharing Phase

Round I:
1. D performs the first two steps as in the commit phase of three round WCS.
2. Each party P_i selects a random value r^i and starts executing an instance of three round WCS protocol to commit r^i, as a dealer. We denote the ith instance of WCS as WCS_i. Let $r_1^i, \ldots, r_n^i$ denote the shares of r^i generated in WCS_i, such that P_i has given r_j^i to P_j during **Round I** of WCS_i.

Round II:
1. For $i = 1, \ldots, n$, party P_i broadcasts the following, for each $j \neq i$: $a_{ij} = r_j^i + \langle u_i, \mathbf{V}_j \rangle = r_j^i + s_{ij}$; and $b_{ij} = r_i^j + \langle u_i, \mathbf{V}_j \rangle = r_i^j + s_{ij}$.
2. Concurrently, **Round II** of WCS_i is executed, for $i = 1, \ldots, n$.

Round III:
1. For each pair (i, j), such that $a_{ij} \neq b_{ji}$, parties do the following:
   - P_i broadcasts $\alpha_{ij} = \langle u_i, \mathbf{V}_j \rangle$; P_j broadcasts $\beta_{ji} = \langle u_j, \mathbf{V}_i \rangle$ and D broadcasts $\gamma_{ij} = \langle u_i, \mathbf{V}_j \rangle = \langle u_j, \mathbf{V}_i \rangle$.
   P_i (P_j) is *unhappy*, if α_{ij} (β_{ji}) mismatches γ_{ij}.
2. Concurrently, **Round III** of WCS_i is executed, for $i = 1, \ldots, n$.

Local Computation (By Each Party):
1. Let Sh be the set of *happy* parties such that their instance of the commit phase of WCS as a dealer is successful. Let Ha_i denote the set of happy parties in the sharing phase of WCS_i for $P_i \in \mathsf{Sh}$.
2. Continue to keep a party P_i in Sh if $\mathcal{P} \setminus (\mathsf{Sh} \cap \mathsf{Ha}_i) \in \Gamma$. Otherwise remove P_i from Sh.
3. Repeat the previous step, till no more parties can be removed from Sh. Now if $\mathcal{P} \setminus \mathsf{Sh} \in \Gamma$, then *the sharing phase succeeds*. Otherwise, it fails and D is discarded.

Reconstruction Phase

Round I:
1. For each $P_i \in \mathsf{Sh}$, run the decommit phase of WCS_i.
2. Every $P_i \in \mathsf{Sh}$ broadcasts the vector obtained from D. Let it be denoted by $\overline{u_i}$.

Local Computation (By Each Party):
1. Let Rec be the set of parties P_i from Sh, such that both the following hold:
   - The decommit phase of WCS_i is successful, with output say $\overline{r^i}$ being accepted as authentic. Let $WCORE_i$ be the $WCORE$, corresponding to WCS_i and let $\overline{r_j^i}$ be the share of $\overline{r^i}$, as disclosed by $P_j \in WCORE_i$ during the decommit phase of WCS_i.
   - Compute $\overline{s_{ij}}$ for every $P_j \in WCORE_i$ as follows:
     (a) $\overline{s_{ij}} = \gamma_{ij}$; if γ_{ij} was broadcasted by D during **Round III** of the sharing phase.
     (b) $\overline{s_{ij}} = a_{ij} - \overline{r_j^i}$; if γ_{ij} was not broadcasted by D during **Round III** of the sharing phase. Here a_{ij} was broadcasted by P_i during the sharing phase.
     Now the computed $\overline{s_{ij}}$'s corresponding to each $P_j \in WCORE_i$ must be consistent with $\overline{u_i}$. Precisely $\overline{s_{ij}} = \langle \overline{u_i}, \mathbf{V}_j \rangle$ must hold, for every $P_j \in WCORE_i$.
2. For every $P_i \in \mathsf{Rec}$, assign $\overline{s_i} = \overline{u_{i1}}$, where $\overline{u_{i1}}$ is the first entry of $\overline{u_i}$.
3. Compute $\overline{s}$ from $\overline{s_i}$'s corresponding to $P_i \in \mathsf{Rec}$ using reconstruction algorithm of LSSS.

Fig. 3. Three Round VSS for Sharing Secret s Tolerating $\mathcal{A}$

Proof. To show that the sharing phase succeeds for an honest D, we prove that $\mathcal{P} \setminus \mathsf{Sh} \in \Gamma$. This is proved by showing that an honest party can never be in $\mathcal{P} \setminus \mathsf{Sh}$ and therefore $\mathcal{P} \setminus \mathsf{Sh}$ contains only a set of corrupted parties. First we note that each honest party P_i will be happy and their instance of WCS will be successful and Ha_i will include all honest parties. Naturally, $\mathcal{P} \setminus (\mathsf{Sh} \cap \mathsf{Ha}_i)$ contains only corrupted parties and will belong to Γ. Thus, all honest parties will be present in Sh. Equivalently, $\mathcal{P} \setminus \mathsf{Sh}$ contains only a set of corrupted parties.   □

Lemma 12. *If the sharing phase succeeds, then* ShHo *is an access set. Moreover, for each* $P_i, P_j \in \mathsf{ShHo}$, $\langle u_i, \mathbf{V}_j \rangle = \langle u_j, \mathbf{V}_i \rangle$. *Furthermore, without loss of generality, let* $\mathsf{ShHo} = \{P_1, \ldots, P_t\}$. *Then there exists a vector* $\boldsymbol{x} = (s^\star, \rho)$, *such that*

$$(s_1, \ldots, s_t)^T = \mathcal{M}_{\mathsf{ShHo}}.\boldsymbol{x}^T.$$

In other words, D will commit the secret $s^\star$ to the parties in ShHo *during the sharing phase. Moreover, if D is honest then $s^\star = s$.*

Proof. Follows using similar arguments as used in our two round VSS and three round WCS.   □

Lemma 13. *If the sharing phase succeeds then* $\mathsf{ShHo} = \mathsf{ReHo}$.

Proof. During the reconstruction phase, every honest $P_i \in \mathsf{Sh}$ will correctly broadcast the vector which it received from D during sharing phase. So we have $\overline{u_i} = u_i$. Now from the correctness property of WCS scheme, the decommit phase of WCS_i, corresponding to the honest P_i will be successful and r^i will be accepted as authentic. So we have $\overline{r^i} = r^i$ and also $\overline{r_j^i} = r_j^i$ for every $P_j \in WCORE_i$. Hence the computed $\overline{s_{ij}}$ will be equal to $s_{ij} = \langle u_i, \mathbf{V}_j \rangle$. So the honest $P_i \in \mathsf{Sh}$ will be present in Rec. Therefore the lemma holds.   □

Lemma 14. *For every* $P_i \in \mathsf{Rec}$, $\overline{s_i}$ *computed during reconstruction phase, is same as the* i^{th} *share of secret* $s^\star$, *which is defined by the shares of the parties in* ShHo *(and hence* ReHo).

PROOF: From the previous two lemmas, the shares of the parties in $\mathsf{ShHo} = \mathsf{ReHo}$ will define a unique secret $s^\star$, which is D's committed secret. Now we have the following two cases:

1. $P_i \in \mathsf{Rec}$ is *honest*: In this case, the lemma holds trivially.
2. $P_i \in \mathsf{Rec}$ is *corrupted*: Since $P_i \in \mathsf{Rec}$, it implies that decommit phase of WCS_i is successful and hence r^i which was committed by P_i during commit phase is accepted as authentic. Now $P_i \in \mathsf{Rec}$ also implies that $\mathcal{P} \setminus (\mathsf{Sh} \cap \mathsf{Ha}_i) \in \Gamma$. Now let CoH_i be the set of *common honest* parties in $(\mathsf{Sh} \cap \mathsf{Ha}_i)$. It is easy to see that CoH_i is an access set, otherwise $\mathcal{A}$ will not satisfy $\mathcal{Q}^3$ condition, which is a contradiction. Now $\mathsf{CoH}_i \subseteq \mathsf{ShHo} = \mathsf{ReHo}$. Also, $\mathsf{CoH}_i \subseteq WCORE_i \subseteq \mathsf{Ha}_i$. Thus, r_j^i revealed by every $P_j \in \mathsf{CoH}_i$ during decommit phase of WCS_i is the correct share of r^i, as given by P_i to P_j during commit phase of WCS_i. Thus, the computed $\overline{s_{ij}}$, corresponding to every $P_j \in \mathsf{CoH}_i$ is equal to s_{ji}. This is because there can be either one of the following two possibilities:
   (a) Both P_i and P_j are happy during sharing phase, but $a_{ij} \neq b_{ji}$. In this case, $\overline{s_{ij}} = \gamma_{ij} = \beta_{ji} = s_{ji}$;

(b) Both P_i and P_j are happy during sharing phase and $a_{ij} = b_{ji}$. In this case, $\overline{s_{ij}} = a_{ij} - r^i_j = b_{ji} - r^i_j = s_{ji}$

Now the shares of the parties in CoH_i define the same secret $s^\star$. This is because, as discussed above, the access set $\mathsf{CoH}_i \subseteq \mathsf{ReHo}$. Since CoH_i is an access set, from the properties of MSP, it follows that s_{ji}'s corresponding to $P'_j s \in \mathsf{CoH}_i$ uniquely define s_i, the ith share of the committed secret $s^\star$ (this can be shown using the same arguments as used in Lemma 6).

On the other hand, $P_i \in \mathsf{Rec}$ also implies that $\overline{u_i}$ revealed by P_i is consistent with all $\overline{s_{ij}} = s_{ji}$'s of $P_j \in \mathsf{CoH}_i$. This further implies that $\overline{u_{i1}}$ is same as s_i because CoH_i is an access set (again this can be shown using the same arguments as used in Lemma 6). □

Theorem 5. *The protocol in Fig. 3 is a three round VSS tolerating non-threshold adversary $\mathcal{A}$ characterized by an adversary structure Γ, where $\mathcal{A}$ satisfies the $\mathcal{Q}^3$ condition. In the protocol, the honest parties perform computation and communication which is polynomial in the size of $\mathcal{M}$.*

Proof. The round complexity can be verified by inspection. Also, it is easy to see that the honest parties perform computation and communication which is polynomial in the size of $\mathcal{M}$. We now show that the protocol satisfies the properties of VSS.

1. **Secrecy:** We have to only consider the case when D is honest. Let the adversary corrupt some $B \in \Gamma$. Then at the end of **Round I** of the sharing phase, adversary learns no information about s from their shares, as B is a non-access set. From the secrecy property of WCS, the adversary will not get any information about r^i's, which are committed by honest P_i's. Hence, at the end of **Round I** of sharing phase, the adversary gains no information about r^i_j's and r^j_i's, corresponding to $P_i, P_j \notin B$. Hence at the end of **Round II**, adversary gains no information about u_i and u_j, as r^i_j's and r^j_i's works as the one-time pad.

   During **Round III**, if $a_{ij} \neq b_{ji}$ or vice-versa, then P_i or P_j is corrupted (as D is honest). Hence, the adversary already knows the share-share $\langle u_i, \mathbf{V}_j \rangle = \langle u_j, \mathbf{V}_i \rangle$. Thus, D's broadcast of γ_{ij} during **Round III** adds no extra information about u_i to adversary's view. Thus, at the end of sharing phase, s remains information theoretically secure.

2. **Correctness:** We have to consider the case when D is honest. If D is honest then the sharing phase will succeed (see Lemma 11). Now by Lemma 12, the parties in ShHo is an access set and defines s. Moreover, by Lemma 14, correct share of s will be reconstructed for every P_i in Rec. These facts guarantee that by applying reconstruction algorithm of the LSSS to the shares of the parties in Rec, secret s will be reconstructed correctly.

3. **Strong Commitment:** We have to consider the case when D is corrupted. The proof is very similar to the proof of correctness. By Lemma 12, the parties in ShHo is an access set and defines some secret $s^\star$, which is D's committed secret. Moreover, from Lemma 13, $\mathsf{ShHo} = \mathsf{RecHo}$. Furthermore, by Lemma 14, correct share of s^* will be reconstructed for every P_i in Rec.

These facts guarantee that by applying reconstruction algorithm of the LSSS to the shares of the parties in Rec, secret $s^\star$ will be reconstructed correctly and uniquely. □

5   Lower Bounds

We now give our lower bound results.

Theorem 6. *Two round perfectly secure VSS is possible if and only if $\mathcal{A}$ satisfies the $\mathcal{Q}^4$ condition.*

Proof. Sufficiency follows from Fig. 1. We now prove the necessity. On the contrary, assume that a two round VSS protocol, say Π, is possible even though $\mathcal{A}$ does not satisfy the $\mathcal{Q}^4$ condition. This implies that there exists B_1, B_2, B_3 and B_4, belonging to the underlying adversary structure Γ, such that $B_1 \cup B_2 \cup B_3 \cup B_4 = \mathcal{P}$. Now consider protocol Π', involving parties P_1, P_2, P_3 and P_4, where party P_i performs the same computation and communication, as done by the parties in B_i in Π, for $i = 1, \ldots, 4$. It is easy to see that if Π is a two round VSS protocol, then $\Pi's$ is also a two round VSS protocol involving four parties, out of which at most one can be corrupted. However, from [5], Π' does not exist. So Π also does not exist. □

Theorem 7. *Any r-round perfectly secure VSS protocol, where $r \geq 3$, is possible if and only if $\mathcal{A}$ satisfies the $\mathcal{Q}^3$ condition.*

Proof. Follows using similar arguments as used in Theorem 6 and by the result of [5]. □

6   Flaw in the Reconstruction Phase of VSS of [4]

In [4], the authors presented a three round VSS tolerating a threshold adversary $\mathcal{A}_t$ with $n = 3t+1$, using a three round WSS protocol as a black-box. However, we now show that there is a flaw in the reconstruction phase of their VSS. Moreover, we also show the modifications to eliminate this flaw. We start with a brief discussion on the WSS and VSS of [4]. *Here we use slightly different notations and steps, that were not there in [4]. However, the current discussion will be valid even with the original notations and steps of [4].* The sharing phase of the WSS of [4] is a special case of the commit phase of our WCS. Precisely the matrix $\mathcal{M}$ here is an $n \times (t + 1)$ *Vandermonde* matrix, whose i^{th} row is $[i^0, i^1, \ldots, i^t]$ and R is the coefficient matrix of a random symmetric bi-variate polynomial $F(x, y)$ of degree-t in x, y, where $F(0,0) = s$. The result of the computation in the WSS of [4] can be viewed as follows (though this view was not presented in [4], the essence is same): if D is not discarded during sharing phase, then there exists a degree-t univariate polynomial, say $f(x)$, such that D has WSS-shared $f(x)$ and each *happy and honest* party P_i has received $f(i)$ from D. Moreover, if D is honest then D will not be discarded and $f(x) = f_0(x) = F(x, 0)$ and hence

$f(0) = s$. Now during reconstruction phase, either $f(x)$ (and hence $f(0) = s$) or $NULL$ will be reconstructed. Moreover, if $f(x)$ is reconstructed then it is reconstructed with the shares revealed by a set of parties WCORE, such that WCORE is a subset of *happy* parties and there exists at least $t+1$ honest parties in WCORE.

Now the VSS protocol of [4] works as follows: During the sharing phase, D selects a random symmetric bi-variate polynomial $F(x, y)$ of degree-t in x, y, where $F(0,0) = s$ and gives each P_i, the degree-t polynomial $f_i(x) = F(x, i)$. Then the parties perform *pair-wise* checking to check the consistency of their common values. To do this, each party P_i acts as a dealer and WSS-shares a degree-t polynomial $f_i^W(x)$ and gives each P_j the share $f_i^W(j)$. Now to do the consistency checking, each P_i broadcasts $a_{ij} = f_i(j) + f_i^W(j)$ and $b_{ij} = f_i(j) + f_j^W(i)$. Each inconsistency (i.e., $a_{ij} \neq b_{ji}$) is resolved by D (by broadcasting $f_i(j)$), as a result of which parties become *happy/unhappy* and the computation proceeds. At the end of sharing phase, all honest parties agree on a set of at least $2t+1$ *happy* parties, say $CORE_{Sh}$, such that the following condition holds:

1. For each $P_i, P_j \in CORE_{Sh}$, we have $f_i(j) = f_j(i)$;
2. Each $P_i \in CORE_{Sh}$ as a dealer, has AWSS-shared a degree-t polynomial $f_i^W(x)$ to at least $2t+1$ parties in $CORE_{Sh}$.

Now notice that there is a subtle point here, which is the basis of the flaw in the reconstruction phase of VSS protocol of [4]. *Even though $f_i(j) = f_j(i)$ is true for every $P_i, P_j \in CORE_{Sh}$ (as both of them are happy), it does not imply that $a_{ij} = b_{ji}$ is true for every $P_i, P_j \in CORE_{Sh}$.* Obviously, if both $P_i, P_j \in CORE_{Sh}$ are *honest*, then $a_{ij} = b_{ji}$. However, if at least one of $P_i, P_j \in CORE_{Sh}$ is *corrupted*, then it may happen that $a_{ij} \neq b_{ji}$, but still both P_i and P_j are happy and are present in $CORE_{Sh}$. More concretely, suppose P_i is *corrupted*, P_j and D are *honest*. Then during **Round II** of sharing phase, P_i may broadcast a_{ij} that is not equal to b_{ji}. But during **Round III**, when D tries to resolve the inconsistency, P_i may broadcast correct $f_i(j)$. That is D broadcasts $\gamma_{ij} = f_i(j)$, P_i broadcasts $\alpha_{ij} = f_i(j)$ and P_j broadcasts $\beta_{ji} = f_j(i)$, such that $\gamma_{ij} = \alpha_{ij} = \beta_{ji}$. So both P_i and P_j will be *happy*. Moreover P_i as a dealer can behave correctly during his instance of WSS to share $f_i^W(x)$, such that P_i satisfies the second property stated above to be in $CORE_{Sh}$.

We now recall the steps of the reconstruction phase of the VSS protocol of [4] in Fig. 4. In [4], the authors claimed that reconstructed $f_i(x)$'s of any $t+1$ parties in $CORE_{Rec}$ define the same bivariate polynomial of degree-t in x and y (see Lemma 6 of [4]). However, we now show that this is not the case. To be precise, consider a setting where D is *honest* and P_i is *corrupted*. During **Round I** of sharing phase, P_i gets $f_i(x) = F(x, i)$. Then P_i as a dealer WSS-shares a degree-t polynomial $f_i^W(x)$. During **Round II**, P_i broadcasts $a_{ij} = f_i'(j) + f_i^W(j)$, instead of $f_i(j) + f_i^W(j)$, corresponding to all P_j's, such that $f_i'(x) \neq f_i(x)$ is another degree-t polynomial. So $a_{ij} \neq b_{ji}$, for *all* P_j's. But then during **Round III**, P_i behaves in such a way that P_i is considered as *happy* along with all other P_j's (this he can do as discussed earlier). P_i also ensures that his WSS instance satisfies the desired property so that P_i is included in $CORE_{Sh}$.

For each $P_i \in CORE_{Sh}$, run the reconstruction phase of WSS_i (the instance of WSS initiated by P_i as a dealer).

Local Computation (By Each Party):

1. Initialize $CORE_{Rec} = CORE_{Sh}$.
2. Remove P_i from $CORE_{Rec}$ if the reconstruction phase of WSS_i outputs $NULL$.
3. If $f_i^W(x)$ is reconstructed during reconstruction phase of WSS_i then compute $f_i(j) = a_{ij} - f_i^W(j)$, for $j = 1, \ldots, n$. Check if the computed $f_i(j)$'s lie on a unique degree-t polynomial. If not then remove P_i from $CORE_{Rec}$. Otherwise, let $f_i(x)$ be the degree-t polynomial.
4. Take $f_i(x)$'s corresponding to any $t+1$ parties in $CORE_{Rec}$, reconstruct $F^\star(x, y)$ and output $s^\star = F^\star(0, 0)$.

Fig. 4. Reconstruction Phase of the VSS Protocol of [4]

Now during reconstruction phase of VSS, suppose the reconstruction phase of WSS_i is successful and hence the WSS-shared polynomial $f_i^W(x)$ is reconstructed correctly. But now when the (honest) parties perform step 3 of the local computation (given in Fig. 4), they will get back $f_i'(j) = a_{ij} - f_i^W(j)$, instead of original $f_i(j)$. Moreover, the computed $f_i'(j)$'s will lie on degree-t polynomial $f_i'(x) \neq f_i(x)$ and P_i will be present in $CORE_{Rec}$. But now notice that $f_i'(x) \neq f_i(x)$ does not lie on the original bivariate polynomial $F(x, y)$. This will further lead to the violation of correctness property of VSS.

Elimination of the Flaw: From the above discussion, it is clear that the reason behind the above flaw is that $a_{ij} = b_{ji}$ may not hold for every $P_i, P_j \in CORE_{Sh}$. To eliminate the above flaw, we modify the step 3 of the local computation of Fig. 4 as follows:

3. If $f_i^W(x)$ is reconstructed during reconstruction phase of WSS_i then compute $f_i(j)$'s as follows:

- $f_i(j) = \gamma_{ij}$; if γ_{ij} was broadcasted by D during **Round III** of sharing phase.
- $f_i(j) = a_{ij} - f_i^W(j)$; if $a_{ij} = b_{ji}$ during sharing phase.

Check if the computed $f_i(j)$'s lie on a unique degree-t polynomial. If not then remove P_i from $CORE_{Rec}$. Otherwise, let $f_i(x)$ be the degree-t polynomial.

Now it is easy to verify that with the above modification, Lemma 6 of [4] will hold.

7   More Efficient 3-round VSS for $n \geq 3t + 1$

In the previous section, we pointed out a flaw in the 3-round VSS of Fitzi et al. [4], and presented how to fix it. The communication complexity of the reconstruction phase of the proposed modified protocol is $\mathcal{O}(n^3)$. This results from the facts that there are n instances of the WSS protocol in the VSS and the communication cost of the reconstruction phase of WSS of [4] is $\mathcal{O}(n^2)$.

On the other hand, if we restrict our three round VSS protocol given in Fig. 3 to threshold adversary, then we get a three round VSS with $n = 3t + 1$ whose communication complexity of reconstruction phase is $\mathcal{O}(n^2)$. This results from the facts that in our VSS, WSS has been replaced by WCS and the communication cost of the decommit phase of WCS is only $\mathcal{O}(n)$. If we compare the definition of WCS and WSS (for formal definition of WSS, see [4]), then we find that in WSS, the dealer D is not allowed to act/play a special role in the reconstruction phase. That is, D is not allowed to reveal the secret and randomness used by him during the sharing phase. During the reconstruction phase, every party reveal their entire view of the sharing phase and a reconstruction function is applied on them to reconstruct either the secret shared during sharing phase or $NULL$. On the other hand, in WCS, D is allowed to act specially in the decommit phase. Precisely, he is allowed to reveal the secret and randomness used by him during commit phase. As a result, the decommit phase of our WCS is conceptually simpler than the reconstruction phase of WSS protocol of [4] and we gain an efficiency of $\Theta(n)$ during the reconstruction phase.

8   Conclusion

In this paper, we resolved the round complexity of VSS tolerating generalized adversary. Our results strictly generalize the results of [4] to non-threshold settings. In our three round protocol, we have not tried to optimize the use of broadcast channel. However, we conjecture that following the techniques of [7], we can design a three round VSS tolerating $\mathcal{Q}^3$ adversary structure, which uses broadcast channel in only one round during the sharing phase.

Acknowledgement. We would like to thank the anonymous referees of ICITS 2011 for several useful comments.

References

1. Ben-Or, M., Goldwasser, S., Wigderson, A.: Completeness Theorems for Non-Cryptographic Fault-Tolerant Distributed Computation (Extended Abstract). In: Proceedings of the 20th Annual ACM Symposium on Theory of Computing, Chicago, Illinois, USA, May 2-4, pp. 1–10. ACM Press, New York (1988)
2. Chor, B., Goldwasser, S., Micali, S., Awerbuch, B.: Verifiable Secret Sharing and Achieving Simultaneity in the Presence of Faults (Extended Abstract). In: Proceedings of the 17th Annual ACM Symposium on Theory of Computing, Providence, Rhode Island, USA, May 6-8, pp. 383–395. ACM Press, New York (1985)
3. Cramer, R., Damgård, I.B., Maurer, U.M.: General secure multi-party computation from any linear secret-sharing scheme. In: Preneel, B. (ed.) EUROCRYPT 2000. LNCS, vol. 1807, pp. 316–334. Springer, Heidelberg (2000)

4. Fitzi, M., Garay, J.A., Gollakota, S., Pandu Rangan, C., Srinathan, K.: Round-optimal and efficient verifiable secret sharing. In: Halevi, S., Rabin, T. (eds.) TCC 2006. LNCS, vol. 3876, pp. 329–342. Springer, Heidelberg (2006)
5. Gennaro, R., Ishai, Y., Kushilevitz, E., Rabin, T.: The Round Complexity of Verifiable Secret Sharing and Secure Multicast. In: Proceedings on 33rd Annual ACM Symposium on Theory of Computing, Heraklion, Crete, Greece, July 6-8, pp. 580–589. ACM Press, New York (2001)
6. Hirt, M., Maurer, U.M.: Complete Characterization of Adversaries Tolerable in Secure Multi-Party Computation. In: Proceedings of the Sixteenth Annual ACM Symposium on Principles of Distributed Computing, Santa Barbara, California, USA, August 21-24, pp. 25–34. ACM Press, New York (1997)
7. Katz, J., Koo, C.-Y., Kumaresan, R.: Improving the round complexity of VSS in point-to-point networks. In: Aceto, L., Damgård, I., Goldberg, L.A., Halldórsson, M.M., Ingólfsdóttir, A., Walukiewicz, I. (eds.) ICALP 2008, Part II. LNCS, vol. 5126, pp. 499–510. Springer, Heidelberg (2008)
8. MacWilliams, F.J., Sloane, N.J.A.: The Theory of Error Correcting Codes. North-Holland Publishing Company, Amsterdam (1978)
9. Maurer, U.M.: Secure multi-party computation made simple. In: Cimato, S., Galdi, C., Persiano, G. (eds.) SCN 2002. LNCS, vol. 2576, pp. 14–28. Springer, Heidelberg (2003)
10. Shamir, A.: How to share a secret. Communications of the ACM 22(11), 612–613 (1979)

Graceful Degradation in Multi-Party Computation
(Extended Abstract)*

Martin Hirt[1], Christoph Lucas[1], Ueli Maurer[1], and Dominik Raub[2]

[1] Department of Computer Science, ETH Zurich, Switzerland
{hirt,clucas,maurer}@inf.ethz.ch
[2] Department of Computer Science, University of Århus, Denmark
raub@cs.au.dk

Abstract. The goal of *Multi-Party Computation* (MPC) is to perform an arbitrary computation in a distributed, private, and fault-tolerant way. For this purpose, a fixed set of n parties runs a protocol that tolerates an adversary corrupting a subset of the participating parties, and still preserves certain security guarantees.

Most MPC protocols provide security guarantees in an *all-or-nothing* fashion. In this paper, we provide the first treatment of MPC with graceful degradation of both security and corruptions. First of all, our protocols provide graceful degradation of security, i.e., different security guarantees depending on the actual number of corrupted parties: the more corruptions, the weaker the security guarantee. We consider all security properties generally discussed in the literature (secrecy, correctness, robustness, fairness, and agreement on abort). Furthermore, the protocols provide graceful degradation with respect to the corruption type, by distinguishing fully honest parties, passively corrupted parties, and actively corrupted parties. Security can be maintained against more passive corruptions than is possible for active corruptions.

We focus on perfect security, and prove exact bounds for which MPC with graceful degradation of security and corruptions is possible for both threshold and general adversaries. Furthermore, we provide protocols that meet these bounds. This strictly generalizes known results on hybrid security and mixed adversaries.

Keywords: Multi-party computation, graceful degradation, hybrid security, mixed adversaries.

1 Introduction

1.1 Secure Multi-Party Computation

Multi-Party Computation (MPC) allows a set of n parties to securely perform an arbitrary computation in a distributed manner, where security means that

---

* The full version of this paper is available at the *Cryptology ePrint Archive*: http://eprint.iacr.org/2011/094. This work was partially supported by the Zurich Information Security Center.

S. Fehr (Ed.): ICITS 2011, LNCS 6673, pp. 163–180, 2011.

secrecy of the inputs and correctness of the output are maintained even when some of the parties are dishonest. The dishonesty of parties is typically modeled with a central adversary who corrupts parties. The adversary can be *passive*, i.e., she can read the internal state of the corrupted parties, or *active*, i.e., she can make the corrupted parties deviate arbitrarily from the protocol.

MPC was originally proposed by Yao [Yao82]. The first general solution was provided in [GMW87], where, based on computational intractability assumptions, security against a passive adversary was achieved for $t < n$ corruptions, and security against an active adversary was achieved for $t < \frac{n}{2}$. In [BGW88, CCD88], information-theoretic security was achieved at the price of lower corruption thresholds, namely $t < \frac{n}{2}$ for passive and $t < \frac{n}{3}$ for active adversaries. The latter bound can be improved to $t < \frac{n}{2}$ if both broadcast channels are assumed and a small error probability is tolerated [RB89, Bea89]. These results were generalized to the non-threshold setting, where the corruption capability of the adversary is not specified by a threshold t, but rather by a so-called adversary structure $\mathcal{Z}$, a monotone collection of subsets of the player set, where the adversary can corrupt the players in one of these subsets [HM97].

All mentioned protocols achieve full security, i.e., secrecy, correctness, and robustness. *Secrecy* means that the adversary learns nothing about the honest parties' inputs and outputs (except, of course, for what she can derive from the corrupted parties' inputs and outputs). *Correctness* means that all parties either output the right value or no value at all. *Robustness* means that the adversary cannot prevent the honest parties from learning their respective outputs. This last requirement turns out to be very strong. Therefore, relaxations of full security have been proposed, where robustness is replaced by weaker output guarantees: *Fairness* means that the adversary can possibly prevent the honest parties from learning their outputs, but then also the corrupted parties do not learn their outputs. *Agreement on abort* means that the adversary can possibly prevent honest parties from learning their output, even while corrupted parties learn their outputs, but then the honest parties at least reach agreement on this fact (and typically make no output). Note that for example [GMW87] achieves secrecy, correctness, and agreement on abort (but neither robustness nor fairness) for up to $t < n$ active corruptions.

1.2   Graceful Degradation

Most MPC protocols in the literature do not degrade very gracefully. They provide a very high level of security up to some threshold t, but no security at all beyond this threshold. There are no intermediate levels of security.[1] Furthermore, a party is considered either fully honest or fully corrupted. There are no intermediate levels of corruptions.

Note that many papers in the literature consider several corruption types, or even several levels of security, but in separate protocols. For example, [BGW88] proposes a protocol for passive security with $t < \frac{n}{2}$, and another protocol for

---

[1] The same observation holds for known protocols for general adversaries.

active security with $t < \frac{n}{3}$. There is no graceful degradation: If in the active protocol, some *passive* adversary corrupts $\lceil \frac{n}{3} \rceil$ parties, the protocol is insecure.

Graceful degradation was first considered by Chaum [Cha89]: He proposed one protocol with graceful degradation of security, namely from information-theoretic security (few corruptions) over computational security (more corruptions) to no security (many corruptions), and another, independent protocol with graceful degradation of corruptions, namely by considering fully honest, passively corrupted, and actively corrupted parties in the same protocol execution. The former protocol (graceful degradation of security, often called *hybrid* security) was recently generalized in [FHHW03, FHW04, IKLP06, Kat07, LRM10]. The latter protocol (graceful degradation of corruptions, often called *mixed* security) was generalized and extended in [DDWY93, FHM98, FHM99, BFH+08, HMZ08].

1.3 Our Focus

In this work, we consider simultaneously graceful degradation of security (i.e., hybrid security) and graceful degradation of corruptions (i.e., mixed adversaries), both in the threshold and in the general adversary setting. In the threshold setting, we consider protocols with four thresholds t^c (for correctness), t^s (for secrecy), t^r (for robustness), and t^f (for fairness).[2] We assume that $t^s \leq t^c$ and $t^r \leq t^c$, since secrecy and robustness are not well defined in a setting without correctness. Furthermore, we assume that $t^f \leq t^s$ since in a setting without secrecy the adversary inherently has an unfair advantage over honest parties.

Furthermore, we also consider graceful degradation with respect to the corruption type: We consider, at the same time, honest parties, passively corrupted parties, and actively corrupted parties (so-called *mixed adversaries*). Such an adversary is characterized by two thresholds t_a and t_p, where up to t_p parties can be passively corrupted, and up to t_a of these parties can even be corrupted actively. Note that t_p denotes the upper bound on the total number of corruptions (active as well as purely passive), and t_a denotes the upper bound on the number of actively corrupted parties (hence, $t_a \leq t_p$).

In the non-threshold setting, security is characterized by four adversary structures $\mathcal{Z}^c$, $\mathcal{Z}^s$, $\mathcal{Z}^r$, $\mathcal{Z}^f$, where correctness, secrecy, robustness, and fairness are guaranteed as long as the set of corrupted players is contained in the corresponding adversary structure.[3] As argued above, we assume that $\mathcal{Z}^s \subseteq \mathcal{Z}^c$, $\mathcal{Z}^r \subseteq \mathcal{Z}^c$ and $\mathcal{Z}^f \subseteq \mathcal{Z}^s$. In order to model both passive and active corruptions, each adversary structure consists of tuples $(\mathcal{D}, \mathcal{E})$ of subsets of the player set, where $\mathcal{E}$ is the set of passively (eavesdropping), and $\mathcal{D} \subseteq \mathcal{E}$ is the set of actively (disruption) corrupted parties. A protocol with adversary structure $\mathcal{Z}$ provides security guarantees for every adversary actively corrupting the parties in $\mathcal{D}$ and passively corrupting the parties in $\mathcal{E}$, for some $(\mathcal{D}, \mathcal{E}) \in \mathcal{Z}$.

---

[2] If the number of corruptions is below multiple thresholds, all corresponding security properties are achieved. In particular, full security is achieved if the number of corruptions is below all thresholds.

[3] As in the threshold case, if the set of corrupted parties is contained in multiple adversary structures, all corresponding security properties are achieved.

Note that the notion of correctness for a security level without secrecy differs from the usual interpretation: The adversary is rushing and may know the entire state of the protocol execution. Hence, input-independence cannot be achieved. Furthermore, for the same reason, we can have probabilistic computations only with adversarially chosen randomness.

1.4   Contributions

We provide the first MPC protocol with graceful degradation in multiple dimensions: We consider all security properties generally discussed in the literature (secrecy, correctness, robustness, fairness, and agreement on abort), and the most prominent corruption types (active, passive). We prove a tight bound on the feasibility of perfectly-secure MPC, both in the threshold and the non-threshold setting, and provide efficient perfectly-secure general MPC protocols matching these bounds.[4] Our main results (Theorems 1 and 2) are a strict generalization of the previous results for perfect MPC, which appear as special cases in our unified treatment. For the sake of simplicity, we do not include fail corruption [BFH+08]. Note that fairness is not discussed in the protocol descriptions, but in Section 4.

Previous results for perfectly secure MPC considered graceful degradation only of corruption levels, i.e., the known protocols always provide full security. Usually, the intuition behind the different corruption types is that passively corrupted parties only aim to break secrecy, whereas actively corrupted parties aim to break correctness (and/or robustness). However, this analogy does not readily extend to mixed adversaries that simultaneously perform passive and active corruptions. Our model separates the different security properties, and therefore allows to make precise statements formalizing the above intuition. This indicates that our model is both natural and appropriate.

As a simple example consider voting. A solution based on a traditional perfectly secure MPC protocol, e.g. [BGW88], achieves secrecy and correctness for up to $t < \frac{n}{3}$ corrupted parties, but provides no guarantees if $t \geq \frac{n}{3}$. However, in voting it is generally much more important that the final tally is correct than to protect the secrecy of votes. Our protocol allows to reduce secrecy to $t = \frac{n}{8}$ corrupted parties, while guaranteeing correctness for $t < \frac{3n}{4}$ actively corrupted parties (and additionally arbitrarily many passively corrupted parties). This protocol is robust for up to $t = \frac{n}{8}$ corruptions. It is also possible to trade correctness for robustness: By reducing the correctness guarantee to $t < \frac{n}{2}$ corruptions, robustness is guaranteed for up to $t = \frac{3n}{8}$ corruptions.

1.5   Model

We consider n parties $1, \ldots, n$, connected by pairwise synchronous secure channels, who want to compute some probabilistic function over a finite field $\mathbb{F}$,

---

[4] The protocols are efficient in the input length, i.e. the threshold protocol is efficient in the number of parties and the size of the circuit to be computed, whereas the protocol for general adversaries is efficient in the size of the adversary structure and the size of the circuit.

represented as a circuit with input, addition, multiplication, random, and output gates. This function can be reactive, where parties can provide further inputs after having received some intermediate outputs. In the main body of this paper, we assume that authenticated broadcast channels are given. The model without broadcast channels is treated in the full version of this paper.

There is a central adversary with unlimited computing power who corrupts some parties passively (and reads their internal state) or even actively (and makes them misbehave arbitrarily). We denote the actual sets of actively (passively) corrupted parties by $\mathcal{D}^*$ ($\mathcal{E}^*$), where $\mathcal{D}^* \subseteq \mathcal{E}^*$. Uncorrupted parties are called *honest*, non-active parties are called *correct*. The security of our protocols is perfect, i.e., information-theoretic with no error probability. The level of security (secrecy, correctness, fairness, robustness, agreement on abort) depends on $(\mathcal{D}^*, \mathcal{E}^*)$.

For ease of notation, we assume that if a party does not receive an expected message (or receives an invalid message), a default message is used instead.

1.6   Outline of the Paper

Our paper is organized as follows: As a main technical contribution, we generalize known protocols for threshold and general adversaries in Sections 2 and 3. In Section 4, we state optimal bounds for MPC, together with proofs of sufficiency. Tightness of the bounds is proven in Section 5.

2   A Parametrized Protocol for Threshold Adversaries

In this section, we generalize the perfectly secure MPC protocol of [BGW88] by introducing two parameters. On an abstract level, our modifications can be described as follows: First, we define the state that is held in the protocol in terms of a parameter that influences the secrecy. In case of [BGW88], this is the degree d of the sharing polynomial (see also [FHM98]). Second, given the parameter d for secrecy, we express the reconstruct protocol in terms of an additional parameter determining the amount of error correction taking place. Traditional protocols correct as many errors as possible. By using a parameter, our protocol may stay below the theoretical limit, thereby providing extended error detection. In case of [BGW88], this parameter is the number e of corrected errors during reconstruction. To our knowledge, such a second parameter has not been considered before. The two parameters must fulfill $d + 2e < n$. Note that by choosing $d + 2e \neq n - 1$, it is possible to reduce robustness for extended correctness. In [BGW88], both parameters are set to $d = e = t$, the maximum number of actively corrupted parties.

In the following, we present the parametrized protocols and analyze them with respect to correctness, secrecy, and robustness. Note that fairness is discussed in Section 4.

2.1   The Underlying Verifiable Secret Sharing

The state of the protocol is maintained with a Shamir sharing [Sha79] of each value. We assume that each party i is assigned a unique and publicly known evaluation point $\alpha_i \in \mathbb{F} \setminus \{0\}$. This implies that the field $\mathbb{F}$ must have more than n elements.

Definition 1 (d-Sharing). *A value s is d-shared when there is a share polynomial $\hat{s}(x)$ of degree d with $\hat{s}(0) = s$, and every party i holds a share $s_i = \hat{s}(\alpha_i)$. We denote a d-sharing of s with $[s]$, and the share s_i with $[s]_i$. A sharing degree d is t-permissive if the shares of all but t parties uniquely define the secret, i.e., $n - t > d$.*

Lemma 1. *Let $d < n$ be the sharing degree. A d-sharing is secret if $|\mathcal{E}^*| \leq d$, and uniquely defines a value if d is $|\mathcal{D}^*|$-permissive.*

Proof. It follows directly from the properties of a polynomial of degree d that secrecy is guaranteed if the number $|\mathcal{E}^*|$ of (actively or passively) corrupted parties is at most d. Furthermore, $n - |\mathcal{D}^*| > d$ implies that there are at least $d + 1$ correct parties whose shares uniquely define a share polynomial.   □

The share protocol takes as input a secret s from a dealer, and outputs a d-sharing $[s]$ (see Figure 1). Due to lack of space, the proof of the following lemma can be found in the full version.

SHARE: Given input s from the dealer, compute a d-sharing $[s]$ of this value.

1. The dealer chooses a random (2-dimensional) polynomial $g(x, y)$ with $g(0, 0) = s$, of degree d in both variables, and sends to party i (for $i = 1, \ldots, n$) the (1-dimensional) polynomials $k_i(y) = g(\alpha_i, y)$ and $h_i(x) = g(x, \alpha_i)$.
2. For each pair of parties (i, j), party i sends $h_i(\alpha_j)$ to party j, and party j checks whether $h_i(\alpha_j) = k_j(\alpha_i)$. If this check fails, it broadcasts a complaint, and the dealer has to broadcast the correct value.
3. If some party i observes an inconsistency between the polynomials received in Step 1 and the broadcasted value in Step 2, it accuses the dealer. The dealer has to answer the accusation by broadcasting both $k_i(y)$ and $h_i(x)$. Now, if some other party j observes an inconsistency between the polynomial received in Step 1 and these broadcasted polynomials, it also accuses the dealer. This step is repeated until no additional party accuses the dealer.
4. If the dealer does not answer some complaint or accusation, or if the broadcasted values contradict, the parties output a default d-sharing. Otherwise, each party i outputs $s_i := k_i(0)$, and the dealer outputs $\hat{s}(x) := g(x, 0)$.[5]

Fig. 1. The Share Protocol

---

[5] That means, in general we discard the second dimension of $g(x, y)$. Yet, in a special context, we will subsequently make use of it.

Lemma 2. *Let $d < n$ be the sharing degree. On input s from the dealer, SHARE correctly, secretly, and robustly computes a d-sharing. If d is $|\mathcal{D}^*|$-permissive, and if the dealer is correct, the sharing uniquely defines the secret s.*

The public reconstruction of a d-shared value s uses techniques from coding theory, which allow a more intuitive understanding of the trade-off between correctness and robustness. It follows from coding theory that a d-sharing is equivalent to a code based on the evaluation of a polynomial of degree d. Such a code has minimal distance $n - d$. Hence, the decoding algorithm can detect up to $n - d - 1$ errors and abort (for correctness), or correct up to $\frac{n-d-1}{2}$ errors (for robustness). In our protocol, we trade correctness for robustness by introducing the correction parameter $e < \frac{n-d}{2}$: Our decoding algorithm provides error correction for up to e errors, and error detection for up to $(n - d) - e - 1$ errors. Note that this trade-off is optimal: If the distance to the correct codeword is greater than $(n - d) - e - 1$, the distance to the next codeword is at most e, and the decoding algorithm would decode to the wrong codeword.

The public reconstruction protocol (Figure 2) proceeds as follows: First, each party broadcasts its share s_i. Then, each party locally "decodes" the broadcasted shares to the closest codeword, and aborts if the Hamming distance between the shares and the decoded codeword is larger than e. Note that during public reconstruction, there is no secrecy requirement.

PUBLIC RECONSTRUCTION : Given a d-sharing $[s]$ of some value s, reconstruct s to all parties.

1. Each party i broadcasts its share s_i. Let $\boldsymbol{s} = (s_1, ..., s_n)$ denote the vector of broadcasted shares.
2. Each party identifies the closest codeword $\boldsymbol{s}_c$ (e.g. using the Berlekamp-Welch algorithm). If the Hamming distance between $\boldsymbol{s}_c$ and $\boldsymbol{s}$ is larger than e, the protocol is aborted. Otherwise, each party interpolates the entries in $\boldsymbol{s}_c$ with a polynomial $\hat{s}_c(x)$ of degree d, and outputs $\hat{s}_c(0)$.[6]

Fig. 2. The Public Reconstruction Protocol

Lemma 3. *Let d be the sharing degree, and e be the correction parameter, where $d + 2e < n$. Given a d-sharing $[s]$ of some value s, PUBLIC RECONSTRUCTION is correct if $|\mathcal{D}^*| < (n - d) - e$, is robust if $|\mathcal{D}^*| \le e$, and always guarantees agreement on abort.*

Proof. Only actively corrupted parties broadcast incorrect shares. Hence, the Hamming distance between the broadcasted shares and the correct codeword is at most $|\mathcal{D}^*|$.

---

[6] That means, in general we discard the vector of corrected shares $\boldsymbol{s}_c$. Yet, in a special context, we will subsequently make use of it.

Correctness: The minimal distance between two codewords is $(n - d)$, and the decoding algorithm corrects up to e errors. Hence, if $|\mathcal{D}^*| + e < (n - d)$, the decoding algorithm never decodes to the incorrect codeword.

Robustness: If $|\mathcal{D}^*| \leq e$, the Hamming distance between the shares and the correct codeword is at most e and the decoding cannot be aborted.

Agreement on abort: The abort decision is only based on broadcasted values. Hence, either all correct parties abort, or all correct parties continue.   □

During PUBLIC RECONSTRUCTION, all parties learn the value under consideration. PRIVATE RECONSTRUCTION, where a value s is disclosed only to a single party k, can be reduced to PUBLIC RECONSTRUCTION using a simple blinding technique ([CDG87]): Party k first shares a uniform random value, which is added to s before PUBLIC RECONSTRUCTION is invoked. Hence, PRIVATE RECONSTRUCTION provides the same security guarantees as PUBLIC RECONSTRUCTION, and additionally provides secrecy of the reconstructed value. Note that the trivial solution, where each party sends its share to party k, does not achieve agreement on abort.

2.2   Addition, Multiplication, and Random Values

Linear functions (and in particular additions) can be computed locally, since d-sharings are linear: Given sharings $[a]$ and $[b]$, and a constant c, one can easily compute the sharings $[a] + [b]$, $c[a]$, and $[a] + c$. Computing a shared random value can be achieved by letting each party i share a random value r_i, and computing $[r] = [r_1] + \ldots + [r_n]$.

The multiplication protocol is more involved. The product c of two shared values a and b is computed as follows [GRR98]: Each party multiplies its shares a_i and b_i, obtaining $v_i = a_i b_i$. This results in a sharing of c with a polynomial $\hat{v}(x)$ of degree $2d$. We reduce the degree by having each party d-share its value v_i (resulting in $[v_i]$), and employing Lagrange interpolation to distributedly compute $\hat{v}(0)$. This results in a d-sharing of the product c.

This protocol is secure only against passive adversaries. An active adversary could share a wrong value $v_i' \neq v_i$. Therefore, each party has to prove that it shared the correct value $v_i = a_i b_i$. This proof requires that a_i and b_i are d-shared, which we achieve by upgrading the d-sharings of a and b, resulting in $[a_i]$ and $[b_i]$ for all i.

Given $[a_i]$, $[b_i]$, and $[v_i]$, it remains to show that $a_i b_i = v_i$, which is equivalent to $z = 0$ for $[z]^{2d} := [a_i][b_i] - [v_i]$, where $[z]^{2d}$ is a $2d$-sharing. Party i knows the sharing polynomial $g(x)$ corresponding to $[z]^{2d}$. However, party i cannot simply broadcast $g(x)$, since this would violate secrecy (the adversary could obtain information about other shares). Therefore, we blind $[z]^{2d}$ by adding a uniformly random $2d$-sharing of 0.

Finally, all parties (locally) check whether $z = 0$, and whether party i broadcasted the correct polynomial $g(x)$, i.e. for party j whether $g(\alpha_j) = [z]_j^{2d}$. Two polynomials of degree $2d$ are equal if they coincide in $2d + 1$ points. So, if party i

broadcasts an incorrect $g(x)$, and if there are at least $2d + 1$ correct parties, at least one correct party detects the cheating attempt and raises an accusation. To prove the accusation, the shares of the corresponding party are reconstructed.

The full description of the multiplication protocol can be found in the full version.

2.3 The Security of the Parametrized Protocol

Considering the security of the subprotocols described above, we can derive the security of the parametrized protocol, denoted by $\pi^{d,e}$ (proof omitted):

Lemma 4. *Let d be the sharing degree, and e be the correction parameter, where $d + 2e < n$. Protocol $\pi^{d,e}$ guarantees* correctness *if $|\mathcal{D}^*| < (n - d) - e$ and $|\mathcal{D}^*| < n - 2d$,* secrecy *if $|\mathcal{E}^*| \leq d$ and correctness is guaranteed,* robustness *if $|\mathcal{D}^*| \leq e$, and* agreement on abort *always.*

3 A Parametrized Protocol for General Adversaries

For general adversaries, we proceed along the lines of the threshold case: We generalize the protocol of [Mau02] and introduce the *sharing specification* $\mathcal{S} = (S_1, \ldots, S_k)$ (corresponding to the sharing degree d), and the *correction structure* $\mathcal{C} = \{C_1, \ldots, C_l\}$ (corresponding to the correction parameter e), both collections of subsets of $\mathcal{P}$.

3.1 The Underlying Verifiable Secret Sharing

The state of the protocol is maintained with a k-out-of-k sharing, where each party holds several summands.

Definition 2 ($\mathcal{S}$-Sharing). *A value s is $\mathcal{S}$-shared for sharing specification $\mathcal{S} = (S_1, \ldots, S_k)$ if there are values $s_1, \ldots, s_k$, such that $s_1 + \ldots + s_k = s$ and, for all i, every (correct) party $j \in S_i$ holds the summand s_i. A sharing specification $\mathcal{S}$ is $\mathcal{D}$-permissive, if each summand is held by at least one party outside $\mathcal{D}$, i.e. $\forall i : S_i \setminus \mathcal{D} \neq \emptyset$.*

Lemma 5. *Let $\mathcal{S}$ be the sharing specification. An $\mathcal{S}$-sharing is secret if $\exists S_i \in \mathcal{S} : S_i \cap \mathcal{E}^* = \emptyset$, and uniquely defines a value if $\mathcal{S}$ is $\mathcal{D}^*$-permissive.*

Proof. Secrecy follows from the fact that $\mathcal{E}^*$ lacks at least one summand s_i. Furthermore, given that $\mathcal{S}$ is $\mathcal{D}^*$-permissive, each summand s_i is held by at least one correct party. Hence, the secret s is uniquely defined by $s = s_1 + \ldots + s_k$. $\qquad\square$

The share protocol takes as input a secret s from a dealer, and outputs an $\mathcal{S}$-sharing of the secret s (see Figure 3). Due to lack of space, the proof of the following lemma can be found in the full version.

Lemma 6. *Let $\mathcal{S}$ be the sharing specification. On input s from the dealer, $\textsc{Share}^{GA}$ correctly, secretly and robustly computes an $\mathcal{S}$-sharing. If $\mathcal{S}$ is $\mathcal{D}^*$-permissive, and if the dealer is correct, the sharing uniquely defines the secret s.*

SHARE$^{\mathbf{GA}}$: Given input s from the dealer, compute an $\mathcal{S}$-sharing of this value.

1. Let $k = |\mathcal{S}|$. The dealer chooses uniformly random summands $s_1, \ldots, s_{k-1}$ and computes $s_k = s + \sum_{i=1}^{k-1} s_i$. Then, the dealer sends s_i to every party $j \in S_i$.
2. For all $S_i \in \mathcal{S}$: Every party $j \in S_i$ sends s_i to every other party in S_i. Then, every party in S_i broadcasts a complaint bit, indicating whether it observed an inconsistency.
3. The dealer broadcasts each summand s_i for which inconsistencies were reported, and the players in S_i accept this summand. If the dealer does not broadcast a summand s_i, the parties use $s_i = 0$.
4. Each party j outputs its share $\{s_i \mid j \in S_i\}$.

Fig. 3. The Share Protocol for General Adversaries

For the public reconstruction[7] of a shared value, we modify the reconstruction protocol of [Mau02]. In our protocol, we trade correctness for robustness by introducing a correction structure $\mathcal{C}$. First, each summand s_i is broadcasted by all parties in S_i. Then, if the inconsistencies can be explained with a faulty set $C \in \mathcal{C}$, the values from parties in C are ignored (corrected), and reconstruction proceeds. Otherwise, the protocol is aborted.

Note that, whenever two sets of possibly actively corrupted parties cover a set $S_i \in \mathcal{S}$, i.e. $S_i \subseteq \mathcal{D}_1 \cup \mathcal{D}_2$, and the parties in $\mathcal{D}_1$ contradict the parties in $\mathcal{D}_2$, then it is impossible to decide which is the correct value. This observation implies an upper bound on $\mathcal{C}$, namely $\forall S \in \mathcal{S}, C_1, C_2 \in \mathcal{C} : S \not\subseteq C_1 \cup C_2$. However, instead of always correcting as many errors as possible, the protocol allows to select a structure $\mathcal{C}$ that remains below this upper bound (i.e. contains smaller sets C). Now, when correcting errors in a set $C \in \mathcal{C}$, we can detect errors in sets $\mathcal{D}$ where $\forall S_i \in \mathcal{S}, C \in \mathcal{C} : S_i \not\subseteq \mathcal{D} \cup C$. Hence, this approach provides a tradeoff between reduced robustness and extended correctness.

PUBLIC RECONSTRUCTION$^{\mathbf{GA}}$: Given an $\mathcal{S}$-sharing of some value s, reconstruct s to all parties.

1. For each summand s_i:
   (a) Each party $j \in S_i$ broadcasts s_i. For $j \in S_i$, let $s_i^{(j)}$ denote the value (for s_i) broadcasted by party j.
   (b) Each party (locally) reconstructs the summand s_i: If there is a value s_i such that there exists $C \in \mathcal{C}$ with $s_i^{(j)} = s_i$ for all $j \in S_i \setminus C$, use s_i. Otherwise abort.
2. Each party outputs the secret $s = s_1 + \ldots + s_k$.

Fig. 4. The Public Reconstruction Protocol for General Adversaries

---

[7] The reduction of private to public reconstruction can be done along the lines of the threshold case.

Lemma 7. *Let S be the sharing specification, and C be the correction structure, where $\forall S \in \mathcal{S}, C_1, C_2 \in \mathcal{C} : S \nsubseteq C_1 \cup C_2$. Given an S-sharing of some value s,* PUBLIC RECONSTRUCTION^{GA} *is correct if $\forall C \in \mathcal{C}, S \in \mathcal{S} : S \setminus C \nsubseteq \mathcal{D}^*$, is robust if $\mathcal{D}^* \in \mathcal{C}$, and always guarantees agreement on abort.*

Proof. Correctness: The condition $\forall C \in \mathcal{C}, S \in \mathcal{S} : S \setminus C \nsubseteq \mathcal{D}^*$ states that for every summand s_i and every set $C \in \mathcal{C}$, there is at least one correct party whose summand is not ignored. Hence, if a value s_i is chosen, it must be the correct one.

Robustness: When reconstructing the summand s_i, all but the actively corrupted parties in $\mathcal{D}^*$ broadcast the same summand s_i. If $\mathcal{D}^* \in \mathcal{C}$, these inconsistencies can be explained with a set in $\mathcal{C}$. Hence, the corresponding set can be ignored and reconstruction terminates without abort.

Agreement on abort: The abort decision is based only on broadcasted values. Hence, either all correct parties abort, or all correct parties continue.   □

3.2   Addition, Multiplication, and Random Values

Linear functions (and in particular additions) can be computed locally, since S-sharings are linear. In particular, given sharings of a and b, and a constant c, one can easily compute the sharings of $a + b$, ca, and $a + c$. Computing a shared random value can be achieved by letting each party i share a random value r_i, and computing a sharing of $r = r_1 + \ldots + r_n$.

For the multiplication of two values a and b, we use the protocol from [Mau02], based on our modified share and reconstruct protocols. The multiplication protocol exploits the fact that $ab = \sum_{i=1}^{k} \sum_{j=1}^{k} a_i b_j$: For each $a_i b_j$, first, all parties who know a_i and b_j compute $a_i b_j$ and share it. Then, all parties choose a (correct) sharing of $a_i b_j$. In the end, each party locally computes the linear function described above. In order to choose a correct sharing of $a_i b_j$, the protocol checks whether all parties that computed $a_i b_j$ shared the same value. If this holds, and if at least one correct party shared $a_i b_j$, all sharings contain the correct value, and an arbitrary one can be chosen. Otherwise, at least one party is actively corrupted, and the summands a_i and b_j can be reconstructed without violating secrecy.

The full description of the multiplication protocol can be found in the full version.

3.3   The Security of the Generalized Protocol from [Mau02]

Considering the security of the subprotocols described above, we can derive the security of the parametrized protocol, denoted by $\pi^{S,C}$ (proof omitted):

Lemma 8. *Let S be the sharing specification, and C be the correction structure, where $\forall S \in \mathcal{S}, C_1, C_2 \in \mathcal{C} : S \nsubseteq C_1 \cup C_2$. The protocol $\pi^{S,C}$ guarantees correctness if $\forall S_i, S_j \in \mathcal{S} : S_i \cap S_j \nsubseteq \mathcal{D}^*$ and $\forall C \in \mathcal{C}, S \in \mathcal{S} : S \setminus C \nsubseteq \mathcal{D}^*$, secrecy if $\exists S_i \in \mathcal{S} : S_i \cap \mathcal{E}^* = \emptyset$ and correctness is guaranteed, robustness if $\mathcal{D}^* \in \mathcal{C}$, and agreement on abort* always.

4   The Main Results

The following theorems state the optimal bounds for perfectly secure MPC with graceful degradation of both security (allowing for hybrid security) and corruptions (allowing for mixed adversaries) for threshold as well as for general adversaries, given broadcast.[8] Furthermore, we show that the bounds are sufficient for MPC by providing parameters for the generalized protocols introduced in Sections 2 and 3, respectively. In the following section, we prove that the bounds are also necessary.

4.1   Threshold Adversaries

We consider a mixed adversary, which is characterized by a pair of thresholds (t_a, t_p): He may corrupt up to t_p parties passively, and up to t_a of these parties even actively. The level of security depends on the number $(|\mathcal{D}^*|, |\mathcal{E}^*|)$ of *actually* corrupted parties; the fewer parties are corrupted, the more security is guaranteed. We consider four security properties, namely correctness, secrecy, robustness, and fairness. Depending on the actual number of corrupted parties, different security properties are achieved. This is modeled with four pairs of thresholds, one for each security requirement, specifying the upper bound on the number of corruptions that the adversary may perform, such that the security requirement is still guaranteed. More specifically, we consider the four pairs of thresholds (t_a^c, t_p^c), (t_a^s, t_p^s), (t_a^r, t_p^r), (t_a^f, t_p^f) and we assume that $(t_a^r, t_p^r) \leq (t_a^c, t_p^c)$ and $(t_a^f, t_p^f) \leq (t_a^s, t_p^s) \leq (t_a^c, t_p^c)$,[9] as secrecy and robustness are not well defined without correctness, and as fairness cannot be achieved without secrecy. Then, correctness with agreement on abort is guaranteed for $(|\mathcal{D}^*|, |\mathcal{E}^*|) \leq (t_a^c, t_p^c)$, secrecy is guaranteed for $(|\mathcal{D}^*|, |\mathcal{E}^*|) \leq (t_a^s, t_p^s)$, robustness is guaranteed for $(|\mathcal{D}^*|, |\mathcal{E}^*|) \leq (t_a^r, t_p^r)$, and fairness is guaranteed for $(|\mathcal{D}^*|, |\mathcal{E}^*|) \leq (t_a^f, t_p^f)$. Trivially, if several of these conditions are satisfied, all corresponding security properties are guaranteed. In particular, full security is guaranteed if the conditions for all four security properties are fulfilled.

Theorem 1. *In the secure channels model with broadcast and threshold adversaries, perfectly secure MPC among n parties with thresholds (t_a^c, t_p^c), (t_a^s, t_p^s), (t_a^r, t_p^r), and (t_a^f, t_p^f), where $(t_a^r, t_p^r) \leq (t_a^c, t_p^c)$ and $(t_a^f, t_p^f) \leq (t_a^s, t_p^s) \leq (t_a^c, t_p^c)$, is possible if*

$$\left(t_a^c + t_p^s + t_a^r < n \ \wedge \ t_a^c + 2t_p^s < n\right) \quad \vee \quad t_p^s = 0.$$

This bound is tight: If violated, there are (reactive) functionalities that cannot be securely computed.

The sufficiency of the bound in Theorem 1 follows basically from Lemma 4 (with $d := t_p^s$ and $e := \max(t_a^r, t_a^f)$). Due to lack of space the proof can be found in the full version. The necessity of the bound is proven in Section 5.

---

[8] The model without broadcast is treated in the full version of this paper.
[9] We write $(t_a^s, t_p^s) \leq (t_a^c, t_p^c)$ as shorthand for $t_a^s \leq t_a^c$ and $t_p^s \leq t_p^c$.

4.2   General Adversaries

The above characterization for threshold adversaries can be extended to general adversaries by providing one adversary structure consisting of tuples $(\mathcal{D}, \mathcal{E})$ of subsets of $\mathcal{P}$ for each security requirement, denoted by $\mathcal{Z}^c$, $\mathcal{Z}^s$, $\mathcal{Z}^r$, and $\mathcal{Z}^f$, respectively. Again, we have the assumption that $\mathcal{Z}^r \subseteq \mathcal{Z}^c$ and $\mathcal{Z}^f \subseteq \mathcal{Z}^s \subseteq \mathcal{Z}^c$, as secrecy and robustness are not well defined without correctness, and as fairness cannot be achieved without secrecy. Then, correctness with agreement on abort is guaranteed for $(\mathcal{D}^*, \mathcal{E}^*) \in \mathcal{Z}^c$, secrecy is guaranteed for $(\mathcal{D}^*, \mathcal{E}^*) \in \mathcal{Z}^s$, robustness is guaranteed for $(\mathcal{D}^*, \mathcal{E}^*) \in \mathcal{Z}^r$, and fairness is guaranteed for $(\mathcal{D}^*, \mathcal{E}^*) \in \mathcal{Z}^f$. Trivially, if several of these conditions are satisfied, all corresponding security properties are guaranteed. In particular, full security is guaranteed if the conditions for all four security properties are fulfilled.

Theorem 2. *In the secure channels model with broadcast and general adversaries, perfectly secure MPC among n parties with respect to $(\mathcal{Z}^c, \mathcal{Z}^s, \mathcal{Z}^r, \mathcal{Z}^f)$, where $\mathcal{Z}^r \subseteq \mathcal{Z}^c$ and $\mathcal{Z}^f \subseteq \mathcal{Z}^s \subseteq \mathcal{Z}^c$, is possible if*

$$\forall (\mathcal{D}^c, \cdot) \in \mathcal{Z}^c, (\cdot, \mathcal{E}_1^s), (\cdot, \mathcal{E}_2^s) \in \mathcal{Z}^s, (\mathcal{D}^r, \cdot) \in \mathcal{Z}^r :$$
$$\left(\mathcal{D}^c \cup \mathcal{E}_1^s \cup \mathcal{D}^r \neq \mathcal{P} \quad \wedge \quad \mathcal{D}^c \cup \mathcal{E}_1^s \cup \mathcal{E}_2^s \neq \mathcal{P} \right) \quad \vee \quad \mathcal{Z}^s = \{(\emptyset, \emptyset)\}.$$

This bound is tight: If violated, there are (reactive) functionalities that cannot be securely computed.

The sufficiency of the bound in Theorem 2 follows basically from Lemma 8 (with $\mathcal{S} := \{\overline{\mathcal{E}^s} \mid (\cdot, \mathcal{E}^s) \in \mathcal{Z}^s\}$ and $\mathcal{C} = \{\mathcal{D} \mid (\mathcal{D}, \cdot) \in \mathcal{Z}^r \cup \mathcal{Z}^f\}$). The proof can be found in the full version. The necessity of the bound is proven in Section 5.

5   Proofs of Necessity

In this section, we prove that the bounds in Theorem 1 and 2 are necessary, i.e., if violated, some (reactive) functionalities cannot be securely computed. Trivially, the impossibility for threshold adversaries follows from the impossibility for general adversaries. The bound for general adversaries (Theorem 2) is violated if $\mathcal{Z}^s \neq \{(\emptyset, \emptyset)\}$ and

$$\exists (\mathcal{D}^c, \cdot) \in \mathcal{Z}^c, (\cdot, \mathcal{E}_1^s), (\cdot, \mathcal{E}_2^s) \in \mathcal{Z}^s, (\mathcal{D}^r, \cdot) \in \mathcal{Z}^r :$$
$$\mathcal{D}^c \cup \mathcal{E}_1^s \cup \mathcal{D}^r = \mathcal{P} \quad \vee \quad \mathcal{D}^c \cup \mathcal{E}_1^s \cup \mathcal{E}_2^s = \mathcal{P}.$$

Due to monotonicity, we can assume that the sets $\mathcal{D}^c, \mathcal{E}_1^s, \mathcal{E}_2^s$, and $\mathcal{D}^r$ are disjoint. Furthermore, since $\mathcal{Z}^s \neq \{(\emptyset, \emptyset)\}$, we can assume that $\mathcal{E}_1^s \neq \emptyset$. We can split the condition according to whether $\mathcal{D}^c \cup \mathcal{E}_1^s \cup \mathcal{D}^r = \mathcal{P}$ or $\mathcal{D}^c \cup \mathcal{E}_1^s \cup \mathcal{E}_2^s = \mathcal{P}$.

1. $\exists (\mathcal{D}^c, \cdot) \in \mathcal{Z}^c, (\cdot, \mathcal{E}_1^s) \in \mathcal{Z}^s, (\mathcal{D}^r, \cdot) \in \mathcal{Z}^r : \mathcal{D}^c \cup \mathcal{E}_1^s \cup \mathcal{D}^r = \mathcal{P} \wedge \mathcal{E}_1^s \neq \emptyset$. We further split this case according to whether $\mathcal{D}^c = \emptyset$ or $\mathcal{D}^r = \emptyset$. Note that, since $\mathcal{Z}^r \subseteq \mathcal{Z}^c$, the case where $\mathcal{D}^c = \emptyset \wedge \mathcal{D}^r \neq \emptyset$ is subsumed by Case 1(b).

   (a) $\exists (\mathcal{D}^c, \cdot) \in \mathcal{Z}^c, (\cdot, \mathcal{E}_1^s) \in \mathcal{Z}^s, (\mathcal{D}^r, \cdot) \in \mathcal{Z}^r :$
   $\mathcal{D}^c \cup \mathcal{E}_1^s \cup \mathcal{D}^r = \mathcal{P} \wedge \mathcal{E}_1^s \neq \emptyset \wedge \mathcal{D}^c \neq \emptyset \wedge \mathcal{D}^r \neq \emptyset$

   (b) $\exists (\mathcal{D}^c, \cdot) \in \mathcal{Z}^c, (\cdot, \mathcal{E}_1^s) \in \mathcal{Z}^s : \mathcal{D}^c \cup \mathcal{E}_1^s = \mathcal{P} \wedge \mathcal{E}_1^s \neq \emptyset \wedge \mathcal{D}^c \neq \emptyset$

(c) $\exists (\cdot, \mathcal{E}_1^s) \in \mathcal{Z}^s : \mathcal{E}_1^s = \mathcal{P} \wedge \mathcal{E}_1^s \neq \emptyset$: Due to monotonicity and $|\mathcal{P}| \geq 2$, this case is identical to Case 2(b).

2. $\exists (\mathcal{D}^c, \cdot) \in \mathcal{Z}^c, (\cdot, \mathcal{E}_1^s), (\cdot, \mathcal{E}_2^s) \in \mathcal{Z}^s : \mathcal{D}^c \cup \mathcal{E}_1^s \cup \mathcal{E}_2^s = \mathcal{P} \wedge \mathcal{E}_1^s \neq \emptyset$. Again, we further split this case according to whether $\mathcal{D}^c = \emptyset$ or $\mathcal{E}_2^s = \emptyset$. Note that the case where $\mathcal{D}^c \neq \emptyset \wedge \mathcal{E}_2^s = \emptyset$ is identical to Case 1(b), and the case where $\mathcal{D}^c = \emptyset \wedge \mathcal{E}_2^s = \emptyset$ is identical to Case 1(c).

(a) $\exists (\mathcal{D}^c, \cdot) \in \mathcal{Z}^c, (\cdot, \mathcal{E}_1^s), (\cdot, \mathcal{E}_2^s) \in \mathcal{Z}^s :$
$\mathcal{D}^c \cup \mathcal{E}_1^s \cup \mathcal{E}_2^s = \mathcal{P} \wedge \mathcal{E}_1^s \neq \emptyset \wedge \mathcal{E}_2^s \neq \emptyset \wedge \mathcal{D}^c \neq \emptyset$

(b) $\exists (\cdot, \mathcal{E}_1^s), (\cdot, \mathcal{E}_2^s) \in \mathcal{Z}^s : \mathcal{E}_1^s \cup \mathcal{E}_2^s = \mathcal{P} \wedge \mathcal{E}_1^s \neq \emptyset \wedge \mathcal{E}_2^s \neq \emptyset$

Case 1(a): $\exists (\mathcal{D}^c, \cdot) \in \mathcal{Z}^c, (\cdot, \mathcal{E}_1^s) \in \mathcal{Z}^s, (\mathcal{D}^r, \cdot) \in \mathcal{Z}^r :$
$$\mathcal{D}^c \cup \mathcal{E}_1^s \cup \mathcal{D}^r = \mathcal{P} \wedge \mathcal{E}_1^s \neq \emptyset \wedge \mathcal{D}^c \neq \emptyset \wedge \mathcal{D}^r \neq \emptyset$$

A state is a requirement for reactive functionalities. We first prove that it is impossible to hold a state in a specific 3-party setting. This proof is inspired by [BFH+08].

Definition 3 (State). *A state for n parties $1, \ldots, n$ is a tuple $(s_1, \ldots, s_n)$ that defines a bit s, where party i holds s_i. A state is* secret *if the state information held by corrupted parties contains no information about the bit s. A state is* correct *if it uniquely defines either s or $\perp$. A state is* robust *if it uniquely defines either 0 or 1.*

Lemma 9. *Three parties A, B, and C cannot hold a state (s_A, s_B, s_C) that defines a bit s providing secrecy in case of a passively corrupted A, correctness and robustness in case of an actively corrupted B, and correctness in case of an actively corrupted C.*

Proof. To arrive at a contradiction, assume that (a, b, c) is a state for $s = 0$. Due to secrecy in case of a passively corrupted A, there exists b' and c' such that (a, b', c') is a valid state for $s = 1$. Due to correctness and robustness in case of an actively corrupted B, the state $(a, \cdot, c)$ must define the value 0 (where $\cdot$ is a placeholder for an arbitrary state information held by B). Due to correctness in case of an actively corrupted C, the state $(a, b', \cdot)$ defines either 1 or $\perp$. As a consequence, with probability greater 0, the state (a, b', c) can be achieved if $s = 0$ and B is actively corrupted, and it can be achieved if $s = 1$ and C is actively corrupted. Hence, it must define both 0 and either 1 or $\perp$, which is a contradiction. □

Given Lemma 9, we can prove the desired bound by reducing the n-party setting to the 3-party setting specified there: Assume we have a perfectly secure n-party state $(s_1, \ldots, s_n)$ for the case $\exists (\mathcal{D}^c, \cdot) \in \mathcal{Z}^c, (\cdot, \mathcal{E}_1^s) \in \mathcal{Z}^s, (\mathcal{D}^r, \cdot) \in \mathcal{Z}^r : \mathcal{D}^c \cup \mathcal{E}_1^s \cup \mathcal{D}^r = \mathcal{P} \wedge \mathcal{E}_1^s \neq \emptyset \wedge \mathcal{D}^c \neq \emptyset \wedge \mathcal{D}^r \neq \emptyset$. By assumption we have that $\mathcal{D}^c$, $\mathcal{E}_1^s$, and $\mathcal{D}^r$ are disjoint.

We obtain a 3-party state (s_A, s_B, s_C) from $(s_1, \ldots, s_n)$ by having A, B, and C emulate the parties in $\mathcal{E}_1^s$, $\mathcal{D}^r$, and $\mathcal{D}^c$ respectively. The state $(s_1, \ldots, s_n)$ tolerates passive corruption of all parties in $\mathcal{E}_1^s$ while maintaining secrecy, active corruption of all parties in $\mathcal{D}^r$ while maintaining correctness and robustness, and active corruption of all parties in $\mathcal{D}^c$ while maintaining correctness. Hence, the resulting state (s_A, s_B, s_C) is secure for the specific corruption setting specified in Lemma 9, which is a contradiction.

Case 1(b): $\exists (\mathcal{D}^c, \cdot) \in \mathcal{Z}^c, (\cdot, \mathcal{E}_1^s) \in \mathcal{Z}^s :$
$$\mathcal{D}^c \cup \mathcal{E}_1^s = \mathcal{P} \ \wedge \ \mathcal{E}_1^s \neq \emptyset \wedge \mathcal{D}^c \neq \emptyset$$

Analogously to the previous section, we prove that it is impossible to hold a state in a specific 2-party setting:

Lemma 10. *Two parties A and B cannot hold a state (s_A, s_B) that defines a bit s providing secrecy in case of a passively corrupted A, and correctness in case of an actively corrupted B.*

Proof. For a contradiction, assume that (a, b) is a state for $s = 0$. Due to secrecy in case of a passively corrupted A, there exists b' such that (a, b') is a valid state for $s = 1$. As a consequence, with probability greater 0, an actively corrupted B can chose between the state (a, b) and (a, b'), violating correctness. □

Given Lemma 10, we can prove the desired bound by reducing the n-party setting to the 2-party setting along the lines of the previous section.

Case 2(a): $\exists (\mathcal{D}^c, \cdot) \in \mathcal{Z}^c, (\cdot, \mathcal{E}_1^s), (\cdot, \mathcal{E}_2^s) \in \mathcal{Z}^s :$
$$\mathcal{D}^c \cup \mathcal{E}_1^s \cup \mathcal{E}_2^s = \mathcal{P} \ \wedge \ \mathcal{E}_1^s \neq \emptyset \wedge \mathcal{E}_2^s \neq \emptyset \wedge \mathcal{D}^c \neq \emptyset$$

We first prove impossibility of computing the logical "and" in a specific 3-party setting.

Lemma 11. *Consider protocols for three parties A (with input $a \in \{0, 1\}$), B (with input $b \in \{0, 1\}$), and C (without input) that compute the logical "and" $z = a \wedge b$ and output it to all parties. There is no such protocol providing secrecy when A or B are passively corrupted, and correctness when C is actively corrupted.*

Proof. To arrive at a contradiction, assume that a secure protocol exists. We consider the random variables T_{AB}, T_{AC} and T_{BC} describing the transcripts of the channels connecting parties A and B, A and C, and B and C, respectively, and T describing the transcript of the broadcast channel, for honest protocol executions.

First, observe that for $a = 0$, we have $z = 0$ independent of b, hence $I(b; T_{AB}, T_{AC}, T | a = 0) = 0$. Analogously, for $a = 1$, A must learn $z = b$, hence $H(b|T_{AB}, T_{AC}, T, a = 1) = 0$. We distinguish two cases, namely when $H(b|T_{AB}, T, a = 1)$ is zero (i) or non-zero (ii).

In case (i), it follows from $I(b; T_{AB}, T_{AC}, T | a = 0) = 0$, that in particular we must have $I(b; T_{AB}, T | a = 0) = H(b|a = 0) - H(b|T_{AB}, T, a = 0) = 0$, and hence $H(b|T_{AB}, T, a = 0) = H(b|a = 0) > 0$. Furthermore, by assumption we have $H(b|T_{AB}, T, a = 1) = 0$. That means that party B can decide if $a = 0$ or $a = 1$ by observing the transcripts T_{AB} and T. This contradicts the secrecy in presence of a passively corrupted party B.

In case (ii), let $(t_{AB}, t_{AC}, t_{BC}, t)$ be a list of transcripts corresponding to a protocol run with $a = 1$ and $b = 0$. It follows from $H(b|T_{AB}, T, a = 1) > 0$ that there are transcripts t'_{AC} and t'_{BC}, such that $(t_{AB}, t'_{AC}, t'_{BC}, t)$ is a list of transcripts corresponding to a protocol run with $a = 1$ and $b = 1$. Thus, when observing t_{AB}, t'_{AC}, and t, party A cannot distinguish whether $b = 1$ and all parties behave correctly, or whether $b = 0$ and party C is actively corrupted provoking a wrong transcript t'_{AC} (which C achieves with non-zero probability). In the first scenario, due to completeness, A must output 1. In the second scenario, due to correctness, party A must output 0 (or abort). This is a contradiction.   □

Given Lemma 11, we can prove the desired bound by reducing the n-party setting to the 3-party setting along the lines of the previous sections.

Case 2(b): $\exists(\cdot, \mathcal{E}_1^s), (\cdot, \mathcal{E}_2^s) \in \mathcal{Z}^s : \ \mathcal{E}_1^s \cup \mathcal{E}_2^s = \mathcal{P} \ \wedge \ \mathcal{E}_1^s \neq \emptyset \wedge \mathcal{E}_2^s \neq \emptyset$

As stated in [BGW88, Kil00], it is impossible to compute the logical "and" with perfect secrecy in a 2-party setting. Again, we can prove the desired bound by reducing the n-party setting to the 2-party setting along the lines of the previous sections.

6   Conclusions and Open Problems

We have provided the first MPC protocols with graceful degradation in multiple dimensions, namely graceful degradation of security, as well as graceful degradation with respect to the corruption type. This covers all common security notions for MPC (correctness, secrecy, robustness, fairness, and agreement on abort), as well as the most prominent corruption types (honest, passive, active), for both threshold and general adversaries. The protocols are strict generalizations (and combinations) of hybrid-secure MPC and mixed adversaries. We derived tight bounds for the existence of perfectly secure MPC protocols for the given settings, and provided protocols that achieve these bounds.

We leave as an open problem to combine additional dimensions of graceful degradation (like, e.g., efficiency) with graceful degradation of security and corruption types (e.g. fail-corruption), as well as to consider other security models (e.g. computational security). Furthermore, in this work, we focus on MPC including reactive functionalities. The bounds for secure function evaluation (SFE) might be slightly weaker.

References

[Bea89]   Beaver, D.: Multiparty protocols tolerating half faulty processors. In: Brassard, G. (ed.) CRYPTO 1989. LNCS, vol. 435, pp. 560–572. Springer, Heidelberg (1990)

[BFH+08] Beerliová-Trubíniová, Z., Fitzi, M., Hirt, M., Maurer, U.M., Zikas, V.: MPC vs. SFE: Perfect security in a unified corruption model. In: Canetti, R. (ed.) TCC 2008. LNCS, vol. 4948, pp. 231–250. Springer, Heidelberg (2008)

[BGW88]   Ben-Or, M., Goldwasser, S., Wigderson, A.: Completeness theorems for non-cryptographic fault-tolerant distributed computation. In: STOC 1988, pp. 1–10. ACM, New York (1988)

[CCD88]   Chaum, D., Crépeau, C., Damgård, I.: Multiparty unconditionally secure protocols. In: STOC 1988, pp. 11–19. ACM, New York (1988)

[CDG87]   Chaum, D., Damgård, I.B., van de Graaf, J.: Multiparty computations ensuring privacy of each party's input and correctness of the result. In: Pomerance, C. (ed.) CRYPTO 1987. LNCS, vol. 293, pp. 87–119. Springer, Heidelberg (1988)

[Cha89]   Chaum, D.: The spymasters double-agent problem: Multiparty computations secure unconditionally from minorities and cryptograhically from majorities. In: Brassard, G. (ed.) CRYPTO 1989. LNCS, vol. 435, pp. 591–602. Springer, Heidelberg (1990)

[DDWY93] Dolev, D., Dwork, C., Waarts, O., Yung, M.: Perfectly secure message transmission. Journal of the ACM 40(1), 17–47 (1993)

[FHHW03] Fitzi, M., Hirt, M., Holenstein, T., Wullschleger, J.: Two-threshold broadcast and detectable multi-party computation. In: Biham, E. (ed.) EUROCRYPT 2003. LNCS, vol. 2656, pp. 51–67. Springer, Heidelberg (2003)

[FHM98]   Fitzi, M., Hirt, M., Maurer, U.M.: Trading correctness for privacy in unconditional multi-party computation (extended abstract). In: Krawczyk, H. (ed.) CRYPTO 1998. LNCS, vol. 1462, pp. 121–136. Springer, Heidelberg (1998)

[FHM99]   Fitzi, M., Hirt, M., Maurer, U.M.: General adversaries in unconditional multi-party computation. In: Lam, K.-Y., Okamoto, E., Xing, C. (eds.) ASIACRYPT 1999. LNCS, vol. 1716, pp. 232–246. Springer, Heidelberg (1999)

[FHW04]   Fitzi, M., Holenstein, T., Wullschleger, J.: Multi-party computation with hybrid security. In: Cachin, C., Camenisch, J.L. (eds.) EUROCRYPT 2004. LNCS, vol. 3027, pp. 419–438. Springer, Heidelberg (2004)

[GMW87]   Goldreich, O., Micali, S., Wigderson, A.: How to play any mental game or a completeness theorem for protocols with honest majority. In: STOC 1987, pp. 218–229. ACM, New York (1987)

[GRR98]   Gennaro, R., Rabin, M.O., Rabin, T.: Simplified VSS and fast-track multiparty computations with applications to threshold cryptography. In: PODC 1998, pp. 101–111. ACM, New York (1998)

[HM97]   Hirt, M., Maurer, U.: Complete characterization of adversaries tolerable in secure multi-party computation. In: PODC 1997, pp. 25–34. ACM, New York (1997)

[HMZ08]   Hirt, M., Maurer, U.M., Zikas, V.: MPC vs. SFE: Unconditional and computational security. In: Pieprzyk, J. (ed.) ASIACRYPT 2008. LNCS, vol. 5350, pp. 1–18. Springer, Heidelberg (2008)

[IKLP06] Ishai, Y., Kushilevitz, E., Lindell, Y., Petrank, E.: On combining privacy with guaranteed output delivery in secure multiparty computation. In: Dwork, C. (ed.) CRYPTO 2006. LNCS, vol. 4117, pp. 483–500. Springer, Heidelberg (2006)

[Kat07]   Katz, J.: On achieving the "best of both worlds" in secure multiparty computation. In: STOC 2007, pp. 11–20. ACM, New York (2007)

[Kil00]   Kilian, J.: More general completeness theorems for secure two-party computation. In: STOC 2000, pp. 316–324. ACM, New York (2000)

[LRM10]   Lucas, C., Raub, D., Maurer, U.: Hybrid-secure MPC: Trading information-theoretic robustness for computational privacy. In: PODC 2010, pp. 219–228. ACM, New York (2010)

[Mau02]   Maurer, U.M.: Secure multi-party computation made simple. In: Cimato, S., Galdi, C., Persiano, G. (eds.) SCN 2002. LNCS, vol. 2576, pp. 14–28. Springer, Heidelberg (2003)

[RB89]   Rabin, T., Ben-Or, M.: Verifiable secret sharing and multiparty protocols with honest majority. In: STOC 1989, pp. 73–85. ACM, New York (1989)

[Sha79]   Shamir, A.: How to share a secret. Communications of the ACM 22(11), 612–613 (1979)

[Yao82]   Yao, A.C.: Protocols for secure computations (extended abstract). In: FOCS 1982, pp. 160–164. IEEE, Los Alamitos (1982)

Quantum Communication Attacks on Classical Cryptographic Protocols
(Invited Talk)

Ivan Damgård

Dept. of Computer Science, Aarhus University

Abstract. In the literature on cryptographic protocols, it has been studied several times what happens if a classical protocol is attacked by a quantum adversary. Usually, this is taken to mean that the adversary runs a quantum algorithm, but communicates classically with the honest players. In several cases, one can show that the protocol remains secure even under such an attack.

However, there are also cases where the honest players are quantum as well, even if the protocol uses classical communication. For instance, this is the case when classical multiparty computation is used as a "subroutine" in quantum multiparty computation. Furthermore, in the future, players in a protocol may employ quantum computing simply to improve efficiency of their local computation, even if the communication is supposed to be classical. In such cases, it no longer seems clear that a quantum adversary must be limited to only classical communication with the honest players. And so the natural question is: what happens to the security if this limitation is dropped?

In this talk, we survey some results from ongoing work that addresses this question, more specifically, we consider security of secret sharing, zero-knowledge protocols and multiparty computation under this new paradigm. In all cases, both positive and negative results can be shown. For instance, a classical threshold secret sharing scheme designed for threshold t is no longer secure in this model, but the same scheme *is* secure with threshold $t/2$.

This is joint work with Jakob Funder, Jesper Buus Nielsen (Dept. of Computer Science, Aarhus University) and Louis Salvail (Université de Montréal).

S. Fehr (Ed.): ICITS 2011, LNCS 6673, p. 181, 2011.

Using Colors to Improve Visual Cryptography for Black and White Images

Roberto De Prisco and Alfredo De Santis

Dipartimento di Informatica
Università di Salerno
84084 Fisciano (SA), Italy

Abstract. Black-and-white visual cryptography (BW-VC) allows the sharing of b&w secret images transforming a secret image into a number of b&w shares. Colored visual cryptography allows the sharing of color images by means of color shares. In this paper we propose a new model, called colored-black-and-white (CBW-VC), in which the secret image is b&w and the shares are color images.

The motivation for the use of this new model is that of constructing schemes to share b&w images using a smaller pixel expansion. Using the CBW-VC model, we provide $(2, n)$-threshold schemes with pixel expansion $m = \lceil \log_3 n \rceil$, improving on the best pixel expansion attainable in the BW-VC model.

For the case of schemes with perfect reconstruction of black pixels we provide a general construction that allows to transform any BW-VC scheme into a CBW-VC scheme whose pixel expansion is $1/3$ of the pixel expansion of the starting BW-VC scheme.

When there are very few participants, namely $n = 2, 3$, the proposed CBW-VC $(2, n)$-threshold schemes have no pixel expansion! We prove that the above two cases are the only ones where it is possible to provide schemes without pixel expansion. That is, we prove that, in the CBW-VC model, it is not possible to construct $(2, n)$-threshold schemes, for $n \geq 4$, and (k, n)-threshold schemes, for $k \geq 3$, without pixel expansion.

1 Introduction

A visual cryptography scheme, or VCS for short, is a special type of secret sharing that allows to share a secret image in such a way that the reconstruction of the secret can be done by the human visual system. The sharing process produces a share for each participant. Each share is an image printed on a transparency. We will denote with $\mathcal{P}$ the set of participants and with n the cardinality of $\mathcal{P}$. The secret image is known by a trusted party, called the dealer. The dealer constructs the n shares and distributes one share to each participant. Certain qualified subsets of participants can "visually" recover the secret image. All other sets of participants, called forbidden, have no information on the secret image. A "visual" recovery for a set $X \subseteq \mathcal{P}$ consists in superposing the shares (transparencies) given to the participants in X. The participants in a qualified set

S. Fehr (Ed.): ICITS 2011, LNCS 6673, pp. 182–201, 2011.

X will be able to see the secret image without any knowledge of cryptography and without performing any cryptographic computation. In most cases the qualified set of participants are all the sets with at least k participants, while all the sets with less than k participants are forbidden. In such cases the schemes are called (k, n)-threshold. In this paper we consider only (k, n)-threshold schemes, although some constructions can be easily extended to any access structure.

Visual cryptography has been devised by Naor and Shamir [12]. Their paper has sparked the "visual cryptography research area" and quite a number of papers have been written on the subject.

The original model used in [12] considers b&w visual cryptography. In b&w visual cryptography the secret image is a b&w image and also the shares are b&w images. The reconstructed image is also a b&w image. The idea is the following: each pixel of the secret image is expanded into some number m of pixels. Sometimes we call such m pixels "subpixels", even though they are regular pixels (a pixel cannot be subdivided). Parameter m is the *pixel expansion* of the scheme. The reconstruction of the secret is obtained by superposing the shares (transparencies) in such a way that pixels are aligned. The human visual system performs an "or" of the pixels: it sees white if all the pixels are white, it sees black if at least one of the superposed pixels is black[1]. The shares are constructed in such a way that when we superpose the shares of a qualified set of participants, among the m subpixels that represent a secret pixel we will find at most ℓ black subpixels, if the secret pixel is white, and at least h black subpixels, if the secret pixel is black, with $0 \le \ell < h \le m$. The far apart are ℓ and h the better will be the reconstructed image. Parameter ℓ and h are used to define the *contrast* of the scheme.

For example, the BW-VC $(2, 2)$-threshold scheme of [12] has pixel expansion $m = 2$ and $\ell = 1$ and $h = 2$. Hence a white secret pixel is reconstructed with one black subpixel and one white subpixel, while a black secret pixel is reconstructed with 2 black subpixels. Figure 1 shows an example with a secret image consisting of 100×170 px (pixels).

Since the pixel expansion is $m = 2$ the shares and the reconstructed image are distorted. In the above example we decided to distort the image over the horizontal axis. Another possibility is to distort it over the vertical axis. For $m > 2$ one can try to distribute the pixel expansion evenly over the two axes. In particular, when m is a square we can avoid distorting the image because each secret pixel can be reconstructed as a matrix of $\sqrt{m} \times \sqrt{m}$ subpixels. In any case, the size of reconstructed image is m times the size of the secret image.

The pixel expansion is a crucial characteristic of the scheme. When the pixel expansion is too large it might be impracticable to use the scheme. For example assume that shares are printed on A4 transparencies. Although modern printers allow to use very tiny pixels, since the shares will have to be superposed manually, to ease the reconstruction it is reasonable to use pixels that are not too small. Assume that the secret image consists of a text string. If, for the desired pixel

---

[1] Many papers represent white with 0 and black with 1; this is why we say that the human visual system performs an "or" operation.

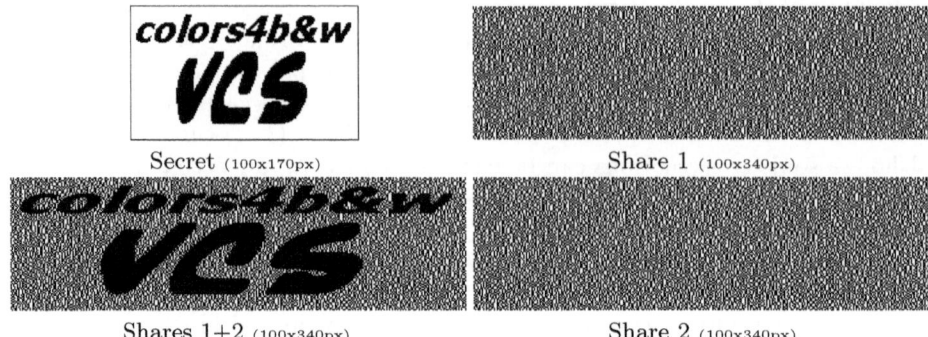

Fig. 1. Sharing and reconstruction for the b&w $(2, 2)$-threshold scheme

size, it is possible to accommodate a certain number z of text characters on a A4 transparency, then the actual string that we can share can be at most z/m characters long. In general, the size of the image that we can share is inversely proportional to m. For this reason it is important that m be as small as possible.

Many papers have tackled the problem of finding BW-VC schemes with optimal (minimum) pixel expansion and several results are known, including some lower bounds on the pixel expansion and schemes achieving the lower bounds. Clearly, we cannot improve on those optimal schemes if we use the BW-VC model. However by allowing the shares to use colors we can construct schemes with smaller pixel expansion. For very specific cases we are able to construct schemes with no pixel expansion. We remark that the probabilistic visual cryptography model proposed in [14] also allows schemes with no pixel expansion, however the reconstruction is only probabilistic, that is, pixels are correctly reconstructed only with some given probability. In [6] it has been shown that the decrease in pixel expansion of a probabilistic scheme is paid with the probability of wrong reconstructions: schemes with a smaller pixel expansion have a greater error probability. In this paper we are concerned with deterministic schemes in which there are no errors in the reconstruction of the secret image.

Some papers (e.g., [7,11,10,13,15]) have considered the generalization of the BW-VC model to color images In this case the secret image, the shares and the reconstructed image are color images. However the use of colors poses several additional difficulties. To overcome these difficulties, almost all the schemes for color images consider black as a special color that can appear without restrictions in the reconstruction. This means that an arbitrary number of the m subpixels can actually be black and only few are colored. Most color schemes heavily exploit the special black color and this makes, except for very few cases, the reconstructed image not recognizable. Moreover, the pixel expansion of color schemes is, not surprisingly, greater than that of BW-VC schemes. For a survey about color visual cryptography see Chapter 12 of [8].

Although the generalization of visual cryptography to color images appears to be quite problematic, the use of colors can be of help in order to share b&w secret images. In this paper we propose to use colors to improve visual cryptography schemes for b&w secret images. That is, while the secret image is b&w, we allow the shares and thus the reconstructed image, to be color images. As before each secret pixel is expanded into m subpixels. Each subpixel can be colored with an arbitrary color. The reconstruction has to guarantee that among the m subpixels we will have at most ℓ black subpixels, if the secret pixel is white, and at least h black subpixels if the secret pixel is black. This requirement is the same as the one that we have for regular b&w cryptography. However using colored shares we aim at reconstructing black as black and white as colored pixels. We call this new model *colored-black-&-white* visual cryptography, or CBW-VC for short, and the we refer to schemes for this model as CBW-VC schemes, or CBW-VCS for short.

Using the CBW-VC model we can improve the pixel expansion of BW-VC schemes; obviously this is possible because the CBW-VC model is more powerful than the BW-VC model. In particular, we provide a construction of CBW-VC $(2, n)$-threshold schemes whose pixel expansion is $m = \lceil \log_3 n \rceil$ improving on the (optimal) pixel expansion of BW-VCS. For the cases of $n = 2, 3$ the schemes have no pixel expansion. For these special cases the reconstructed image will have exactly the same size of the original one, white pixels will be reconstructed as colored pixels and black pixels will be reconstructed as black pixels. That is, the image will be as the original one, but the white background will be substituted with a mixture of colored pixels.

We also prove that the above two particular cases are the only ones for which we can construct schemes with no pixel expansion. More specifically, we prove that it is not possible to construct CBW-VC $(2, n)$-threshold schemes, for $n \geq 4$, and CBW-VC (k, n)-threshold schemes, for $k \geq 3$, using $m = 1$.

As it happens for b&w images, among schemes with the same contrast, the reconstructed image is more clearly visible when black pixels are reconstructed with only black pixels. Schemes that have this property are called schemes with perfect reconstruction of black pixels (PB-VCS).

We provide a general construction that allows to take any PB-BW-VC (k, n)-threshold scheme with perfect reconstruction of black pixels and transform it into a PB-CBW-VC (k, n)-threshold scheme with perfect reconstruction of black pixels. The pixel expansion of the resulting PB-CBW-VCS is $m = \lceil m'/3 \rceil$ where m' is the pixel expansion of the starting PB-BW-VCS. The construction works for any access structure and not just threshold schemes.

This paper is organized as follows. Section 2 describes the model that we use while Section 3 recalls previous relevant work . Section 4 provides the schemes for the case of $k = 2$, Section 5 describes the impossibility result and, finally, Section 6 describes the general construction for (k, n)-threshold schemes with perfect reconstruction of black pixels. Section 7 contains concluding remarks and directions for future work.

2   The Model

In order to deal with colored pixels we need to use a color model. Using the RGB color model a color is represented as a triple (x, y, z), with $0 \leq x, j, z \leq L$, for a fixed threshold L, where x, y and z are, respectively the amount of red, green and blue light present in the color. The RGB color model is a standard color model and has been used also in some other papers that tackle colored visual cryptography (the interested reader can look at Chapter 12 of [8] for a survey on colored visual cryptography).

Typically, for computers, we have $L = 255$ and we can represent 3^{256} different colors. When we superpose two colored pixels the resulting color is a function of the two colored pixels. A good approximation of the resulting color is given by the following operator add:

$$\text{add}(\chi_1, \chi_2) = \left(\text{int}\left(\frac{x_1 x_2}{L}\right), \text{int}\left(\frac{y_1 y_2}{L}\right), \text{int}\left(\frac{z_1 z_2}{L}\right)\right).$$

In this paper we will use only the 8 full intensity colors black, red, green, blue, cyan, magenta, yellow and white, denoted by, respectively, $\bullet$, R, G, B, C, M, Y and $\circ$. Thus, for simplicity of notation, we assume that $L = 1$. A white light contains all colors and is represented by $\circ = (1,1,1)$. The color black is obtained when there is no light at all, and thus it is represented by $\bullet = (0,0,0)$. The colors red, green and blue are represented, respectively, by R $= (1,0,0)$, G $= (0,1,0)$ and B $= (0,0,1)$. The colors cyan, magenta and yellow are the "complement" of, respectively, blu, green and red, and thus are represented by C $= (0,1,1)$, M $= (1,0,1)$ and Y $= (1,1,0)$. The add operator can be simplified to:

$$\text{add}(\chi_1, \chi_2) = (x_1 x_2, y_1 y_2, z_1 z_2)$$

The add operator can be easily extended to vectors of colors and also to matrices: we add the colors in each column and the result is a vector whose length is equal to the number of columns. See the following for an example.

A secret image, consisting of b&w pixels, has to be shared among a set $\mathcal{P} = \{1, \ldots, n\}$ of *participants*. A trusted party, which is called the *dealer* and is not a participant, knows the secret image. The dealer has to distribute the *shares* to the n participants in the form of printed transparencies. Some subsets of $\mathcal{P}$, called *qualified sets* have to be able to "visually" recover the secret image, by superposing their shares (transparencies) and holding the stacked set of transparencies to the light. Other subsets of $\mathcal{P}$, called *forbidden sets*, must not be able to get any information on the secret image from their shares, neither by superposing the transparencies nor by any other computation. In this paper we consider (k, n)-threshold schemes for which the qualified sets are all the subsets of $\mathcal{P}$ with cardinality at least k. All the subsets with less than k participants are forbidden.

Each pixel appears in n versions called *shares*, one for each transparency. Each share is a collection of m pixels. We allow the pixels of the shares to have one of the full intensity colors in the palette $\mathcal{P}al_{\text{COL}} = \{\circ, R, G, B, C, M, Y, \bullet\}$. Notice that for regular b&w schemes the colors of pixels in the shares are restricted to $\mathcal{P}al_{\text{BW}} = \{\circ, \bullet\}$.

A visual cryptography scheme (VCS) is described by two collections $\mathcal{C}_\circ$ and $\mathcal{C}_\bullet$ of $n \times m$ matrices with elements in $\mathcal{P}al_{\text{COL}}$. A matrix M in one of such collections is called a distribution matrix and is just a representation of the pixels in the shares: each row corresponds to a share (row i is the share of participant i) and the m elements of the row provide the colors of the m pixels into which the secret pixel has to be expanded. Often the m pixels in a row are called "subpixels" because they represent the secret pixel in a share. The superposition operation is given by the **add** of the rows corresponding to the shares. For example, here is a matrix M and the resulting **add**(M):

$$M = \begin{bmatrix} \circ\,\circ\,\mathbf{Y}\,\mathbf{M}\,\bullet\,\mathbf{R}\,\mathbf{R} \\ \circ\,\mathbf{G}\,\mathbf{C}\,\circ\,\mathbf{R}\,\mathbf{R}\,\mathbf{G} \\ \circ\,\mathbf{B}\,\mathbf{B}\,\mathbf{G}\,\mathbf{R}\,\mathbf{R}\,\mathbf{B} \end{bmatrix}$$

$$\text{add}(M) = \quad \circ\,\bullet\,\mathbf{B}\,\bullet\,\bullet\,\mathbf{R}\,\bullet$$

Given a vector v of elements in $\mathcal{P}al_{\text{COL}}$ (or in $\mathcal{P}al_{\text{BW}}$) we denote with $w_x(v)$, the number of elements of v equal to x and with $w_{\bar{x}}(v)$ the number of elements of v different from x. For example, $w_\bullet(v)$ is the number of elements of v equal to $\bullet$, $w_{\bar{\bullet}}(v)$ is the number of elements of v different from $\bullet$ and $w_\circ(v)$ is the number of elements of v equal to $\circ$.

Next we provide a formal definition of a VCS. Notice that this definition works both for the regular BW-VC model in which the shares are restricted to be b&w and in the CBW-VC model in which the shares can have colored pixels. For the BW-VC model the shares palette is $\mathcal{P}al_{\text{BW}}$, while for the CBW-VC model the shares palette is $\mathcal{P}al_{\text{COL}}$.

Definition 1. *A (k, n)-threshold VCS is defined by two collections $\mathcal{C}_\circ$ and $\mathcal{C}_\bullet$ of $n \times m$ distribution matrices that must satisfy the following conditions. There must exist two integers ℓ and h, with $0 \leq \ell < h \leq m$, such that:*

1. *(Contrast property) Any qualified set X, $|X| \geq k$, can recover the secret image by stacking the transparencies assigned to the participants in X. Formally, for any $M \in \mathcal{C}_\circ$, we have that $w_\bullet(\text{add}(M|X)) \leq \ell$ and for any $M \in \mathcal{C}_\bullet$, we have that $w_\bullet(\text{add}(M|X)) \geq h$.*
2. *(Security property) Any forbidden set X, $|X| < k$, has no information on the secret image. Formally, the two collections of $|X| \times m$ matrices, $\mathcal{D}_\circ = \{M|X,$ for each $M \in \mathcal{C}_\circ\}$, and $\mathcal{D}_\bullet = \{M|X,$ for each $M \in \mathcal{C}_\bullet\}$, are indistinguishable in the sense that they contain the same matrices with the same frequencies.*

Let M be a distribution matrix. Given a subset X of participants we denote by M_X the submatrix of M consisting of all the rows of M that represent shares of participants in X. A scheme is used in the following way: if the secret pixel is of color $\circ$ (resp. $\bullet$), then the dealer randomly chooses one of the matrices in $\mathcal{C}_\circ$ (resp. $\mathcal{C}_\bullet$) and uses it as the distribution matrix. Often, but not always, the distribution collections contain all the matrices that can be obtained by permuting the columns of a given *base matrix*. In such cases the scheme can be described by two base matrices $B_\circ$ and $B_\bullet$: $\mathcal{C}_\circ$ (resp. $\mathcal{C}_\bullet$) is obtained be permuting in all possible ways the columns of $B_\circ$ (resp. $B_\bullet$).

The first property in Definition 1 is the contrast property and the second one is the security property. The security property guarantees that forbidden sets of participants have no information about which collection has been used to encode the pixel because with the information provided by the shares, any of the collections is equally likely to have been used to encode the pixel.

The contrast property requires that in the reconstruction of a white pixel the number of black subpixels ($w_\bullet$) is sufficiently small (at most ℓ), whereas in the reconstruction of a black pixel the number of black subpixels is sufficiently large (at least h). Notice that this property is the same as the one that we have for regular b&w schemes. In the case of regular b&w scheme, however, we have that the shares can only have b&w subpixels and thus $w_\circ + w_\bullet = m$; in the case of colored b&w schemes we can have $w_\circ + w_\bullet < m$ because some pixels of the reconstruction can be colored. Clearly it is always the case that $w_\bullet + w_{\bar\bullet} = m$.

As we have already said, the main focus of this paper is the pixel expansion m. We would like m to be as small as possible. We refer the reader to [9] for a discussion about the contrast. Using $\alpha = (h - \ell)/m$ as the definition of the contrast, we have that all the schemes presented in this paper have contrast $\alpha = 1/m$.

3   Previous Work

Visual cryptography has been introduced by Naor and Shamir [12]. Quite a number of papers have followed [12]. Many papers have studied the construction of schemes with optimal pixel expansion and both constructions and lower bounds are known. Other papers have studied the contrast of the schemes, the sharing of multiple secret images, the prevention of cheating. Some papers have studied the generalization to color images. We will recall only the results that are necessary for this paper. The interested reader can look at [8] for surveys about visual cryptography and pointers to the literature.

A particular class of schemes consists of those schemes for which the reconstruction of the black pixels is perfect, that is, schemes for which $h = m$. Schemes with perfect reconstruction of black pixels are important because, among schemes with equal contrast, they provide a reconstruction of the secret that is more clearly visible. We will refer to such schemes as PB-BW-VCS for the BW-VC model and as PB-CBW-VCS for the CBW-VC model.

3.1   Lower Bounds on the Pixel Expansion

Ateniese et al. [1] have proved the following lower bound:

Theorem 1. *[1] In any (k, n)-threshold* BW-VCS *with pixel expansion m, we have that*

$$\binom{n}{k-1} \leq \binom{m}{\lfloor m/2 \rfloor} \tag{1}$$

and $m = \Omega(k \log n)$.

For the case of $k = 2$ the above theorem can be restated as follows.

Theorem 2. *In any $(2, n)$-threshold* BW-VCS *with pixel expansion m, we have that*

$$n \leq \binom{m}{\lfloor m/2 \rfloor} \tag{2}$$

and $m = \Omega(\log n)$.

Eisen and Stinson [9] have studied schemes with specified "whiteness" and "blackness" levels of reconstructed pixels. The whiteness and blackness levels are given by the thresholds ℓ and h. The following theorem (Theorem 9.1 of [9][2]) holds.

Theorem 3. *[9] In any $(2, n)$-threshold* BW-VCS *with pixel expansion m and thresholds ℓ and h, if $m - \ell \geq (n - 1)(m - h)$ then*

$$m = n(m - \ell) - \frac{n(n - 1)}{2}(m - h).$$

When $h = m$, the condition $m - \ell \geq (n - 1)(m - h)$ is always satisfied and thus for schemes with perfect reconstruction of black pixels we have that $m = n(m - \ell)$. If we are not interested in the threshold ℓ or if we want a bound that does not depend on ℓ we can minimize the left side of this equality over all possible values of ℓ. Since for schemes with perfect reconstruction of black pixels we have that $h = m$ and thus that $0 \leq \ell \leq m - 1$ we have the following theorem.

Theorem 4. *In any $(2, n)$-threshold* PB-BW-VCS *with pixel expansion m we have that $m \geq n$.*

3.2   Schemes without Perfect Reconstruction of Black Pixels

Proof of existence of schemes with optimal pixel expansion are cited in [1]. The proofs are based on perfect hash families. However there is no explicit construction of optimal schemes.

Bose and Mukerjee [5] have provided specific constructions, for $n \leq 70$, of $(2, n)$-threshold schemes with optimal pixel expansion, that is with m that matches Equation (2) of Theorem 2. We will refer to such schemes as $\mathcal{S}_{2,n}^{\mathrm{BM}}$.

Section 6.1 of [1] provides a construction of $(2, n)$-threshold schemes with pixel expansion $m = 2\lceil \log_2 n \rceil$. Such a pixel expansion matches the asymptotic lower bound of Theorem 2. We will refer to such schemes as $\mathcal{S}_{2,n}^{\mathrm{A}}$.

---

[2] We remark that Theorem 9.1 of paper [9] literally says: If $\hat{h} \geq (n - 1)\hat{\ell}$ then $m = n\hat{h} - \frac{n(n-1)}{2}\hat{\ell}$. We have used $\hat{\ell}$ and $\hat{h}$ because paper [9] uses a different definition for the thresholds h and ℓ. With the definition used in this paper, they correspond to $\hat{\ell} = m - h$ and $\hat{h} = m - \ell$. Using this transformation we get the theorem reported in the text.

3.3   Schemes with Perfect Reconstruction of Black Pixels

The $(2, n)$-threshold scheme in the original paper by Naor and Shamir [12] has
pixel expansion $m = n$ and has perfect reconstruction of black pixels. Hence it is
optimal. The scheme is the following: the base matrix $B_\circ$ consists of one column
of white pixels and $n - 1$ columns with black pixels, while the base matrix $B_\bullet$ is
the identity $n \times n$ matrix with the substitutions $0 \leftrightarrow \circ$ and $1 \leftrightarrow \bullet$. We will refer
to such schemes as $\mathcal{S}_{2,n}^{\mathrm{NS}}$.

Also the (n, n)-threshold scheme of [12] is with perfect reconstruction of black
pixels. The scheme has pixel expansion $m = 2^{n-1}$ and is the following: the base
matrix $B_\circ$ consists of all the columns with an even number of $\bullet$ pixels while the
base matrix $B_\bullet$ consists of all the columns with an odd number of $\bullet$ pixels. We
will refer to such schemes as $\mathcal{S}_{n,n}^{\mathrm{NS}}$.

Blundo et al. [2] have generalized the above two constructions to (k, n)-
threshold schemes for any k, $2 \leq k \leq n$. The construction specifies the mul-
tiplicity $\mu_{b,j}$ of the columns with j black pixels in each base matrix B_x, where
$x \in \{\circ, \bullet\}$. We will refer to such schemes as $\mathcal{S}_{k,n}^{\mathrm{B}}$. The pixel expansion of the
$(3, n)$-threshold is $m = (n - 1)^2$ and for the $(n - 1, n)$ is $m = (n - 2)2^{n-2} + 1$.
In general we have the following bounds on the pixel expansion of the schemes
$\mathcal{S}_{k,n}^{\mathrm{B}}$.

Lemma 1.   *[2] The pixel expansion m of the schemes $\mathcal{S}_{k,n}^{\mathrm{B}}$ satisfies*

$$\binom{n-1}{k-1} 2^{k-2} + 1 \leq m \leq \left(\binom{n-1}{k-1} - 1 \right) 2^{k-1} + 1.$$

All of the above PB-BW-VCS have $\ell = m - 1$, and, obviously, $m = h$.

Table 1 provides a summary of the relevant known results. The companion table to the right summarizes the pixel expansion improvements obtained in this
paper.

Table 1. Summary of known relevant results (and to the right a summary of the results
of this paper)

Known results	Lower bound	Construction		This paper
		BW-VCS		CBW-VCS
$k = 2$	$m = \Omega(\log_2 n)$ [1]	$m = 2\lceil \log_2 n \rceil$ [1]		$m = \lceil \log_3 n \rceil$
		PB-BW-VCS		PB-CBW-VCS
$k = 2$	$m \geq n$ [9]	$m = n$ [12]		$m = \lceil m'/3 \rceil$
$k = 3$	-	$m = (n-1)^2$ [2]		where m' is the
$4 \leq k \leq n - 2$	-	Lemma 1		pixel expansion of
$k = n - 1$	-	$m = (n-2)2^{n-2} + 1$ [2]		any (k, n)-threshold
$k = n$	-	$m = 2^{n-1}$ [12]		PB-BW-VCS.

4   CBW-VC $(2, n)$-Threshold Schemes

In this section we will provide a construction of CBW-VC $(2, n)$-threshold schemes. The construction gives schemes with pixel expansion $m = \lceil \log_3 n \rceil$. We start by first describing two simple cases, for $n = 2, 3$, and then we provide the generalization to any n.

Let us start with the case $n = 2$. There are several ways to implement a $(2, 2)$-threshold CBW-VCS. We report only a scheme that uses the 3 colors R,G and B. It is possible to obtain similar schemes using the following sets of colors: $\{R, G, B, C, M, Y\}$, $\{R, G\}$, $\{R, B\}$, $\{G, B\}$, $\{Y, B\}$, $\{M, G\}$, and $\{C, R\}$.

Construction 5 (Scheme $(2, 2)$-RGB). *The following collections of distribution matrices describe a $(2, 2)$-threshold CBW-VCS with a shares palette equal to $\{R, G, B, \bullet\}$.*

$$\mathcal{C}_\circ = \left\{ \begin{bmatrix} R \\ R \end{bmatrix}, \begin{bmatrix} G \\ G \end{bmatrix}, \begin{bmatrix} B \\ B \end{bmatrix} \right\} \qquad \mathcal{C}_\bullet = \left\{ \begin{bmatrix} R \\ G \end{bmatrix}, \begin{bmatrix} G \\ R \end{bmatrix}, \begin{bmatrix} R \\ B \end{bmatrix}, \begin{bmatrix} B \\ R \end{bmatrix}, \begin{bmatrix} G \\ B \end{bmatrix}, \begin{bmatrix} B \\ G \end{bmatrix} \right\}.$$

It is easy to see that both the security and the contrast property are satisfied, and that $m = 1$, $\ell = 0$ and $h = 1$. The contrast is $\alpha = 1$. Figure 2 shows an example of use of the $(2, 2)$-RGB scheme: a secret b&w image, the two shares and the reconstructed secret image. All the images have size 100×170 pixels (px).

Secret $(100 \times 170\text{px})$ Share 1 $(100 \times 170\text{px})$ Share 2 $(100 \times 170\text{px})$ Shares 1+2 $(100 \times 170\text{px})$

Fig. 2. Sharing and reconstruction for the $(2, 2)$-RGB scheme. The mixture of pixels is made up of red, green and blue pixels. You will not see the colors if the paper has been printed in b&w.

We remark that with a regular BW-VC schemes we cannot obtain schemes without pixel expansion. The $(2, 2)$-threshold CBW-VC scheme is without pixel expansion; this means that the reconstructed image is the same size as the original one. Figure 3 shows the reconstructed image obtained with the $(2, 2)$-threshold BW-VCS $\mathcal{S}_{2,n}^{\text{NS}}$: the first two with pixel expansion $m = 2$ and a distortion of the image, and the third one with pixel expansion $m = 4$ (obtained by using the concatenation of two $\mathcal{S}_{2,n}^{\text{NS}}$) that avoids the distortion but makes the image 4 times bigger. In a regular BW-VCS the reconstructed image is a black image over a mixture of b&w pixels. In the CBW-VCS the reconstructed image is a black image over a mixture of colored pixels (R,G and B in the example).

Next we provide a $(2, 3)$-threshold scheme.

Construction 6 (Scheme $(2, 3)$-RGB). *The following collections of distribution matrices describe a $(2, 3)$-threshold CBW-VCS with a shares palette equal to $\{R, G, B\}$.*

$$m = 2 \text{ (200x170px)}$$

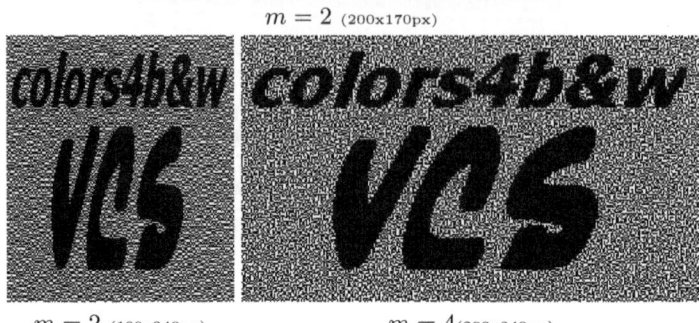

$$m = 2 \text{ (100x340px)} \qquad\qquad m = 4 \text{(200x340px)}$$

Fig. 3. Reconstructed images for regular $(2,2)$-threshold BW-VCS

$$C_\circ = \left\{ \begin{bmatrix} R \\ R \\ R \end{bmatrix}, \begin{bmatrix} G \\ G \\ G \end{bmatrix}, \begin{bmatrix} B \\ B \\ B \end{bmatrix} \right\} \qquad C_\bullet = \left\{ \begin{bmatrix} R \\ G \\ B \end{bmatrix}, \begin{bmatrix} G \\ R \\ B \end{bmatrix}, \begin{bmatrix} B \\ G \\ R \end{bmatrix} \right\}.$$

As before, it is easy to see that both the security and the contrast property are satisfied, and that $m = 1$, $\ell = 0$ and $h = 1$. The contrast is $\alpha = 1$. As for the $(2,2)$-threshold schemes also in this case we have that the reconstructed image is a black image over a mixture of colors. In this case the mixture of colors is made up of the three colors R,G and B. Figure 4 shows the shares and the reconstructed images.

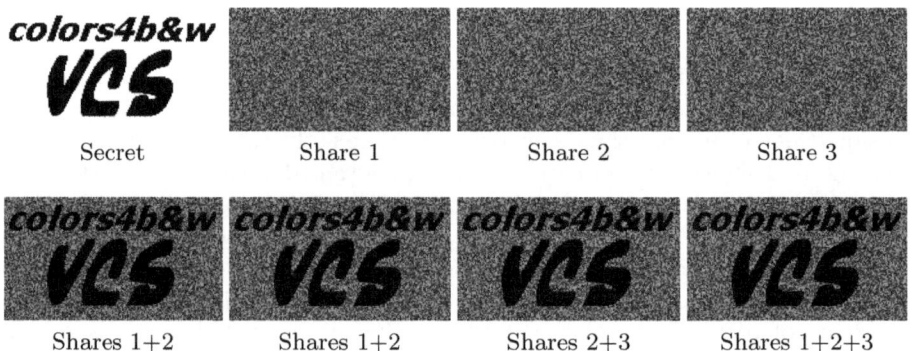

| Secret | Share 1 | Share 2 | Share 3 |

| Shares 1+2 | Shares 1+2 | Shares 2+3 | Shares 1+2+3 |

Fig. 4. Shares and reconstructed images for the $(2,3)$-threshold CBW-VCS. The mixture of pixels is made up of red, green and blue pixels. All images are 100x170 pixels. You will not see the colors if the paper has been printed in b&w.

Finally, we present a generalization of the technique used for the particular cases $n = 2, 3$. For $n \geq 4$ we have to start expanding the secret pixels into $m \geq 2$ subpixels and the contrast of the reconstructed image degrades as n increases.

Construction 7. *Let* $m = \lceil \log_3 n \rceil$. *Consider the set* $\mathcal{S}$ *of all the strings of length* m *over the alphabet* $\Sigma = \{\mathsf{R}, \mathsf{G}, \mathsf{B}\}$. *These are* $3^m \geq n$. *Choose any* n *such strings and denote them* $s_1, s_2, \ldots, s_n$. *The collections of distribution matrices of the scheme are:*

$$
\mathcal{C}_\circ = \left\{ \begin{bmatrix} s_1 \\ s_1 \\ s_1 \\ \cdots \\ \cdots \\ s_1 \\ s_1 \\ s_1 \end{bmatrix}, \begin{bmatrix} s_2 \\ s_2 \\ s_2 \\ \cdots \\ \cdots \\ s_2 \\ s_2 \\ s_2 \end{bmatrix}, \begin{bmatrix} s_3 \\ s_3 \\ s_3 \\ \cdots \\ \cdots \\ s_3 \\ s_3 \\ s_3 \end{bmatrix}, \ldots\ldots\ldots, \begin{bmatrix} s_{n-1} \\ s_{n-1} \\ s_{n-1} \\ \cdots \\ \cdots \\ s_{n-1} \\ s_{n-1} \\ s_{n-1} \end{bmatrix}, \begin{bmatrix} s_n \\ s_n \\ s_n \\ \cdots \\ \cdots \\ s_n \\ s_n \\ s_n \end{bmatrix} \right\}
$$

$$
\mathcal{C}_\bullet = \left\{ \begin{bmatrix} s_1 \\ s_2 \\ s_3 \\ \cdots \\ \cdots \\ s_{n-2} \\ s_{n-1} \\ s_n \end{bmatrix}, \begin{bmatrix} s_n \\ s_1 \\ s_2 \\ \cdots \\ \cdots \\ s_{n-3} \\ s_{n-2} \\ s_{n-1} \end{bmatrix}, \begin{bmatrix} s_{n-1} \\ s_n \\ s_1 \\ \cdots \\ \cdots \\ s_{n-4} \\ s_{n-3} \\ s_{n-2} \end{bmatrix}, \ldots\ldots\ldots, \begin{bmatrix} s_3 \\ s_4 \\ s_5 \\ \cdots \\ \cdots \\ s_n \\ s_1 \\ s_2 \end{bmatrix}, \begin{bmatrix} s_2 \\ s_3 \\ s_4 \\ \cdots \\ \cdots \\ s_{n-1} \\ s_n \\ s_1 \end{bmatrix} \right\}.
$$

Some examples will clarify the construction. Let $n = 4$. We have that $m = 2$ and the set $\mathcal{S}$ consists of 9 strings: $\mathcal{S} = \{\mathsf{RR}, \mathsf{RG}, \mathsf{RB}, \mathsf{GG}, \mathsf{GR}, \mathsf{GB}, \mathsf{BB}, \mathsf{BR}, \mathsf{BG}\}$. We choose the following 4 strings of $\mathcal{S}$: $\{\mathsf{RR}, \mathsf{BB}, \mathsf{GG}, \mathsf{RG}\}$. The collections of distribution matrices are:

$$
\mathcal{C}_\circ = \left\{ \begin{bmatrix} \mathsf{RR} \\ \mathsf{RR} \\ \mathsf{RR} \\ \mathsf{RR} \end{bmatrix}, \begin{bmatrix} \mathsf{BB} \\ \mathsf{BB} \\ \mathsf{BB} \\ \mathsf{BB} \end{bmatrix}, \begin{bmatrix} \mathsf{GG} \\ \mathsf{GG} \\ \mathsf{GG} \\ \mathsf{GG} \end{bmatrix}, \begin{bmatrix} \mathsf{RG} \\ \mathsf{RG} \\ \mathsf{RG} \\ \mathsf{RG} \end{bmatrix} \right\} \quad \mathcal{C}_\bullet = \left\{ \begin{bmatrix} \mathsf{RR} \\ \mathsf{GG} \\ \mathsf{BB} \\ \mathsf{RG} \end{bmatrix}, \begin{bmatrix} \mathsf{RG} \\ \mathsf{RR} \\ \mathsf{GG} \\ \mathsf{BB} \end{bmatrix}, \begin{bmatrix} \mathsf{BB} \\ \mathsf{RG} \\ \mathsf{RR} \\ \mathsf{GG} \end{bmatrix}, \begin{bmatrix} \mathsf{GG} \\ \mathsf{BB} \\ \mathsf{RG} \\ \mathsf{RR} \end{bmatrix} \right\}
$$

Here is another example. Let $n = 10$, then we have that $m = 3$ and $\mathcal{S} = \{\mathsf{RRR}, \mathsf{GGG}, \mathsf{BBB}, \mathsf{RGB}, \mathsf{RBG}, \mathsf{BGR}, \mathsf{BRG}, \mathsf{GRB}, \mathsf{GBR}, \mathsf{RRG}, \mathsf{RGR}, \mathsf{GRR}, \mathsf{RRB}, \mathsf{RBR}, \mathsf{BRR}, \mathsf{GGR}, \mathsf{GRG}, \mathsf{RGG}, \mathsf{GGB}, \mathsf{GBG}, \mathsf{BGG}, \mathsf{BBR}, \mathsf{BRB}, \mathsf{RBB}, \mathsf{BBG}, \mathsf{BGB}, \mathsf{GBB}\}$. We choose the following 10 elements of $\mathcal{S}$: $\{\mathsf{RGB}, \mathsf{RBG}, \mathsf{BGR}, \mathsf{BRG}, \mathsf{GRB}, \mathsf{GBR}, \mathsf{RRG}, \mathsf{RGR}, \mathsf{GRR}, \mathsf{RRB}\}$. The collections of distribution matrices are:

$$
\mathcal{C}_{\circ} = \left\{
\begin{bmatrix} RGB \\ RGB \\ RGB \\ RGB \\ RGB \\ RGB \\ RGB \\ RGB \\ RGB \\ RGB \end{bmatrix},
\begin{bmatrix} RBG \\ RBG \\ RBG \\ RBG \\ RBG \\ RBG \\ RBG \\ RBG \\ RBG \\ RBG \end{bmatrix},
\begin{bmatrix} BGR \\ BGR \\ BGR \\ BGR \\ BGR \\ BGR \\ BGR \\ BGR \\ BGR \\ BGR \end{bmatrix},
\begin{bmatrix} BRG \\ BRG \\ BRG \\ BRG \\ BRG \\ BRG \\ BRG \\ BRG \\ BRG \\ BRG \end{bmatrix},
\begin{bmatrix} GRB \\ GRB \\ GRB \\ GRB \\ GRB \\ GRB \\ GRB \\ GRB \\ GRB \\ GRB \end{bmatrix},
\begin{bmatrix} RRG \\ RRG \\ RRG \\ RRG \\ RRG \\ RRG \\ RRG \\ RRG \\ RRG \\ RRG \end{bmatrix},
\begin{bmatrix} RGR \\ RGR \\ RGR \\ RGR \\ RGR \\ RGR \\ RGR \\ RGR \\ RGR \\ RGR \end{bmatrix},
\begin{bmatrix} GRR \\ GRR \\ GRR \\ GRR \\ GRR \\ GRR \\ GRR \\ GRR \\ GRR \\ GRR \end{bmatrix},
\begin{bmatrix} GRB \\ GRB \\ GRB \\ GRB \\ GRB \\ GRB \\ GRB \\ GRB \\ GRB \\ GRB \end{bmatrix},
\begin{bmatrix} RRB \\ RRB \\ RRB \\ RRB \\ RRB \\ RRB \\ RRB \\ RRB \\ RRB \\ RRB \end{bmatrix}
\right\}
$$

$$
\mathcal{C}_{\bullet} = \left\{
\begin{bmatrix} RGB \\ RBG \\ BGR \\ BRG \\ GRB \\ GBR \\ RRG \\ RGR \\ GRR \\ RRB \end{bmatrix},
\begin{bmatrix} RRB \\ RGB \\ RBG \\ BGR \\ BRG \\ GRB \\ GBR \\ RRG \\ RGR \\ GRR \end{bmatrix},
\begin{bmatrix} GRR \\ RRB \\ RGB \\ RBG \\ BGR \\ BRG \\ GRB \\ GBR \\ RRG \\ RGR \end{bmatrix},
\begin{bmatrix} RGR \\ GRR \\ RRB \\ RGB \\ RBG \\ BGR \\ BRG \\ GRB \\ GBR \\ RRG \end{bmatrix},
\begin{bmatrix} RRG \\ RGR \\ GRR \\ RRB \\ RGB \\ RBG \\ BGR \\ BRG \\ GRB \\ GBR \end{bmatrix},
\begin{bmatrix} GBR \\ RRG \\ RGR \\ GRR \\ RRB \\ RGB \\ RBG \\ BGR \\ BRG \\ GRB \end{bmatrix},
\begin{bmatrix} GRB \\ GBR \\ RRG \\ RGR \\ GRR \\ RRB \\ RGB \\ RBG \\ BGR \\ BRG \end{bmatrix},
\begin{bmatrix} BRG \\ GRB \\ GBR \\ RRG \\ RGR \\ GRR \\ RRB \\ RGB \\ RBG \\ BGR \end{bmatrix},
\begin{bmatrix} BGR \\ BRG \\ GRB \\ GBR \\ RRG \\ RGR \\ GRR \\ RRB \\ RGB \\ RBG \end{bmatrix},
\begin{bmatrix} RBG \\ BGR \\ BRG \\ GRB \\ GBR \\ RRG \\ RGR \\ GRR \\ RRB \\ RGB \end{bmatrix}
\right\}
$$

Theorem 8. *Construction 7 gives a $(2, n)$-threshold scheme with pixel expansion $m = \lceil \log_3 n \rceil$, $\ell = 0$ and $h = 1$.*

Proof. Let $s_1, s_2, \ldots, s_n$ be the strings used for the construction of the scheme. Security property: For any participant i, the set $\mathcal{D}_{\circ} = \{M|i, \text{ for each } M \in \mathcal{C}_{\circ}\}$, and $\mathcal{D}_{\bullet} = \{M|i, \text{ for each } M \in \mathcal{C}_{\bullet}\}$, are both equal to the set $\{s_1, s_2, \ldots, s_n\}$. Contrast property: Take any two participants i and j. If the secret pixel is white then we have that the shares of i and j are both equal to one of the base strings, say s_k, with $k \in 1, 2, .., n$. Hence we have that $w_{\bullet}(\text{add}(s_k, s_k)) = 0$, that is $\ell = 0$.

If the secret pixel is black then we have that the two shares of i and j are equal to two different base string s_{k_1} and s_{k_2}. Since the two strings are different we have that $w_{\bullet}(\text{add}(s_{k_1}, s_{k_2})) \geq 1$, because there will be at least one position in which they differ. Recall that the superposition of two different colors in the set Σ gives black. Hence $h = 1$.

Finally the pixel expansion is $m = \lceil \log_3 n \rceil$ because each matrix in the collections has $\lceil \log_3 n \rceil$ columns.

Comparison of BW-VCS *and* CBW-VCS. The CBW-VC model is more powerful than the BW-VC model. This allows to get schemes with smaller pixel expansion, with the drawback, if it can be considered so, of the presence of colored pixels in the reconstruction. In the BW-VC model the $(2, n)$-threshold schemes have pixel expansion that is lower bounded by (2) of Theorem 2. For $n \leq 70$, the $\mathcal{S}_{2,n}^{\text{BM}}$ provided in [5] have optimal pixel expansion in the BW-VC model. In general, Theorem 2 states that the pixel expansion of BW-VC schemes is lower bounded by $m = \Omega(\log n)$. Using the CBW-VC model we can construct schemes that have pixel expansion $\lceil \log_3 n \rceil$. Although there is no improvement from an asymptotic point of view, $\lceil \log_3 n \rceil$ is much smaller than the lower bound (2) of Theorem 2. Table 2 shows the explicit value of the lower bound of Theorem 2 and the pixel expansion of CBW-VC schemes, for small values of n.

Table 2. Pixel expansion comparison

n	2	3	4	5	6	7	8	9	10	11	12	13	14	15	16	17	18	19
Eq. (2), Th. 2, $m \geq$	2	3	4	4	4	5	5	5	5	6	6	6	6	6	6	6	6	6
Const. 7, $m =$	1	1	2	2	2	2	2	2	3	3	3	3	3	3	3	3	3	3

n	20	21	22	23	24	25	26	27	28	29	30	31	32	33	34	35
Eq. (2), Th. 2, $m \geq$	6	7	7	7	7	7	7	7	7	7	7	7	7	7	7	7
Const. 7, $m =$	3	3	3	3	3	3	3	3	4	4	4	4	4	4	4	4

5   Impossibility Result

In this section we prove that the extra power of the CBW-VC model allows to construct schemes without pixel expansion only for the cases of $(2, 2)$-threshold and $(2, 3)$-threshold schemes. Indeed we show in this section that it is not possible to construct $(2, n)$-threshold schemes, for $n \geq 4$, nor (k, n)-threshold schemes, for $k \geq 3$, without pixel expansion.

The CBW-VC model used in this paper exploits only the 8 full intensity colors. The impossibility proofs that we provide work even if we relax this restriction and allow the model to use any color. So, only for this section, we assume that the colors are triples of values (x, y, z), where x, y, z are real numbers such that $0 \leq x, y, z \leq 1$. In the following we will use $\star$ to denote a number in the interval $[0, 1]$ and $+$ to denote a positive number in the interval $]0, 1]$.

Theorem 9. *In the* CBW-VC *model it is not possible to construct a* $(2, n)$-*threshold scheme, for* $n \geq 4$, *with pixel expansion* $m = 1$.

Proof. By contradiction assume that such a scheme exists and let $\mathcal{C}_\circ, \mathcal{C}_\bullet$ be the collections of distribution matrices. Let B be a distribution matrix for a black secret pixel, that is $B \in \mathcal{C}_\bullet$. Since $m = 1$ matrix B has one column and it must be that $\ell = 0$ and $h = 1$. This means that $\text{add}(B|X) = \bullet = (0, 0, 0)$ for any qualified set X. It also means that $\text{add}(W|X) = \circ = (1, 1, 1)$ for any $W \in \mathcal{C}_\circ$.

Claim 1: B cannot have two pixels that are equal, with the exception of black pixels. Indeed if there are two pixels that are equal and are different from the black pixel the qualified set of 2 participants corresponding to those two pixels would reconstruct a black pixel as a colored pixel violating the contrast property.

Claim 2: Any pixel in B cannot be •, that is, cannot have the form $(0,0,0)$. Indeed such a triple, for the security property has to appear also in any distribution matrix W for the white color. But this violates the contrast property because all the qualified sets that contain a participant that gets • as a share for the white pixel from W would not be able to reconstruct white pixels.

Claim 3: Any pixel in B cannot have the form $(+,+,+)$, and thus, in particular, cannot be ○. Indeed if $(+,+,+)$ appears in a row of B then all other $n-1 \geq 3$ rows of B should be $(0,0,0)$ because any qualified set must reconstruct black pixels as black. But by Claim 2, we know that this is not possible.

Claim 4: Any pixel in B cannot have one component equal to 0 and two components equal to $+$. Indeed if $(0,+,+)$ appears in a row of B then all other $n-1 \geq 3$ rows of B should be $(+,0,0)$ because any qualified set must reconstruct black pixels as black. We know, by Claim 1, that this is not possible. We get the same contradiction for the other two cases $(+,0,+)$ and $(+,+,0)$.

By Claims 1-4, we have that all the pixels of B must be different and each must have one of the forms $(0,0,+)$, $(0,+,0)$, $(+,0,0)$. However since B has at least $n \geq 4$ rows, this is impossible. This implies that B cannot exists, and thus the collection $C_\bullet$ must be empty. This means that the scheme does not exists.

Theorem 10. *In the* CBW-VC *model it is not possible to construct a (k,n)-threshold scheme, for $k \geq 3$, with pixel expansion $m = 1$.*

Proof. By contradiction assume that such a scheme exists and let $C_\circ, C_\bullet$ be the collections of distribution matrices. Let B be a distribution matrix for a black secret pixel, that is $B \in C_\bullet$. Since $m = 1$ matrix M has one column:

$$ B = \begin{bmatrix} (\star,\star,\star) \\ (\star,\star,\star) \\ \cdots \\ (\star,\star,\star) \\ (\star,\star,\star) \end{bmatrix}, $$

where $\star$ is a placeholder for the color component. Since $m = 1$ we must have $\ell = 0$ and $h = 1$. This means that it must be $\mathsf{add}(B|X) = \bullet = (0,0,0)$ for any qualified set X. It also means that $\mathsf{add}(W|X) = \circ = (1,1,1)$ for any $W \in C_\circ$.

Claim 1: Any pixel in B cannot be •. Indeed for the security property such a pixel should appear also in any distribution matrix $W \in C_\circ$. Then we would have $\mathsf{add}(W|X) = \bullet = (0,0,0)$ for any qualified set X that contains the black pixel and this violates the contrast property.

Claim 2: Any pixel in B cannot have 2 components equal to 0, that is cannot have the form $(0,0,+)$, $(0,+,0)$ or $(+,0,0)$. For the sake of contradiction, assume that B has such a pixel. Assume that the pixel is $(0,0,+)$; the following reasoning is valid, with the obvious modifications, also for the other cases, so the assumption is without loss of generality. In order to have $\mathsf{add}(B|X) = (0,0,0)$ for any qualified set X that contains the participant with $(0,0,+)$, it must have one of the other pixels equal to $(\star, \star, 0)$. That is matrix B must have the following pair of pixels:

$$B = \begin{bmatrix} \cdots \\ (0,0,+) \\ \cdots \\ (\star,\star,0) \\ \cdots \end{bmatrix}.$$

Since $k \geq 3$, for the security property the same pair of pixels must appear in a distribution matrix $W \in \mathcal{C}_\circ$ for the white color. But this implies that $\mathbf{add}(W|X) = (0,0,0)$ for any qualified set that contains those two rows. This violates the contrast property. Hence the claim is true.

Claim 1 and 2 imply that the pixels in matrix B must have either the form $(+,+,+)$ or one of the forms $(0,+,+),(+,0,+),(+,+,0)$. We now distinguish two cases: $k = 3$ and $k \geq 4$.

Case $k = 3$: Matrix B cannot have pixels of the form $(+,+,+)$. Indeed if this was the case it would be impossible to have $\mathbf{add}(B) = \bullet$. Indeed since $k = 3$ and pixels can only be $(+,+,+)$ or have at most one component equal to 0, superposing 3 pixels will always yield at least one component greater than 0. This means that pixels must have one component equal to 0 and the other two components equal to $+$. Since $k = 3$ the only possible form for matrix B is

$$B = \begin{bmatrix} (0,+,+) \\ (+,0,+) \\ (+,+,0) \end{bmatrix}.$$

Consider now any two rows of B, for example the first and the second. By the security property we have that the same two rows must appear in a matrix $W \in \mathcal{C}_\circ$. That is, there is $W \in \mathcal{C}_\circ$ such that

$$W = \begin{bmatrix} (0,+,+) \\ (+,0,+) \\ (\star,\star,\star) \end{bmatrix}.$$

The third row of W cannot be $(+,+,0)$ otherwise we would have $\mathbf{add}(W) = \bullet$ and this violates the contrast property. Hence it must be either

$$W = \begin{bmatrix} (0,+,+) \\ (+,0,+) \\ (0,+,+) \end{bmatrix} \quad \text{or} \quad W = \begin{bmatrix} (0,+,+) \\ (+,0,+) \\ (+,0,+) \end{bmatrix}.$$

In both cases we have two pixels that are equal. For the security property such a pair of pixels should appear also in B. But this contradicts the fact that B must have 3 different pixels. Hence we have that matrix B cannot exist. This concludes the proof for the case $k = 3$.

Case $k \geq 4$: Assume that matrix B has one pixel of the form $(+,+,+)$. Let X be a qualified set, it must be the case that the matrix $B|X$ contains the following pixels:

$$
B = \begin{bmatrix} \text{....} \\ (+,+,+) \\ \text{....} \\ (0,+,+) \\ \text{....} \\ (+,0,+) \\ \text{....} \\ (+,+,0) \\ \text{....} \end{bmatrix}.
$$

This is necessary in order to have $\mathbf{add}(B|X) = \bullet$. By the security property, since $k \geq 4$ the triple of pixels $(0,+,+),(+,+,0),(+,+,0)$ must appear also in any matrix $W \in \mathcal{C}_o$. That is for any matrix $W \in \mathcal{C}_o$ we have

$$
W = \begin{bmatrix} \text{....} \\ (0,+,+) \\ \text{....} \\ (+,0,+) \\ \text{....} \\ (+,+,0) \\ \text{....} \end{bmatrix}.
$$

However this implies that $\mathbf{add}(W|X) = \bullet$ for any qualified set S that contains those 3 pixels and this violates the contrast property. Hence we have that B cannot exist, and this concludes the proof for $k \geq 4$.

6   PB-CBW-VC (k, n)-Threshold Schemes

In this section we present a technique that allows to take any BW-VCS with perfect reconstruction of black pixels and transform it into a CBW-VCS with perfect reconstruction of black pixels. The technique works only for schemes with perfect reconstruction of black pixels and not for schemes that do not have this property. The idea is to group the b&w pixels in triplets and transform each triplet into a color. Since each triplet of b&w pixels is transformed into 1 colored pixel, the pixel expansion of the constructed scheme is $m = \lceil m'/3 \rceil$, where m' is the pixels expansion of the starting scheme. Let us start by describing the transformation from a b&w distribution matrix M' to a color distribution matrix M.

Transformation 11. *Let M' be an $n \times m'$ b&w distribution matrix. Let $\hat{M}'$ be the matrix obtained from M' by adding 0,1 or 2 columns with all black pixels to M' so that the number $\hat{m} = 3\lceil m'/3 \rceil$ of columns of $\hat{M}'$ is a multiple of 3. It is not important where these columns are added but to make things easier let us assume that these added columns are appended as last columns of $\hat{M}'$. To obtain the transformed distribution matrix M, group the $\hat{m} = 3z$ columns of M into z groups of 3 columns. For each row (triplet) in each group substitute the 3 b&w pixels with the colored pixel specified by the following tables:*

Triplet in matrix $\hat{M}'$			Color in matrix M
1	2	3	
○	○	○	○
●	○	○	Y
○	●	○	M
○	○	●	C

Triplet in matrix $\hat{M}'$			Color in matrix M
1	2	3	
●	●	○	B
●	○	●	G
○	●	●	R
●	●	●	●

Let us see an example of the above transformation. Below are shown a 5×7 b&w distribution matrix M', its 5×9 padded version $\hat{M}'$ with pixels grouped in 3 blocks of 3 pixels each, and the corresponding 5×3 color matrix M:

$$M' = \begin{bmatrix} ○ & ● & ○ & ● & ● & ○ & ● \\ ● & ● & ○ & ● & ○ & ● & ○ \\ ● & ● & ● & ● & ● & ● & ○ \\ ○ & ● & ● & ● & ○ & ○ & ● \\ ○ & ○ & ● & ○ & ● & ○ & ○ \end{bmatrix} \qquad \hat{M}' = \begin{bmatrix} ○ & ● & ○ & ● & ● & ○ & ● & ● & ● \\ ● & ● & ○ & ○ & ○ & ● & ○ & ● & ● \\ ○ & ○ & ● & ● & ● & ● & ○ & ● & ● \\ ○ & ● & ● & ○ & ○ & ○ & ● & ● & ● \\ ● & ○ & ○ & ○ & ● & ○ & ○ & ● & ● \end{bmatrix} \qquad M = \begin{bmatrix} M & B & ● \\ G & C & R \\ C & ● & R \\ R & ○ & ● \\ Y & M & R \end{bmatrix}$$

Since matrices $\hat{M}'$ and M are closely related the following holds. Let $z' = \text{add}(M')$ and let z be the vector obtained by transforming vector z' with Transformation 11. Then we have that $z = \text{add}(M)$. For the above example we would have that $z' = [●●●|●●●|●●●]$ and $z = [●●●]$ and $\text{add}(M) = [●●●]$. As another example let $X = \{2, 3, 5\}$ and consider the matrix $\hat{M}'|X$. Let $z' = \text{add}(\hat{M}'|X)$. We have that $z' = [●○●|●●●|○●●]$ and thus $z = [G●R]$. We also have $\text{add}(M) = [G●R]$. With an abuse of notation we can write that $\text{add}(M') = \text{add}(\hat{M}') = \text{add}(M)$.

We are now ready to present the construction of PB-CBW-VC (k, n)-threshold schemes.

Construction 12. *Let S' be a* BW-VCS *with perfect reconstruction of black pixel whose collections of distribution matrices are $\mathcal{C}'_o$ and $\mathcal{C}'_●$ and let m' be the pixel expansion of S'. The* CBW-VCS *scheme S is defined by the two collections $\mathcal{C}_o$ and $\mathcal{C}_●$ obtained from $\mathcal{C}'_o$ and $\mathcal{C}'_●$ by applying Transformation 11 to every matrix in the collections.*

Theorem 13. *Construction 12 provides a* PB-CBW-VC (k, n)-*threshold schemes with pixel expansion $m = \lceil m'/3 \rceil$, where m' is the pixel expansion of the starting* PB-BW-VC (k, n)-*threshold scheme.*

Proof. Let S' be the starting BW-VCS with collections $\mathcal{C}'_o$ and $\mathcal{C}'_●$ and let m' be the pixel expansion of S. Let S be the scheme obtained from S' using Construction 12.

Safety property. Let X be a non-qualified set of participants. Consider the sets of matrices $\{M|X \text{ with } M \in \mathcal{C}'_o\}$ and $\{M|X \text{ with } M \in \mathcal{C}'_●\}$. By the safety property for S' we have that A and B contain the same matrices each with the same frequency. Since each matrix $\mathcal{C}'_o$ is transformed into a matrix of $\mathcal{C}_●$ and each matrix of $\mathcal{C}'_●$ is transformed into a matrix of $\mathcal{C}_o$ we have that also the sets $\{M|X : M \in \mathcal{C}_o\}$ and $\{M|X : M \in \mathcal{C}_●\}$ have the same matrices with the same frequencies. Hence the safety property for S' is also satisfied.

Contrast property. Let X be a qualified set of participants. Consider any matrix $M \in \mathcal{C}_{\bullet}$ and let M' be the corresponding matrix in $\mathcal{C}'_{\bullet}$. By the construction we have that $\mathsf{add}(M|X) = \mathsf{add}(M'|X)$. Since S' is with perfect reconstruction of the black pixels we have that $\mathsf{add}(M'|X)$ is made up of m' black pixels. Hence $\mathsf{add}(M|X)$ is made up of $m = \lceil m'/3 \rceil$ black pixels. This implies that $h = m$.

Similarly, consider any matrix $M \in \mathcal{C}_{\circ}$ and let M' be the corresponding matrix in $\mathcal{C}'_{\circ}$. By the construction we have that $\mathsf{add}(M|X) = \mathsf{add}(M'|X)$. By the contrast property of S' we have that $\mathsf{add}(M'|X)$ contains at least one white pixels. Since $\mathsf{add}(M'|X) = \mathsf{add}(M|X)$, we have that $\mathsf{add}(M|X)$ must contain at least one pixel that is not black. This implies that we can set $\ell = m - 1$.

Comparison of PB-BW-VCS *and* PB-CBW-VCS. For the case of schemes with perfect reconstruction of black pixels we have that the CBW-VC model allows to decrease the pixel expansion of a factor of $1/3$ with respect to the BW-VC model. The improvement does not make any difference from an asymptotic point of view, but, especially for small values of k and n, it makes the schemes more practicable. Table 3 shows explicitly the pixel expansion of the best schemes for small values of k and n.

Table 3. Pixel expansion comparison for small values of k and n

	$(2, n)$			$(3, n)$			$(n-1, n)$			(n, n)	
n	m BW-VCS	m CBW-VCS	n	m BW-VCS	m CBW-VCS	n	m BW-VCS	m CBW-VCS	n	m BW-VCS	m CBW-VCS
2	2	1	2	-	-	2	-	-	2	2	1
3	3	1	3	4	2	3	3	1	3	4	2
4	4	2	4	9	3	4	9	3	4	8	3
5	5	2	5	16	6	5	25	9	5	16	6
6	6	2	6	25	9	6	65	22	6	32	12

7   Conclusions and Future Work

In this paper we have proposed a new model for black and white visual cryptography. In this new model the shares are allowed to be color images. Exploiting this model we can construct schemes that have smaller pixel expansion. There are a number of future work directions. For example one can try to find schemes in this new model with smaller pixel expansion or prove lower bounds on the pixel expansion. Another direction is to investigate the relationship between this new model and the b&w model. Yet another one is to study the contrast in the proposed model.

References

1. Ateniese, G., Blundo, C., De Santis, A., Stinson, D.R.: Visual Cryptography for General Access Structures. Information and Computation 129(2), 86–106 (1996)
2. Blundo, C., De Bonis, A., De Santis, A.: Improved Schemes for Visual Cryptography. Designs, Codes and Cryptography 24, 255–278 (2001)
3. Blundo, C., De Santis, A.: Visual Cryptography Schemes with Perfect Reconstruction of Black Pixels. Comput. & Graphics 22(4), 449–455 (1998)
4. Blundo, C., De Santis, A., Stinson, D.R.: On the Contrast in Visual Cryptography Schemes. Journal of Cryptology 12(4), 261–289 (1999)
5. Bose, M., Mukerjee, R.: Optimal $(2, n)$ visual cryptography schemes. Designs, Codes and Cryptography 40, 255–267 (2006)
6. Cimato, S., De Prisco, R., De Santis, A.: Probabilistic Visual Cryptography Schemes. The Computer Journal 49(1), 97–107 (2006)
7. Cimato, S., De Prisco, R., De Santis, A.: Colored visual cryptography without color darkening. Theoretical Computer Science 374(1-3), 261–276 (2007)
8. Cimato, S., Yang, C.-N. (eds.): Visual Cryptography and Secret Image Sharing. Digital Imaging and Computer Vision book series. CRC Press (to appear)
9. Eisen, P.A., Stinson, D.R.: Threshold Visual Cryptography Schemes with Specified Whiteness Levels of Reconstructed Pixels. Designs, Codes and Cryptography 25, 15–61 (2002)
10. Hou, Y.-C.: Visual Cryptography for Color Images. Pattern Recognition 36, 1619–1629 (2003)
11. Koga, H., Yamamoto, H.: Proposal of a Lattice-Based Visual Secret Sharing Scheme for Color and Gray-Scale Images. IEICE Trans. on Fundamentals of Electronics, Communication and Computer Sciences 81-A(6), 1262–1269 (1998)
12. Naor, M., Shamir, A.: Visual Cryptography. In: De Santis, A. (ed.) EUROCRYPT 1994. LNCS, vol. 950, pp. 1–12. Springer, Heidelberg (1995)
13. Verheul, E.R., van Tilborg, H.C.A.: Constructions and properties of k out of n visual secret. Designs, Codes, and Cryptography 11, 179–196 (1997)
14. Yang, C.-N.: New visual secret sharing schemes using probabilistic method. Pattern Recognition Letters 25(4), 481–494 (2004)
15. Yang, C.-N., Laih, C.-A.: New Colored Visual Secret Sharing Schemes. Designs, Codes and Cryptography 20, 325–335 (2000)

Digital Fingerprinting under and (Somewhat) beyond the Marking Assumption

(Invited Talk)

Alexander Barg[1,2] and Grigory Kabatiansky[2]

[1] Department of ECE and Institute for Systems Research, University of Maryland,
College Park, MD 20742, USA
[2] Institute for Information Transmission Problems, Russian Academy of Sciences,
Moscow, Russia
abarg@umd.edu,kaba@iitp.ru

Abstract. This paper is an extended abstract of the invited talk given by the first-named author.

In the first part of the talk we give a general introduction to collusion-resistant fingerprinting, discussing problem statements and different sets of assumptions for the digital fingerprinting problem.

In the second part we discuss in more detail a combinatorial version of the fingerprinting problem, known as *parent-identifying codes*. Most earlier works on digital fingerprinting rely on the so-called *marking assumption*, under which the attackers cannot modify the coordinates in which their fingerprints are identical. We introduce a version of parent-identifying codes for collusion attacks that do not necessarily follow the marking assumption. We show existence of such codes for coalitions of arbitrary size t. Some exact answers are obtained for $t = 2$ pirates.

1 The Fingerprinting Problem

Digital fingerprinting is a technique motivated by the task of protecting copyrighted contents against unauthorized distribution. The contents is provided to the users of the system with registration information embedded in it in the form of fingerprints. The problem arises if a group of t users (pirates) attempts to create an unregistered copy of the data by combining their fingerprints into a fingerprint that does not permit their identification by the content owner. The goal of the owner is to design fingerprints in a way that, under certain assumptions, enables him to identify at least some members of the pirate coalition from an unregistered fingerprint.

We assume that M users of the system are provided with fingerprints given by n-words over a finite alphabet $\mathcal{Q} = \{0, 1, \ldots, q-1\}$. The mapping $[M] \to \mathcal{Q}^n$ defines a code $\mathcal{C}$ of length n. A t-subset $U = \{u^1, \ldots, u^t\} \subset \mathcal{C}$ is called a *coalition* of size t. A *collusion attack* occurs when several uses (pirates) form a coalition U to create an unregistered fingerprint y with the purpose of making it impossible to identify any members of U based on observing y. The vector y is formed as

S. Fehr (Ed.): ICITS 2011, LNCS 6673, pp. 202–205, 2011.
© Springer-Verlag Berlin Heidelberg 2011

a function of U (the attack map). The *fingerprinting problem* calls for designing codes resilient to collusion attacks.

Collusion attacks. Let $U_i = \{u_i^1, \ldots, u_i^t\}$ be the set of the ith coordinates of the elements of U. Coordinate $i, 1 \leq i \leq n$ is called *undetectable* for U if all vectors in U have the same value in it, i.e., if $|U_i| = 1$, and is called *detectable* otherwise. Denote by $D(U)$ the set of detectable coordinates for a coalition U.

Let $U \subset \mathcal{C}$ be a coalition. Suppose that $y_i \in U_i$ for all $i = 1, \ldots, n$. Under this restriction the set of attack vectors for U forms the subset

$$\langle U \rangle = \{(y_1, \ldots, y_n) \in \mathcal{Q}^n : y_i \in U_i, \; i = 1, \ldots, n\} \tag{1}$$

called the *narrow-sense envelope* of the coalition. The elements of $\langle U \rangle$ are called *descendants* of U, and for any of the descendants $y \in \langle U \rangle$ the elements of U are called its *parents*.

A code $\mathcal{C}$ has the *t-identifiable parent property* (is a *t-IPP* code) if for any $y \in \bigcup_{U \subset \mathcal{C}, |U| \leq t} \langle U \rangle$ it is possible to find at least one of its parents, i.e. if

$$\bigcap_{U \subset \mathcal{C}, |U| \leq t, y \in \langle U \rangle} U \neq \emptyset.$$

t-IPP codes permit unconditional identification of pirates under the narrow-sense attack (1).

A more potent attack assumes that the pirates can change detectable coordinates to any symbols of the alphabet $\mathcal{Q}$ or make them unreadable. Define the *wide-sense envelope* $\langle U \rangle_w$ of the coalition U as

$$\langle U \rangle_w = \{(y_1, \ldots, y_n) \in \mathcal{Q}^n \cup \{*\} : \; y_i = u_i, i \notin D(U)\} \tag{2}$$

Codes that permit recovery of the pirates for this problem with an arbitrary small error probability of identification are called *collusion-secure* or *fingerprinting*.

The attacks (1) and (2) rely on the so-called **marking assumption**, under which the pirates cannot modify the coordinates in which their fingerprints are identical. Lifting this restriction results in stronger attack strategies by the pirates. We call a coordinate i of y a *mutation* if $y_i \notin U_i$. Assume that the coalition U forms y following the IPP attack rule (1) except for ϵn coordinates that can deviate from this rule. A code $\mathcal{C} \subset \mathcal{Q}^n$ is called (t, ϵ)-IPP (*robust t-IPP code*) if it guarantees exact identification of at least one member of the pirate coalition of size at most t for any collusion attack with at most ϵn mutations.

The *rate* of the fingerprinting code is defined as $R = R(\mathcal{C}) \triangleq \log_q |\mathcal{C}|/n$. One of the main questions for the fingerprinting problem is that of the maximum attainable rate $R_q(t)$ of codes under various attacks. We mention some of the known results for this problem in the next section.

2   Existence of Fingerprinting Codes: Results on the Rate

IPP codes for two pirates were introduced by Hollmann et al. [10] who also proved that $R_q(2) > 0$ for all $q \geq 3$. More generally, [5] showed that $R_q(t) > 0$

for all $q \geq t + 1$. The main tool for the proof is the notion of partially hashing functions introduced in [5] as a characterization of the IPP property. Upper bounds on the rate of t-IPP codes were found in [1,7].

The existence of high-rate fingerprinting codes resilient against the wide-sense attack (2) was shown in [8,4]. The strongest results to-date [2,9,11] give sequences of fingerprinting codes of rate $\Theta(t^{-2})$ which is also asymptotically tight [2].

A *multilevel fingerprinting problem* was introduced recently in [3]. Under this version, the set of $M = M_1 M_2$ users is partitioned into M_1 groups of size M_2 each. It is assumed that the pirate coalitions can be of small size (up to t_2 users) or of a larger size $t_1 > t_2$. The codes are designed in such a way that for small coalitions the distributor is capable of identifying at least one of the pirates, while for larger coalitions it identifies a group that contains one of the pirates. Paper [3] proves existence of two-level fingerprinting codes with asymptotically positive rate. The concept of multilevel fingerprinting parallels the idea of unequal error protection of message symbols in information theory. The proof in [3] makes use of this analogy.

Existence results for robust t-IPP codes [6] depend on the exact nature of the attack strategy. We consider attacks under which an ϵ proportion of coordinates in the attack y can take any values from the alphabet $\mathcal{Q}$ or become erased (unreadable). These coordinates may be within the set $D(U)$ of detectable coordinates or outside it. This set of assumptions results in several somewhat distinct generalizations of the t-IPP property. In the talk we show existence of robust t-IPP codes for all $t \leq q - 1$ and some positive proportion of the runaway (mutant) coordinates. The proofs involve relations between IPP codes and combinatorial arrays with separating properties such as perfect hash functions and hash codes, partially hashing families and separating codes.

For $t = 2$ we find the exact proportion of mutant coordinates (for several error scenarios) that permits unconditional identification of parents.

Acknowledgments. The research of A. Barg is partially supported by the National Science Foundation. The research of G. Kabatiansky is partially supported by Russian Foundation for Fundamental Research.

References

1. Alon, N., Stav, U.: New bounds on parent-identifying codes: the case of multiple parents. Combinatorics, Probability and Computing 13(6), 795–807 (2004)
2. Amiri, E., Tardos, G.: High rate fingerprinting codes and fingerprinting capacity. In: Proc. 20th ACM-SIAM Sympos. Discrete Algorithms (SODA 2009), pp. 336–345 (2009)
3. Anthapadmanabhan, N.P., Barg, A.: Two-level fingerprinting: Stronger definitions and code constructions. In: Proc. IEEE Int. Sympos. Inform. Theory (ISIT 2010), Austin, TX, pp. 2528–2532 (2010)
4. Barg, A., Blakley, G.R., Kabatiansky, G.: Digital fingerprinting codes: Problem statements, constructions, identification of traitors. IEEE Trans. Inform. Theory 49(4), 852–865 (2003)

5. Barg, A., Cohen, G., Encheva, S., Kabatiansky, G., Zémor, G.: A hypergraph approach to the identifying parent property: the case of multiple parents. SIAM J. Discrete Math. 14, 423–431 (2001)
6. Barg, A., Kabatiansky, G.: Robust parent-identifying codes and combinatorial arrays (2010) (preprint)
7. Blackburn, S.: An upper bound on the size of a code with the k-identifiable property. J. Combinatorial Theory Ser. A 102, 179–185 (2003)
8. Boneh, D., Shaw, J.: Collusion-secure fingerprinting for digital data. IEEE Trans. Inform. Theory 44(5), 1897–1905 (1998)
9. Dumer, I.: Equal-weight fingerprinting codes. In: Chee, Y.M., Li, C., Ling, S., Wang, H., Xing, C. (eds.) IWCC 2009. LNCS, vol. 5557, pp. 43–51. Springer, Heidelberg (2009)
10. Hollmann, H.D.L., van Lint, J.H., Linnartz, J.P., Tolhuizen, L.M.G.M.: On codes with the identifiable parent property. J. Combinatorial Theory Ser. A 82(2), 121–133 (1998)
11. Huang, Y., Moulin, P.: Saddle-point solution of the fingerpinting capacity game. In: Proc. IEEE International Symposium on Information Theory (ISIT 2009), Seoul, Korea, pp. 2256–2260 (2009)

Communication Optimal Multi-valued Asynchronous Byzantine Agreement with Optimal Resilience

Arpita Patra[1,*] and C. Pandu Rangan[2]

[1] Department of Computer Science, Aarhus University, Denmark
arpita@cs.au.dk, arpitapatra10@gmail.com
[2] Department of Computer Science and Engg., IIT Madras, India
prangan55@gmail.com

Abstract. Byzantine Agreement (BA) and Broadcast (BC) are considered to be the most fundamental primitives for fault-tolerant distributed computing and cryptographic protocols. An important variant of BA and BC is Asynchronous Byzantine Agreement (ABA) and Asynchronous Broadcast (called as A-cast) respectively. Most often in the literature, protocols for ABA and A-cast were designed for a single bit message. But in many applications, these protocols may be invoked on *long message* rather than on single bit. Therefore, it is important to design efficient *multi-valued* protocols (i.e. protocols with *long message*) which extract advantage of directly dealing with long messages and are far better than multiple invocations to existing protocols for single bit. In synchronous network settings, this line of research was initiated by Turpin and Coan [27] and later it is culminated in the result of Fitzi et al. [15] who presented the first ever *communication optimal* (*i.e. the communication complexity is minimal in asymptotic sense*) multi-valued BA and BC protocols with the help of BA and BC protocols for short message. It was left open in [15] to achieve the same in asynchronous settings.

In [21], the authors presented a communication optimal multi-valued A-cast using existing A-cast [6] for small message. Here we achieve the same for ABA which is known to be harder problem than A-cast. Specifically, we design a *communication optimal*, optimally resilient (*allows maximum fault tolerance*) multi-valued ABA protocol, based on the existing ABA protocol for short message.

Keywords: Asynchronous Byzantine Agreement, Multi-valued, Unbounded Computing Power.

1 Introduction

The problem of Byzantine Agreement (BA) (also popularly known as consensus) was introduced in [22] and since then it has emerged as the most fundamental problem in distributed computing. It has been used as a building block for

---

* Financial Support from Center for Research in Foundations of Electronic Markets (CFEM) Denmark Acknowledged. The work was done when the author was a PhD student at IIT Madras, India.

S. Fehr (Ed.): ICITS 2011, LNCS 6673, pp. 206–226, 2011.

several important secure distributed computing tasks such as Secure Multiparty Computation (MPC) [4,5,26], Verifiable Secret Sharing (VSS) [10,4,26] etc. In practice, BA is used in almost any task that involves multiple parties, like voting, bidding, secure function evaluation, threshold key generation etc [14]. Informally, a BA protocol allows a set of parties, each holding some input bit, to agree on a common bit, even though some of the parties may act maliciously in order to make the honest parties disagree.

An important variant of BA problem is asynchronous BA (known as ABA) that studies the BA problem in asynchronous network which is known to be more realistic than synchronous network. The works of [3,25,6,11,8,7,1,23] have reported different ABA protocols. In this paper, we focus on ABA, specifically on the communication complexity of the problem.

Our Model.   We follow the network model of [8,7]. Specifically, our ABA protocol is carried out among a set of n parties, say $\mathcal{P} = \{P_1, \ldots, P_n\}$, where every two parties are directly connected by a secure channel and t out of the n parties can be under the influence of a *computationally unbounded Byzantine (active) adversary*, denoted as $\mathcal{A}_t$. We assume $n = 3t + 1$ which is the minimum number of parties required to design any ABA protocol [17]. The adversary $\mathcal{A}_t$, completely dictates the parties under its control and can force them to deviate from the protocol in any arbitrary manner. The parties not under the influence of $\mathcal{A}_t$ are called *honest or uncorrupted*.

The underlying network is asynchronous, where the communication channels between the parties have arbitrary, yet finite delay (i.e. the messages are guaranteed to reach eventually). To model this, we assume that $\mathcal{A}_t$ controls the network and may delay messages between any two honest parties. However, it cannot read or modify these messages as the links are private and authenticated, and it also has to eventually deliver all the messages by honest parties. In asynchronous network, the inherent difficulty in designing a protocol comes from the fact that a party can not distinguish between a slow sender (whose message is simply delayed in the network) and a corrupted sender (who did not send the message at all). So a party can not wait for the values sent by all parties, as waiting for all of them may turn out to be endless. Hence the values of up to t (potentially honest) parties may have to be ignored for computation at any step.

Definitions.   We now define ABA and its variant formally.

Definition 1 (ABA [8]). *Let Π be an asynchronous protocol executed among the set of parties $\mathcal{P}$, with each party having a private binary input. We say that Π is an ABA protocol tolerating $\mathcal{A}_t$ if the following hold, for every possible behavior of $\mathcal{A}_t$ and every possible input: (a)* **Termination***: All honest parties eventually terminate the protocol. (b)* **Correctness***: All honest parties who have terminated the protocol hold identical outputs. Furthermore, if all honest parties had same input, say ρ, then all honest parties output ρ.*

We now define (ϵ, δ)-ABA protocol, where both ϵ and δ are negligibly small values and are called error probabilities of the ABA protocol. Throughout our paper, we assume $\epsilon = 2^{-\Omega(\kappa)}$ and $\delta = 2^{-\Omega(\kappa)}$, where κ is called as the error parameter. To achieve the above bounds for error probabilities, our protocol will operate on finite Galois field $\mathbb{F} = GF(2^\kappa)$.

Definition 2 $((\epsilon, \delta)$-ABA). *An ABA protocol Π is called (ϵ, δ)-ABA if: (a) Π satisfies* **Termination** *described in Definition 1, except with an error probability of ϵ and (b) Conditioned on the event that every honest party terminates Π, protocol Π satisfies* **Correctness** *property described in Definition 1, except with error probability δ.*

The ABA and (ϵ, δ)-ABA can be executed for long messages and these type of protocols will be referred as *multi-valued* protocols. The important parameters of any ABA protocol are: (a) **Resilience**: It is the maximum number of corrupted parties (t) that the protocol can tolerate and still satisfy its properties; (b) **Communication Complexity**: It is the total number of bits communicated by the *honest* parties in the protocol; (c) **Computation Complexity**: It is the computational resources required by the honest parties during a protocol execution; and (d) **Running Time**: An informal, but standard definition of the running time of an asynchronous protocol is provided in [8,7].

The History of ABA. From [22,17], any ABA protocol tolerating $\mathcal{A}_t$ is possible if and only if $n \geq 3t + 1$. Thus any ABA protocol designed with $n = 3t+1$ parties is called as *optimally resilient*. By the seminal result of [13], any ABA protocol, irrespective of the value of n, must have some *non-terminating* runs/executions, where some honest party(ies) may not terminate at all. So in any (ϵ, δ)-ABA protocol with non-zero ϵ, the probability of the occurrence of a non-terminating execution is at most ϵ (these type of protocols are called $(1 - \epsilon)$-terminating [8,7]). On the other hand in any $(0, \delta)$-ABA protocol, the *probability* of the occurrence of a non-terminating execution is *asymptotically zero* (these type of protocols are called *almost-surely terminating*, a term coined in [1]). In Table 1, we summarize the best known ABA protocols in the literature.

Table 1. Summary of the Best Known Existing ABA Protocols

Ref.	Type	Resilience	Communication Complexity (CC) in bits	Expected Running Time (ERT)
[6]	$(0, 0)$-ABA	$t < n/3$	$\mathcal{O}(2^n)$	$\mathcal{C} = \mathcal{O}(2^n)$
[11,12]	$(0, 0)$-ABA	$t < n/4$	$\mathcal{O}((nt + t^7) \log |\mathbb{F}|)$[a]	$\mathcal{C} = \mathcal{O}(1)$
[8,7]	$(\epsilon, 0)$-ABA	$t < n/3$	Private[b]: $\mathcal{O}(\mathcal{C}n^{11}(\log \kappa)^4)$[c] A-cast[d]: $\mathcal{O}(\mathcal{C}n^{11}(\log \kappa)^2 \log n)$	$\mathcal{C} = \mathcal{O}(1)$
[1]	$(0, 0)$-ABA	$t < n/3$	Private: $\mathcal{O}(\mathcal{C}n^6 \log |\mathbb{F}|)$ A-cast: $\mathcal{O}(\mathcal{C}n^6 \log |\mathbb{F}|)$	$\mathcal{C} = \mathcal{O}(n^2)$
[20]	$(\epsilon, 0)$-ABA	$t < n/3$	Private: $\mathcal{O}(\mathcal{C}n^6 \log \kappa)$ A-cast: $\mathcal{O}(\mathcal{C}n^6 \log \kappa)$	$\mathcal{C} = \mathcal{O}(1)$
[20]	Multi-valued[e] $(\epsilon, 0)$-ABA	$t < n/3$	Private: $\mathcal{O}(\mathcal{C}n^5 \log \kappa)$ A-cast: $\mathcal{O}(\mathcal{C}n^5 \log \kappa)$	$\mathcal{C} = \mathcal{O}(1)$

[a] Here $\mathbb{F}$ is the finite field over which the ABA protocol of [11,12] works. It is enough to have $|\mathbb{F}| \geq n$ and therefore $\log |\mathbb{F}|$ can be replaced by $\log n$. In fact in the remaining table, $\mathbb{F}$ bears the same meaning.
[b] Communication over private channels between pair of parties in $\mathcal{P}$.
[c] In this table, κ is the error parameter of the protocols.
[d] Total number of bits that needs to be A-casted (see more discussion on A-cast in subsection 2.1 under section 2).
[e] This protocol allows to reach agreement on $(t + 1)$ bits concurrently.

Multi-valued ABA. In many applications, ABA protocols are invoked on *long messages* rather than on single bit. For example, in asynchronous MPC (AMPC) [5,7,19], where typically lot of ABA invocations are required, many of the invocations can be parallelized and optimized to a single invocation with a long message. All existing protocols for ABA [25,3,6,11,12,8,7,1,20] are designed for single bit message. A naive approach to design multi-valued ABA for $\ell > 1$ bit message is to parallelize ℓ invocations of existing ABA protocols dealing with single bit. This approach requires a communication complexity that is ℓ times the communication complexity of the existing protocols for single bit and hence is not very efficient. More intelligent techniques need to be called for in order to gain in terms of communication complexity.

In synchronous network, Turpin and Coan [27] are the first to report a multi-valued BC protocol based on the access to a BC protocol for short message. Recently, Fitzi et al. [15] have designed *communication optimal* BA and BC protocols for large message using BA and BC protocol (respectively) for small message. While all existing synchronous BA protocols required a communication cost of $\Omega(\ell n^2)$ bits, the BA protocols of [15] communicate $\mathcal{O}(\ell n + poly(n, \kappa))$ bits to agree on an ℓ bit message. For a sufficiently large ℓ, the communication complexity expression reduces to $\mathcal{O}(n\ell)$, which is a clear improvement over $\Omega(\ell n^2)$. A brief discussion on the approach used in [15] for designing BA protocol is presented in **Appendix A**.

Designing *communication optimal*, multi-valued ABA and A-cast protocol was left as an interesting open question in [15]. The problem of A-cast has been resolved in [21]. In this paper, we settle the case for ABA which is known to be harder than A-cast. Our ABA calls for much more involved techniques than A-cast of [21]. To the best of our knowledge, ours is the first ever attempt to design multi-valued ABA.

Our Contribution. We propose a *communication optimal, optimally resilient, multi-valued (ϵ, δ)-ABA* protocol that attains a communication complexity of $\mathcal{O}(\ell n + poly(n, \kappa))$ bits to agree on an ℓ bit message. Our protocol requires $\mathcal{O}(n^3)$ invocations to ABA protocol for small messages (we may use any one of the ABA protocols listed in Table 1; the most communication efficient ABA is listed in the last row of the same table). For sufficiently large ℓ, the communication complexity of our protocol becomes $\mathcal{O}(\ell n)$ bits. From the result of [15], any BA protocol in synchronous networks with $t \in \Omega(n)$, requires to communicate $\Omega(n\ell)$ bits for an ℓ bit message. The same lower bound holds for asynchronous networks as well. Therefore our ABA is *communication optimal* for large enough ℓ. The degree of n and κ (and therefore the bound on ℓ for which our protocol is communication optimal) in the term $poly(n, \kappa)$ depends on the ABA for short message under use.

In our ABA protocol, we employ *player-elimination* framework introduced in [16] in the context of MPC. So far player-elimination was used only in MPC and AMPC. Hence our result shows the first non-MPC application of the technique. Apart from this, we present a novel idea to expand a set of $t + 1$ parties, with all the honest party(ies) in it holding a common message m, to a set of $2t + 1$

parties with all honest parties in it holding m. Moreover, the expansion process requires a communication complexity of $\mathcal{O}(\ell n + poly(n, \kappa))$ bits, where $|m| = \ell$. This technique may be useful in designing communication efficient protocols for many other form of consensus problems.

2   Communication Optimal (ϵ, δ)-ABA Protocol

We now present our novel (ϵ, δ)-ABA protocol with $n = 3t + 1$, called Optimal-ABA. The protocol allows the honest parties in $\mathcal{P}$, each having input message of ℓ bits, to reach agreement on a common message $m^* \in \{0, 1\}^\ell$ containing ℓ bits. Moreover, if all the honest parties have same input m, then they agree on m at the end. We first describe the existing tools used in Optimal-ABA.

2.1   Tools Used

Hash Function [15,9].   A *keyed* hash function $\mathcal{U}_\kappa$ maps arbitrary strings in $\{0, 1\}^*$ to κ bit string with the help of a κ bit random key. So $\mathcal{U}_\kappa : \{0, 1\}^* \to \{0, 1\}^\kappa$. $\mathcal{U}_\kappa$ can be implemented as follows: Let m and r be the input to $\mathcal{U}_\kappa$, where m is an ℓ bit string that need to be hashed/mapped and r is the hash key selected from $\mathbb{F}$. Without loss of generality, we assume that $\ell = poly(\kappa)$. Then m is interpreted as a polynomial $f_m(x)$ over $\mathbb{F}$, where the degree of $f_m(x)$ is $\lceil \ell/\kappa \rceil - 1$. For this, m is divided into blocks of κ bits and each block of κ bits is interpreted as an element from $\mathbb{F}$. Then these field elements are considered as the coefficients of $f_m(x)$ over $\mathbb{F}$. Finally, $\mathcal{U}_\kappa(m, r) = f_m(r)$. We now have the following important well-known theorem.

Theorem 1 (Collision Theorem [15]). *Let m_1 and m_2 be two ℓ bit messages. The probability that $\mathcal{U}_\kappa(m_1, r) = \mathcal{U}_\kappa(m_2, r)$ for a randomly chosen hash key r is $\frac{\ell 2^{-\kappa}}{\kappa} = 2^{-\Omega(\kappa)}$ which is negligible.*

A-cast or Asynchronous Broadcast.   In brief, an A-cast protocol allows a sender $S \in \mathcal{P}$ to send some message M identically to all the parties in $\mathcal{P}$. An A-cast protocol satisfies two properties: (1) **Termination:** If S is honest, then all honest parties in $\mathcal{P}$ will eventually terminate; If any honest party terminates, then all honest parties will eventually terminate. (2) **Correctness:** If the honest parties terminate, then they do so with a common output M^*; (b) Furthermore, if the sender S is honest then $M^* = M$. The first ever protocol for A-cast is due to Bracha [6] and the protocol is error free in both termination and correctness. The A-cast protocol of [6] is t resilient with $t < n/3$ and communicates $\mathcal{O}(n^2)$ bits to A-cast a *single bit* in constant running time. The other protocol for A-cast is reported in [21]. This protocol has error in both correctness and termination; but it communicates $\mathcal{O}(\ell n)$ bits for an ℓ bit input where $\ell = \omega(n^2(n \log n + \kappa))$. For simplicity, in our ABA protocol we will prefer to use A-cast of [6]. We use the following syntax to invoke A-cast: A-cast($S, \mathcal{P}, M$). The description of Bracha's A-cast protocol is available in [7].

Notation 1 (Convention for Using A-cast:). *By saying that 'P_i A-casts M', we mean that P_i as a sender, initiates A-cast($P_i, \mathcal{P}, M$). Similarly 'P_j receives*

M from the A-cast of P_i' will mean that P_j terminates A-cast$(P_i, \mathcal{P}, M)$, with M as the output. By the property of A-cast, if some honest party P_j terminates A-cast$(P_i, \mathcal{P}, M)$ with M as the output, then every other honest party will eventually do so, irrespective of the behavior of the sender P_i.

Asynchronous Verifiable Secret Sharing (AVSS). An AVSS scheme consisting of two phases, namely sharing phase and reconstruction phase, can be viewed as a *distributed commitment mechanism* where a (possibly corrupted) special party in $\mathcal{P}$, called *dealer* (denoted as D), *commits* a secret $s \in \mathbb{F}$ in the sharing phase, where commitment information is distributed among the parties in $\mathcal{P}$. Later in reconstruction phase, the commitment s can be *uniquely* and privately reconstructed by any specific party, say $P_\alpha \in \mathcal{P}$ (we may call it as P_α-private-reconstruction) even in the presence of $\mathcal{A}_t$. Here P_α is called *receiver* party. Moreover, if D and P_α are honest, then secrecy of s from $\mathcal{A}_t$ is maintained throughout. AVSS is implemented by a pair of protocols (Sh, Rec) and it has three properties called, **Termination, Correctness** and **Secrecy** (for a formal definition of AVSS, refer to [7,19]).

If an AVSS satisfies its **Termination** and/or **Correctness**, except with error probability $\rho = 2^{-\Omega(\kappa)}$, then we arrive at the notion of statistical AVSS. From [8], statistical AVSS tolerating $\mathcal{A}_t$ is possible iff $n \geq 3t + 1$. The best known communication efficient statistical AVSS with $n = 3t + 1$ is due to [19]. We use the following syntax to invoke AVSS: AVSS-Share$(D, \mathcal{P}, s)$ (protocol for sharing phase) and AVSS-Rec$(D, \mathcal{P}, s, P_\alpha)$ (protocol for reconstruction phase).

Agreement on a Common Subset (ACS). In our (ϵ, δ)-ABA protocol, we come across the following situation: There exists a set of parties $\mathcal{R} \subseteq \mathcal{P}$ with $|\mathcal{R}| \geq t + 1$, such that each party in $\mathcal{R}$ is asked to A-cast (AVSS-Share) some value(s). While the honest parties in $\mathcal{R}$ will eventually do the A-cast (AVSS-Share), the corrupted parties in $\mathcal{R}$ may or may not do the same. So the (honest) parties in $\mathcal{P}$ want to agree on a *common* set $\mathcal{T} \subset \mathcal{R}$, with $1 \leq |\mathcal{T}| \leq |\mathcal{R}| - t$, such that A-cast (AVSS-Share) instance of each party in $\mathcal{T}$ will be eventually terminated by the (honest) parties in $\mathcal{P}$. For this, the parties use ACS primitive (stands for Agreement on Common Subset), presented in [5]. The ACS protocol will use $|\mathcal{R}|$ instances of ABA invoked on single bit. We may use the best known communication efficient $(\epsilon, 0)$-ABA of [20] for this purpose. We use the following syntax for invoking ACS: ACS$(\mathcal{R}, |\mathcal{T}|)$.

Theorem 2. *The communication complexity of ACS is equal to $|\mathcal{R}|$ executions of ABA protocol each invoked on a single bit.*

2.2   Protocol Optimal-ABA

Our protocol Optimal-ABA uses the so-called *player-elimination framework*, along with several novel ideas. So far player-elimination [16] has been used *only* in the context of synchronous and asynchronous MPC [16,2,24]. Ours is the first non-MPC application of player-elimination. We would refer it by *party-elimination*, rather than player-elimination in our context (as we use the term party in place of player). In the party-elimination framework, the computation of Optimal-ABA is divided into t segments, where in each segment the parties agree on an $\frac{\ell}{t}$ bit, considering $\frac{\ell}{t}$ bits of their original input as the *input message* of the segment. In particular, the parties divide their original message into t blocks, each of size $\frac{\ell}{t}$ bits and in α^{th} segment $\mathcal{S}_\alpha$, the parties reach agreement on an $\frac{\ell}{t}$ bit message, considering *only* the αth block as the input message. Each segment terminates eventually with the parties having common output of $\frac{\ell}{t}$ bits; moreover if the honest parties start a segment with the same block of $\frac{\ell}{t}$ bits, then they agree on that common input.

The computation of a segment is carried out in a *non-robust* fashion, in the sense that if all the parties including the corrupted parties behave according to the protocol then the segment successfully achieves its task; otherwise the segment may fail in which case it outputs a *triplet of parties* among which *at least one is corrupted*. In the former case, the next segment will be taken up for computation for reaching agreement with next block of $\frac{\ell}{t}$ bits as input. In the latter case, the same segment will be repeated among the set of parties after excluding the parties in the triplet and this continues until the segment becomes successful. It is to be noted that though the computations in a segment may be done among a *subset* of parties from $\mathcal{P}$ (as parties in triplet might be eliminated from $\mathcal{P}$), the agreement in the segment is finally attained over all honest parties in $\mathcal{P}$. It is now easy to see that the t segments may fail at most t times *in total* as t is the upper bound on the number of corrupted parties. After t failures, all the corrupted parties will be removed and therefore there will be no more failure.

We denote the input of party P_i by $m_i \in \{0,1\}^\ell$, which is divided into t blocks, with α^{th} block being denoted by $m_{i\alpha}$, for $\alpha = 1, \ldots, t$. At the beginning of our protocol, we initialize two dynamic variables $n' = n$ and $t' = t$ and one dynamic set $\mathcal{P}' = \mathcal{P}$. $\mathcal{P}'$ denotes the *set of non-eliminated* parties and contains n' parties, out of which at most t' can be corrupted. In every segment $\mathcal{S}_\alpha$ the computation is structured into three main phases: (a) **Checking Phase**, (b) **Expansion Phase** and (c) **Output Phase**. The segment failure may occur *only in the second phase* and hence *only* the first two phases of a segment may be repeated several times (bounded by t); once the first two phases are successful for a segment, the segment will always be successfully completed after robustly executing the third phase. So at the end of segment $\mathcal{S}_\alpha$, every honest party will agree on a common $\frac{\ell}{t}$ bits, denoted by m_α^*. Moreover if the honest parties start with common input (i.e. $m_{i\alpha}$'s are equal for all honest parties), then m_α^* will be same as that common input.

1. **Checking Phase:** Here the parties, on having private input message of $\frac{\ell}{t}$ bits each (i.e. $m_{i\alpha}$'s), jointly perform some computation in order to determine and agree on a set of $t' + 1$ parties called $\mathcal{P}'_{ch} \subseteq \mathcal{P}'$, such that the honest parties in $\mathcal{P}'_{ch}$ hold a common ℓ/t bit message, say m_α^*. In case of failure due to the inconsistencies among the inputs of the honest parties, the parties abort any further computation for current segment and agree on a predefined message $m_\alpha^\dagger$. So in this case current segment terminates with all honest parties agreeing on common output $m_\alpha^* = m_\alpha^\dagger$. On the other hand, if $\mathcal{P}'_{ch}$ is generated and agreed among the parties, then the computation for current

segment proceeds to the next phase. It is to be noted that $\mathcal{P}'_{ch}$ will be *always obtained* if the initial messages of the honest parties in $\mathcal{P}'$ are same.

2. **Expansion Phase:** Here the parties in $\mathcal{P}'_{ch}$ on holding a common message m^*_α help other parties to receive m^*_α. Specifically here the parties jointly perform some computation in conjunction with the parties in $\mathcal{P}'_{ch}$ to expand $\mathcal{P}'_{ch}$ to a set of $2t'+1$ parties, denoted by $\mathcal{P}'_{ex}$ (with $\mathcal{P}'_{ch} \subset \mathcal{P}'_{ex} \subseteq \mathcal{P}'$) such that all honest parties in $\mathcal{P}'_{ex}$ hold m^*_α. *The expansion technique is the most crucial and novel part of our protocol.* But the computation of this phase is non-robust and hence either one of the following is guaranteed: (a) $\mathcal{P}'_{ex}$ is constructed successfully or (b) a triplet of parties (P_i, P_j, P_k) is obtained, such that at least one of the three parties is corrupted. If the former case happens, then parties proceed to execute **Output Phase**. If the latter case happens, then n' and t' are reduced by 3 and 1 respectively and the current segment is repeated from the beginning (from the **Checking Phase**) with updated n' and t' and $\mathcal{P}' = \mathcal{P}' \setminus \{P_i, P_j, P_k\}$. Note that n', t' and $\mathcal{P}'$ always satisfy: $n' = 3t'+1$ and $|\mathcal{P}'| = n'$.

3. **Output Phase:** Here the parties in $\mathcal{P}'_{ex}$ help the parties in $\mathcal{P} \setminus \mathcal{P}'_{ex}$ (**not** $\mathcal{P}' \setminus \mathcal{P}'_{ex}$) to learn the common ℓ/t message m^*_α held by the honest parties in $\mathcal{P}'_{ex}$. After this phase, current segment terminates with common output m^*_α and the parties proceed to the computation of next segment. The implementation of this phase is very similar to the implementation of the Output Phase of [21] and the Claiming Stage of the BA protocol of [15].

Now the overall structure of Optimal-ABA is presented below.

Protocol Optimal-ABA($\mathcal{P}$)

Code for P_i: Every party in $\mathcal{P}$ executes this code.

1. Set $n' = n$, $t' = t$ and $\mathcal{P}' = \mathcal{P}$. Initialize $\alpha = 1$.
2. While $\alpha \leq t$, do the following for segment $\mathcal{S}_\alpha$ with input $m_{i\alpha}$ and with n', t' and $\mathcal{P}'$ to agree on m^*_α:
   (a) **Checking Phase:** Participate in the code Checking, presented in Fig. 1 to determine and agree on $\mathcal{P}'_{ch} \subseteq \mathcal{P}'$ of size $t'+1$ such that all the honest parties in $\mathcal{P}'_{ch}$ hold common $\frac{\ell}{t}$ bits, say m^*_α. If $\mathcal{P}'_{ch}$ is generated then proceed to the next phase. Otherwise set m^*_α to some predefined value $m^\dagger_\alpha \in \{0,1\}^{\frac{\ell}{t}}$, set $\alpha = \alpha + 1$ and terminate the current segment with output m^*_α.
   (b) **Expansion Phase:** Participate in code Expansion presented in Fig. 2 to expand $\mathcal{P}'_{ch}$ to contain $2t'+1$ parties, denoted by $\mathcal{P}'_{ex}$ such that $\mathcal{P}'_{ch} \subset \mathcal{P}'_{ex} \subseteq \mathcal{P}'$ and all honest parties in $\mathcal{P}'_{ex}$ hold m^*_α. If $\mathcal{P}'_{ex}$ is generated successfully then proceed to the next phase. Otherwise output a triplet (P_m, P_l, P_k), set $n' = n' - 3$, $t' = t' - 1$ and $\mathcal{P}' = \mathcal{P}' \setminus \{P_m, P_l, P_k\}$ and repeat the current segment.
   (c) **Output Phase:** Participate in code Output presented in Fig. 3 and output m^*_α upon termination, set $\alpha = \alpha + 1$ and terminate the current segment.
3. Output m^* which is the concatenation of $m^*_1, \ldots, m^*_t$ and terminate the protocol.

In the sequel, we will pursue an in-depth discussion on the implementation and properties of each of the above three phases.

Checking Phase. As mentioned before, the aim of this phase is to either agree on a set $\mathcal{P}'_{ch}$ of size $t' + 1$ such that all the honest parties in $\mathcal{P}'_{ch}$ hold common message, say m^*_α, or decide that such set may not exist. When all the honest parties start with same input message, $\mathcal{P}'_{ch}$ can be always found out and agreed upon. To achieve the above task, every party hashes his message with a random key and A-casts the (random key, hash value) pair. The parties then agree on a set $\mathcal{I}$ of $n' - t'$ parties whose A-cast will be eventually received by every honest party. This can be achieved by executing an instance of ACS.

Now every party P_i prepares a response vector $\overrightarrow{v_i}$, indicating whether the hash value of every $P_j \in \mathcal{I}$ is indeed the hash value of his own message $m_{i\alpha}$ with respect to P_j's hash key (this should ideally be the case, when P_i and P_j are honest and their input messages are identical, i.e. $m_{i\alpha} = m_{j\alpha}$). P_i A-casts $\overrightarrow{v_i}$. Now the parties again agree on a set of $n' - t'$ parties, say $\mathcal{J}$ whose A-cast with their $\overrightarrow{v_i}$ has been terminated. *Now notice that if all honest parties start with common input, then the vectors of the honest parties in $\mathcal{J}$ would be identical and would have at least $t' + 1$ 1's at the locations corresponding to the $t' + 1$ honest parties in $\mathcal{I}$.* So now the parties try to find a set of at least $t' + 1$ parties in $\mathcal{J}$, whose vectors are identical and have *at least $t' + 1$ 1's in them*. If found, then any subset of $t' + 1$ parties from that set (say $t' + 1$ parties with smallest index) will be considered as $\mathcal{P}'_{ch}$. It is easy to show that $\mathcal{P}'_{ch}$ will be *always obtained* if the initial messages of the honest parties in $\mathcal{P}'$ are same. Moreover it can be shown that the honest parties in $\mathcal{P}'_{ch}$ hold common message, say m^*_α with very high probability (see Lemma 2). But if $\mathcal{P}'_{ch}$ is not found, then the honest parties know that their input messages are inconsistent and hence they agree that such set can not be found. The steps performed so far are enough for achieving the goal of our current phase.

But we need to do some more task for the requirement of next phase i.e. **Expansion Phase.** In **Expansion Phase**, we require that every honest party P_j in $\mathcal{P}'$ should hold a distinct *secret* random hash key and hash value of the message corresponding to every party P_i in $\mathcal{I}$, such that the hash key and hash value that P_j has received from P_i should not be known to anybody other than P_i and P_j. Though achieving this in synchronous network is easy, it needs some amount of effort in asynchronous network. We do this by using AVSS-Share and AVSS-Rec. The code that implements this phase is now given in Fig. 1.

Before proving the properties of **Checking Phase**, we define the following:

Event E: *Let E be an event in an execution of Checking, defined as follows: All invocations of AVSS scheme initiated by the parties in $\mathcal{I}$ have been terminated with correct output. More clearly, E means that all the invocations of AVSS initiated by the parties in $\mathcal{I}$ will satisfy termination and correctness property. It is easy to see that E occurs with very high probability of $(1 - 2^{-\Omega(\kappa)})$.* □

In the sequel, all the lemmas for all the three phases are proved conditioned on event E.

Lemma 1 (Termination of Checking Phase). *In a segment $\mathcal{S}_\alpha$, an execution of **Checking Phase** will be terminated, except with probability $2^{-\Omega(\kappa)}$,*

Checking

To avoid notational clutter, we assume that $\mathcal{P}'$ is the set of first n' parties

Code for $P_i \in \mathcal{P}'$: Every party in $\mathcal{P}'$ executes this code

1. On having input $m_{i\alpha}$,
   (a) choose a random hash key r_i from $\mathbb{F}$ and A-cast $(r_i, \mathcal{V}_i)$ where $\mathcal{V}_i = \mathcal{U}_\kappa(m_{i\alpha}, r_i)$;
   (b) choose n' random hash keys $r_{i1}, \ldots, r_{in'}$ from $\mathbb{F}$ and commit $(r_{ij}, \mathcal{V}_{ij})$ where $\mathcal{V}_{ij} = \mathcal{U}_\kappa(m_{i\alpha}, r_{ij})$, by executing AVSS-Share$(P_i, \mathcal{P}', r_{ij})$ and AVSS-Share$(P_i, \mathcal{P}', \mathcal{V}_{ij})$.
2. Participate in AVSS-Share$(P_j, \mathcal{P}', r_{jk})$ and AVSS-Share$(P_j, \mathcal{P}', \mathcal{V}_{jk})$ for every $P_j \in \mathcal{P}'$ and $k = 1, \ldots, n'$.
3. Participate in ACS$(\mathcal{P}', n' - t')$ to agree on a set of $n' - t'$ parties from $\mathcal{P}'$, denoted as $\mathcal{I}$, whose A-cast and the $2n'$ instances of AVSS-Share will be eventually terminated (by the honest parties in $\mathcal{P}'$).
4. Wait to receive $(r_j, \mathcal{V}_j)$ from the A-cast of every $P_j \in \mathcal{I}$.
5. Wait to terminate all $2n'$ instances of AVSS-Share of every party in $\mathcal{I}$. Participate in AVSS-Rec$(P_j, \mathcal{P}', r_{jk}, P_k)$ and AVSS-Rec$(P_j, \mathcal{P}', \mathcal{V}_{jk}, P_k)$ for every $P_j \in \mathcal{I}$ and every $P_k \in \mathcal{P}'$ for P_k-private-reconstruction of $(r_{jk}, \mathcal{V}_{jk})$.
6. Obtain $(r_{ji}, \mathcal{V}_{ji})$ pair from AVSS-Rec$(P_j, \mathcal{P}', r_{ji}, P_i)$ and AVSS-Rec$(P_j, \mathcal{P}', \mathcal{V}_{ji}, P_i)$ corresponding to every $P_j \in \mathcal{I}$.
7. Construct n length vector $\overrightarrow{v_i}$, where $\overrightarrow{v_i}[j] = \begin{cases} \bot & \text{If } P_j \notin \mathcal{I} \\ 1 & \text{If } P_j \in \mathcal{I} \text{ and } \mathcal{V}_j = \mathcal{U}_\kappa(m_{i\alpha}, r_j). \\ 0 & \text{If } P_j \in \mathcal{I} \text{ and } \mathcal{V}_j \neq \mathcal{U}_\kappa(m_{i\alpha}, r_j). \end{cases}$
   A-cast $\overrightarrow{v_i}$.
8. Participate in ACS$(\mathcal{P}', n' - t')$ to agree on a set of $n' - t'$ parties from $\mathcal{P}'$, denoted as $\mathcal{J}$, whose A-cast with an n length vector has been terminated.
9. Check whether there is a unique set of at least $t' + 1$ parties in $\mathcal{J}$ such that their vectors are identical and have at least $t' + 1$ 1's in them (Note that this can be done in polynomial time).
   (a) If yes, then let $\mathcal{P}'_{ch}$ be the set containing exactly $t' + 1$ parties (say the parties with first $t' + 1$ smallest indices) out of those parties. Let $\overrightarrow{v}$ be the n length vector, where $\overrightarrow{v}[i] = 1$ if the ith location of the vectors of all parties in $\mathcal{P}'_{ch}$ is 1, otherwise $\overrightarrow{v}[i] = \bot$. Moreover, let $\mathcal{I}_1 = \{P_i \in \mathcal{I} \text{ such that } \overrightarrow{v}[i] = 1\}$. Assign $m^*_\alpha = m_{i\alpha}$ if $P_i \in \mathcal{P}'_{ch}$.
   (b) If not, then decide that $\mathcal{P}'_{ch}$ can not be found.

Fig. 1. Code for Checking Phase

where termination means that the code either outputs a set $\mathcal{P}'_{ch}$ of size $t' + 1$ or decide that such set can not be constructed.

Proof: Conditioned on event E, an execution of **Checking Phase** will always terminate if both the executions of ACS terminate and all the instances of A-cast terminate. Since A-cast has no error in termination and each execution of ACS terminates except with probability $2^{-\Omega(\kappa)}$, an execution of **Checking Phase** will terminate except with negligible probability. $\qquad\square$

Lemma 2 (Correctness of Checking Phase). *In an execution of* **Checking Phase** *in a segment* $\mathcal{S}_\alpha$, *the honest parties in* $\mathcal{P}'_{ch}$ *(if it is found) hold a common message* m^*_α, *except with probability* $2^{-\Omega(\kappa)}$. *Moreover, if the honest parties start* $\mathcal{S}_\alpha$ *with common message* m_α, *then* $\mathcal{P}'_{ch}$ *will always be found with* $m^*_\alpha = m_\alpha$.

Proof. We prove the first part of the lemma. If $\mathcal{P}'_{ch}$ contains exactly one honest party, then first part is trivially true with m^*_α being the input message of the sole honest party in $\mathcal{P}'_{ch}$. So let $\mathcal{P}'_{ch}$ contain at least two honest parties. We now show that the messages of every pair of honest parties (P_i, P_j) in $\mathcal{P}'_{ch}$ are same. Recall that the response vectors $\vec{v_i}$ and $\vec{v_j}$ of P_i and P_j are identical and have at least $t' + 1$ 1's in them. Moreover, $\mathcal{I}_1$ contains all P_k's such that $\vec{v_i}[k] = \vec{v_j}[k] = 1$. Evidently, $|\mathcal{I}_1| \geq t + 1$. So there is at least one *honest* party in $\mathcal{I}_1$, say P_k, such that $\vec{v_i}[k] = \vec{v_j}[k] = 1$. This implies that $\mathcal{V}_k = \mathcal{U}_\kappa(m_{i\alpha}, r_k)$ and $\mathcal{V}_k = \mathcal{U}_\kappa(m_{j\alpha}, r_k)$ holds for P_i and P_j respectively, where P_i has received $(\mathcal{V}_k, r_k)$ from P_k (by A-cast) and P_j has received $(\mathcal{V}_k, r_k)$ from P_k (by A-cast). Now by **Collision Theorem** (Theorem 1), it follows that $m_{i\alpha} = m_{k\alpha}$ and $m_{j\alpha} = m_{k\alpha}$, except with probability $2^{-\Omega(\kappa)}$. Consequently $m_{i\alpha} = m_{j\alpha}$, except with probability $2^{-\Omega(\kappa)}$. Now let us fix an honest party, say P_i in $\mathcal{P}'_{ch}$. If P_i's value is equal to every honest P_j's value in $\mathcal{P}'_{ch}$, then it means that all honest parties in $\mathcal{P}'_{ch}$ hold a common message m^*_α, except with negligible error probability.

We now prove the second part. When all honest parties start with same input m_α, the vectors of all honest parties in $\mathcal{J}$ will have 1 at the locations corresponding to the honest parties in $\mathcal{I}$. Since there are at least $t' + 1$ honest parties in both $\mathcal{I}$ and $\mathcal{J}$, $\mathcal{P}'_{ch}$ can always be found and now it is easy to see that all honest parties in $\mathcal{P}'_{ch}$ will hold m_α.   □

Expansion Phase. If $\mathcal{P}'_{ch}$ is found and agreed upon in previous phase, then the parties proceed to expand $\mathcal{P}'_{ch}$ in order to obtain $\mathcal{P}'_{ex}$. For that we first initiate $\mathcal{K} = \mathcal{P}'_{ch}$ and $\overline{\mathcal{K}} = \mathcal{P}' \setminus \mathcal{K}$. Then $\mathcal{K}$ will be expanded to contain $2t' + 1$ parties and we will assign $\mathcal{K}$ to $\mathcal{P}'_{ex}$ when $\mathcal{K}$ contains $2t' + 1$ parties. We call the $\mathcal{K}$ containing $t' + 1$ parties as 'initial' $\mathcal{K}$ and likewise the $\mathcal{K}$ containing $2t' + 1$ parties as 'final' $\mathcal{K}$. The expansion (transition from 'initial' $\mathcal{K}$ to 'final' $\mathcal{K}$) takes place in a sequence of t' iterations. In each iteration, either $\mathcal{K}$ is expanded by one or in case of failure a conflict triplet is returned. In the latter case, the current segment fails and it is again repeated (from **checking phase**) with renewed value of n', t' and $\mathcal{P}'$ (i.e. after excluding the parties in the triplet from $\mathcal{P}'$).

So this phase starts as follows: First an injective mapping $\varphi : \mathcal{K} \to \overline{\mathcal{K}}$ is defined. Now a party $P_i \in \mathcal{K}$ sends his message m^*_α to party $\varphi(P_i) \in \overline{\mathcal{K}}$. A party $P_i \in \overline{\mathcal{K}}$ on receiving a message m^*_α from $\varphi^{-1}(P_i) \in \mathcal{K}$, calculates vector $\vec{v_i}$ with the (key, hash value) pair of the parties only in $\mathcal{I}_1$ ($\perp$ is placed at all other locations) and with m^*_α as the message. P_i then A-casts $\texttt{Matched-}P_i$ if $\vec{v_i}$ is identical to $\vec{v}$ (which was calculated in Checking). Otherwise let k be the minimum index in $\vec{v_i}$ such that $\vec{v_i}[k] \neq \vec{v}[k]$, then P_i A-casts a conflict triplet $(\varphi^{-1}(P_i), P_i, P_k)$. Clearly, one of the three parties in the triplet must be corrupted. The parties now invoke an instance of ACS to agree on a single party, say P_l from $\overline{\mathcal{K}}$ whose A-cast has been terminated. Such a party from $\overline{\mathcal{K}}$

can always be found as there exists at least one honest $P_m \in \mathcal{K}$ which will be mapped to another honest $P_l = \varphi(P_m) \in \overline{\mathcal{K}}$ and P_l will eventually receive m_α^* from P_m and successfully A-cast some message (see Lemma 4).

Now there are two cases. If $(\varphi^{-1}(P_l), P_l, P_k)$ is received from the A-cast of P_l, then the computation stops here and the triplet $(\varphi^{-1}(P_l), P_l, P_k)$ is returned. If Matched-P_l is received from the A-cast of P_l, then P_l is included in $\mathcal{K}$ and excluded from $\overline{\mathcal{K}}$. P_l now finds a unique party from the set of parties in $\overline{\mathcal{K}}$ that was never mapped before (say the unmapped party with smallest index) and sends m_α^* to it. Again the party who receives the message, calculates response vector with the received message and A-casts either a conflict triplet or Matched signal. Then the parties invoke an instance of ACS to agree on a single party from $\overline{\mathcal{K}}$ whose A-cast has been terminated and this process continues until either $|\mathcal{K}|$ becomes $2t' + 1$ or the segment is failed with some triplet in some iteration. Though it is non-intuitive that in every iteration the parties will be able to agree on a single party from $\overline{\mathcal{K}}$ by executing ACS, this will indeed happen and we prove this in Lemma 4. If $\mathcal{K}$ becomes of size $2t' + 1$, it is assigned to $\mathcal{P}'_{ex}$. The code for this phase is given in Fig. 2. We now prove the properties of **Expansion Phase**.

Lemma 3. *In a segment $\mathcal{S}_\alpha$, in any iteration of* while *loop (in an execution of* **Expansion Phase***), no two different parties in $\mathcal{K}$ are mapped to the same party in $\overline{\mathcal{K}}$. Also in case* while *loop is completed with $\mathcal{K}$ containing $2t' + 1$ parties, only the last entrant in 'final' $\mathcal{K}$ is not mapped to any party.*

Proof. From the protocol steps, it is clear that a party in $\mathcal{K}$ is mapped only once. Now we show that no pair (P_i, P_j) in $\mathcal{K}$ is mapped to same party. This is true as φ is injective and also every time a party P_i from $\mathcal{K}$ is mapped to a party P_k in $\overline{\mathcal{M}}$ (set of unmapped parties), P_k is never mapped again as it is immediately transferred to $\mathcal{M}$ (set of mapped parties).

Now we show that there will be enough number of parties in $\overline{\mathcal{M}}$ to be mapped in all iterations, except the last one. We consider the worst case, where the while loop is executed completely for t' iterations (as 'initial' $|\mathcal{K}|$ is $t' + 1$ and t' more parties have to enter to make 'final' $\mathcal{K}$ of size $2t' + 1$), without outputting any triplet. Now as per the protocol, at the beginning of the while loop, $\mathcal{K} = t' + 1$, $\overline{\mathcal{K}} = 2t'$, $\mathcal{M} = t' + 1$ and $\overline{\mathcal{M}} = 2t' - (t' + 1) = t' - 1$. In i^{th} iteration, a party, say P_l from $\mathcal{M}$ (hence from $\overline{\mathcal{K}}$) enters into $\mathcal{K}$ and gets mapped to an unmapped party in $\overline{\mathcal{M}}$ (hence in $\overline{\mathcal{K}}$). As a result: (a) $|\mathcal{K}|$ increases by 1, (b) $|\overline{\mathcal{K}}|$ decreases by 1, (c) $|\mathcal{M}|$ remains same and (d) $|\overline{\mathcal{M}}|$ decreases by 1. So after $t' - 1$ iterations, the following hold: (a) $|\mathcal{K}| = 2t'$, (b) $|\overline{\mathcal{K}}| = t' + 1$, (c) $|\mathcal{M}| = t' + 1$ and (d) $|\overline{\mathcal{M}}| = 0$. Hence $\overline{\mathcal{M}}$ becomes empty only after the mapping is done in $(t' - 1)^{th}$ iteration. In the last iteration (t'^{th}), another party from $\mathcal{M}$ (hence from $\overline{\mathcal{K}}$) is finally included in $\mathcal{K}$ which need not be mapped to any more party as $\mathcal{K}$ becomes exactly $2t' + 1$ at this point.   □

Lemma 4. *In a particular execution of* **Expansion Phase** *in a segment $\mathcal{S}_\alpha$, $|\mathcal{K}|$ will increase by one with probability at least $(1 - 2^{-\Omega(\kappa)})$, in every iteration of* while *loop until the* while *loop is completed due to $|\mathcal{K}| = 2t' + 1$ or broken due to the output of a triplet.*

Expansion

Code for $P_i \in \mathcal{P}'$: Every party in $\mathcal{P}'$ executes this code

1. Assign $\mathcal{K} = \mathcal{P}'_{ch}$ and $\overline{\mathcal{K}} = \mathcal{P}' \setminus \mathcal{K}$.
2. Define an injective mapping $\varphi : \mathcal{K} \rightarrow \overline{\mathcal{K}}$ where $\overline{\mathcal{K}} = \mathcal{P}' \setminus \mathcal{K}$ as follows: the party with smallest index in $\mathcal{K}$ is associated with the party with smallest index in $\overline{\mathcal{K}}$. Let $\mathcal{M} = \varphi(\mathcal{K})$ ($\subset \overline{\mathcal{K}}$, as $|\mathcal{K}|$ is exactly $t' + 1$) be the set of currently *mapped* parties in $\overline{\mathcal{K}}$. Let $\overline{\mathcal{M}} = \overline{\mathcal{K}} \setminus \mathcal{M}$ be the set of currently *unmapped* partied in $\overline{\mathcal{K}}$.
3. If $P_i \in \mathcal{K}$, then send m_α^* to $\varphi(P_i)$.
4. If $P_i \in \overline{\mathcal{K}}$ and has received message m_α^* from $\varphi^{-1}(P_i) \in \mathcal{K}$, then calculate vector $\overrightarrow{v_i}$
   of length n as follows: $\overrightarrow{v_i}[j] = \begin{cases} \bot & \text{If } P_j \notin \mathcal{I}_1 \\ 1 & \text{If } P_j \in \mathcal{I}_1 \text{ and } \mathcal{V}_{ji} = \mathcal{U}_\kappa(m_\alpha^*, r_{ji}). \text{ Recall that} \\ 0 & \text{If } P_j \in \mathcal{I}_1 \text{ and } \mathcal{V}_{ji} \neq \mathcal{U}_\kappa(m_\alpha, r_{ji}). \end{cases}$
   $(r_{ji}, \mathcal{V}_{ji})$ pair was obtained by P_i in Checking from AVSS-Rec$(P_j, \mathcal{P}', r_{ji}, P_i)$ and AVSS-Rec$(P_j, \mathcal{P}', \mathcal{V}_{ji}, P_i)$. If $\overrightarrow{v_i}$ is identical to $\overrightarrow{v}$ then A-cast Matched-P_i; otherwise let k be the minimum index in $\overrightarrow{v_i}$ such that $\overrightarrow{v_i}[k] \neq \overrightarrow{v}[k]$, then A-cast (P_j, P_i, P_k), where $P_j = \varphi^{-1}(P_i)$.
5. `while` $|\mathcal{K}| < 2t' + 1$ do:
   (a) Participate in an instance of ACS$(\mathcal{M}, 1)$ to agree on a single party from $\mathcal{M}$ whose A-cast has been terminated. Let the party be P_l.
   (b) If (P_m, P_l, P_k) is received from A-cast of P_l, then stop any further computation and output the triplet (P_m, P_l, P_k).
   (c) If Matched-P_l is received from A-cast of P_l, then set $\mathcal{K} = \mathcal{K} \cup \{P_l\}, \overline{\mathcal{K}} = \overline{\mathcal{K}} \setminus \{P_l\}$ and $\mathcal{M} = \mathcal{M} \setminus \{P_l\}$.
   (d) Define a mapping, which maps P_l to the party in $\overline{\mathcal{M}}$ with the smallest index, say P_m. Set $\overline{\mathcal{M}} = \overline{\mathcal{M}} \setminus \{P_m\}$ and $\mathcal{M} = \mathcal{M} \cup \{P_m\}$.
   (e) If $P_i = P_l$, then send m_α^* to P_m.
   (f) If $P_i = P_m$ and P_i has received message m_α^* from P_l, then calculate vector $\overrightarrow{v_i}$ of length n in the same way as in step 4. If $\overrightarrow{v_i}$ is identical to $\overrightarrow{v}$ then A-cast Matched-P_i; otherwise let k be the minimum index in $\overrightarrow{v_i}$ such that $\overrightarrow{v_i}[k] \neq \overrightarrow{v}[k]$, then A-cast (P_l, P_i, P_k).
6. Set $\mathcal{P}'_{ex} = \mathcal{K}$. If $P_i \in \mathcal{P}'_{ex}$, then consider m_α^* as the final message.

Fig. 2. Code for the Expansion Phase

Proof. To prove the lemma, we show that in every iteration of the `while` loop, the parties will be able to agree on a single party (using ACS) from $\overline{\mathcal{K}}$ (except with negligible probability, as the instance of ACS may not terminate with negligible probability), whose A-cast will be terminated. In other words, we assert that in every iteration of the `while` loop, there will exist one party from $\overline{\mathcal{K}}$ who will eventually A-cast a response. Moreover, this will be true, until the `while` loop is either over or broken due to the output of a triplet. For this, we claim that in every iteration of `while` loop, there must be an honest party, say P_i, belonging to $\mathcal{K}$, such that P_i is mapped to another honest party, say P_j, belonging to $\overline{\mathcal{K}}$. Moreover, honest P_i's message will eventually reach to honest P_j, who will then A-cast his response, which is either an n length vector or a triplet of parties.

At the time of entering into the loop for the first time, assume that among $t' + 1$ parties in $\mathcal{K}$ there are $0 \leq c \leq t'$ corrupted parties. So the remaining $t' - c$ corrupted parties are in 'initial' $\overline{\mathcal{K}}$. In the worst case, c corrupted parties and $t' - c$ honest parties from $\mathcal{K}$ may be mapped to c honest parties and $t' - c$ corrupted parties, respectively from $\overline{\mathcal{K}}$. Still $\mathcal{K}$ contains at least one honest party which is bound to be mapped to another honest party from $\overline{\mathcal{K}}$, as there is no other unmapped corrupted party in $\overline{\mathcal{K}}$. So our claim holds for first iteration. In general in i^{th} iteration, there are $t' + i$ parties in $\mathcal{K}$ out of which say c with $0 \leq c \leq t'$ are corrupted parties. So extending the previous argument for this general case, there are i honest parties in $\mathcal{K}$ who are mapped to i honest parties in $\overline{\mathcal{K}}$. Among these i mappings, $i - 1$ might correspond to previous $i - 1$ iterations. But still one mapping is left for i^{th} iteration. Now let the mapping be from honest $P_j \in \mathcal{K}$ to honest $P_k \in \overline{\mathcal{K}}$.

So P_j's message reaches to P_k eventually and P_k tries to prepare $\overrightarrow{v_k}$ with received message and the (key, hash value) of the parties in $\mathcal{I}_1$. Conditioned on event E, P_k will receive the (key, hash value) of the parties in $\mathcal{I}_1$. Once P_k prepares his vector, he A-casts his response (which could be either Matched-P_k, if $\overrightarrow{v_k} = \overrightarrow{v}$ or a triplet of parties if $\overrightarrow{v_k} \neq \overrightarrow{v}$). If P_k's response is Matched-P_k, then $|\mathcal{K}|$ will be incremented by 1; otherwise, the loop will be broken with a triplet as output. $\qquad\Box$

Lemma 5 (Termination of Expansion Phase). *In a segment $\mathcal{S}_\alpha$, an execution of* **Expansion Phase** *will terminate, except with probability $2^{-\Omega(\kappa)}$, where termination means that the code either outputs a triplet or a set $\mathcal{P}'_{ex}$ of size $2t' + 1$.*

Proof: From Lemma 4, in every iteration of the while loop, there will exist one party from $\overline{\mathcal{K}}$ who will eventually A-cast a response. Now conditioned on event E, the termination of an execution of **Expansion Phase** depends on the termination of the invoked ACS protocols and the A-casts. A-cast has no error in termination. The invocations of ACS (there can be at most t' invocations corresponding to t' iterations of while loop) will terminate, except with probability $2^{-\Omega(\kappa)}$. Therefore, an execution of **Expansion Phase** terminates, except with probability $2^{-\Omega(\kappa)}$. $\qquad\Box$

Lemma 6 (Correctness-I of Expansion Phase). *In an execution of* **Expansion Phase** *in a segment $\mathcal{S}_\alpha$, all the honest parties in $\mathcal{P}'_{ex}$ (if found) will hold a common message m^*_α, which was also the common message held by the honest parties in $\mathcal{P}'_{ch}$, except with probability $2^{-\Omega(\kappa)}$. Moreover if the honest parties start $\mathcal{S}_\alpha$ with same input message m_α, then $m^*_\alpha = m_\alpha$.*

Proof: Let us consider party P_f, who is the first *honest* party to enter into 'initial' $\mathcal{K}$ during the **Expansion phase**. Recall that P_f enters into $\mathcal{K}$ (hence $\mathcal{P}'_{ex}$) when it receives a message $\overline{m^*}$ from some already existing (possibly corrupted) party P_j in $\mathcal{K}$ and P_f's generated $\overrightarrow{v_f}$ is identical to $\overrightarrow{v}$. We claim that $\overline{m^*_\alpha} = m^*_\alpha$, except with error probability $2^{-\Omega(\kappa)}$. Consider an honest $P_k \in \mathcal{K}$ and an honest P_l in $\mathcal{I}_1$ with $\overrightarrow{v}[l] = 1$ (there is at least one such honest P_l as $|\mathcal{I}_1| \geq t' + 1$). By **Collision Theorem**, $m_{k\alpha} = m_{l\alpha} = m^*_\alpha$, except with error probability $2^{-\Omega(\kappa)}$. Now since

$\overrightarrow{v_f} = \overrightarrow{v}$, it implies that $\overrightarrow{v}_f[l] = 1$, as $\overrightarrow{v}[l] = 1$. This further implies that $\overline{m_\alpha^*} = m_{l\alpha}$. Hence it implies that $\overline{m_\alpha^*} = m_\alpha^*$ holds, with very high probability. This is because the key and hash value pair $(r_{lf}, \mathcal{V}_{lf})$ is not known to anyone (including possibly corrupted P_j) other than P_f and P_l. Hence with very high probability, P_f has received m_α^* from P_j.

Now let P_s be the second honest party to enter into 'initial' $\mathcal{K}$. P_s may receive its message either from P_f or from any party belonging to 'initial' $\mathcal{K}$. In both cases, P_s's message will be m_α^*, except with negligible error probability. In general, if an honest party P_i enters into 'initial' $\mathcal{K}$ at sometime, then its message will be equal to m_α^*, except with negligible error probability.   □

Lemma 7 (Correctness-II of Expansion Phase). *In an execution of* **Expansion Phase** *in a segment* $\mathcal{S}_\alpha$, *if a triplet* (P_m, P_l, P_k) *is* A-casted *by* P_l *then at least one of* P_m, P_l *and* P_k *is corrupted, except with error probability* $2^{-\Omega(\kappa)}$ *where* $P_m \in \mathcal{K}, P_l \in \overline{\mathcal{K}}$ *and* $P_k \in \mathcal{I}_1$.

Proof. Let P_m, P_l and P_k be honest, where $P_m \in \mathcal{K}, P_l \in \overline{\mathcal{K}}$ and $P_k \in \mathcal{I}_1$. Since $P_k \in \mathcal{I}_1$, it implies that $\overrightarrow{v}(k) = 1$ holds. Also $P_m \in \mathcal{K}$ implies that $\overrightarrow{v}_m(k) = 1$. This further implies that m_α^* held by P_m is same as $m_{k\alpha}$ held by P_k, except with error probability $2^{-\Omega(\kappa)}$ (from **Collision Theorem**). Now during **Expansion phase**, P_m sends his m_α^* to P_l and P_l computes $\overrightarrow{v}_l$ with respect to the received m_α^* and the pairs $(r_{jl}, \mathcal{V}_{jl})$, corresponding to every $P_j \in \mathcal{I}_1$. On computing $\overrightarrow{v}_l$, party P_l will find that $\overrightarrow{v}_l(k) = \overrightarrow{v}(k)$, except with negligible error probability. This is because P_k is honest and hence $\mathcal{V}_{kl}$ is the hash value of $m_{k\alpha}$, with respect to the hash key r_{kl}. However, as shown above, m_α^* received by P_l from P_m is same as $m_{k\alpha}$, except with negligible error probability. So P_l will find that $\mathcal{V}_{kl} = \mathcal{U}_\kappa(m_\alpha^*, r_{kl})$. Hence P_l will not A-cast triplet (P_m, P_l, P_k). So if at all P_l A-casts (P_m, P_l, P_k), then at least one of P_m, P_l and P_k is corrupted.   □

Output Phase. Once the parties agree on $\mathcal{P}'_{ex}$, with all honest parties in it holding some common m_α^*, we need to ensure that m_α^* propagates to all (honest) parties in $\overline{\mathcal{P}_{ex}} = \mathcal{P} \setminus \mathcal{P}'_{ex}$, in order to reach agreement on m_α^*. This is achieved in code **Output** (presented in Fig. 3) with the help of the parties in $\mathcal{P}'_{ex}$. A simple solution could be to ask each party in $\mathcal{P}'_{ex}$ to send his m_α^* to all the parties in $\overline{\mathcal{P}_{ex}}$, who can wait to receive $t'+1$ same m_α^* and then accept m_α^* as the message. This solution will work as there are at least $t'+1$ honest parties in $\mathcal{P}'_{ex}$. But clearly, this requires a communication complexity of $\mathcal{O}(\frac{\ell}{n} \cdot n^2) = \mathcal{O}(\ell n)$ bits for each segment (and thus $\mathcal{O}(\ell n^2)$ bits for our ABA protocol; this violates our promised communication complexity bound for Optimal-ABA). Hence, we adopt a technique proposed in [15] for designing a BA protocol in synchronous settings with $n = |\mathcal{P}| = 2t + 1$ parties. Now the technique proposed in [15] requires a set of parties, say $\mathcal{H} \subset \mathcal{P}$ such that all the honest parties in $\mathcal{H}$ hold the same message and the majority of the parties in $\mathcal{H}$ are honest. Under this condition the technique allows the set of honest parties in $\mathcal{P} \setminus \mathcal{H}$ to obtain the common message of the honest parties in $\mathcal{H}$ with a communication cost of $\mathcal{O}(\ell n)$ bits. In our context $\mathcal{P}'_{ex}$ has all the properties of $\mathcal{H}$. Hence we adopt the technique of [15] in our context in the following way: Every $P_i \in \mathcal{P}'_{ex}$ sets $d = t'+1$ and $c = \lceil \frac{\ell+1}{td} \rceil$

and transforms his message m_α^* (with $|m_\alpha^*| = \frac{\ell}{t}$) into a polynomial $p(x)$ of degree $d-1$ over $GF(2^c)$. Now if somehow a party $P_j \in \overline{\mathcal{P}_{ex}}$ receives d values on $p(x)$, then he can interpolate $p(x)$ and receive m_α^*. For this, party $P_i \in \mathcal{P}_{ex}'$ sends i^{th} value on $p(x)$, namely $p_i = p(i)$ to every $P_j \in \overline{\mathcal{P}_{ex}}$. As the corrupted parties in $\mathcal{P}_{ex}'$ may send wrong p_i, P_j should be able to detect correct values. For this, every $P_i \in \mathcal{P}_{ex}'$ also sends hash values of $(p_1, \ldots, p_n)$ for a random hash key to every $P_j \in \overline{\mathcal{P}_{ex}}$. Now P_j can detect 'clean' values with the help of the hash values and eventually P_j will receive d 'clean' values (possibly from $d = t' + 1$ honest parties in $\mathcal{P}_{ex}'$) using which he can compute m_α^*.

Output

i. **Code for P_i:** Every party in $\mathcal{P}$ (not $\mathcal{P}'$) will execute this code.

1. If $P_i \in \mathcal{P}_{ex}'$, do the following to help the parties in $\overline{\mathcal{P}_{ex}} = \mathcal{P} \setminus \mathcal{P}_{ex}'$ to compute m_α^*:
   (a) Set $d = t' + 1$ and $c = \lceil \frac{\ell+1}{td} \rceil$.
   (b) Interpret m_α^* as a polynomial $p(x)$ of degree $d-1$ over $GF(2^c)$. For this, divide m_α^* into blocks of c bits and interpret each block as an element from $GF(2^c)$. These elements from $GF(2^c)$ are the coefficients of $p(x)$.
   (c) Send $p_i = p(i)$ to every $P_j \in \overline{\mathcal{P}_{ex}}$, where p_i is computed over $GF(2^c)$.
   (d) For every $P_j \in \overline{\mathcal{P}_{ex}}$, choose a random distinct hash key R_{ij} from $\mathbb{F}$ and send $(R_{ij}, \mathcal{X}_{ij1}, \ldots, \mathcal{X}_{ijn})$ to P_j, where for $k = 1, \ldots, n$, $\mathcal{X}_{ijk} = \mathcal{U}_\kappa(p_k, R_{ij})$. Here, to compute $\mathcal{X}_{ijk}$, interpret p_k as a c bit string.
   (e) Terminate this code with m_α^* as output.
2. If $P_i \in \overline{\mathcal{P}_{ex}}$, do the following to compute m_α^*:
   (a) Call p_k received from party $P_k \in \mathcal{P}_{ex}'$ as 'clean' if there are at least $t' + 1$ P_j's in $\mathcal{P}_{ex}'$, corresponding to which $\mathcal{X}_{jik} = \mathcal{U}_\kappa(p_k, R_{ji})$ holds, where $(R_{ji}, \mathcal{X}_{ji1}, \ldots, \mathcal{X}_{jin})$ is received from $P_j \in \mathcal{P}_{ex}'$.
   (b) Wait to receive d 'clean' p_k's and upon receiving, interpolate $d-1$ degree polynomial $p(x)$ using those 'clean' values, interpret m^* from $p(x)$ and terminate this protocol with m_α^* as the output.

Fig. 3. Code for **Output Phase**

Lemma 8 (Termination of Output Phase). *An execution of* **Output Phase** *in any segment $\mathcal{S}_\alpha$ will terminate, except with probability $2^{-\Omega(\kappa)}$.*

Proof: From the steps of the code **Output**, the parties in $\mathcal{P}_{ex}'$ always terminate after performing the steps as mentioned in step 1(a)-1(d) of the code. So we now have to prove that the parties in $\mathcal{P} \setminus \mathcal{P}_{ex}'$ terminate, except with negligible error probability. To show this, we first assert that if all the honest parties in $\mathcal{P}_{ex}'$ hold common m_α^*, then the above event happens with no error; but the parties in $\mathcal{P}_{ex}'$ hold common m_α^*, except with negligible error probability (from Lemma 6). Hence it will follow that the parties in $\mathcal{P} \setminus \mathcal{P}_{ex}'$ terminate, except with negligible error probability.

Now we are left to show that the parties in $\mathcal{P} \setminus \mathcal{P}_{ex}'$ terminate without error when all the honest parties in $\mathcal{P}_{ex}'$ hold common m_α^*. Consider an honest party P_i in $\overline{\mathcal{P}_{ex}}$. Clearly, P_i terminates if it receives $d = t' + 1$ 'clean' values eventually.

To assert that P_i will indeed receive $d = t' + 1$ 'clean' values, we first show that the value p_k received from every honest P_k in $\mathcal{P}'_{ex}$ will be considered as 'clean' by P_i. Consequently, since there are $t' + 1$ honest parties in $\mathcal{P}'_{ex}$, P_i will eventually receive $t' + 1$ 'clean' values even though the corrupted parties in $\mathcal{P}'_{ex}$ may never send any value to P_i. If the honest parties in $\mathcal{P}'_{ex}$ have common m^*_α, they will generate same $p(x)$ and therefore same $p_k = p(k)$. Hence, $\mathcal{X}_{jik} = \mathcal{U}_\kappa(p_k, R_{ji})$ will hold, with respect to $(R_{ji}, \mathcal{X}_{jik})$ of every honest P_j in $\mathcal{P}'_{ex}$. As there are at least $d = t' + 1$ honest parties in $\mathcal{P}'_{ex}$, the p_k received from honest $P_k \in \mathcal{P}'_{ex}$ will be considered as 'clean' by P_i. This proves our claim.   □

Lemma 9 (Correctness of Output Phase). *Every honest party in $\mathcal{P}$ will output a common message m^*_α in an execution of* **Output Phase** *in a segment $\mathcal{S}_\alpha$, except with probability $2^{-\Omega(\kappa)}$. Moreover, if the honest parties start $\mathcal{S}_\alpha$ with same input m_α, then $m^*_\alpha = m_\alpha$.*

Proof: Lemma 6 shows that all the honest parties in $\mathcal{P}'_{ex}$ will output same m^*_α with very high probability. So we are left to prove that all the honest parties in $\overline{\mathcal{P}_{ex}}$ will output same m^*_α as well.

So let $P_i \in \overline{\mathcal{P}_{ex}}$ be an honest party. Now the p_k value of each honest $P_k \in \mathcal{P}'_{ex}$ will be eventually considered as 'clean' value by honest P_i. This is because there are at least $t' + 1$ honest parties in $\mathcal{P}'_{ex}$, who hold same m^*_α and therefore same $p(x)$ (and hence $p(k)$). So $\mathcal{X}_{jik} = \mathcal{U}_\kappa(p_k, R_{ji})$ will hold, with respect to $(R_{ji}, \mathcal{X}_{jik})$ of every honest P_j in $\mathcal{P}'_{ex}$. A corrupted $P_k \in \mathcal{P}'_{ex}$ may send $\overline{p_k} \neq p_k$ to P_i, but $\overline{p_k}$ will not be considered as a 'clean' value with very high probability. This is because, in order to be considered as 'clean' value, $\overline{p_k}$ should satisfy $\mathcal{X}_{jik} = \mathcal{U}_\kappa(\overline{p_k}, R_{ji})$ with respect to $(R_{ji}, \mathcal{X}_{jik})$ of at least $t + 1$ P_j's from $\mathcal{P}'_{ex}$. The test will fail with respect to an honest party from $\mathcal{P}'_{ex}$ with very high probability according to **Collision Theorem** (see Theorem 1). Thus though the test may pass with respect to all corrupted parties in $\mathcal{P}'_{ex}$ (at most t), the test will fail for every honest party from $\mathcal{P}'_{ex}$ with high probability. Hence, honest P_i will reconstruct $p(x)$ using d 'clean' values (which he is bound to get eventually), with very high probability. The second part is easy to follow.   □

Properties of Optimal-ABA. We now prove the properties of Optimal-ABA.

Lemma 10. *In Optimal-ABA, in total there can be t segment failures. The* **Checking Phase** *and* **Expansion Phase** *may be executed for at most $2t$ times. But* **Output Phase** *may be executed at most t times, once for each segment.*

Proof: Since there are t corrupted parties, in total there can be t segment failures. These t failures may occur within a single segment or they may be distributed across t segments. After t failures, all corrupted parties will be removed from $\mathcal{P}$ and hence segment failure can not occur any more.

Since a segment may fail in **Expansion Phase**, there can be $2t$ executions of **Checking Phase** and **Expansion Phase** of which at most t may be non-robust executions (conflict triplet is found) and remaining t may be robust executions. Since segment can not fail in **Output Phase**, this phase may be executed at most t times, once for each segment.   □

Lemma 11 (Termination of Optimal-ABA). *Protocol Optimal-ABA will terminate eventually, except with probability $2^{-\Omega(\kappa)}$.*

Proof: This follows from Lemma 1, Lemma 5 and Lemma 8 and the fact that event E occurs with very high probability.   □

Lemma 12. *Conditioned on the event that segment $\mathcal{S}_\alpha$ terminates, every honest party outputs common m_α^* at the end of $\mathcal{S}_\alpha$, except with probability $2^{-\Omega(\kappa)}$. Moreover if the honest parties start $\mathcal{S}_\alpha$ with same input message m_α, then $m_\alpha^* = m_\alpha$.*

Proof: $\mathcal{S}_\alpha$ may terminate at the end of **Checking Phase** or at the end of **Output Phase**. If $\mathcal{S}_\alpha$ terminates at the end of **Checking Phase**, then every party assigns $m_\alpha^* = m_\alpha^\dagger$, where $m_\alpha^\dagger$ is a predefined value. Hence in this case the first part of the lemma holds without any error. Now let $\mathcal{S}_\alpha$ terminate at the end of **Output Phase**. Here we show that every party in $\mathcal{P}$ outputs common m_α^* at the end of **Output Phase** of $\mathcal{S}_\alpha$. By **Correctness of the Output Phase** (Lemma 9), given event E, all honest parties in $\mathcal{P}$ will hold common m_α^*, except with negligible error probability. Now since event E happens with very high probability, it follows that the parties in $\mathcal{P}$ will hold common m_α^*, except with negligible error probability.

The second part of the lemma follows from Lemma 2, 6 and 9.   □

Lemma 13 (Correctness of Optimal-ABA). *Conditioned on the event that Optimal-ABA terminates, every honest party outputs common m^* at the end of Optimal-ABA, except with probability $2^{-\Omega(\kappa)}$. Moreover if the honest parties start Optimal-ABA with same input message m, then $m^* = m$.*

Proof: This follows from Lemma 12 and the fact that m^* is the concatenation of $m_1^*, \ldots, m_t^*$.   □

Theorem 3. *Optimal-ABA is a (ϵ, δ)-ABA protocol.*

Proof: Follows from Lemma 11 and Lemma 13.   □

Theorem 4. *Optimal-ABA privately communicates $\mathcal{O}(\ell n + n^4 \kappa)$ bits and requires $\mathcal{O}(n^3)$ invocations to ABA (for single bit) and AVSS protocols (for one field element) to agree on an ℓ bit message.*

Proof: In Optimal-ABA, **Checking Phase** and **Expansion Phase** may be executed for at most $2t$ times and **Output Phase** may be executed t times (by Lemma 10).

In a single execution of **Checking Phase**, there are at most $2n'^2$ instances of AVSS. Moreover, there are two executions of ACS to agree on a set of parties of size $t' + 1$ and n' A-cast of n length response vectors. Since $n' = \mathcal{O}(n)$, the total communication complexity during one execution of **Checking Phase** is $2n^2 \cdot \text{AVSS} + 2n \cdot \text{ABA} + n^4$ bits.

During the execution of **Expansion Phase**, the most expensive step in terms of communication complexity is the execution of ACS, which will be executed t' times (the maximum number of iterations of `while` loop) in the `while` loop.

Since $t' = \mathcal{O}(n)$, this step requires a communication complexity of $n^2 \cdot$ ABA. Moreover, during **Expansion Phase** each party in $\mathcal{K}$ will privately send his ℓ/t bit message to exactly one party in $\overline{\mathcal{K}}$ to which it is mapped. As $|\mathcal{K}| = \mathcal{O}(n)$, this step requires a communication cost of $\mathcal{O}(n\ell/t)$ bits.

A single execution of **Output Phase** requires $\mathcal{O}(n'^2 c + n'^3 \kappa)$ bits of private communication. Now $\mathcal{O}(n'^2 c + n'^3 \kappa) = \mathcal{O}(\ell + n'^3 \kappa)$ as $c = \lceil \frac{\ell+1}{td} \rceil = \lceil \frac{\ell+1}{tt'} \rceil$ and $n' = \mathcal{O}(n)$, $t' = \mathcal{O}(n)$.

So executing **Checking Phase** and **Expansion phase** $2t = \Theta(n)$ times and executing **Output Phase** t times require a communication complexity of $\mathcal{O}(\ell n + n^4 \kappa)$ bits plus $\mathcal{O}(n^3)$ invocations to ABA and AVSS protocols.   □

3   Open Problems

The communication complexity of Optimal-ABA shows that the protocol is communication optimal for sufficiently large ℓ and the bound on ℓ depends on the communication complexity of the underlying ABA and AVSS protocols. One may try to design communication optimal ABA protocol for all values of ℓ (if possible) using completely different approach.

References

1. Abraham, I., Dolev, D., Halpern, J.Y.: An almost-surely terminating polynomial protocol for asynchronous Byzantine Agreement with optimal resilience. In: PODC, pp. 405–414 (2008)
2. Beerliová-Trubíniová, Z., Hirt, M.: Perfectly-secure MPC with linear communication complexity. In: Canetti, R. (ed.) TCC 2008. LNCS, vol. 4948, pp. 213–230. Springer, Heidelberg (2008)
3. Ben-Or, M.: Another advantage of free choice: Completely asynchronous agreement protocols. In: PODC, pp. 27–30 (1983)
4. Ben-Or, M., Goldwasser, S., Wigderson, A.: Completeness theorems for non-cryptographic fault-tolerant distributed computation. In: STOC, pp. 1–10 (1988)
5. Ben-Or, M., Kelmer, B., Rabin, T.: Asynchronous secure computations with optimal resilience. In: PODC, pp. 183–192 (1994)
6. Bracha, G.: An asynchronous $\lfloor(n-1)/3\rfloor$-resilient consensus protocol. In: PODC, pp. 154–162 (1984)
7. Canetti, R.: Studies in Secure Multiparty Computation and Applications. PhD thesis, Weizmann Institute, Israel (1995)
8. Canetti, R., Rabin, T.: Fast asynchronous Byzantine Agreement with optimal resilience. In: STOC, pp. 42–51 (1993)
9. Carter, L., Wegman, M.N.: Universal classes of hash functions. Journal of Computer and System Sciences 18(4), 143–154 (1979)
10. Chor, B., Goldwasser, S., Micali, S., Awerbuch, B.: Verifiable secret sharing and achieving simultaneity in the presence of faults. In: STOC, pp. 383–395 (1985)
11. Feldman, P., Micali, S.: An optimal algorithm for synchronous Byzantine Agreemet. In: STOC, pp. 639–648 (1988)
12. Feldman, P., Micali, S.: An optimal probabilistic protocol for synchronous Byzantine Agreement. SIAM Journal of Computing 26(4), 873–933 (1997)

13. Fischer, M.J., Lynch, N.A., Paterson, M.: Impossibility of distributed consensus with one faulty process. JACM 32(2), 374–382 (1985)
14. Fitzi, M.: Generalized Communication and Security Models in Byzantine Agreement. PhD thesis, ETH Zurich (2002)
15. Fitzi, M., Hirt, M.: Optimally efficient multi-valued Byzantine Agreement. In: PODC, pp. 163–168 (2006)
16. Hirt, M., Maurer, U.M., Przydatek, B.: Efficient secure multi-party computation. In: Okamoto, T. (ed.) ASIACRYPT 2000. LNCS, vol. 1976, pp. 143–161. Springer, Heidelberg (2000)
17. Lynch, N.A.: Distributed Algorithms. Morgan Kaufmann, San Francisco (1996)
18. Patra, A., Choudhary, A., Rabin, T., Rangan, C.P.: The round complexity of verifiable secret sharing revisited. In: Halevi, S. (ed.) CRYPTO 2009. LNCS, vol. 5677, pp. 487–504. Springer, Heidelberg (2009)
19. Patra, A., Choudhary, A., Rangan, C.P.: Efficient statistical asynchronous verifiable secret sharing with optimal resilience. In: Kurosawa, K. (ed.) Information Theoretic Security. LNCS, vol. 5973, pp. 74–92. Springer, Heidelberg (2010)
20. Patra, A., Choudhary, A., Pandu Rangan, C.: Efficient asynchronous Byzantine Agreement with optimal resilience. In: PODC, pp. 92–101 (2009)
21. Patra, A., Rangan, C.P.: Communication optimal multi-valued asynchronous broadcast protocol. In: Abdalla, M., Barreto, P.S.L.M. (eds.) LATINCRYPT 2010. LNCS, vol. 6212, pp. 162–177. Springer, Heidelberg (2010)
22. Pease, M., Shostak, R.E., Lamport, L.: Reaching agreement in the presence of faults. JACM 27(2), 228–234 (1980)
23. Pfitzmann, B., Waidner, M.: Unconditional Byzantine Agreement for any number of faulty processors. In: Finkel, A., Jantzen, M. (eds.) STACS 1992. LNCS, vol. 577, pp. 339–350. Springer, Heidelberg (1992)
24. Prabhu, B.S., Srinathan, K., Pandu Rangan, C.: Trading players for efficiency in unconditional multiparty computation. In: Cimato, S., Galdi, C., Persiano, G. (eds.) SCN 2002. LNCS, vol. 2576, pp. 342–353. Springer, Heidelberg (2003)
25. Rabin, M.O.: Randomized Byzantine generals. In: FOCS, pp. 403–409 (1983)
26. Rabin, T., Ben-Or, M.: Verifiable secret sharing and multiparty protocols with honest majority. In: STOC, pp. 73–85 (1989)
27. Turpin, R., Coan, B.A.: Extending binary Byzantine Agreement to multivalued Byzantine Agreement. Information Processing Letters 18(2), 73–76 (1984)

Appendix A: Approach Used in the BA of [15]

Here we briefly recall the approach used in [15] for designing the communication optimal multi-valued BA protocol in synchronous settings. The protocol of [15] requires $n = 2t + 1$ parties. So $|\mathcal{P}| = 2t + 1$. The BA protocol was structured into three stages: (a) Checking, (b) Consolidation and (c) Claiming Stage. In the Checking Stage, the parties in $\mathcal{P}$ compare their respective messages and jointly determine an accepting subset $\mathcal{P}_{acc} \subseteq \mathcal{P}$ of size at least $n - t$, such that all 'accepting' parties hold the same message, and all (honest) parties holding this message are 'accepting'. This stage can be aborted when inconsistencies among honest parties are detected. If this stage is not aborted then the BA protocol proceeds to Consolidation Stage where the parties in $\mathcal{P}_{acc}$ help to decide on a happy subset $\mathcal{P}_{ok} \subseteq \mathcal{P}$, such that all 'happy' parties hold the same message, and the majority of 'happy' parties are honest. Also this stage may be aborted in case of inconsistencies among the honest parties' inputs. Consolidation Stage is very important and introduces new ideas. But a careful checking will reveal that the same ideas can not be implemented in asynchronous network even for $n = 3t + 1$ parties. That is why we introduce a new sets of ideas in our ABA protocol. Finally, if Consolidation Stage is not aborted then BA protocol of [15] proceeds to the last stage called Claiming Stage. In the Claiming Stage, the parties in $\mathcal{P}_{ok}$ distribute their common message to the unhappy parties i.e. the parties in $\mathcal{P} \setminus \mathcal{P}_{ok}$. This stage will never be aborted and hence at the end every party will output a common value. If the BA protocol aborts during Checking and Consolidation Stages then every party decides on a predefined default value.

Author Index

GPSR Compliance

The European Union's (EU) General Product Safety Regulation (GPSR) is a set of rules that requires consumer products to be safe and our obligations to ensure this.

If you have any concerns about our products, you can contact us on ProductSafety@springernature.com

In case Publisher is established outside the EU, the EU authorized representative is:

Springer Nature Customer Service Center GmbH
Europaplatz 3
69115 Heidelberg, Germany

Batch number: 09474011

Printed by Printforce, the Netherlands